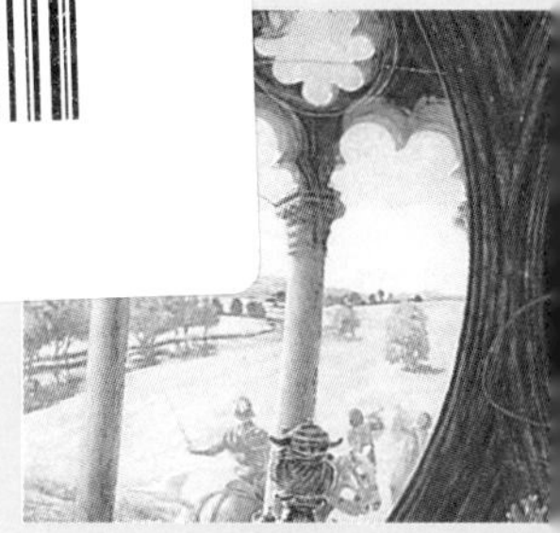

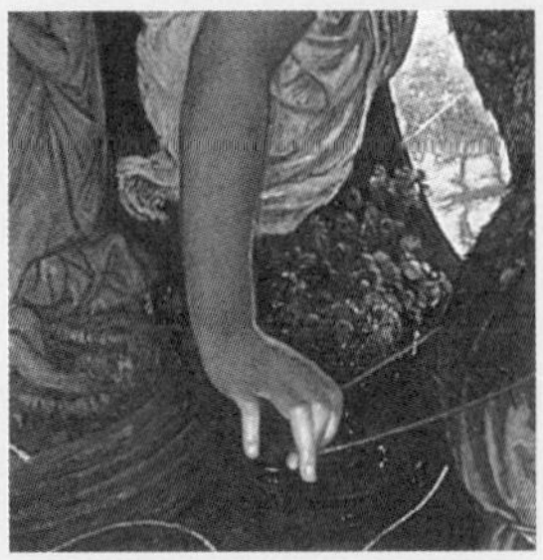

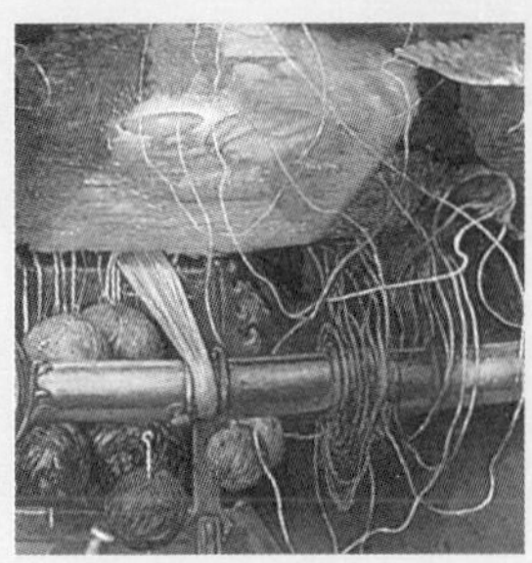

THE WORLD IN PAINT

Modern Art and Visuality

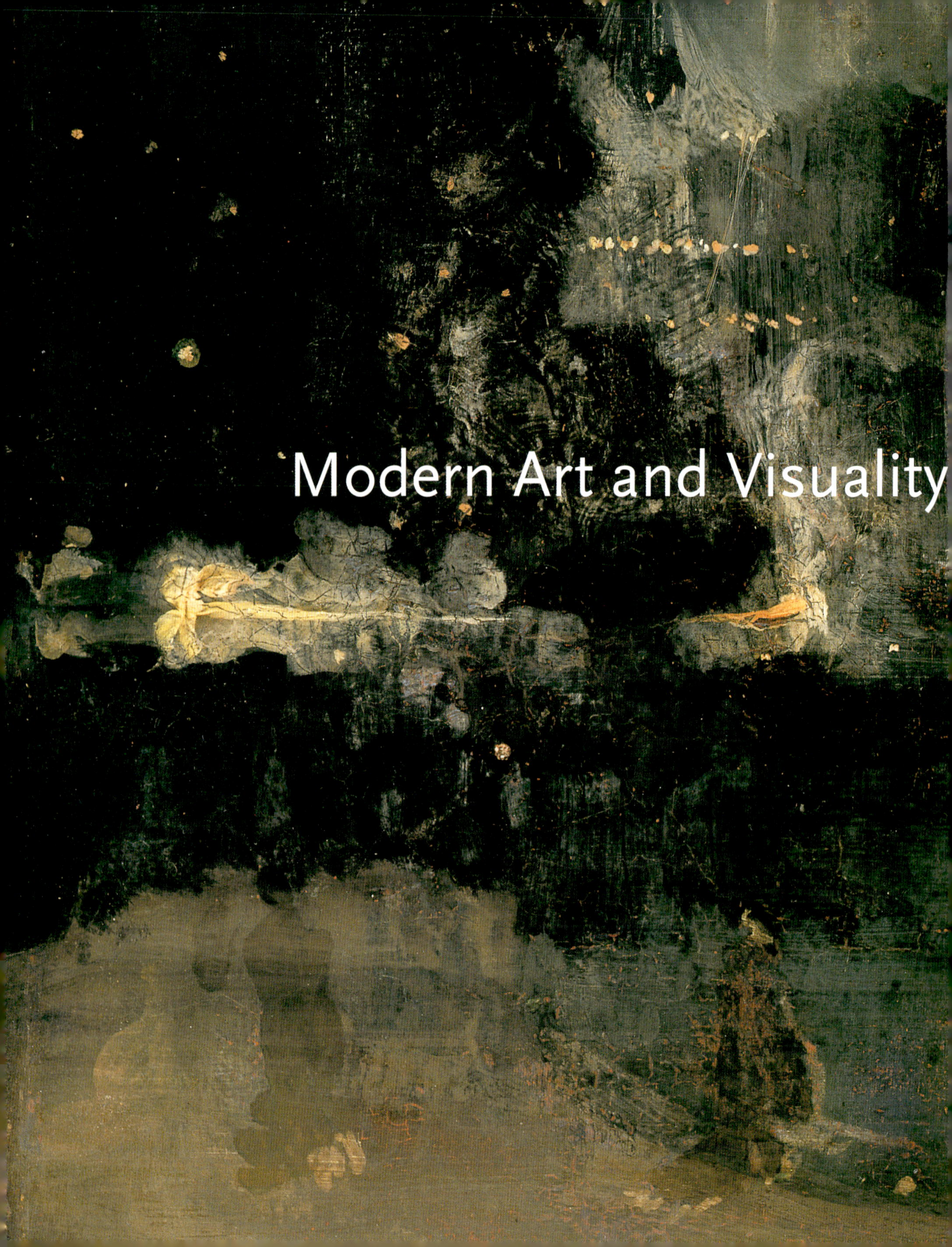

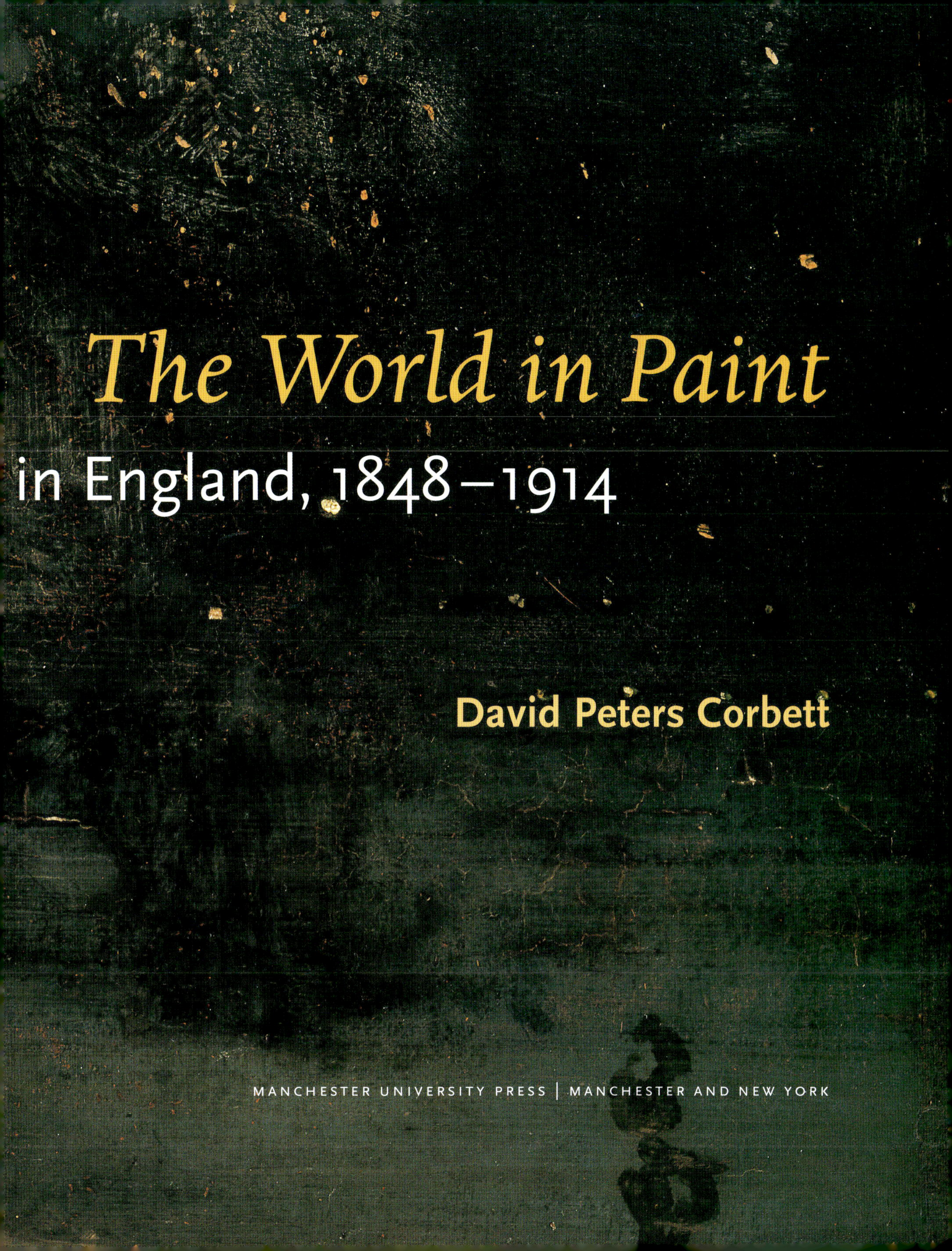

The World in Paint in England, 1848–1914

David Peters Corbett

MANCHESTER UNIVERSITY PRESS | MANCHESTER AND NEW YORK

British Library
Cataloguing-in-Publication Data
A catalogue record for this book is available
from The British Library.

Printed in China

First published in the UK in 2004 by
Manchester University Press,
Oxford Road, Manchester M13 9NR, UK
www.manchesteruniversitypress.co.uk

Co-publisher edition by special arrangement
with The Pennsylvania State University Press,
University Park, PA 16802-1003

CIP data applied for
ISBN 0-7190-6964-5 hardback
ISBN 0-7190-6965-3 paperback

To Susan, Henry and Araminta
and
to the memory of my father

THERE IS AN ENGLISH SCHOOL OF PAINTING. This is what first strikes a visitor to any International Exhibition of the Fine Arts. . . . Passing through the galleries set apart for Germany, Austria, Italy, Spain, Belgium, Holland, even for the United States or for Scandinavia, you might imagine yourself to be still in France, and you are, in fact, always amongst artists who live in Paris, or who have studied in Paris, or who follow, at least from afar off, either the discipline of her school or the revolutionary movement of Parisian art circles. . . . But on reaching the English pictures you feel, on the contrary, that you are no longer amongst fellow-countrymen and it is doubtful even whether they may be your contemporaries.

—*Robert de la Sizeranne,* English Contemporary Art, *1898*

Contents

Illustrations

Lane, 1894), reproduced by courtesy of the Director and Librarian, the John Rylands University Library of Manchester

56. Charles Ricketts, "Some Diver of the Colchian Caves," Oscar Wilde, *The Sphinx,* with decorations by Charles Ricketts (London: Elkin Mathews and John Lane, 1894), reproduced by courtesy of the Director and Librarian, the John Rylands University Library of Manchester
57. Sidney Starr, *The City Atlas,* oil on canvas, 1889, National Gallery of Canada, Ottawa, Gift of the Massey Collection of English Painting 1946
58. Philip Wilson Steer, *A Summer's Evening,* oil on canvas, c. 1887–88, private collection. Photo: Witt Library, Courtauld Institute of Art, University of London
59. Walter Sickert, *Little Dot Hetherington at the Bedford Music Hall,* oil on canvas, c. 1888–89, private collection, © Estate of Walter Sickert, 2003. All rights reserved, DACS. © 2004 Artists Rights Society (ARS), New York/DACS, London
60. Walter Sickert, *Vesta Victoria at the Old Bedford,* oil on canvas, c. 1890, private collection, © Estate of Walter Sickert, 2003. All rights reserved, DACS
61. Walter Sickert, *The P. S. Wings in the O. P. Mirror,* oil on canvas, c. 1889, Musée des Beaux Arts, Rouen, © Estate of Walter Sickert, 2003. All rights reserved, DACS
62. Walter Sickert, *Gatti's Hungerford Palace of Varieties: Second Turn of Katie Lawrence,* oil on canvas, c. 1903–4, Yale University Art Gallery, Mary Gertrude Abbey Fund, © Estate of Walter Sickert, 2003. All rights reserved, DACS. © 2004 Artists Rights Society (ARS), New York/DACS, London
63. Walter Sickert, *The Gallery of the Old Bedford,* oil on canvas, c. 1895, National Museums Liverpool (Walker Art Gallery), © Estate of Walter Sickert, 2003. All rights reserved, DACS
64. Walter Sickert, *The Studio: Painting of a Nude,* oil on canvas, 1906, private collection, © Estate of Walter Sickert, 2003. All rights reserved, DACS
65. Walter Sickert, *Dawn, Camden Town,* oil on canvas, c. 1909, Harewood House Trust. Reproduced by the kind permission of the Earl and Countess of Harewood and Trustees of the Harewood House Trust, © Estate of Walter Sickert, 2003. All rights reserved, DACS

Acknowledgments

I HAVE INCURRED MANY DEBTS DURING THE WRITING OF THIS BOOK. The University of York Innovation and Research Priming Fund helped me begin the research in 1997, when I thought I was going to write another sort of book entirely. A semester as Visiting Research Fellow in the Graduate Program in Visual and Cultural Studies at the University of Rochester in 1997 helped me see what it was I actually wanted to do and provided a marvelous context for the exchange of ideas relating to theory and methodology and to visual culture. I benefited from the spectacular collections of the Yale Center for British Art on two occasions, firstly while I was a Paul Mellon Fellow there in the summer of 1998, and then again during 2000–2001, when I returned for a stimulating period as Visiting Associate Professor in the Yale Department of the History of Art. A summer as a Clark Fellow at the Sterling and Francine Clark Art Institute in Williamstown in 2001 allowed me to complete a first draft and to gauge how far there was still to go. I made the very final adjustments in the highly stimulating and congenial setting of Clare Hall, Cambridge, as a Visiting Fellow in 2003.

On these and other occasions I have benefited from conversations with, and the support of, many individuals. During my time in New Haven, I was fortunate enough to enjoy regular conversations with Tim Barringer, Alex Nemerov, Patrick McCaughey, and Christopher Wood that touched on the book and its associated methodological matters. I must also record a debt of gratitude to Tim for having the idea of inviting me to teach in New Haven—and then making it happen. Alex was enormously helpful and stimulating in talking with me about Art History, methodology, and neglected art. Janet Wolff not only talked to me about the historiography of modern English art and let me read her work in progress, but she also read a near final version of the manuscript for me. Michael Ann Holly and Keith Moxey were helpful interlocutors first in Rochester and then in Williamstown. Brian Allen listened to me as the project developed and smiled on it at its end. At York, Jason Edwards demonstrated just what an advantage it is to have an expert on Aestheticism down the corridor; Jeanne Nuechterlein shared her own work on the northern Renaissance with me. Lawrence Rainey has been stimulating and inventive as a colleague in the English Department. Elizabeth Prettejohn had a number of conversations about the material with me, was generous in all sorts of ways, and also read a near final draft. My footnotes document a profound debt to her scholarship on the nineteenth century. Kenneth McConkey also read a near final draft and talked to me about it. Paul Barlow, Roger Cardinal, Caroline Van Eck, Paul Edwards, Gillian Forrester, Alastair Grieve, Mark Hallett, John Hatcher, Ysanne Holt, Ludmilla Jordanova, Michael Leja, Morna O'Neill, Lara Perry, Anna Gruetzner Robins, Jason Rosenfeld, Fiona Russell, Jon Shirland, Debora Silverman, Paul Smith, Catherine Soussloff, Lisa Tickner, Colin Trodd, Malcolm Warner, Shearer West, Michael White, and Rebecca Zurier all had conversations about aspects of the material with me. My footnotes again reveal that in many cases their own work has been a stimulus and that I have often relied on their scholarship. Many students have contributed to my ideas, sometimes by arguing against them, sometimes by pushing them further than I was able to do myself. I must single out especially all those who took my graduate seminar on the material both at York and at Yale. All errors that remain are, of course, my own.

The British Academy generously allowed me a grant toward the cost of prints and permissions, which made this aspect of the preparation of the book enormously easier and for which I am extremely grateful. At Penn State, Gloria Kury has been always engaged, stimulating in response, and encouraging, as well as a fountain of energy—everything one would want in an editor. Alison Whittle at Manchester has proved her equal. I am grateful to both for their help, encouragement, generosity, and support.

I am grateful to the following for permission to use material in Chapters 1, 4, and 5 that originally appeared in rather different form elsewhere: Blackwell Publishing for material in the journal *Art History* 21, no. 1 (1998) and 24, no. 1 (2001); Manchester University Press for material in *English Art, 1860–1914* (2000), ed. David Peters Corbett and Lara Perry; and Sulis Press for material in *The Great London Vortex: Modernist Literature and Art,* ed. Paul Edwards (2003).

Finally, my family put up with the book for a lot longer than I had any right to expect them to and my dedication once again records the debt.

YORK, 1997–2003

Introduction

No task is harder than this of translation from colour into speech, when the speech must be so hoarse and feeble, when the colour is so subtle and sublime.

—ALGERNON CHARLES SWINBURNE (on Whistler), "Notes on Some Pictures of 1868," *Essays and Studies*, 1875

In May 1900, during a trip he made to Spain with his friend and mentor—the artist, connoisseur, and collector Charles Ricketts—Thomas Sturge Moore, himself a poet, art critic, and occasional graphic artist, found himself standing in front of Titian's *Bacchanal* in the Prado (see fig. 51).[1] Struck by the painting, as Ricketts was (and probably under Ricketts's influence), Moore began to plan what his critics have considered one of his finest poems. "Lines on Titian's 'Bacchanal' in the Prado at Madrid" was published in *The Gazelles and Other Poems* in 1904. In the poem, Moore concentrated on the sleeping figure of the bacchante in the foreground of the picture and made her a symbol of the ideal identity of the self and the world:

Her flushed face
Breathes up toward open sky with fast-closed lids,—
As though, half-conscious, her complexion knew
Where stirred the tree-tops, where the blue was vast.
. . . torso, loins and thighs,
All hued as clouds are that the morning face.[2]

But this unity, it seems, is precarious, achievable only through the renunciation of consciousness—or its intermittence. In Moore's poem it is not the controlling self but the body, deprived of conscious awareness and hence transformed into a natural object, all stolid reflective surface rather than depth, that knows the world:

Sleep,
Sleep, oh, and wake no more; Bacchus has kissed
Thy lips, thine eyes, thy brow; thy joy and his
But lately were as one, therefore sleep on:
Be all past woes forgotten in thy dream![3]

The final lines make this negation of consciousness a precondition for understanding the world. A perpetual absence of the self, personified as the figure of night, promises access to a transcendent and perfected reality:

When the night finds thee, mayest thou still be sleeping!
She then, for ever and for aye, will take thee
To her deep dwelling and unechoing halls;
How could she leave thee? She who owns them all—
Owns all the stars, whose beauty is complete,
Whose joy is perfect, and whose home is peace;
While all their duty is to shine for love.[4]

Endings like this, which are typical of Moore's poetry, imply the disclosure of some final meaning that will resolve the circumstances of the poem in a revelation of mystery, an uncovering of the deep meaning of the world.[5] This disclosure is, in Frank Kermode's definition of late-nineteenth-century Symbolism, "the image as a radiant truth out of space and time."[6] In "Lines on Titian's 'Bacchanal,'" promised revelation arises out of the nature of Titian's painting. It is the mystery and silence of the visual, the apparent identity of image and the thing depicted, that Moore translates into the verbal by attributing precisely those qualities of silence and identity to the bacchante and her revelatory surrender of consciousness. Like the bacchante, the painting is "half-conscious," reflecting the world back to itself. The "complexion" of its paint surface "knows" the world, but in a mysterious, mute fashion. This amounts to a strong claim on behalf of the visual. Moore brings forward its nonlinguistic register as a means—one superior to language—for understanding reality. Moreover, paint's very superficiality, its literal concentration on the surface of experience, its abjuration of depth, allows it to do this. The surface of the visual and the world itself are identical, inseparable elements in understanding.

As the circumstances under which he saw the *Bacchanal* might suggest, the "aesthetic partnership" of Charles Ricketts and Charles Shannon strongly influenced Moore at this time.[7] Ricketts was a leading member of an English generation concerned above all with cultivating "exquisite taste, refined manners and obscure interests" as "an end in themselves."[8] Indeed, Ricketts's and Shannon's fastidious connoisseurial celebration of the visual qualities of works of art exemplifies the role of Aestheticism in English culture at the close of the nineteenth century. Aestheticism as such is not my focus in this book, but it does play a central role in the history I propose here: it emerged as a response to

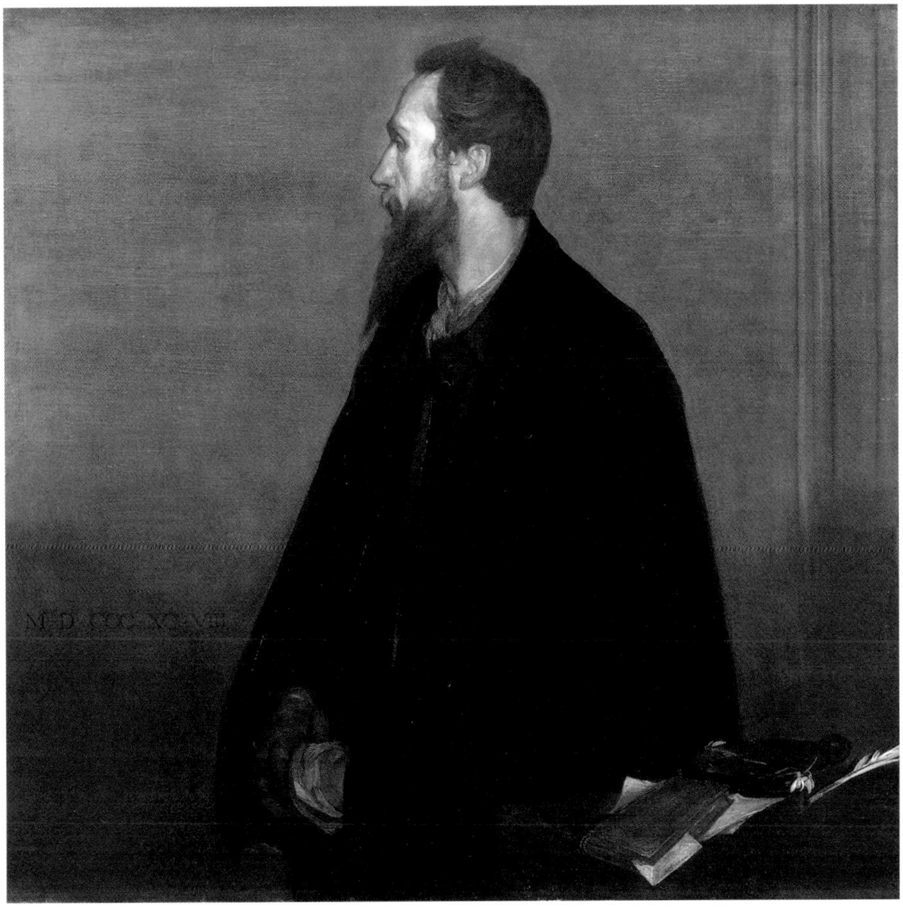

FIGURE 1. Charles Haslewood Shannon, *Portrait of Charles Ricketts*, 1898

structural shifts in the art world and in society as a whole. Faced with the fragmentation and diversification of potential audiences in the decades after 1860 and the commodification of art within capital, artists and aestheticians theorized a "natural" or essential split between the interests of art and those of its consumers, so that "art was always a thing exclusively for the expert."[9] Ricketts reflects the tensions induced by this process of modernization in the contemporary art world. He conducted his career entirely within the commercialized systems of the late nineteenth century, yet his art and aesthetics suppress this experience and define themselves as hermetic practices operating outside and beyond it. "I am turning away from the 20th century," he wrote of Shannon's 1898 portrait of him (fig. 1), adding, "to think only of the 15th. . . . I look as if I had written to Ariosto, the book at my side has been sent to me by Aretino."

That evocation of a desired past only served to conjure up the absolute integrity of the work of art, its place outside the desiccated logic of the everyday, its concern with its own imagination.[10]

In 1911 Ricketts wrote the introduction to the catalogue of a large and ambitious London exhibition he had organized at the Grafton Galleries. According to J. G. P. Delaney, his biographer, the introduction—"A Century of Art, 1810–1910"—constituted "an act of homage to the great imaginative artists of the nineteenth century and an answer to Roger Fry's Post-Impressionist Exhibition held at the same venue the previous year."[11] Ricketts detested the willing embrace of modernity he detected in the art of Impressionism and Post-Impressionism, its "valueless" striving for novelty and its contempt for tradition.[12] He challenged the emergent modernist lineage of 1910 by championing the search for "beauty" conducted by the artists he admired—Alfred Stevens, G. F. Watts, Dante Gabriel Rossetti, and Puvis de Chavannes—in opposition to the modern. In his essay, Ricketts argued that art in the nineteenth century had been sundered from its culture and confined to the margins without any clearly defined or acknowledged social role. He wrote, "the modern mind has had little hope, less trust, and no belief in art; it has hugged other ideals"—above all, those of materialism and the machine.[13] The absence of patronage and a secure place for the arts within culture had pushed the artist into the commodified, reified practices characteristic of the late-nineteenth-century art world: "If former centuries might be described as eras of Church and State patronage, the nineteenth century is that of isolated and unsupported effort. . . . the moderns have been forced into a direct appeal to the private purchaser, and to the creating of a fashion or appetite for the kind of art which each artist wished to do."[14]

Ricketts's own experience is closely matched here. He spent the early part of his career in commercial graphic work to support Shannon, who, unencumbered by financial obligations, was to reinvent the old masters for modern purposes (and later to burst upon an appreciative world). This telling dichotomy enslaved Ricketts throughout his life. He was an active entrepreneur in the art world, and, as the proprietor of the Vale Press, a proponent of commercial publishing ventures. He was also a highly sophisticated and self-conscious aesthete, one devoted to connoisseurship and to the idea of the beautiful made and consumed outside the systems of commerce. His periodical, *The Dial* (1889–97), promoted Continental *Symbolisme* within a frankly commercial form of publication that he struggled to remake as hermetic. This combination exemplifies the anxieties modernization brought out in late-nineteenth-century art practice as a whole (fig. 2).[15]

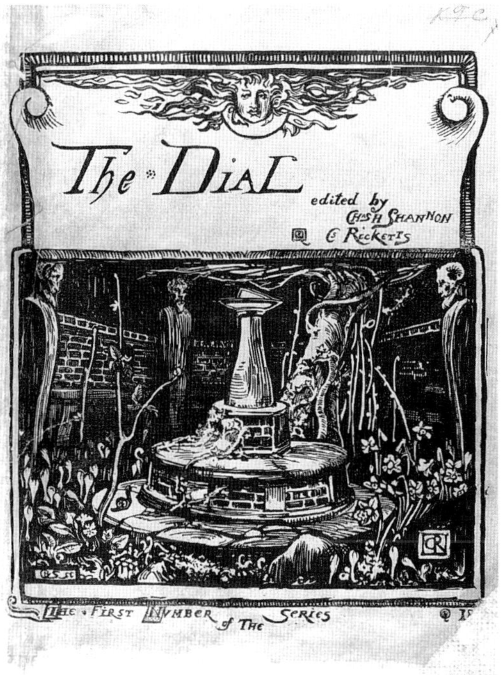

FIGURE 2. Charles Ricketts and Charles Shannon, cover, *The Dial* 1 (1889)

And yet this self-conscious refusal of the modern is also misleading. Given the pressure of modernity on Ricketts's life and career, it is perhaps not entirely surprising that his analysis in "A Century of Art" should be virtually identical with the account offered later by advanced modernism. In fact, literary historian Peter Bürger calls upon exactly this transition from patronage to the individual artistic entrepreneur operating in the cultural marketplace for the historical framework of his *Theory of the Avant-Garde.*[16] For Bürger, the avant-garde emerges in response to the perceived marginalization of art within culture and explicitly aims to return art to life, to render art relevant and appropriate to the circumstances of experience once again. Ricketts's analysis, too, culminates with his desire to achieve "a closer contact between art and the business of life."[17] He imagines a moment when art's exile from the center of cultural practice will end, when the dichotomy between the hermetic concerns of art and the concerns of life will collapse into an identity in which art belongs once more to lived experience. In this sense, Ricketts's sense of the strains on modern artistic practice is comparable to the diagnoses of later modernists, a connection to which I will return at the end of Chapter 5.

Ricketts holds that the cultural marginalization of art had resulted "between the years 1810–1910 . . . [in] a century of continuous effort to renew the language of painting," but he conceives the nature of that renewal in late Romantic terms. Ricketts believes that the nineteenth century was "a new Renaissance . . . an epoch of hope and endeavour among the artists," and Stevens, Watts, and Puvis are said to be among the proofs of this statement.[18] But they eschew modernist aspirations, however obsessive their search for new expression and languages in art and whatever the circumstances provoking them into that search. Instead, they and the other nineteenth-century masters Ricketts admires "have been devoted to the search after beauty, beauty of fact, beauty of emotion and thought, and to the revaluation of the scope of art as the emotional equal of the great literature of our time."[19] The terms in which art responds to its cultural estrangement therefore reflect the late Romantic symbolism for which Ricketts stands. Puvis "like all great masters paints . . . those moods of ecstasy in which we find the love of beauty and ease and grace."[20] Watts has the power to express what is suppressed and hidden, what lies beneath the surface of experience: "The invisible! The pulsations in the air about a spiritual manifestation, the peculiar rhythm belonging to 'les gestes insolites,' the appeal to our emotions by some intuitive use of line, mass, tone, and colour, or expression,—this poetic, or emotional gift has been at the command of the master in many of his imaginative designs."[21] Watts is "conscious of that something in the human force beyond . . . literalness of rendering"; he is "a painter who [can] turn his pigment into something more than the stuff one squeezes out of tubes . . . the artist who . . . 'renders the invisible by the visible.'"[22] As in the work of Rossetti and Burne-Jones, "those interpreters of passion as it hides away in the modern human mind, troubled, isolated, and coiled upon itself," "passion and the love of beauty" in Watts "is no longer outward and expansive, but something which remembers and regrets."[23] Ricketts resorts to a Symbolist language that looks not at the world that surrounds it but at a different creation, one imagined as a revelation of reality's inner workings. Art of Ricketts's sort seeks a representation that will access those aspects of experience elided or covered over by the dominant materialism of industrial capitalism. We can legitimately see him as engaged on that quest to find the eternal beneath the contingent and fleeting that Baudelaire famously identified as the founding principle of modernism[24]—the urgent desire to strip away the veil of matter and to suggest or evoke something of greater truth beneath.[25]

In this project, the capacity of the visual to comprehend the world and reveal its realities plays a central role.[26] As in Moore's "Lines on Titian's 'Bacchanal,'" the visual is highly valued because it can seem to *be* the world—that is, unmediated reality—and thus the means of directly accessing and understanding experience.[27] Writing toward the end of his life in some notes for a memoir, Moore celebrated this aspect of Shannon's practice, his visual acuity, his capacity to "look." He wrote, "Intellectuals generally only look at a work of art long enough to recognize its general character and place it in the catalogue of their knowledge, [but] he made a point of looking at everything as though he had never seen anything like it before. 'The fresh eye is the seeing eye' he would say. The eye that thinks it knows all about it only recognizes[,] never discovers."[28] When you look with the "seeing eye," you "discover" the world itself. That discovery is an act of revelation, an uncovering and bringing into comprehension of the depths of reality.[29] The visual is both the precise distillation of the world and the channel through which its ultimate, deeper meanings can be revealed and brought to consciousness. The visual thus carries the promise of revelation that Moore persistently seeks in his poetry and that pervades the intellectual life of the Ricketts circle and the English art world at the end of the nineteenth century.

This position poses certain difficulties. How can reality be communicated and not simultaneously betrayed? Shannon objects to the "intellectual" analysis of works of art because of its enthrallment to the generalizing and cataloguing abstraction of words, an abstraction that belies "the fresh eye," innocently looking. The summary communication of language, sunk in the depths of social rather than transcendent meaning, constantly threatens to distort or traduce the purity of perception assured by the visual. The visual needs translation through the verbal, but the verbal is labile and inadequate, both in its capacity to effect that translation and in its impotence before the meanings that require description. "Words are the most abused and most hackneyed of all art's mediums. We lie and cheat and bore our fellows with them," as Moore put it.[30] As a member of the group around Ricketts, Moore shared its preoccupation with these issues. If language was fallen, the visual still held out the promise of immediacy, revelation, and understanding, the possibility of a direct, "unmediated" world, a representation that was exactly the thing itself.

The Visual

Although Ricketts and his circle were active from the late 1880s onward, they inherited interests that had begun to develop much earlier. The most influential account of the history of the visual during the nineteenth century is that offered by Jonathan Crary, whose 1990 book, *Techniques of the Observer,* posits a "reorganization of vision" as a result of "events and forces, especially in the 1820s and 1830s, that produced a new kind of observer."[31] Wishing to break down the conventional identification of modernity in the visual with the emergence of formal modernism in French painting during the 1870s, Crary describes "a crucial systemic shift . . . well under way by 1820" that underlies both "modernist painting of the 1870s and 1880s and the development of photography after 1839" (5). He contends that

> *[w]hat takes place from around 1810 to 1840 is an uprooting of vision from the stable and fixed relations [of the Enlightenment, which] subsisted as an objective ground of visual truth. [In its place] a variety of discourses and practices—in philosophy, science, and in procedures of social normalization—tend to abolish the foundations of that ground in the early nineteenth century. In a sense, what occurs is a new valuation of visual experience: it is given an unprecedented mobility and exchangeability, abstracted from any founding site or referent.* (14)

I find Crary's sense of the labile and fictional nature of vision persuasive. In this book, however, I am interested in aspects of visual history not discussed by Crary, in the consequences of these shifts in understanding vision for practicing painters, and in how these consequences played out in England as a continuity of attempts to create a modern art. Crary's analysis reflects a dependence on the French experience for definitions of "modernism," a dependence that dominates scholarship to this day. In the conventional account, Edouard Manet and Impressionism in the 1870s and 1880s inaugurate modernism in painting, which is marked by formal deformation and experimentation in relation to cultural shifts that rendered much of the texture of everyday experience indeterminate and uncertain.[32] Crary's study suggests an earlier point of origin than is often acknowledged for the cultural forces at work, but the art-historical location of modern painting in late-nineteenth-century France remains undisturbed.

It is a central premise of this book that the definition of modernity in painting can be rethought by attending to the history of English painting from the mid-nineteenth century to the First World War. In concert with Crary, I identify the emergence of a new climate of possibility for the visual, this time specifically in the case of England, by the 1840s. At a moment when Victorians shared a widespread cultural concern about the nature of modernity, many of the artists, thinkers, and writers whom I discuss in the following chapters held that the visual might be a direct means of understanding the world and, to borrow T. J. Clark's phrase, "a way of storing knowledge" about it.[33] It became possible to imagine the visual as a way of knowing and communicating truths about experience and the world that no longer seemed available by other means. If the visual allowed access to reality in some direct, unmediated way, then it might also offer a means by which to answer the culture's pressing questions about modernity—about its nature, about how to evaluate it, about how any understanding might be communicated to wider audiences, and about how that might be done so that alternative values to those offered by the modern might be promulgated or at least raised. Many Victorians saw such a diagnosis as a profound necessity, and the putative capacity of the visual (including painting) to make it promised the solution to an important cultural conundrum.

Throughout the late nineteenth century, the purpose and status of the arts within a modernizing society seemed problematic. How should art function when the dominant values were disinclined to grant importance to an activity that yielded so little in economic terms and offered only expendable experiences, such as pleasure or relaxation? Was art no more than "a mere ornamental fringe on the social garment," as G. F. Watts feared[34]—a sort of aesthetic sweetmeat, distraction for the tired entrepreneur or the economically disengaged cadre of middle-class women, a brief frisson to counter the serious business of life? Or could it make more profound and telling interventions in human existence? The knot that held together modern values, the denigration of art, and the visual's potential to understand the world also ensnared the ambitions of many mid- to late Victorian and early-twentieth-century artists.

Even while the visual seemed to hold out a positive solution to these questions, the early nineteenth century, as Crary argues, also saw the beginning of a deeply rooted skepticism about the unmediated nature of visual knowledge. The idea that the visual had some direct access to reality was, in these circumstances, never more than a desirable possibility, a leap of faith, a supportive fiction about painting and its relationship to the world. With changes in contemporary theories of knowledge, it proved increasingly difficult to make that leap or embrace that fiction. As it became evident that the physical processes of human sight were themselves labile, involving complex distortions before images even registered themselves on the brain, it also became harder to ignore the mediated nature of visual representation or its role in formulating, rather than merely reporting, understanding. Other developments in nineteenth-century science, too, led to a switch in attention from the visible to the invisible worlds. In contrast to the analysis of the physical sciences, which focused on penetrating to the deepest, most arcane levels of reality, the visual increasingly appeared preoccupied with surface, with mere phenomenal appearance. Reality, it seemed (at least in the caustic light cast by Victorian science), took place at a level below that which sight could register, in the movement of invisible but pervasive particles through the universe, a process too deep for vision, which was now merely one of a number of ephemeral manifestations riding on the deceptive surface of the world.

These intersecting pressures on the cultural understanding of the visual resulted in the shifting and complex climate of possibility that is my subject in this book. *The World in Paint* addresses the way in which painters between 1848 and 1914 responded to these pressures, both positive and disabling, in their quest to achieve a modern art, one suitable for its "age" (to use a common contemporary formulation)—that is, an art that would reflect upon and diagnose the character and values of modern experience for its audience. The brutal absolutism of the historiographical distinctions we have inherited from the modernist period conceals the continuity of these concerns, enforcing an unbridgeable divide between late-nineteenth-century art and English modernism as it emerged around 1910. In what follows, I argue that it is possible to trace a "tradition" or unfolding project in English painting between 1848 and the outbreak of the First World War. The history of that project is the history of the struggle to imagine the visual as a medium capable of registering and understanding modern experience against a cultural situation that offered both powerfully positive and negative versions of its potential.[35]

I want to be clear about the extent of my claims here. Our ability to identify and describe the cultural processes by which scientific and other modes of understanding may interact with the imaginative representation of the world has been furthered by Gillian Beer's work on the interrelationships between Victorian science and other aspects of the cultural scene. In her best-known book, *Darwin's Plots* (1983), Beer looks at the responses of novelists to evolutionary theory: "with varying degrees of self awareness they . . . tested the extent to which [the theory] can provide a determining fiction by which to read the world."[36] Elsewhere, she writes:

The reception of ideas outside the immediate circle of co-workers is not systematic. This realization may be a nuisance for those of us raised in scholarly habits of mind but its acceptance is a precondition for any worthwhile analysis of the movement of ideas across fields within any historical culture. We must not look for intact ideas being transferred from setting to setting: ideas rarely remain intact when they change context. Instead we need to study how ideas are reimagined in response to other needs and to the thickness—in Geertz's term—of enquiry and debate elsewhere. We need also to be aware of the inertia of old thoughts to which new ideas can be accommodated.[37]

This strikes me as a very helpful summary of the issues at stake in doing this sort of work. As they make their way into the consciousness of even highly educated nonspecialist audiences, new theories or modes of understanding, whether scientific or otherwise, tend to change in uneven and unsystematic ways, acquiring different complexities and histories in new contexts. The Victorian cultural scene and its attitudes toward language and the visual are enormously complex. Ideas that had an impact, often implicitly, on the status of representation constantly circulated through the cultural and intellectual elites who made up the art world. In the process of dispersal and accommodation to understanding, these ideas were subject to interpretation and reinterpretation, to redaction, and to something very like what Harold Bloom has called "misprision"[38]—as well as to the inertia of received opinion. But, that said, the notions that concern me differ in an important sense from those of Beer's study, for I am not dealing with concepts remotely as systematic as Darwinian theory. These ideas were not clearly formulated by anyone outside the practice of painting. Their means of assertion was not language but paint, form, color, and shape on the surface of a canvas. In the light of our inclination to privilege linguistic over all other forms of argument or expression, they tend to seem negatives rather than positives, ghostly possibilities arising from the absence of strong claims elsewhere, shadows that drift in to occupy vacant cultural space. In fact, it may well be that they are best understood as concepts that supported, in a nonverbal way, painters' desire to claim their own practice as the most fundamental and, in this case, the most truthful in its relationship to reality and contemporary needs. They were a set of floating possibilities, a mental climate about the visual arts, expressed most forcefully in the manipulation of pigment on a surface.

When the generations from the Pre-Raphaelite moment of 1848 onward came to confront the requirements of practice, though, an altogether more rigorous testing of their viability took place. Faced with the need to produce work fit to bear out these "determining fictions" about the visual arts, however hazily held, the promise of the visual was enacted and thought through in the detail of paint on the canvas. I argue that, in response, some significant paintings from the early 1850s and after embody, first, an evolving dialectical duel between the competing claims of language and the visual, and subsequently, a series of meditations on the competence of the visual to serve as a way of knowing the world. Faced with the empty canvas, painters repeatedly found themselves obliged to overcome negative evaluations of vision and to argue—through the materiality of their work itself—that knowledge about reality might be gained from their handling of pigment on the flat plane of the canvas. In the process, paint became both the demonstration and the principal metaphor through which the feasibility of successfully communicating "reality" was measured and explored—a crucial issue for any painter who took the nature of modern experience as a subject. The working-out of this tradition of possibility and inquiry over sixty years of English art is the central theme of this book.

But such a subject and such claims beg important questions. "He frequently gives me quite a thrill of pleasure," said Albert Moore of his close friend and confrere, James McNeill Whistler, adding, "by means of the manipulation of his paint."[39] Such a statement, made as part of Moore's pretrial deposition in the 1878 case of *Whistler v. Ruskin,* is hard to resist quoting (if only in the hope of entertaining as well as persuading the reader). It makes a serious point, however. Moore's enthusiasm is aroused by the substance of paint itself, pushed around or—in Whistler's case—diluted to a thin liquid and washed onto the flat surface of a canvas. But how can such an activity generate meaning? Is the "thrill of pleasure" it can provide its only virtue, an instant of sensuous enjoyment, brief, trivial, and meaningless? Or can paint instruct us, tell us truths about the world because, in some manner, it can inquire into reality and thus enlighten us in ways other forms of knowledge cannot? The question of whether painting could know the world through its materiality concerned the several generations of painters and thinkers about art who are my subjects here.[40]

Art history, as a discipline, has shied away from addressing such questions too explicitly, embarrassed perhaps by the possibility that its object of study might after all exist only to serve something as frivolous as sensuous pleasure and hence prove its own investigation indulgent or irresponsible. It has preferred to shore up the suspect edifice of the physical work with the somber buttresses supplied by the archive, the social history of the object, or such things as psychoanalysis or semiotics—in other words, the serious business of scholarly inquiry, a weighty undertaking that no one could accuse of frivolity. In what follows, I invoke the historical as a principal agent of explanation and may thus risk stabilizing this disruptive potential of the visual in my turn. Nonetheless, the argument I put forward concerns itself with how we are to handle this embarrassing fact of the materiality of the work of art and the questions it brings in its wake: about the meanings we can plausibly attribute to color, pigment, line, and form, as well as the value of pleasure and even the fearsome spectre of the aesthetic, which twenty years of the social history of art have encouraged us to ignore.

The wholesale rejection of the theories of Clement Greenberg that took place in the 1970s and after, and its corollary, the rise of the social history of art to art-historical orthodoxy, have combined to marginalize inquiry into these visual qualities of the artwork. At its height, the sociohistorical approach refused the visual aspects of the painting in the name of moral probity. The visual was equated with the aesthetic, and the aesthetic was no more than a repressive mystification that covered over the realities of power, status, and oppression. A concern with the visual aspect of works of art seemed proof of dubious or culpable tastes and was damned by association with the connoisseurs who served the marketplace.[41] So-called high modernism, conceived as the apogee of formalism, was defined as an approach that impeded critical activity and encouraged a lack of self-consciousness or awareness of anything outside the two dimensions of the canvas, thus allowing art to serve discreditable purposes. The visual stood accused—and was better ignored.

And yet, a powerful interest in visuality, of course, *is* historically a characteristic of modernist painting. Greenberg famously identified the irreducible physical facts of the medium as the defining conditions of modernist art: he pronounced that "the limitations that constitute the medium of painting [are] the flat surface, the shape of the support, the properties of pigment."[42] The "ineluctable flatness of the support," above all, is the "fundamental . . . condition" toward which modernism "orientated itself."[43] Moreover, there is arguably nothing specific to modernism about either the physical facts of the medium or their manipulation.[44] We do not have to accept Greenberg's argument about modernism to accept that the material aspects of painting are fundamental to its capacity to generate meaning. *All* painting must signify, if it has meaning at all, through these founding qualities of its physical constitution.[45] To say this is not to propose a "formalism"—at least not if we take the term to mean that we should confine the significance of the work of art purely to its visible fabric without reference to the history and culture in which it takes part. Rather, if works of art do in fact *mean* in culture, then they must surely do so through the physical characteristics that are unique to them as objects. The problem becomes one of how to connect historical circumstance with the physical surfaces of paintings. An identification of a self-conscious awareness of the mediating role of paint in representation, along with an anxiety to reconcile that knowledge with the belief in painting's immediacy and truthfulness in accounting for the world, lies at the heart of my readings of English painting from the Pre-Raphaelites on. It is a historical argument and not a purely visual one.

To describe English painting in this way is to trespass against received wisdom. Not only am I suggesting that the visual and its manipulation play important roles in the way English artists tackled the pressing question of how to acknowledge and explore their own modernity, but I am also implying that the conventional identification (and often dismissal) of their art as "literary" is misleading. The art-historical division between a visually experimental and mobile French "modernism" and a dully literary, anecdotal, or narrative English "realism" will not stand up to much hard scrutiny. A self-consciousness about technique and paint surface—and an explicit drive for innovation as a means to express novel circumstances—marks English painting from the eighteenth century on, and from at least the 1840s it is preoccupied with the visual as a response to contemporary experience. What distinguishes the "tradition" I posit here is precisely the continuity of endeavor we can trace from the moment of Pre-Raphaelitism to the English modernism of the First World War. This art thought about its ability to understand and communicate the character of its culture, its "modernity," as a function of formal innovation and self-consciousness. The creation of new visual languages seemed essential to meet the needs of new conditions of experience. New configurations of paint and facture took on the responsibility of diagnosing, comprehending, and transcending the realities of that modernity. The visual in English painting turns out to be both complicit with language and frequently opposed to it, placing its own forms of meaning and knowledge against a problematic linguistic version.

But to say this is to get ahead of my argument. The promise held out by the ideas I am advancing is the historicization of the visual facts of painting, an inquiry into how line, color, and the formal events of facture assume meanings specific to a time and to a culture. In the case of English painting in my period, these meanings turn out to be involved with a response to the culture's modernity and to the status of knowledge available about it. Such a historicization requires answers to some fundamental questions. How did this particular historical moment conceptualize the visual? What was the significance of the material characteristics of an artwork? In what ways were the possible manipulations of paint "read" and understood by the artist and his or her contemporaries?[46] Answers to such questions need to be rigorously historical but also require a close attention to the nature of the visual, to the marks made by brush or knife, and to the visual's function within the painting as a whole, what Georges Didi-Huberman calls "a semiology . . . of events, accidents, and singular features of the pictorial image," an analytic inquiry into the materiality of paint.[47] The problem with much art history in practice is its inclination to derive social meaning from context and institutional environment alone and to ignore the nature of the object and the capacity of the visual to generate cultural meaning. This book is an attempt to imagine how such an inquiry might look in the context of English painting between the mid-nineteenth century and the First World War. It addresses how painting's materiality signifies in this specific historical moment and reads the meaning of paintings made at the time through the terms raised by that analysis. In doing so, it proposes an account of the complex emergence of a modern painting in England during these years.

Visuality, Modernity, Unmediation

In order to formulate both the nature of the questions for my time and place and the answers that the painters I discuss gave to them, I have drawn throughout on the three concepts in the title of this section. I want to introduce them now briefly before I move on to the historical material. The first, "visuality," signifies that the visual is not an innocent category but one that is formed through and in culture and history.[48] Hal Foster uses the word to contrast the physical facts of sight with the ways in which they are understood and augmented at any historical moment.[49] Foster asserts that vision, "the mechanism of sight," differs from visuality, "its historical techniques."[50] Such a distinction opens up the type of inquiry, exemplified by Crary's investigation into the "hegemonic set of discourses and practices in which vision took shape in the nineteenth century" (*Techniques,* 7), that scrutinizes the social formation of vision. Building on these definitions, Nicholas Mirzoeff has proposed visuality as the intersection of visual technologies (by which he means oil paint, among other things), the individual, and society, "an interaction of the visual sign, the technology that enables and sustains that sign, and the viewer."[51] If we accept these definitions, visuality is the construction of vision at a particular historical moment and the meanings that accrue to it through its operation. In the first sense I am using here, "visuality" accordingly names the ways in which meaning is attributed in culture both to vision and to the visual character of objects. There is a second sense of the term, however: one may speak of visuality as the asserted material qualities of a work of art. In this sense, a painting's visuality is its facture, the way in which pigment and its visual characteristics are explicitly manipulated in order to construct the picture as an artifact possessing meaning.[52] Visuality refers, then, to the visual assemblage of the material object rather than to any discursive meaning that might arise from the narrative or subject matter of a picture. One might speak, in this sense, of the "pure" visuality of, say, much

Aesthetic painting. I use visuality in both these senses in what follows and trust to context to make the meaning clear.

"Modernity" is my second concept, and it leads me to a set of related words that I use throughout the book. The terms "modernity" and "modern" figure throughout my discussion because they point to a self-conscious ambition among the artists I deal with to develop a practice adequate to their contemporary life. This does not imply a modern subject matter. Instead, I mean by this a desire to achieve a painting that takes as its subject matter the psychic character of cultural experience, aware all the while that the nature of that experience is in flux, so that it continually touches on novelty and transformation. The art that answers to these conditions is modern but not necessarily modernist. I reserve that word for the formally experimental art produced in the few years before the First World War.[53] I am not arguing for stylistic connections but rather a shared and developing response to a cultural situation. Whatever forms it takes, the "tradition" I trace strives to achieve a modern art expressive of an understanding of contemporary experience, one able to comprehend, evaluate, and communicate what were taken to be the realities of that experience. The question for artists throughout this period was how successfully such a project—to define and understand modern life—could be conducted in what one of the tradition's major figures, Walter Sickert, called the "gross material" substance of paint.[54]

The ways in which artists found themselves responding to this situation take us to the last of my central concepts. "Mediation" names the ways in which representation figures the world for comprehension. In any act of understanding, there are three terms involved: the world, the medium or technology through which perception takes place, and the observing self, the same trio we have seen operating in definitions of visuality. The raw materials of what is thought of or experienced as reality (which themselves perhaps have only an imaginative status) are processed through some technology, through a physiological operation, or through a concept or preconception and are presented to the self through the prism provided by that medium. There is no comprehension of the world without some version of this triad. There is good reason to think of an explicit awareness of mediation, in this sense, as a sign of cultural modernity. The perception that knowledge is contingent, partial, and invested marks the style of cognition we associate with the culture of the late nineteenth and early twentieth centuries. An awareness that concepts, language, or other forms of representation are the intermediaries to understanding is a primary impulse for the self-consciousness and reflexivity of strictly modernist art—

as well as of much cultural production that we think of as "Victorian," "Aestheticist," or "fin-de-siècle."[55]

In the work that she has initiated on the meanings of glass as a modernizing substance in the nineteenth century, Isobel Armstrong has produced some compelling formulations of this awareness in Victorian culture. Armstrong sees the omnipresence of this invisible but reflective medium from the 1830s onward as having "provoked, if not a crisis of mediation, acute awareness of an intensely mediated culture": "As transparency mediates the gaze, its lucidity is itself the result of a highly mediated process. Glass is a *transitive* material, and in the nineteenth century it became insistently so, a material which made one intensely aware that, in the movement between one state and another, there is a third term. The world is triangulated."[56] Under such circumstances, the visual itself becomes self-aware. The desire to apprehend the world directly is constantly undermined by the return of the materiality of representation and the technologies of sight, so that there arises "an intense anxiety of mediation, a scientific, philosophical, aesthetic and civic problem to the Victorians," one in which representation is imagined, like glass, as "an invisible membrane, a barrier," or, most commonly and pressingly, "a middle, an equivocating, difficult substance," interposing itself between vision and the world.[57] One does not need to accept the full extent of these claims to see that, from the perspective I am proposing, these changes are part of much wider sets of shifts and developments in Victorian culture. Armstrong indeed connects the technological development of glass in the early part of the nineteenth century to "the beginnings of an avidly scopic culture—a culture of *looking*" in ways that support the claims I make here for the cultural importance of the visual as well as a pervasive awareness of the role of mediation in the act of representation.[58]

I have found it useful to extend the idea of mediation to its corollary, or opposite, which I call "unmediation." Unlike visuality and modernity, unmediation is my neologism and is best explained through its appearance in what follows. I use it to describe the major trope through which late-nineteenth-century artists sought to express the dream that the visual can diagnose and communicate realities about the world. For some, it served as a focus of self-consciousness and as the major means of inquiring into the persuasiveness of such a claim for the visual. Painting, with its technologies of pigment and application, is imagined as outside the systems of mediation, direct and immediate in its relationship with the world and hence able to provide through its visual character an authentic knowledge denied to other forms of understanding. It results from the desire to believe that the distribution of pigment on the surface of a canvas could elicit a sensuous "thrill of pleasure" that would provide a complex knowledge about lived experience. This fantasy of immediacy gives rise to strategies and responses in paintings, ways of asserting and insisting on an unmediated access to reality as a principal thematic strand in their makeup. The unsustainablity of the dream provokes its own tradition.[59]

Language, Representation, and Commodification

I want to look now at some of the important ways in which the changing modernity of the culture during the nineteenth and early twentieth centuries proved formative for the history I am tracing. This structure helps clarify the main historical developments that underpin my analysis: the rise of ideas inimical to early-nineteenth-century claims for language as a means of knowledge and the corresponding gain in potential for the visual; the role of John Ruskin's early writing in preparing the ground for such a development; the increasing challenge to this idea of the visual mounted by developments in areas of Victorian science from optics to astronomy; and the ways in which these ideas in circulation within the culture intersected with the commodification and commercialization of the art world itself. Although I place considerable emphasis on the effect of suspicion about language, I see it as only one (although perhaps the most immediate) contribution to the climate of possibility I identify around the visual. The fate of language and visuality expresses the wider history of theories of knowledge within the society.

Nineteenth- and twentieth-century history has, in keeping with the understanding of cultural modernity, been told in terms of "revolution" and a prolonged "crisis" composed of successive or parallel crises in diverse areas, among them religion, language, administration, and the theory of knowledge. The nineteenth century sees repeated attempts both to hold back the processes of change and to modernize the practical arrangements of existence, so that reflection and understanding move at different paces than, and are opposed to, technology and administration. Partly, this is a history of failed promise, as attempts to shore up the ruins of understanding repeatedly collapse. The hope "that scientific and historical knowledge would provide synthetic and normative foundations for modern life" of the sort that "philosophy and religion" provided in earlier societies came to be acknowledged as unsustainable, as the processes of nineteenth-century thought moved toward the questioning of objectivity and its replacement by a mediated world, one dependent on the operation of subjectivity and understanding in order to achieve a knowable form.[60] The corollary of this is the perception that "nature" exceeds the bounds of the thinkable—that we have merely a fragmentary grasp of the realities we seek to understand, each shard of understanding won from an acknowledgment of our own situated and partial viewpoint in reaching it. By the early twentieth century, "in the human sciences, philosophy and the arts we find the shared assumption that consciousness is not fully transparent to itself. It is regulated by mechanisms that define reality as we ordinarily know it."[61] The contingency of knowledge and understanding is installed as a central characteristic of the world.

Language, like other totalizing systems, came under pressure from such developments. By the 1840s, the confidence in the identity of language and the world of an earlier Romantic idealism had substantially eroded. The belief (influentially argued by Samuel Coleridge) that language could be "a mirror of some antecedently existing fact," a spiritual "revelation" of a divinely ordered reality, collapsed under the pressure of this emergent skepticism about the structure of knowledge, one that gained momentum as the century progressed.[62] W. David Shaw, for instance, in his study of "the connections . . . between Victorian poetics and changing theories of language and knowledge," proposes a shift from an initial belief that the knowledge offered by language directly reflects nature, through agnosticism, philosophical questioning of the status of representation in thought, and intermittent attempts to recuperate the earlier immediacy of relationship, to a late Victorian obsession with the autonomy of representation from the world it purports to describe. In this final style of "pure presentation . . . as in art for art's sake, there is no pretence of re-presenting or of analogizing anything," but instead "a mere symbolic shorthand like the algebraic notations of the mathematical physicist." Language and the representation of the world in language-based systems such as science are acknowledged as media that do not transmit their subjects but offer perspectives through which we can observe them: "a symbolic shorthand . . . a kaleidoscope of fictions which renounce any pretence of duplicating anything."[63] "The scientist does not merely record," comments Sally Shuttleworth, glossing George Eliot's opinions in *Daniel Deronda* (1876): "he actively constructs a schema within which his observations are placed." Such a view "threatens the comforting conception of science as the unquestionable transcription of the unchanging external world."[64]

From a related point of view, Linda Dowling has seen the new historical linguistics of the nineteenth century as corroding established values and certainties, a process she speaks of as "a Victorian cultural crisis." Like Shaw and Shuttleworth, she traces a change from certainty to skepticism in the nineteenth century, as a view of "language as a system blindly obeying impersonal philological rules in isolation from . . . human values and experience" ate away at Victorian foundations of belief.[65] In this spirit, the linguist and writer on the nature of myth, Max Müller, addressing the Royal Institution in 1863, set out "to determine the sway, if any, which language as such exercises over our thoughts." He concluded that words have a "variable" relation to things, and thus detached language from the world by installing it as a medium. "The mischief," he wrote, "begins when language forgets itself, and makes us mistake the word for the Thing, the Quality for the Substance, the *Nomen* for the *Numen*."[66] Such views, too, raised suspicions about the primacy of language as a means of understanding. Once words are understood to be only arbitrarily connected to things, language appears as a medium, interposing a screen of interpretation between the world and our understanding of it. These developments, entirely antipathetic to the identity of language and world as it was conceived in the Romantic idealist tradition, proved profoundly unsettling to the evaluation of language in the culture.

The impact of linguistics on views of language was matched by that of other areas of scientific investigation. The German physicist Hermann von Helmholtz, whose theories had an enormous influence in late-nineteenth-century Britain and who has featured largely in the considerable literature on the interaction of science and cultural representation in the period, concerned himself, as part of an extended scientific inquiry, with optics as well as with general theories of scientific understanding.[67] Beer speaks of "the prevalence of Helmholtzian physiological optics and acoustics as a reference point in English Victorian intellectual life." His ideas were indeed widely known and influential, providing criteria for judgment over a range of debates.[68] In a series of books and articles explicitly indebted to Helmholtz, John Tyndall, his interpreter and popularizer in Britain, put forward the argument for the preeminence of scientific authority and understanding, and, in particular, its superiority to the authority and understanding offered by language.[69] Tyndall's inaugural address on the "advancement of science," delivered in 1874, opens with a reprint of Helmholtz's "Opinions of an Eminent Scientist," which had first appeared in the widely read magazine *Nature*. In this text, Helmholtz had deemed language fundamentally inferior to scientific analysis as a way of understanding the world:

The past progress of education of civilized nations has had its central point in the study of language. Language is the great instrument through possession of which man is most distinctly separated from the lower animals; through the use of which he is able to share the experience and knowledge of other individuals of his time, as also those of past generations. . . . But while language is the means of handing down and preserving truth once recognized, we must not forget that its study teaches nothing of how fresh truth is to be found. . . . Thus all these [language-based] studies do not themselves lead us to the proper source of knowledge—do not bring us face to face with the reality which we seek to know.[70]

The combination in the scientific method of abstraction from individual experience and the generation of universal laws to describe the cosmos allowed scientists like Helmholtz and Tyndall to assert their method's superiority as a means of understanding the operations and nature of reality. Giving his own version of this argument in his 1871 *Fragments of Science for Unscientific People,* Tyndall argued that although the journey was incomplete, science had made great strides toward the "complete intellectual mastery of nature." He continued: "Were they facts only, without logical relationship, science might, as a means of discipline, suffer in comparison with language. But the whole body of phenomena is instinct with law; the facts are hung on principles, and the value of physical science as a means of discipline consists in the motion of the intellect, both inductively and deductively, along the lines of law marked out by phenomena."[71] Writing for a popular educated audience, Tyndall is always tactful in the claims he makes for science, but the meaning of this challenge to the capacity of language to account for the world is nonetheless very clear. As a means of understanding the realities of the universe, or of accounting for experience and perception within it, language, in its traditional humanistic guise, is a flawed and inadequate instrument when compared with the refined questionings of scientific method. Well before this skeptical late Victorian intellectual landscape had come about, the solidity of language as a form of knowledge about the world had become porous and begun to dissolve away. It seemed impossible by the 1850s to believe in the rich idealist identity of language and the world when theories of both language and knowledge increasingly stressed the disconnection of the two.[72]

This uncertainty about the status of language was reinforced from the 1860s onward by other structural developments in the culture. As the century approached its final quarter, a progressive accommodation of the art world to capitalist norms and processes operating elsewhere in society became increasingly evident, a process that Griselda Pollock has summed up as "the economic modernization of artistic practice by capitalist forms of production."[73] Dragged along by pervasive structural developments in bourgeois culture, the art world evolved its own versions of the attributes of capitalist production. Art underwent a process of fragmentation into ever smaller competing markets, the elaboration of the competitive machinery of publicity and market image, and the reification and professionalization of art and artists as commodities. Jasper Milvain, "the literary man of 1882"—and thus the character in George Gissing's novel of 1891, *New Grub Street,* who best represents the decision to embrace and exploit this situation—sums up the new dispensation early on. Milvain declares that "literature nowadays is a trade . . . your successful man of letters is your successful tradesman. He thinks first and foremost of the markets."[74] Milvain adds, "I maintain that we people of brains are justified in supplying the mob with the food it likes. . . . Let us use our wits to earn money, and make the best we can of our lives. If only I had the skill, I would produce novels out-trashing the trashiest that ever sold fifty thousand copies."[75]

Significantly, in Gissing's account, *language* is associated with the market.[76] Not only under threat from skepticism about its ontological claims to express the realities of the world, language has also become tied in with the processes of modernity as they played out for artists and writers in the closing decades of the century. To the degree that language became associated with modernity, literally constitutive of New Grub Street and all it stood for, it came to seem, or be reinforced as, a fallen medium, one that was corrupt because irretrievably bound in with the systems it might otherwise have diagnosed. The result would have a powerful impact on the valuation of art itself, as "the late Victorian awareness of a shift from production to consumption" that accompanied this process brought the attention of artists, writers, and thinkers to bear on its implications.[77]

One outcome of this professionalization and modernization of artistic practice was the connection of works of visual art to a flood of discourse, words written and spoken to defend and explicate the visual artifacts that were supposedly prior.[78] The outpouring of words in reviews, catalogue entries, defenses, letters to the press, articles (and, famously, lawsuits), under which the pure object of late-nineteenth-century art threatened to disappear, makes it clear that there were more words about art around at precisely the moment when art was being claimed as an "autonomous" practice, free from the commercial and professional contexts in which language was incontestably the master and the means to success and authority.[79] Kate Flint has discussed the spectacular growth of professional art criticism both as a necessary mediator "between public and artist" that appeared once the visual self-consciousness of paintings began to demand a certain level of sophistication from its spectators and as a frank commodification of that role.[80] Commerce, primarily, constituted this world, and words were the means by which the visual arts were connected most clearly to that reality—the raw material from which a sellable commodity could be invented.

The Promise of the Visual

By the mid-nineteenth century, then, the status of knowledge was under question. As a result, "in every cultural domain," as Dorothy Ross puts it in a discussion of the response of the human sciences to the "new subjectivity of knowledge," "this new uncertainty led to efforts to reconstruct knowledge, value, and representation."[81] The visual arts were no different from any other inquiry into the world in this respect, and artists and thinkers about the visual accordingly began to consider its possibilities as a means of reintegrating the role of representation with knowledge about the world. In that scene of possibility, other factors were also in play. Ben Knights has traced the survival of Romantic ideas of cultural leadership by thinkers and writers fully integrated into their society into the Victorian age. Coleridge's argument for an intellectual "clerisy" having "an ideal role in relation to society as a whole" is perpetuated in the work of such "sages" as Thomas Carlyle, Matthew Arnold, John Stuart Mill, Ruskin, and John Henry Newman as a "defensive reaction" to the marginalization of art in bourgeois culture.[82] The Victorian desire for a moral polity, one that could deal honestly with the circumstances of life according to the Christian dispensation, was bound into this broader effort to preserve the role of art in modernity. Carlyle, the first great prophet of the century, had thundered against the dominant values of the culture. "Were we required to characterise this age of ours by any single epithet," he wrote in "Signs of the Times" (1829), "we should be tempted to call it . . . the Mechanical Age . . . the age which, with its whole undivided might, forwards, teaches and practises the great art of adapting means to ends."[83] Art became the possible route by which other values than those dominant in the culture could be made active. Art could diagnose and express the realities of experience for the citizens of this modernity, the artist filling a vatic role as a conduit of truths for the whole of society. "'I' is not always the author speaking of himself," declared Alfred Tennyson, "but the voice of the human race speaking through him."[84] For Ruskin, the painter can be a priest whose ethical leadership depends on the force of his imagination. But such a claim assumes not only that art's re-creation of experience can provide us with greater insights than experience itself but also that this re-creation must issue in action. If the artist is a sage and the interpreter of the culture to its citizens, then the work of art becomes the pattern of action and its purest instance. Art *is* action: the "artist becomes hero . . . the work of art becomes the quintessential deed."[85] For those concerned with the visual arts, it seemed that the visual itself might fill that active function, reconceive modernity, and revalue the possibilities of representation.

The most influential thinker about the visual in this way was Ruskin. In the first volumes of *Modern Painters* (begun in 1843), Ruskin takes up the search for alternative values and posits apprehension of the natural world through the medium of vision as their source.[86] For Ruskin, both vision and the natural stand for an integrity and authenticity of experience uncompromised by the corrupting influence of nineteenth-century materialism:[87]

> *Nothing to look at! That is indeed—you will find, if you consider of it—our sorrowful case. The vast extent of the advertising frescoes of London, daily refreshed into brighter and larger fresco by its billstickers, cannot somehow sufficiently entertain the popular eyes . . . even the excitement of the shop-window, with its unattainable splendours, or too easily attainable impostures, cannot maintain itself in the wearying mind of the populace, and I find my charitable friends inviting the children, whom the streets educate only into vicious misery, to entertainments of scientific vision, in microscope or magic lantern; thus giving them something to look at, such as it is;—fleas mostly; and the stomachs of various vermin; and people with their heads cut off and set on again;— still* something, *to look at.*[88]

In this passage the visual is opposed not only to the corrupted modernity of "the streets" and the popular visual culture of advertising, billboards, and the display of consumer goods but also to the inadequate alternatives offered by "scientific" vision. In contrast, painting depends on another, purer, vision, one that Ruskin claims is direct in its access to the world, unmediated in its apprehension of the realities of the physical universe. He contends, "The whole technical power of painting depends on our recovery of what may be called the *innocence of the eye;* that is to say, of a sort of childish perception of these flat stains of colour, merely as such, without consciousness of what they signify,— as a blind man would see them if suddenly gifted with sight."[89] In *Techniques of the Observer,* Crary identifies this "innocence" with a more general modernization of ideas about vision in the nineteenth century that posited their own form of "'pure' perception": the reduction of vision to the reception of light by the retina, to "pure" sensation without any implication of "historical codes and conventions of seeing" that were understood as after the fact and separate from the elemental processes of sight (96). Ruskin's version of these ideas was based on a belief in the capacity of the purified eye to apprehend the reality of the world directly as visual experience. The world is perceived before any social vision as "flat stains of colour," like the painter's canvas itself. His famous word pictures, like the celebration of the technical power of color in painting and perception in *Modern Painters,* seem designed to express this elemental understanding of the visual. The innocent eye, concludes Crary, imagines a situation in which the "subjectivity of the observer" is argued away (69).

In a study of "the autobiographical impulse" in Ruskin, Jay Fellows traces the history of Ruskin's attitude toward the self and objections to its encroachment on the world. In the early part of his career, Ruskin was adamantly opposed to the intrusion of the self into observation because its presence seems to distort the accurate understanding of what is experienced. He resists and persistently theorizes away the self who observes in favor of its separation from the world, expressed through the trope of seeing, observation, the distance between what is seen and the self that does the seeing. His preference is therefore for what Fellows calls "a condition of voyeuristic invisibility," that is, for the individual to become "an optical system without a sense of self." The self must become "annulled," become "less than nothing," so that the reality of experience can be directly apprehended.[90] Taking up Fellows's points, Lindsay Smith has written of the "repression of consciousness" in Ruskin's thought that the making of art "allows the negative self to penetrate a perceived object in order to enhance . . . the illusion of non-involvement" and to produce an artist whose highest ambition is to negate his own self before the realities he delineates.[91] Ruskin wants an art that directly relates to the world, free of the dissembling codes of post-Renaissance mimesis. "He wants," says Smith, "to dispense with conventions of picture-making which influence vision in order to recover what he considers primary optical 'facts' . . . that which exists prior to sophisticated and preconceived orderings of the visual field."[92]

Ruskin's influence was pervasive, and *Modern Painters* provided a powerful model of the relationship of the visual to reality that held an intuitive appeal for artists. For the generation that came of age with the Pre-Raphaelite moment of the late 1840s, not only was language under suspicion but a highly influential and appealing claim for the visual was also in circulation as an alternative. The visual—from the perspective Ruskin offered—could stand for the possibility of transcending modernity, overcoming the instrumental values presented by developments in other areas of the culture.[93] "In modernity," Jay Bernstein has argued, "beauty is not only alienated from truth, but grieves its loss."[94] I am suggesting that we might see visuality as fulfilling a similar function. The visual, penetrating into realities that language no longer seemed convincingly able to reveal, acquired a potentiality, a scene of opportunity and ambition, that it had not possessed before. But that potential had to evade the fact of its compensatory role, its grieving for a loss it attempted to disguise as plenitude. Although vision as a central value in Ruskin promised to allow modernity to be assessed and rethought by a successful modern painting, it was a gift that brought with it a weary self-consciousness, a negative of itself against which potential had to be continually asserted.

Against this background, intellectuals and artists from the 1840s onward began to develop theories of art that would support its independence from the fallen state of modern life. From at least as early as the appearance of the Pre-Raphaelites in 1848, Victorian artists were preoccupied with the obligation to find a new visual language to match the new conditions of experience that accompanied modernity. The artist, wrote G. F. Watts in a typical formulation, "can produce no great work unless he impress the character of his age upon his production, not necessarily taking his subjects from it (better if he can), but taking the impress of its life."[95] Aware that circumstances and the pace of change meant that existing regimes of representation no longer served to account for the realities of experience, that "the turmoil and complications of modern life make an artist's task incomparably more difficult and artificial" so that "we can no longer be the *unconscious* voice of our time," as Frederic Leighton put it, artists from the Pre-Raphaelite Brotherhood on consciously sought to evolve and refine new visual languages suitable for the task of expressing the age.[96] In this project, Ruskin's thought gave them hope as well as a forbidding task. The visual, mobilized in the form of painting, was to conjure the reality of modern experience directly for the spectator, to be the conscious "unconscious" voice of its time.

How this type of thinking operated in practice can be seen in the opinions and reception of a major artist of the late nineteenth century. In keeping with the opinions of the early Pre-Raphaelites, Edward Burne-Jones, like many of his peers, criticized the character of new, modernized forms of knowledge throughout his life, whether financial, scientific, or emotional. "As I looked at its gigantic wearisomeness," he wrote of that celebrated symbol of modernity, the Crystal Palace, "at its length of cheerless monotony, iron and glass, glass and iron, I grew more and more convinced of the powerlessness of such material to effect an Architecture . . . give me *The Light of the World* and the apse of

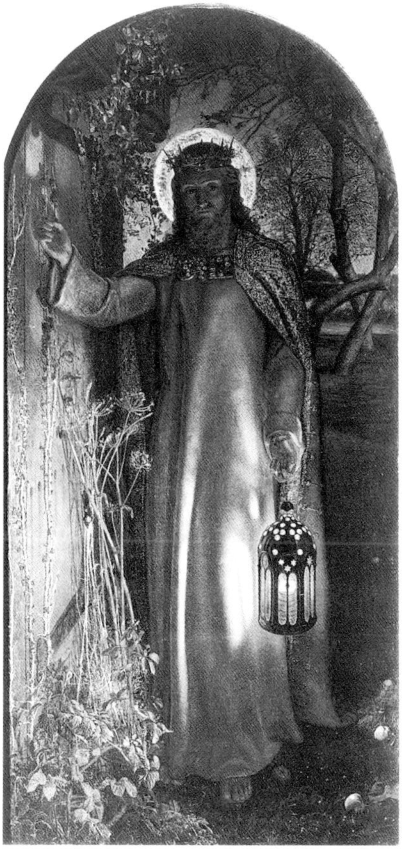

FIGURE 3. William Holman Hunt, *The Light of the World,* 1851–53, retouched 1858, 1886

Westminster."[97] The evocation here of William Holman Hunt's painting of 1851–53 (fig. 3), like the soaring thirteenth-century apse of Westminster Abbey, opposes a self-consciously symbolic and spiritual image to the gross monumentality of the Crystal Palace. Spirituality is thought to allow an access to authentic human experience that modern materialism cannot. This perspective, which owed much to Ruskin's ideas of prophetic imagination and an ethical and priestly role for the artist, gave a characteristic tenor to Burne-Jones's statements about his own ambitions: "when I work hard and paint visions and dreams and symbols for the understanding of people, I shall hold my head up better," he wrote in 1856.[98] His assertions that "I shall try to live less and less in [the world]: altogether out of it if possible" or that his art was "a reflection of a reflection of something purely imaginary" thus gain a different inflection from that of the "escapism" normally attributed to them.[99] Burne-Jones's "escape" has a critical edge. In his own mind, he escapes to "that strange land that is more true than real."[100]

Burne-Jones's contemporaries also recognized this impulse readily enough and identified the dreamwork of his art as a critical act with a direct relevance to modernity. Julia Cartwright, writing on Burne-Jones's "life and work" for the *Art Annual* in 1894, began with the statement that "the art of Burne-Jones from first to last has been a silent and unconscious protest against the most striking tendencies of the modern world." She was quite clear what these tendencies were and what the virtues were of setting art against them:

In an age when the scientific spirit has penetrated into every department of life, when skilful execution and experimental research supply the lack of ideas and atone for poverty of invention among our painters, this master, almost alone among his peers, has revealed an imaginative faculty of the rarest description. In a period which is essentially prosaic, when realism has invaded both art and fiction, and material prosperity seems to be the end and aim of all endeavour, he has remained a poet and an idealist. . . . From the dulness and ugliness of the present he turns with all the passionate ardour of his being to the forgotten past, and there, in the myths and fairy-tales of the old world, he finds the food after which his soul hungers. There his love of beauty is satisfied, his imagination finds itself at home.[101]

For Cartwright, art provides the sustenance that life under Victorian materialism fails to offer, and this necessary nourishment is spiritual, defined as those uncommercial currents of the human soul that appear to lack use value in economic terms: "imagination," "invention," "idealism." "All stories told or written have arisen out of life's experience," wrote the art critic J. E. Phythian, "each, in some degree is true to it; and the truest, in the deepest sense of the word, are not always those that merely recite facts."[102] It was the French art critic Robert de la Sizeranne who provided the fullest exposition of this viewpoint:

It is perfectly true that [Burne-Jones] does not paint dresses from Worth, or furniture from the stores. He should be congratulated thereupon. But it is an immense error, made by realists in search of modern superficiality, to think that his works suggest fewer contemporary pictures, fewer existing interests, because they are further apart from our daily life than the illustrations of the Graphic and the Illustrated London News. This is proved by the permanent impression they leave on anyone who has seen them. For myself, I never looked at some of his works without a revival of the anxieties and realities of the passing hour.[103]

Sizeranne goes on to discuss *Love Among the Ruins* (1894, fig. 4) as an example of this effect, concluding that, as he looked at it, "our thoughts were with the present, with the ruins amidst which we live, which are all too real" and linking the

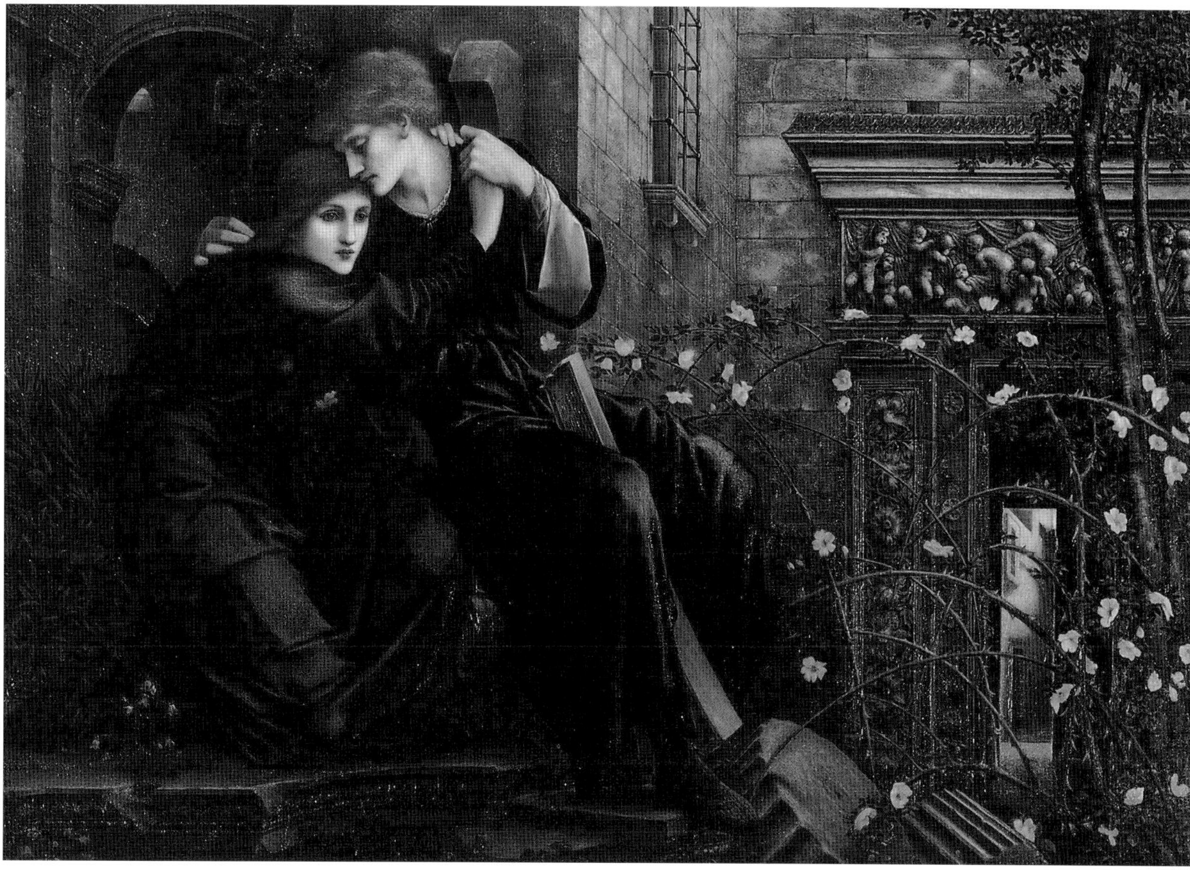

FIGURE 4. Edward Burne-Jones, *Love Among the Ruins,* 1894

painting's subject directly to an account of late-nineteenth-century despair at modernity's dismantling of certainties.[104] For commentators like Sizeranne, Burne-Jones's devotion to the unreality of his fictional worlds allows him a vantage point from which the realities of contemporary experience can be rescued from their normal obscurity and rendered visible. The escapism of the art is a tool through which "the natural reaction from an age of rationalism and materialism" can offer consolation as well as diagnosis and critique.[105]

Burne-Jones's art, then, was conceived by contemporaries and by the artist himself as a form of knowledge, a critical understanding of his time and culture—one that depended on the capacity of painting to function as a means of knowing the contemporary world. That is its "visuality." Sizeranne's evocation of the effect of *Love Among the Ruins* is predicated on a belief in painting's ability to feed emotional information about the conditions of experience back to the spectator. The paintings are thought to be mirror images of the spectator's experience, but they are *true* images that increase information about that condition by illuminating, focusing, and diagnosing what is experienced but not necessarily understood. Seen in this light, the idea of Burne-Jones as the anti-naturalist who fled modernity, the painter who demanded that all his viewers had "to pass through the golden gate of his dreams," has a specific meaning.[106] Burne-Jones's visual "reflection of a reflection of something purely imaginary" can image the intangible world of value and meaning, everything that materialism cannot see or touch, and serve as the route to apprehensions of deeper realities than mimesis will allow. It was into the breach opened up by the implication of language in modernity that this positive sense of the visual as a potential space of alternative values, where the reality of experience might be identified and interrogated on behalf of the audience, inserted itself. The artwork, one concerned only with the kinds of knowledge that a pure visuality could offer, stood against the modernity of its culture and promised an access to realities that culture denied.

Visuality and Uncertainty

So far I have concentrated on introducing factors that kept open the attractions of the visual, however complexly, for several generations of artists and thinkers. But as these developments worked to reinforce that scene of possibility, other processes within the culture were challenging it with equal or greater authority. Beer has described the shifts in late Victorian culture that, after the 1850s, led the visual to become a scene of anxiety and uncertainty for much contemporary thought and understanding. She argues for two related processes at work in the period. On the one hand, "vision was, in a quite new way, subordinate to the invisible."[107] The reception of the second law of thermodynamics accustomed the culture to think of a universe that contained a finite amount of energy and in which and through which energy moved as the constant motion of "material particles" presenting themselves to the senses as physical bodies, or as light, sound, or heat.[108] From this perspective, vision became a deceptive mode in which to encounter the realities of the universe, because it was in the invisible that the real occurred, out of immediate reach and susceptible to human access only through the mysticisms of "Mr Sludge, 'The Medium'"—"The First Fact / We're taught is, there's a world beside this world, / With spirits, not mankind for tenantry"—or the abstract theories of high scientific speculation that were as inimical to the visual as a form of knowledge as to language.[109]

The invisible, in this context, was the medium of our existence—"extensive, out of human control . . . not amenable to analysis yet replete with phenomena."[110]

On the other hand, the same science that was in the process of consigning reality to this invisible realm that was so resistant to sensual apprehension was, at the same time, developing a theoretical and practical optics that allowed understanding of the mechanics of sight to be pursued to a hitherto unimaginable degree.[111] The results of this development, however, were merely to confirm in another idiom the uncertainty and suspicion about the capacities of vision that the speculations of the physicists had produced in the realm of theory. Vision was revealed as a fundamentally mediated set of processes.[112] Again, it was the work of Helmholtz that proved most influential. The work on optics Helmholtz undertook effectively challenged ideas of the direct connection of vision to the external world. In Helmholtz's hands, optics, in keeping with other areas of Victorian science, became a confirmation of the active and constructed nature of all forms of knowledge. For Helmholtz, "the visual image . . . is a sign, no passive copy of external things such as a photographic image, but rather a purely symbolic representation constructed by the mind to facilitate our physical interaction with things."[113] Mere physiological priority was no defense, for Helmholtz posited an empiricist theory of vision in which the physiological ability to apprehend the world depends on learned skills and capacities. When Robert Brudenell Carter, who had been Hunterian Professor of Pathology and Surgery at the Royal College of Surgeons, published *Eyesight, Good and Bad: A Treatise on the Exercise and Preservation of Vision* in 1880, he made an absolute division between the strictly physiological registration of visual events on the retina and the processing of vision in the brain. While he compared the first to "the common camera-obscura of the photographer," the brain, which "interprets the visual appearance and completes the act of seeing," remains outside the remit of his inquiry: "how this completion is effected we do not at present know."[114] The possibility of a direct connection between the world and our apprehension through vision had been denied, and the brain's comprehension of what was seen had become a mediated principle, interposing a screen of interpretation between the world and its image. As the eye, distorting its object as it registered it, passed the coded information to which it reduced the world along to the brain, the processes of interpretation came into play to replace the direct access of earlier ideas of vision with a highly interpreted, almost fictional account.

Describing the "downgrading" of the authority of the eye in this way in the work of Helmholtz, Beer cites the following passage from Charles Darwin:

Helmholtz [writes Darwin], whose judgement no one will dispute, after describing in the strongest terms the wonderful powers of the human eye adds these remarkable words: "That which we have discovered in the way of inexactness and imperfection in the optical machine and in the image of the retina, is as nothing in comparison with the incongruities which we have just come across in the domain of the sensations. One might say that nature has taken delight in accumulating contradictions in order to remove all foundation from the theory of a pre-existing harmony between the external and internal worlds."[115]

It is clear that vision, as much as language, was under stress in the last half of the nineteenth century. Flint, whose book *The Victorians and the Visual Imagination* (2000) develops Beer's arguments, reinforces this position. A central plank of her thesis is that "though the visual was, indeed, of paramount importance to the Victorians, it was a heavily problematised category." Flint builds up from this insight a series of impressive analyses of the Victorian imaginative interaction "between the material and the invisible worlds" and a variety of dualities that stand in for this division—knowable and hypothesized; body and mind; body and spirit; figured and imaginative. In this dualism, "the essential vehicle, the mediating instrument," was "the eye: something that itself partook of this dual function, both subjective and objective."[116]

This duality, a veil of suspicion cast over the visual, had its counterpart as well in the public sphere. If the rank commercialism of Gissing's "Grub Street" compromised language by association, the same was true of the popularization and commercialization of visual media throughout the latter half of the nineteenth century. Popular culture and the cultures of commerce were never simply creatures of the word. Regenia Gagnier speaks of "the art of advertising" as, by the 1890s, reflecting a "crisis of images," and the final decades of the century saw the expansion of advertising and of visual as well as linguistic copy as a prime means of the dissemination of contemporary commerce, instrumentality, and the commodification of objects and value.[117] Well before the end of the century, the visual could no more escape the implications of this accommodation to means-end values than could language, as Ruskin's strictures on the "vast extent of the advertising frescoes of London" demonstrate.[118]

Such evidence adds complexity to my account of the potentiality of the visual as it was imagined by the artists and writers of the later nineteenth century. There was no unproblematic immediacy. Language does indeed come under stress from midcentury on, and, partly as a result of this and partly as a consequence of other factors such as the influence of Ruskin's early writings, the visual comes, potentially and for some people, to assume the role of privileged mode of understanding that language had been forced to renounce. But because the visual is under pressure as much as language, that scene of possibility is a more complex one than this observation alone can explain. The result is a situation in which the potential of the visual to deal successfully with experience was held to as a means of overcoming the values of modernity, but in which that possibility was constantly under attack. What emerges is an interplay between potential and disablement, a set of unfolding tensions from which springs the complex of ideas that I am tracing around the visual.

When Robert de la Sizeranne published his book *English Contemporary Art* in 1898, he reacted to one aspect of these tensions. He was most struck by the impact of English color's frank disregard of "the law . . . of the harmony of tones" familiar on the Continent.[119] English color was too strong, so that, for example, "with very few exceptions Burne-Jones' colours have a false brilliancy, which is called richness in his own land, but on the French side of the Channel is looked upon as mere tinsel" and "in the lesser masters the violence of their colouring becomes insupportable." Sizeranne offered a cultural explanation for this:

The English collect violent colours and do not harmonise them. This results in some measure from the education given to their eye by the objects around them and the colour of the atmosphere in which they live. London, buried in fog almost all the year, has little colouring in itself, but such colours as are to be found stand out all the more vividly on the unbroken grey tones, and make a harsh discord. On the blackness of houses coated with soot, and of prison-like palaces, glare the raw red of the soldiers' uniforms, the flaunting red of the letter-boxes, the vinous red of the shoe-blacks, the sealing-wax red of parasols and omnibus advertisements. The omnibuses streaked with green, canary-yellow, scarlet advertisements, roll through the town like wandering palettes, distracting and exasperating the colour senses. . . . The background being weaker, the foreground seems stronger. There is no relation, no transition between them. The violent shock of these two tonalities confuses the eye, which loses all idea of harmonies.[120]

This testifies to a powerful sense of the importance of color within English culture by the end of the century. For Sizeranne it assumes a central role in the passage of modern experience into representation. Color is pervasive in the English visual world, but it is color harsh, brutal, and violent, dependent upon the flashing signals of advertising and the shocking rawness of chemical hues splashed across the surface of the London fog.

The overt materiality of English painters, for Sizeranne, results from this environmental context. He perceives the "English school" as wielding a specific facture: "the English method in general is heavy, trivial, laboured, dry, limited, in thick, close touches, *tight;* the labour is apparent, the constraint is surmised, the pains taken by the painter are felt by the spectator."[121] And the painters I discuss in the following chapters are regularly concerned with the role of technique and facture in their work. For these artists, meaning in the visual arts inheres in the character of paint itself; consequently, it involves them in the aspect of artworks that is most distinctive, their material character as visual objects. Yet the themes I take up run strongly through words as well as images, and this book is often concerned with the life of metaphors of materiality and its meanings. It is how pigment is understood and theorized in painting that concerns me for large parts of the argument. As a consequence, I spend a great deal of time in what follows analyzing text—both literary and discursive—as painters and their fellow travelers begin to think about and thematize these issues. Overall, I argue for a situation in which the potential of the visual to deal truthfully with reality was prized as a possible alternative to the values that reigned in modernity but in which that potential was constantly being undercut. The result is a very thickly layered interweaving of possibility and disablement, a set of tensions out of which a modern painting in England arose.

I believe that what I propose will point up historical continuities that are often ignored and will allow us to see the work of certain painters as powerful and sophisticated in ways that have not hitherto been obvious. But the book makes no claims to be comprehensive; it consists instead of a series of roughly chronological case studies that overlap as well as advance the narrative. It is in the nature of books to make their subjects somewhat neater than they actually are. I hope these overlaps resist that tendency and help break down the lure of "a linear view of change" that would distort the history of English painting over these years by insisting on a neat sequence of "development" or "evolution" from a misguided past to a "correct" modernist present.[122]

Chapter 1 is the first of five interpretive chapters, very broadly chronological, that trace the unfolding history of how the climate of possibility I describe was thought through in painting. I begin with an account of the ambition of the founding Pre-Raphaelites in 1848–50 to produce a new art that would prove adequate to the novel conditions of modernity. I connect this to the possibilities believed to lie in the visual, arguing for Pre-Raphaelitism's investment in the remaking of representation through the invention of a new painting—new both technically and in subject matter. I then go on to track the darkening of this initially optimistic vision in the later work of Rossetti and, through a discussion of Burne-Jones, show how relationships that had been posited straightforwardly in 1850 had become complex for the second wave of Pre-Raphaelite painters. The original duality of Pre-Raphaelite expression in both words and images comes to seem by the 1870s a combat between language as implicated in a corrupt modernity and the visual as opposed to it. This chapter also introduces Aestheticism's pivotal role in my argument.

Chapter 2 takes up the question of Aestheticism and explores the function of the visual in Walter Pater and a number of artists of the 1870s and 1880s. I trace the working-through of claims for the visual in Frederic Leighton, G. F. Watts, Albert Moore, and James McNeill Whistler. In their diverse ways, each of these artists sought to balance the claims of painting; this led to a number of distinct but related solutions to the problems posed by the theoretical existence of a purely visual painting. This leads me to spend some time considering Aestheticist theories that saw art as anchored in its own materiality and that claimed this as the basis of authority and achievement.

Chapter 3 deals with Charles Ricketts in his 1890s role as the illustrator of Oscar Wilde. I argue that Ricketts's work both resists and supports Wilde and that this fact is readable in the context of the themes of the book. I then go on to discuss the role of portraiture, particularly Watts's project from the 1850s onward to summarize nineteenth-century history through a gallery of portraits of its most significant figures—a prime example of belief in the visual as a means of recording contemporary reality—and then take this on into the critique of the claims for the visual embodied in Wilde's *Picture of Dorian Gray,* before going back to Ricketts and completing my argument about the contest and disagreement between word and image.

Chapter 4 continues the chronological unfolding of the narrative, looking at the appearance of Impressionist techniques and subject matter in England during the 1880s and 1890s and their connection with Symbolist art and its concerns. Through Walter Sickert, an artist who is involved with both, I trace them into the twentieth century. I argue for a thematics of the visual in Sickert's work, closely tied to a realist project to describe the facts of modern experience, but also engaged in a nuanced investigation into paint's adequacy as a vehicle for such an ambition. Sickert inherits some of the solutions to the problems posed for working painters by the potentiality of the visual. His painting continues to work through the issues they raise and to give them visual expression in ways that are of crucial importance for the emergence of a formal modernism in England.

Chapter 5 carries the "tradition" up to 1914. It hopes to demonstrate the continuity within English painting that can connect Rossetti with English modernism before the First World War. The Camden Town Group, the Vorticists, the Bloomsbury Group, and other exponents of various English modernisms are thus put back into a history of which they are a part, and I show the ways in which the project to be "modernist" up to 1914 was deeply indebted to this modern prehistory. The chapter also attempts to discriminate among the various uses to which modernism puts its visual inheritance. There is a sustained discussion of the representation of modern life in the work of Camden Town, Vorticism, and the Bloomsbury painters, and their differences are related to different uses of the visual and material characteristics of the paint itself, differences that I argue are explicitly operative within their work. With this claim in mind, I conclude with a consideration of some of the consequences of my arguments for our understanding of periodization in English painting during these years and a summary of the implications of the book.

Lisa Tickner has recently noted that the advent of Roger Fry's "Manet and the Post-Impressionists" exhibition in 1910 marked the turning point in the adoption of aesthetics antipathetic to the standards and character of Victorian painting: "since then," she comments, "it has been very difficult to write about Victorian art—as *art*—at all."[123] Historical understanding, under the spell cast by the glamour of French modernism, has relegated English painting to the margins of both modernity and aesthetics. The consequences have included an unhelpful periodization that has suppressed the continuity of English painting from the mid-nineteenth century to the formal modernism that appeared before the First World War and a denigration of the aesthetic quality of so much of this art. The complexity, sophistication, and excitement of this work as a response to modern experience and as an innovative and independent visual program have been too little recognized. *The World in Paint* attempts to contribute to remedying that situation and to encourage the recognition of English painting both as a major modern art and as "*art*—at all."

"Not Material *Enough for the Age*"

PRE-RAPHAELITE WORDS AND IMAGES

In 1854, William Holman Hunt's painting *The Awakening Conscience* (1853–56, fig. 5) was exhibited at the Royal Academy. It is one of the best known of all Pre-Raphaelite works, and in many ways it exemplifies the ambitions of the early Pre-Raphaelites. Hunt's painting is highly realized and intensely detailed, crammed from top to bottom with precise delineations of matter and material possessions, from the surface characteristics of rosewood, fabric, and hair to the silvered sheen of the mirror against the back wall. A hard, penetrating light bathes every corner of the room, rendering all the details of these objects clear and open to our scrutiny. We can even see the rim of dried mud adhering to the right shoe of the man lounging in his chair. An image of clear vision, his companion starts up from his lap, eyes wide open to receive enlightenment, her gaze fixed on the brilliant clarity of the scene beyond the window. Reflected back for us in the mirror, every minute detail of the exterior world is made available to our sight.

In working so hard to present clarity to its viewers, Hunt's picture seems to chime with Ruskin's famous call, at the end of the first volume of *Modern Painters* (1843), for an art that would bring into focus the smallest instances of reality in the visible world. Artists, says Ruskin, "should go to Nature in all singleness of heart, and walk with her laboriously and trustingly, having no other thoughts but how best to penetrate her meaning, and remember her instruction; rejecting nothing, selecting nothing, and scorning nothing; believing all things to be right and good, and rejoicing always in the truth."[1] Early Pre-Raphaelite painting embraced this idea of fidelity to the physical details of the material world as the vehicle by which a truthful and accurate account of reality could be achieved. Hunt's minute description of the furnishings of this London house, the clothes of its inhabitants, and the incidentals of its environment is rendered to express fully the social realities they embody. Accordingly, *The Awakening Conscience* has been recently read as a prime example of early Pre-Raphaelite painting's concern with social and cultural modernity. Like Dante Gabriel Rossetti's long-contemplated and finally abandoned *Found* (begun 1859, fig. 6), Hunt deals with the theme of the "fallen woman," "an urgent problem in the modern city."[2] This was also the reading proposed by Ruskin, who in 1854 wrote a vigorous defense of Hunt's work in a letter to *The Times:*

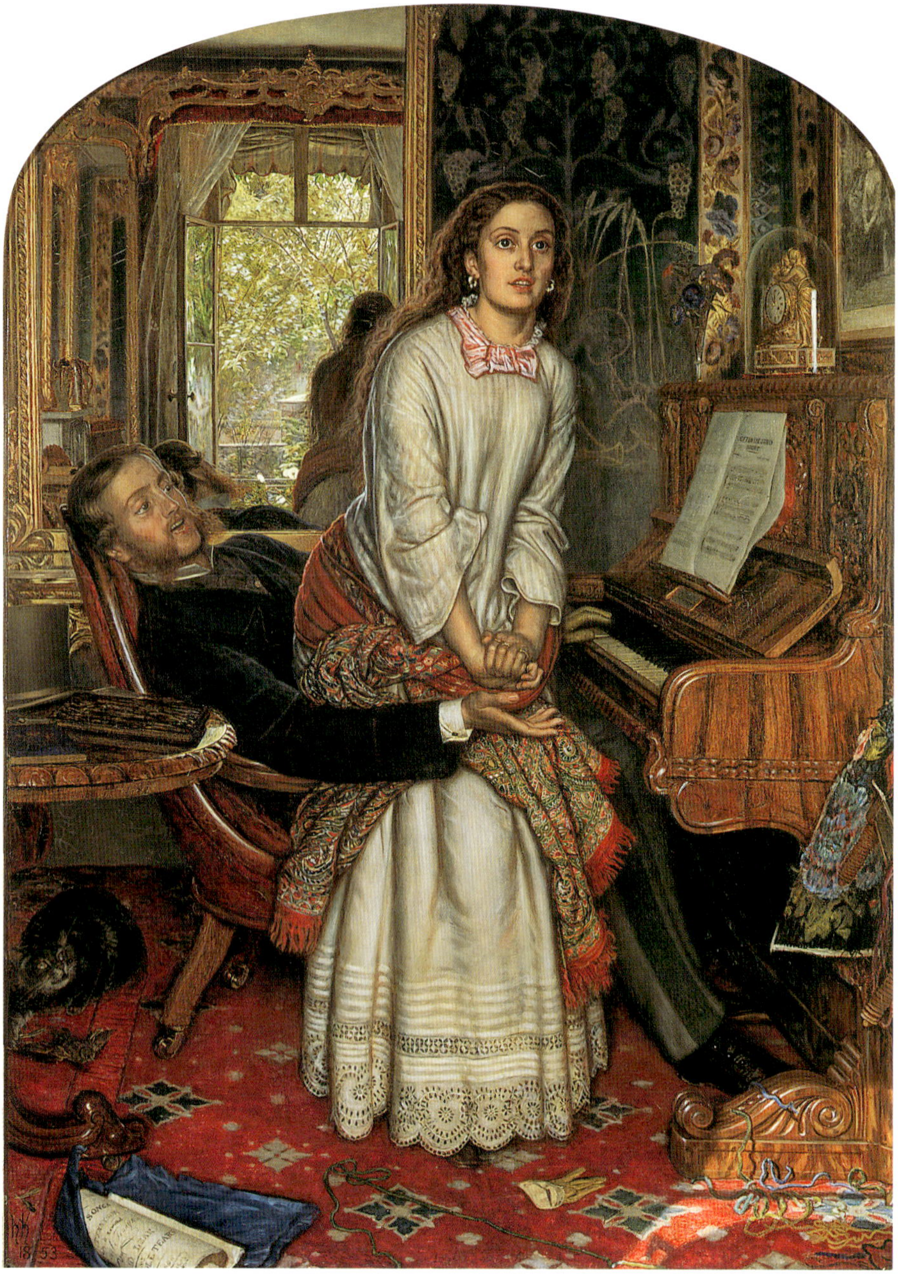

FIGURE 5. William Holman Hunt, *The Awakening Conscience*, 1853–56

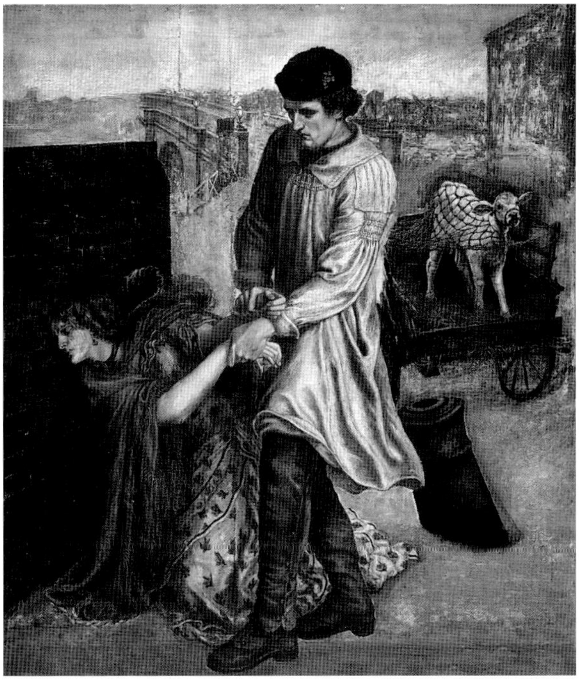

FIGURE 6. Dante Gabriel Rossetti, *Found*, begun 1859

The poor girl has been sitting singing with her seducer; some chance words of the song, "Oft in the stilly night," have struck upon the numbed places of her heart; she has started up in agony; he, not seeing her face, goes on singing, striking the keys carelessly with his gloved hand. . . . There is not a single object in all that room—common, modern, vulgar . . . but it becomes tragical, if rightly read. That furniture so carefully painted, even to the last vein of the rosewood—is there nothing to be learnt from that terrible lustre of it, from its fatal newness; nothing there that has the old thoughts of home upon it, or that is ever to become a part of home?

The capacity of the painting "to meet full in the front the moral evil of the age" depends on its realization of the material circumstances in which evil is enacted: "the very hem of the poor girl's dress, at which the painter has laboured so closely, thread by thread, has story in it, if we think how soon its pure whiteness may be soiled with dust and rain, her out-cast feet failing in the street."[3] Ruskin connects the highly realized detailing of the material description to the moral theme and thereby epitomizes the ambition of early Pre-Raphaelitism to register social reality through an innovative account of the physical world. This linkage relies on the clarity that the painting works to achieve, a point on which Ruskin several times insists. If the "seducer" cannot see the woman's face, the spectator can, and that moment of seeing focuses the whole painting. Sight in Hunt's picture operates as a form of knowledge, sweeping up the meaning of this modern conversation piece through its display of material signifiers. The dawning awareness written on the woman's features carries the clear message so painstakingly woven into the painting's many details.

The World in Paint

Observers noted these themes of materiality, clarity, and vision in the new art of the Pre-Raphaelite Brotherhood even before Hunt's painting appeared.[4] Writing in 1850, the editor of *The Critic,* Edward William Cox, had announced a departure "from our usual plan of noticing the periodicals under one heading" in order to review the first two numbers of the new Pre-Raphaelite monthly magazine, *The Germ.* Cox cited extracts from some of the anonymous contributions (by Dante Gabriel Rossetti, Coventry Patmore, and Christina Rossetti) to demonstrate that "the contents . . . are the production of no common minds" before concluding with a passage that connected the magazine to more general issues: "The Germ has our heartiest wishes for its success; but we scarcely dare to *hope* that it may win the popularity it deserves. The truth is that it is too good for the time. It is not *material* enough for the age."[5] In a later review of the two final issues of the magazine, Cox glossed what he meant by this, arguing that "we cannot contemplate this young and rising school in art and literature without the most ardent anticipations of something great to grow from it, something new and worthy of our age": "The Germ was not wantonly so entitled, for it abounded with the promise of a rich harvest. . . . But we expressed . . . our fear lest the very excellence of this magazine should be fatal to its success. It was too good—that is to say, too refined and of too lofty a class, both in its art and its poetry—to be sufficiently popular to pay even the printer's bill."[6]

This is an interesting response to *The Germ.* Cox's assertions signal the magazine's role as the expression of a group endeavor and a focused intellectual and artistic program, something that other reviewers at the time also deemed worthy of comment. "English artists have hitherto worked each one by himself, with too little of common purpose, too little of distinct and steadily pursued intellectual object," wrote *The Guardian,* welcoming the fact that "here, at last, we have a school" and suggesting that its "success . . . would be a national blessing."[7] This sense of group identity defined the Brotherhood and underlay their characteristically modern view of art as a practice in which innovation and revelation played a crucial role.[8] According to William Michael Rossetti, the P.R.B. was motivated by dissatisfaction with existing artistic conventions: "the temper of these striplings, after some years of the current academic training, was the temper of rebels: they meant revolt, and produced revolution."[9]

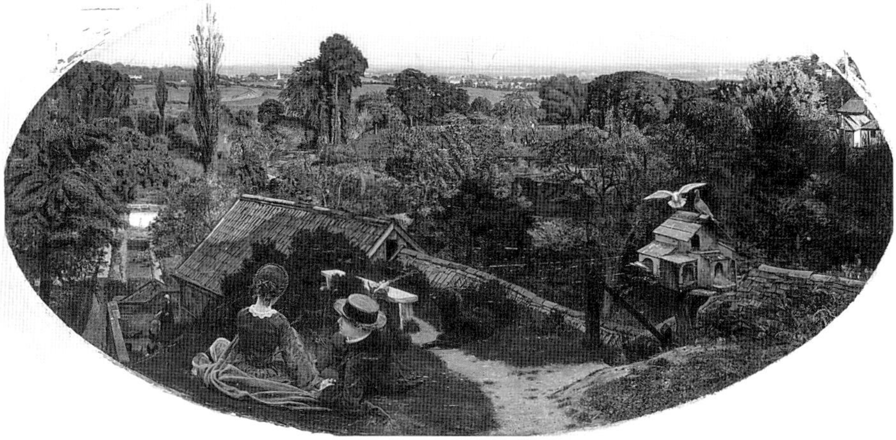

FIGURE 7. Ford Madox Brown, *An English Autumn Afternoon,* 1852–54

Although William Michael Rossetti wrote this with the benefit of hindsight, his comments usefully clarify the hopes in 1850 for "this young and rising school" to be "something new and worthy of our age." For the P.R.B., innovation in art and literature was directed at replacing what they thought of as the exhausted strategies of the tradition with a new art, one capable of dealing adequately with contemporary conditions and experience. Pre-Raphaelite art aimed to revivify the culture's deadened systems of representation and to reinvent them as revelatory expressions of a spiritual or human dimension that seemed absent from modern life.[10] Like Carlyle, who in 1843 had written in the opening pages of *Past and Present* of the stunned "enchantment" and spiritual impoverishment of "the English Nation" struggling to "get to know the meaning of *its* strange new Today," the P.R.B. sought "the eternal inner Facts of this Universe . . . Nature's right truth" as an answer to the pressing questions of modern existence and its representation.[11] The many attempts of the Brotherhood's artists to produce pictures of modern life express this quest—from *The Awakening Conscience* and *Found* to Ford Madox Brown's *English Autumn Afternoon* (1852–54, fig. 7), *The Last of England* (1852–55, Birmingham Museums and Art Gallery), and *Work* (1852–65, Manchester City Art Galleries), as well as Millais's *The Rescue* (1855, National Gallery of Victoria, Melbourne) and F. G. Stephens's *Mother and Child* (1854–56, Tate Britain, London, unfinished).[12] Theirs was to be an innovative and committed art in which the visual would function as the vehicle by which the meaning of contemporary reality,

Carlyle's "the right Inner True," would be clarified and revealed to the nation, becoming what Ruskin called "art in some sort compassionate, exhortant, or communicative, and useful . . . as a record of what was done among men in your day."[13] In this sense, Cox's comment that *The Germ* was "not *material* enough" might reflect its repudiation of materialist values and its attempt to achieve a critical perspective on contemporary experience.

Such ambitions raise the central question that confronted the P.R.B. If their art meant to provide a new order of visual representation that could deal with modern experience in this revelatory way, then how could that goal be achieved? In what sense could the visual arts diagnose, communicate, and reform the lived realities of mid-nineteenth-century life, and exactly how could "a national school" advance the question of "the condition of England"? Without an answer to such questions, the P.R.B. would risk becoming like those "dilettanti" found "pasturing" among the "mutilated black Ruin" of modernity whom Carlyle had anathematized in *Past and Present*.[14]

A possible answer seems to emerge from the second theme raised by Cox's *Germ* reviews. This is the fascination of the founding Pre-Raphaelites with an alternative materiality to that of their age, one formed from the material constitution of the medium in which they operated, whether words or images or, in the case of Dante Gabriel Rossetti, both. Jerome McGann has recently suggested that we should understand Rossetti through a sense of his "art of embodied practice" and has described Rossetti's "proper subject" as "the cognitive nature of immediated sensual perception," by which he means a sharply intellectual inquiry into materiality.[15] Rossetti himself spoke of Pre-Raphaelitism as a "materialist" art. His materialism, in this sense of a close, reflective engagement with the sensual world, is evident from very early in his career.[16] F. G. Stephens's later description of Rossetti's first appearance at the Royal Academy Schools tries to capture the young artist's embroilment in the physical and material details of the world:

Rather below the middle height and with a slightly rolling gait, Rossetti came forward among his fellows with a jerky step, tossed the falling hair back from his face, and, having both hands in his pockets, faced the student world with an insouciant *air which savoured of defiance, mental pride and thorough self-reliance. A bare throat, a falling, ill-kept collar, boots not over familiar with brushes, black and well-worn habiliments, including, not the ordinary frock or jacket "of the period," but a very loose dress-coat which had once been new—these were the outward and visible signs of a mood which cared even less for appearances than the art-student of those days was accustomed to care.*[17]

Stephens's strategy in this description is to refer the materiality of Rossetti's self-presentation back to his inward "mood," an inner truth that spurns the materialism of "appearances" but nonetheless finds itself ideally figured through their "outward and visible signs." In effect, Stephens proposes a mechanism that connects the materiality of appearance with the "inner Facts," allowing matter to signify and communicate adequately the eternal realities of experience.

Writing this down in the 1890s, Stephens kept faith with the beliefs of the youthful P.R.B. "Despite differences," wrote Hunt of his relationship with Rossetti in his account of the Brotherhood, "we both agreed that a man's work must be the reflex of a living image in his own mind, and not the icy double of the facts themselves."[18] In 1850 Stephens had set out this same claim as a quasi-official manifesto of the group in an essay he wrote for the second number of *The Germ*. In "The Purpose and Tendency of Early Italian Art," Stephens's understanding of art before Raphael turns on what he takes to be its fundamental realism, its faithful representation of the truths of nature. From this, he reasons that a clear-sighted modern art will only arise from attention to the material reality of the visible world:

An unprejudiced spectator of the recent progress and main direction of Art in England will have observed, as a great change in the character of the productions of the modern school, a marked attempt to lead the taste of the public into a new channel by producing pure transcripts and faithful studies from nature, instead of conventionalities and feeble reminiscences from the Old Masters; an entire seeking after originality in a more humble manner than has been practised since the decline of Italian Art in the Middle Ages.[19]

Stephens imagines the painter, spiritually honed and refined by "a firm attachment to truth in every point of representation," delineating the reality of experience, cultivating "the power of representing an object, that its entire intention may be visible, its lesson felt."[20] His model—the same one that operates in his reminiscence of Rossetti's student life—is one of the penetration of understanding into reality through the self's inward purity and innocence. The artist perceives and represents the truth through burnishing the mirror of his own identity. "Believe that there is that in the fact of truth, though it be only in the character of a single leaf earnestly studied, which may do its share in the great labour of the world," says Stephens: "remember that it is by truth alone that the Arts can ever hold the position for which they were intended."[21] In order to yield its significance, the leaf must be "earnestly studied," unlocked through the artist's inner attention.

Stephens posits, then, a relationship central to the aesthetic thought of the early P.R.B. that forms the intellectual justification for the claim that art is able to account for its age. "The subject was a modern one," says one of Rossetti's surrogate narrators of a painting he executes in the short story "St Agnes of Intercession" (of which I shall have more to say below), "and indeed it has often seemed to me that all work, to be truly worthy, should be wrought out of the age itself, as well as out of the soul of its producer, which must needs be a soul of the age."[22] This resonates with Cox's "something new and worthy of our age" as well as with the type of engagement urged by Carlyle and others, including Ruskin.[23] But it differs from them in sharing the mechanism of Stephens's description. For Rossetti's protagonist, the expression of the realities of "the age" and the expression of the artistic self are imagined as identical. The answer that early Pre-Raphaelitism proposes to the question of how its innovative modern art could achieve the goal of dealing with modern experience, and thus prove itself worthy of the task of diagnosing and communicating those realities, is the one Stephens gives: the artist should look within himself, and by his attention to that *necessarily* reflective mirror of the "soul of the age," he will express the age itself.

In the following sections of this chapter, I will address how these formulations of the new art's ambitions influenced the Pre-Raphaelites' understanding of the role of the visual arts in representing and assessing modern experience. I will contend that early on, Rossetti felt uneasy with the mechanism proposed. The short stories he conceived for *The Germ* in 1849 and 1850—and his subsequent paintings of the 1860s and 1870s—significantly respond to that skepticism. I argue that this development, usually read in terms of the emergence of Aestheticism in England, can fruitfully be seen as the growth of an anxiety about the capacity of the visual to express the reality of the world. For Rossetti, his dual character as a creator allowed this anxiety to be allayed or at least kept to one side. Still, his painting after 1859 seeks to assert a "materialist" ground for valuing the visual as a form of knowledge. For the second wave of Pre-Raphaelite artists, however, Rossetti's solution proved hard to sustain. I go on to discuss Burne-Jones's works of the late 1870s as self-conscious inquiries into the adequacy of the visual. Burne-Jones takes up the challenge implied by these claims and endeavors to work through the possibility that they might be substantiated in the activity of painting. He does so by developing Rossetti's assertion of the identity of representation, the observer, and the world as a central trope of his own work. Whatever the success of this attempt to reconnect the terms of the triad, that identity springs apart again in other works

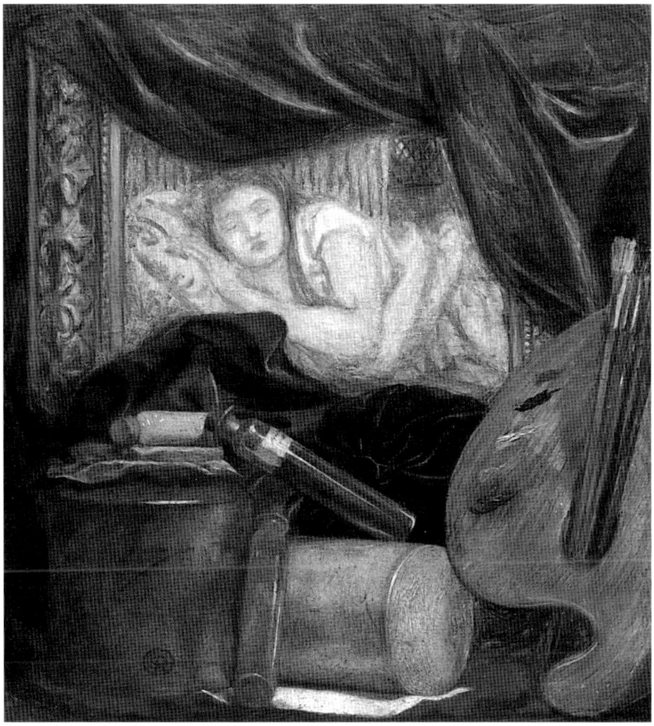

FIGURE 8. Dante Gabriel Rossetti, *Bottles,* 1848

of late Pre-Raphaelitism, as the ambition it expresses proves increasingly difficult to sustain.

Hand and Soul

Rossetti executed two early works in oils in 1848 when, after leaving the RA Schools, he was briefly a pupil of Ford Madox Brown. One is a still-life study of pickle jars, bottles, and vials, all framed by the repoussoir elements of a large palette and stacked brushes (1848, fig. 8).[24] It is a conventional subject and, predictably, Rossetti balked at the task. Nevertheless, the effect of the vials (which contain paint in the three primary colors) and of the markings on the surface of the palette is suggestively self-reflexive.[25] Alastair Grieve remarks of this painting that Rossetti's "sudden introduction to colour seems to have led him to question deeply its language," so that he was able "to use it in an unconventional way for symbolic and decorative purposes."[26] William Bell Scott famously remembered Rossetti working shortly afterwards on his first major oil painting, *The Girlhood of Mary Virgin* (1848–49, fig. 9), using an innovative technique: "He was painting in oils with water-colour brushes, as thinly as in water-colour, on canvas which he had primed with white till the surface was as smooth as card-

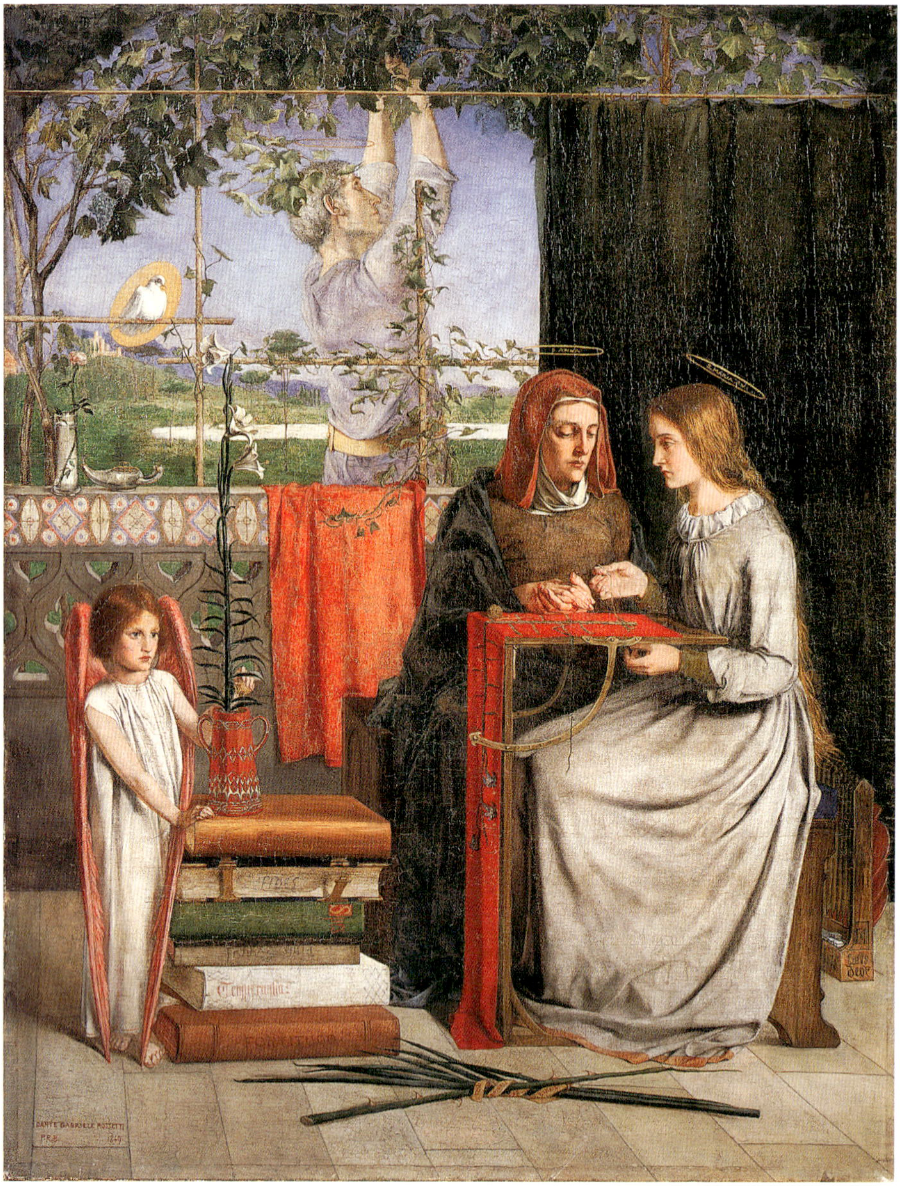

FIGURE 9. Dante Gabriel Rossetti, *The Girlhood of Mary Virgin,* 1848–49

board, and every tint remained transparent."[27] Elizabeth Prettejohn has recently connected these early works by Rossetti to a broader series of "experiments with media and techniques" in both paint and drawing that give a "cohesive look to the early P.R.B. oils." She demonstrates how emphatic the use of the physical trace of the medium, applied "stroke by individual stroke," was for the

Brotherhood's artists, producing "a coherent whole not by the imposition of an overall pictorial harmony, but by the accumulation and juxtaposition of numberless equally emphasised touches."[28]

The P.R.B. painters were able to evolve this technique because of the availability of modern industrial colors and pigments. They owed a particular debt to the work of George Field, a color-maker and theorist who had produced a range of "unusually pure and transparent colours" that made possible techniques like those adopted by Rossetti in *The Girlhood of Mary Virgin,* in which pigment was applied thinly over a white ground "to achieve an unprecedented brilliance of hue."[29] Hunt and Millais also used this technique on their painting expeditions to the rural hinterland of London in the summer of 1851, when they painted the landscape backgrounds for what in due course became *The Light of the World* (1851–53, see fig. 3) and *The Hireling Shepherd* (1851–52, fig. 10), in the case of Hunt, and *A Huguenot, on St Bartholomew's Day* (1851–52, Makins Collection), in that of Millais.[30] The chromatic brilliance and the extraordinary level of detail in *The Hireling Shepherd* seemed to contemporaries to achieve, through "novelty of effect," an unprecedented "truth." William Michael Rossetti discerned "a feeling of the country . . . such as we do not remember to have seen before," while Stephens, picking up Hunt's declaration that the painting aimed to reproduce "the sunlight brightness of the day itself," thought that the realization of this sunlight in the picture was "an entirely new thing in art."[31] These comments indicate the extent to which those close to the Pre-Raphaelite painters believed that technical innovation was meant to work in the service of inner truth. Under their influence, there came to be an acknowledged connection between the interest in the technical enlargement of the painter's chromatic vocabulary and an opposition to the materialism of the culture. This was made explicit in the 1875 revised edition of Field's *Grammar of Colouring,* first published in 1850: "If, in this utilitarian age, we are asked, 'What is the use of colour?' we are constrained, however reluctantly, to answer: 'Not any.' . . . In the colours which pervade creation . . . our merciful Creator has superadded beauty to utility . . . the works of the Almighty are designed so as to surround us with everything that shall make this work-day world one in which the higher faculties of the mind may be exercised."[32] If color has no utilitarian use, then its purpose is to bring us into contact with an area of value outside the prosaically material. Pre-Raphaelite technical experimentation and innovation in the early 1850s served a similar function.

But if the founding Pre-Raphaelites thought of their project to represent the modern as a visual one, language and the literary also featured as equal

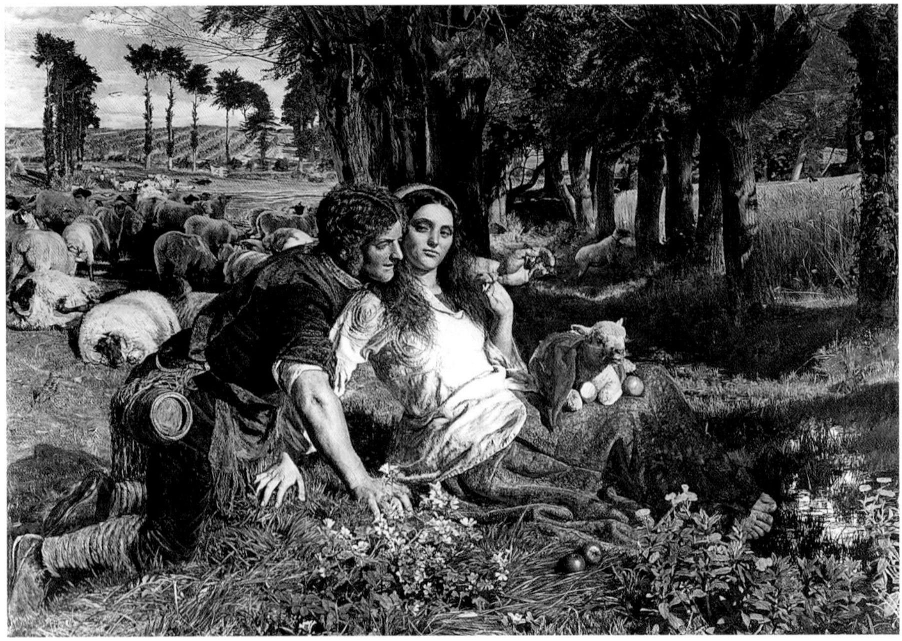

FIGURE 10. William Holman Hunt, *The Hireling Shepherd,* 1851–52

partners in their reformulation of the arts. *The Germ* printed more poetry and discursive prose than examples of visual art, and P.R.B. enthusiasm extended to Keats or *The Arabian Nights* as readily as to the rather nebulous category of "early Italian" painters. William Michael Rossetti identified "Holman-Hunt, Woolner, and Stephens" as "reading men" and Millais and Collinson as "both . . . capable of writing with point, and even in verse," and he thought that the early P.R.B. had been built out of words.[33] Dante Gabriel Rossetti persuaded a number of these artistic colleagues to write for *The Germ,* and from the first he himself created "double works of art" in both words and images.[34] This versatility distinguished him from his less fortunate colleagues and successors. "A picture," Rossetti said, "is a painted poem," and his currency in both arts allowed him a flexibility denied to them.[35] But this facility also brought the question of the relative capacities of language and the visual explicitly into play in his work. *The Girlhood of Mary Virgin,* the first painting to carry the P.R.B. initials, was typical of his early visual art: it was exhibited accompanied by two sonnets that detailed the iconography of the painting and conducted the reader through its symbolic order and theology. The relationship between text and image appears relatively straightforward in this case, with the sonnets glossing a primary visual object. But that simplicity is deceptive. Rossetti's sonnets usefully open up some of the complexities of word and image relationships for the early Pre-Raphaelites.

The concept of glossing itself raises these issues. Rossetti's poems seem to assume what Michael Baxandall has called an "ostensive" relationship to the image; that is, they explicitly point out the important aspects of the painting.[36] Both sonnets begin with this ostensive gesture toward the work: "This is that blessed Mary," "These are the symbols."[37] The implication is that the visual precedes the linguistic register, which exists in order to explicate it. The spectator is logically prior to the reader, because access to the understanding that the work contains inheres in the act of viewing rather than in that of reading text. The image comes before the word.[38] This is perhaps complex enough as a relationship. But if the visual precedes the verbal, then on what grounds does it require linguistic explication? What status do the sonnets have if not that of the clarification and identification of meanings and significances that are not clear from the visual object itself? If it *is* the case that the painting requires this exposition, then surely its priority is irretrievably compromised. Indeed, this tangle of implications complicates the claim that the visual provides access to reality. The ontological complexities of the relationship between language and visual understanding underline how problematic any such claim must be. The visual cannot conduct the spectator into the inner truths so dear to Pre-Raphaelite ambition, at least not merely by virtue of its own achievements and without the aid of language. For Rossetti, the uncertainty that this situation expresses became the focus of meditation and inquiry during the early years of the Brotherhood.

While he was working on *The Girlhood of Mary Virgin* and its companion piece, *Ecce Ancilla Domini!* (1849–50, Tate Britain, London), Rossetti was writing his short story "Hand and Soul," published in January 1850 in the first number of *The Germ*.[39] This fiction, which has received considerable notice as an important statement of Rossetti's Pre-Raphaelite aesthetics, deals with an early Italian painter, Chiaro dell'Erma, and his artistic history, and it proposes a solution to the conundrum of the visual's access to truth.[40] Chiaro's struggles to achieve a satisfactory art closely mirror Pre-Raphaelite hopes: "conceiving art almost . . . for himself, and loving it deeply, he endeavoured from early boyhood towards the imitation of any objects offered in nature."[41] Chiaro passes through a series of possibilities, making art that is sensuous, moral, and symbolic by turns but achieving success with none. His final idiom marries "cold symbolism and abstract impersonation" to "the presentment of some moral greatness that should impress the beholder" (26). But this ambition to attain a direct relationship to contemporary moral needs proves vain. When, in this style, Chiaro paints "a number of tall, narrow frescos, presenting a moral allegory of Peace" in the entranceway to a church, the rival factions of "the two greatest houses of the feud in Pisa" turn on each other as they leave a service, "and there was so much blood cast up the walls on a sudden, that it ran in long streams down Chiaro's paintings" (28). So much for the effectiveness of visual allegories, thinks Chiaro, of Peace or of anything else. Confronted by this failure of "the hope that I nourished in this my generation of men," Chiaro despairs:

I am as one who, through the whole night, holding his way diligently, hath smitten the steel unto the flint, to lead some whom he knew darkling; who hath kept his eyes always on the sparks that himself made, lest they should fail; and who, towards dawn, turning to bid them that he had guided God speed, sees the wet grass untrodden except of his own feet. . . . Am I not as a cloth drawn before the light, that the looker may not be blinded; but which sheweth thereby the grain of its own coarseness; so that the light seems defiled, and men say, "We will not walk by it." Wherefore through me they shall be doubly accursed, seeing that through me they reject the light. (29)

This is the climactic moment of the story, when Chiaro's visuality unfolds into darkness, "defiling" and reject[ing] the light." This complex moment turns on the mediation of the visual, "the grain" of the "cloth drawn before the light" that allows vision to take place but intrudes on its own constitution, the materiality of its coarse grain interposed between reality and its understanding. For Chiaro, that mediation appears disabling, anxious, a "dark" negative that prevents him from realizing his ambition. Confronted by his failure to speak directly and productively to his time, Chiaro experiences a displacement of the visual in the form of "a vision" in his studio. His soul appears to him as a woman, "an image . . . of thine own soul within thee" (30). The advice she offers reiterates the claim that expressing the inner self will also express external reality: "In all that thou doest, work from thine own heart, simply . . . set the hand and the soul to serve man with God" (31). The narrative presents this spiritual moment as if it can serve as an effective closure, matter translated into "vision."

Despite the importance accorded it by William Michael Rossetti and subsequent commentators, "Hand and Soul" does not resolve the issues it raises. The "soul," appearing to Chiaro, displaces the complex question of how a contemporary visual art might be meaningful to the interiority of the artist (as we have seen Rossetti, Stephens, and Hunt displace it already). Because this is an assertion or aspiration rather than a demonstration, the story remains unconvincing. Rossetti reaffirms the need the Pre-Raphaelites perceived for a spiritual understanding of experience and the modern age, and Chiaro's vision conveys this, but it leaves unresolved the problem of how such an understanding is to be achieved or disseminated.

Rossetti continued to examine this theme in the second of his short stories, "St Agnes of Intercession," which was meant to be included in *The Germ*—although Rossetti put it aside when the periodical failed and took it up again only in 1870 or later.[42] "St Agnes" deals with a central Rossettian moment, the confrontation with the double, the "bogie" whose face is eerily identical to the protagonist's own.[43] It is an odd story: the extensive revisions that appear to have been made when it was taken up have left traces of difference in tone, mood, and the nature of the action that are still evident in the final text. But although William Michael Rossetti felt that "it does not seem to be intended to bear an equal weight of moral or spiritual significance" as "Hand and Soul,"[44] it appears to me to have been made over by Rossetti in his later revisions into an important commentary on the early ambitions of the P.R.B. In fact, it amounts to a more reflective consideration of the central issues.

Written in a pastiche style derived from the stories of Edgar Allan Poe and E. T. A. Hoffmann and heralded by a cod epigraph purporting to be from *Tristram Shandy,* "St Agnes of Intercession" inserts from the first an ironic distance between its narrative voice and its central figure, another young artist.[45] The first-person narrative recounts the disturbing circumstances surrounding this character's revelation of a previous existence. The middle section of the tale describes how he discovers his own likeness and that of his fiancée, replicated respectively in a self-portrait and a portrait of his mistress by an early Italian painter with whom he has experienced a long affinity: "that it *was* my portrait,—that the St Agnes was the portrait of Mary,—and that both had been painted by myself four hundred years ago,—this now rose up distinctly before me as the one and only solution of so startling a mystery."[46] For my purposes, though, this gothic moment is less interesting than the development, around the core narrative, of some of the ideas that I have identified in "Hand and Soul" and that directly relate to the ambitions of the early Pre-Raphaelites.[47] These developments provide a clearer statement of the relationship to reality that "Hand and Soul" offers in a more muddled, complex way. The surrounding tale, however, casts serious doubt on the basis of that clarity.

The central events of "St Agnes of Intercession" are framed by two sections of unequal length that deal with a more modern setting and form a counterpoint to the supernatural events set in Italy. The extended prologue to the Italian section of the story deals first with the narrator's "earliest recollections . . . the London winter evenings" (557) and subsequently with his very Rossetti-like education and the circumstances of his first exhibition, showing an equivalent of *The Girlhood of Mary Virgin.*[48] Like Rossetti, the narrator is impatient with the "toil rigidly exact and dealing often with trifles" (ibid.) of his early art education: "I cared even too little for what could be taught me by others," so that "my original designs greatly outnumbered my school-drawings" (558). Struck by one of his sister's friends, Mary Arden, whose "beauty seemed to grow on my sight by gazing, as the stars do in water," the youthful art student executes a painting "with all the energy of which I was capable" (ibid.). Apart from the fact that Mary sits for the painting, we learn little about it. We do know, however, that it differs in an important way from *The Girlhood of Mary Virgin*. We gather from the reaction of a self-obsessed and snobbish art critic that the picture conforms to early P.R.B. ambitions, manifesting an "uncompromising adherence to nature as then present before me, which I had attempted throughout" (561), causing it to stand out among the conventional paintings that surround it on exhibition at the Royal Academy. This effect is produced from a striking but hidden motif: "The subject was a modern one, and indeed it has often seemed to me that all work, to be truly worthy, should be wrought out of the age itself, as well as out of the soul of its producer, which must needs be a soul of the age" (558). This passage combines the aspirations of Chiaro dell'Erma with an acknowledgment of the essential modernity of aim that inspired them. For Rossetti, all subjects will be colored by the character of the time in which they are made. They will all be "modern," whatever the ostensible subject matter. Chiaro's painting of the soul is here confirmed as the mechanism through which "the age" itself comes into vision and becomes available for painting. The self is identical to its age, and its expression is therefore necessarily "wrought out of the age itself"—a notion that reflects on the central conceit of the story, with its identities spanning four hundred years. This particular aspect of the narrative suggests a desire to dramatize the claim for unity with the spiritually effective art of the past that was more baldly stated in "Hand and Soul." Moreover, the visual takes up the burden of revelation and understanding, although we never actually learn what this "modern" subject is. The narrator's gaze in the first section of the tale is lively and vivid, though often frustrated: Mary Arden's "beauty seemed to grow on my sight by gazing," he says, and in the gallery he fruitlessly seeks his own painting: "my gaze also passed uneasily, but without encountering the object of its solicitude" (560).

When he does encounter it, it almost slips away: "As we were shaking hands, a part of the 'line' opposite to where we stood was left bare by a lapse in the crowd. 'There seems to be an odd-looking picture,' said my companion. I looked in the same direction: the press was closing again; I caught only a glimpse of the canvas, but that sufficed: it was my own picture, *on the line!*" (561). Here, sight and the visual achievement to which it gravitates preserve the possibility of revelation. To have a painting hung "on the line" was to have pride of place in the exhibition, the painting available to the spectators' line of sight and not "skied" (that is, hung out of easy vision).

A much shorter section at the end matches this initial section of the story. The narrator, his health broken by the experience of revelation he has endured during his trip to Italy, is slowly nursed back to health in London. The story ends with the ringing of London bells and his first shaky steps out into the familiar city, a moment presented as a return to mental stability after the disequilibrium of his Italian experience. The passage, which is truncated in comparison to the leisurely opening, is worth quoting in full:

I set out hastily in the well-known direction of Mary's house. While I walked through the crowded streets, the sense of reality grew upon me at every step, and for the first time during some months I felt a man among men. Any artist or thoughtful man whatsoever, whose life has passed in a large city, can scarcely fail, in course of time, to have some association connecting each spot continually passed and repassed with the labours of his own mind . . . wherever in the daily walk through the thronged and jarring city, the soul has read some knowledge from life, or laboured towards some birth within its own silence, there abides the glory of that hour, and the cloud rests there before an unseen tabernacle. And thus now, with myself, old trains of thought and the conceptions of former years came back as I passed from one swarming resort to another, and seemed, by contrast, to wake my spirit from its wild and fantastic broodings to a consciousness of something like actual existence; as the mere reflections of objects, sunk in the vague pathless water, appear almost to strengthen it into substance. (570)

This passage puts away the events of the Italian sojourn and returns the narrator to the sanity of modern life in the urban environment of his "earliest recollections." Like Poe's protagonist in "The Man of the Crowd," but to different effect, the narrator returns to the landscape of the city and "actual existence." As he does so, the "mere reflections" of the world are claimed as realizations, "strengthen[ing] it into substance."

There are echoes here of earlier statements, and these go some way toward bringing this rather abrupt conclusion into harmony with what has gone before. The final lines recall the narrator's earlier description, quoted above, of Mary, whose "beauty seemed to grow on my sight by gazing, as the stars do in water." The reference to the cloud before the tabernacle picks up a phrase at the beginning of the story during the account of the narrator's reluctant art training: "what was then the precise shape of the cloud within my tabernacle, I could scarcely say now; or whether through so thick a veil I could be sure of its presence there at all" (557).[49] In these two passages, Rossetti evokes a number of instances in the Old Testament when God appears to Moses in the form of a "cloudy pillar . . . at the tabernacle door" (Exodus 33:9). But whereas the first reference is facetious in its context, the second very seriously suggests revelation, the bringing into vision of the unseen and mysterious. At the end of the story, Rossetti's narrator offers the modern and urban as a site of revelation and clarity, sweeping aside the supernatural and unsettling context of the central sections of the story.

The abbreviated nature of this final urban epiphany, however, leaves open the possibility that the narrator is mistaken in this apparent clarity and return to health. The two rhyming passages I have cited both evoke images of understanding that are veiled and opaque, not clear; revelation appears in them as the occult and the unseen. The veil of the tabernacle was the cloth that separated "the Holy Place" from "the Most Holy Place," where the Ark of the Covenant and the inmost mysteries were stored. The veil conceals the moment of revelation, as does God's fiery pillar of cloud. In the concluding passage, the revelation the narrator optimistically derives from this analysis of "the thronged and jarring city" remains stubbornly "unseen," opaque and indistinct. It remains inarticulate within the story, inasmuch as the protagonist hurriedly informs us that this possibility of reading "some knowledge from life" resides in perambulation through the city, but we do not see this revelation accomplished. Like the "mere reflections of objects, sunk in the vague pathless water" that reflect in their turn Mary's "beauty," augmented by the narrator's gaze, the recovery of truth and experience through attention to the modern is fluid, partial, and misleading. And like the claims of "Hand and Soul," it is asserted rather than demonstrated.

From this point of view, the supernatural events of the story acquire the greatest meaning because they are the most fully realized and intense. They also present knowledge—and, by implication, the knowledge of modernity that the protagonist seeks—as unknowable and inaccessible: "The tremendous experience of that moment, the like of which has never, perhaps, been known to any other man must remain undescribed; since the description, read calmly at common leisure, could seem but fantastic raving. . . . After that first incapable pause, during which I stood rooted to the spot, I could no longer endure to look on the picture, and turning away, fled back through the rooms and into the street" (566).

In the first section of the story, the narrator's sight is constantly in play, though not necessarily effective. The impact of this encounter, however—when the narrator finally sees what he has sought—causes him to shut down his visual sense: "I drew the blinds before my windows, and covered my face to think" (566). He adds, "as I again lay back and hid my now burning and fevered face, I repeated . . . aloud:—'How unsearchable are Thy judgements, and Thy ways past finding out!'" (567). And in his dream, "in the place of my picture, which I could not see, there hung the St Agnes of Perugia" (ibid.). The dream culminates with an anti-revelation, in which vision and the visual turn out after all to be the agents of non-understanding rather than discovery:

I was going upstairs to my room at home, where I thought Mary was waiting to sit for her portrait. The staircase was quite dark; and as I went up, the voices of several persons I knew passed by me, as if they were descending; and sometimes my own among them. I had reached the top, and was feeling for the handle of the door, when it was opened suddenly by an angel; and looking in, I saw, not Mary, but a woman whose face was hidden with white light, and who had a lamb beside her that was bleating aloud. She knelt in the middle of the room, and I heard her say several times: "O Lord, it is more than he can bear. Spare him, O Lord, for her sake whom he consecrated to me." After this, music came out of heaven, and I thought to have heard speech; but instead, there was silence that woke me. This dream must have occurred repeatedly in the course of the night, for I remember waking up in perfect darkness, overpowered with fear, and crying out in the words which I had heard spoken by the woman; and when I woke in the morning, it was from the same dream, and the same words were on my lips. (ibid.)

The emphasis here is ultimately on language, the "words . . . on my lips." The visual becomes a negative—the blinding light that hides the mysterious woman's face. Words are cried out "in darkness," so that neither the light nor the dark carries anything but delusion, incomprehension, and fear.[50]

In "St Agnes of Intercession," the impossibility of revelation is more central than the final evocation of the modern cityscape, which therefore appears brutally resistant to the spiritualized understanding proposed by the P.R.B. in

1848–50 as the means through which modernity might be represented and understood. Revising his early text of 1850 in the 1870s, Rossetti seems to have reworked the tale to emphasize the impossibility of deep interpretation. There is a franker, more forthright statement of the necessity of confronting and understanding the modern than in "Hand and Soul"—as well as a harsher skepticism about the capacity of the painter's art to achieve it. The early Pre-Raphaelite project imagined the visual as capable—through innovation—of revelation, of understanding the deep realities of the age. In the full version of "St Agnes," the visual is merely the medium of darkness, proffering a bemused incomprehension before the object of its inquiry.

The Surface of Meaning

This skepticism about the capacity of the visual to penetrate to the inner meanings of the world and to carry the perceptions of a spiritualized understanding of experience proved crucial for the subsequent evolution of Rossetti's art. When he returned to the manuscript of "St Agnes of Intercession" in 1870 and made the revisions I have discussed, Rossetti's work as a painter had long since shifted decisively away from the public context of early Pre-Raphaelitism and toward interiority. Other members of his immediate artistic circle show similar developments. Among the works of the other founding Pre-Raphaelites, Millais's painting *The Blind Girl* (1854–56, fig. 11) also marks this moment of transformation in the Brotherhood's interests. By shifting the focus of attention in the painting away from the social and historical concerns of the early P.R.B. toward a newly intense fascination with the senses as a subject in their own right, Millais imagines a context in which modern life and experience can be recast into an imaginative and largely autonomous realm of sensation.[51] Millais's subject matter develops a drawing of the previous year, *The Blind Man* (1853, fig. 12), that more clearly perpetuates the social interests of the first phase of Pre-Raphaelite activity. Clearly set in a contemporary city environment reminiscent of the London conjured up in the closing paragraphs of "St Agnes of Intercession," Millais's blind man readily becomes the occasion for social observation and comment.[52] But *The Blind Girl* is less precisely placed[53] and inaugurates a turn away from the social. Although the clothing, the concertina, and the demeanor of the two girls all locate them socially in a way understood by contemporary commentators on the painting, Millais goes some way toward abstracting them from context by placing them in a landscape.[54]

The corollary of this reduction of social immediacy is the augmentation of the sensorium, its extension in every direction through the repertoire of touch

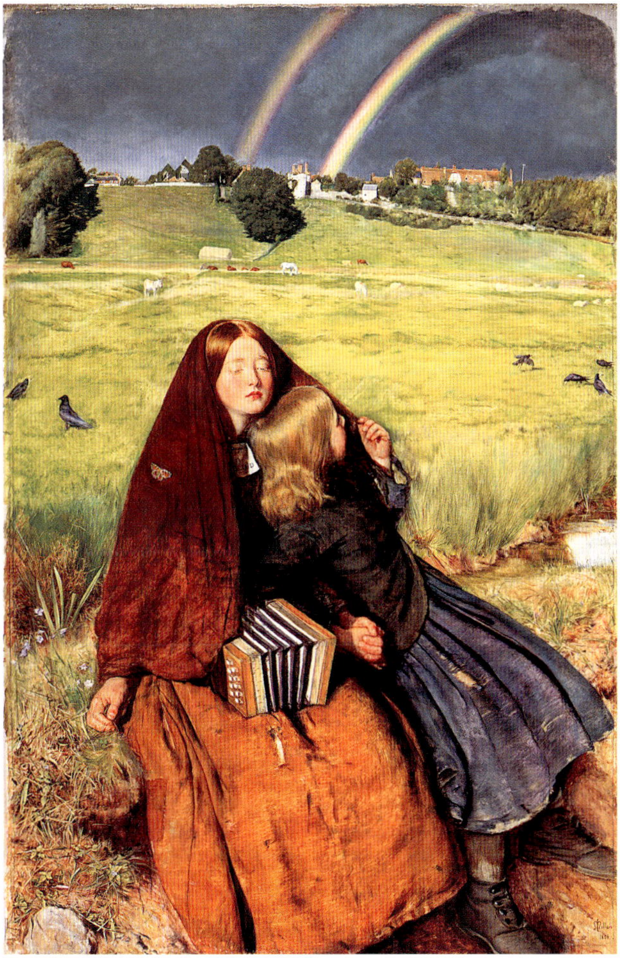

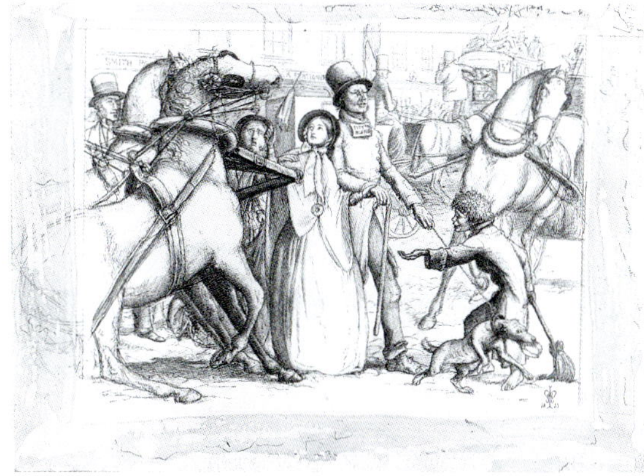

FIGURE 12. John Everett Millais, *The Blind Man,* 1853

FIGURE 11. John Everett Millais, *The Blind Girl,* 1854–56

(the prominence and movements of the two girls' hands, the butterfly, and the tactility of the tears in the coarse fabric of their skirts), smell (the harebells and forget-me-nots), hearing (the concertina, the rooks cawing in the background), and, overwhelmingly, sight.[55] Millais uses the brilliant palette of the P.R.B. to assert an intensity of vision, an aspect of the painting that was obvious to the (unsympathetic) *Athenaeum* critic who thought he saw "sweetmeat rainbows of lollypop colours" and "raw green fields."[56] The younger, sighted, girl turns and peers around the edge of her sister's shawl to gaze at the double rainbow glowing above.[57] Her attention directs ours, asking us to consider the materiality of the world and the capacity of representation to partake of that vivid materiality, looking out from social reality and toward another, more intense aspect of experience. Like the younger sister, *The Blind Girl* turns its own gaze away from social themes and toward a newly vivid concern with the materiality of the world and representation.

Flint interprets *The Blind Girl* typologically as an evocation of inner vision contrasted with "the gross materialism of the age."[58] But in fact the turn seems to be *toward* materiality in this other, spiritualized, aspect. The painting's inwardness, if that is what it is, is surely an entirely shallow or superficial version of that quality. Both girls are fixed in concentration on the physical and material world that surrounds them. The blind girl's inward gaze is no gaze at all, after all; her hand, delicately holding the stem of a forget-me-not, draws her attention. The contrast to the vulgar materialism of the time resides in "the visible, material world" rather than outside or beyond it.[59] The slightly later *Autumn Leaves* (1855–56, fig. 13), with its looser paintwork and apparent renunciation of Pre-Raphaelite detail and precision in describing the world, pushes that interest in surface and tactility further. Although its newly broad brushwork has traditionally been accounted for by the change in circumstances brought about by Millais's marriage, this reading of his art seems increasingly unpersuasive.[60] It is the materiality of the visible, including the substance of paint itself, that is being signaled, and here Millais extends the interests of *The Blind Girl*. Whereas the first painting constituted a theoretical argument for this position, *Autumn Leaves* begins to instantiate it and pushes it through from content to technique. Effie Millais caught the nature of this movement when she reported Millais's intention in beginning work: "he wished to paint a picture full of beauty and without subject."[61]

The same imperatives and solutions that Millais engages in these two key paintings of the Pre-Raphaelite turn appear in Rossetti's works from the later 1850s. Many recent commentators have remarked on the self-reflexivity of the paintings of women that Rossetti began to make at that time—women who, in the words of F. G. Stephens, are "amorously, mystically, or moodily lost in dreams, or absorbed by thoughts too deep for words."[62] *Bocca Baciata* (1859, fig. 14) is widely acknowledged as "a landmark in the emerging Aestheticism of the post–Pre-Raphaelite era" because of its preoccupation with the pleasure of the visual, its emphasis on "sheer visual delight as an end in itself."[63] These terms signal the appearance in English painting of the ideas normally referred to as Aestheticism. I shall discuss the nature and importance of Aestheticism further in the next chapter: there I deal with the impact of the ideas of Walter Pater (and others) and with the expression of Aestheticist ideas in painting. For now, I want only to note the interest that Aestheticism takes in the physical and material constitution of art objects as part of a wider interest in the notion of

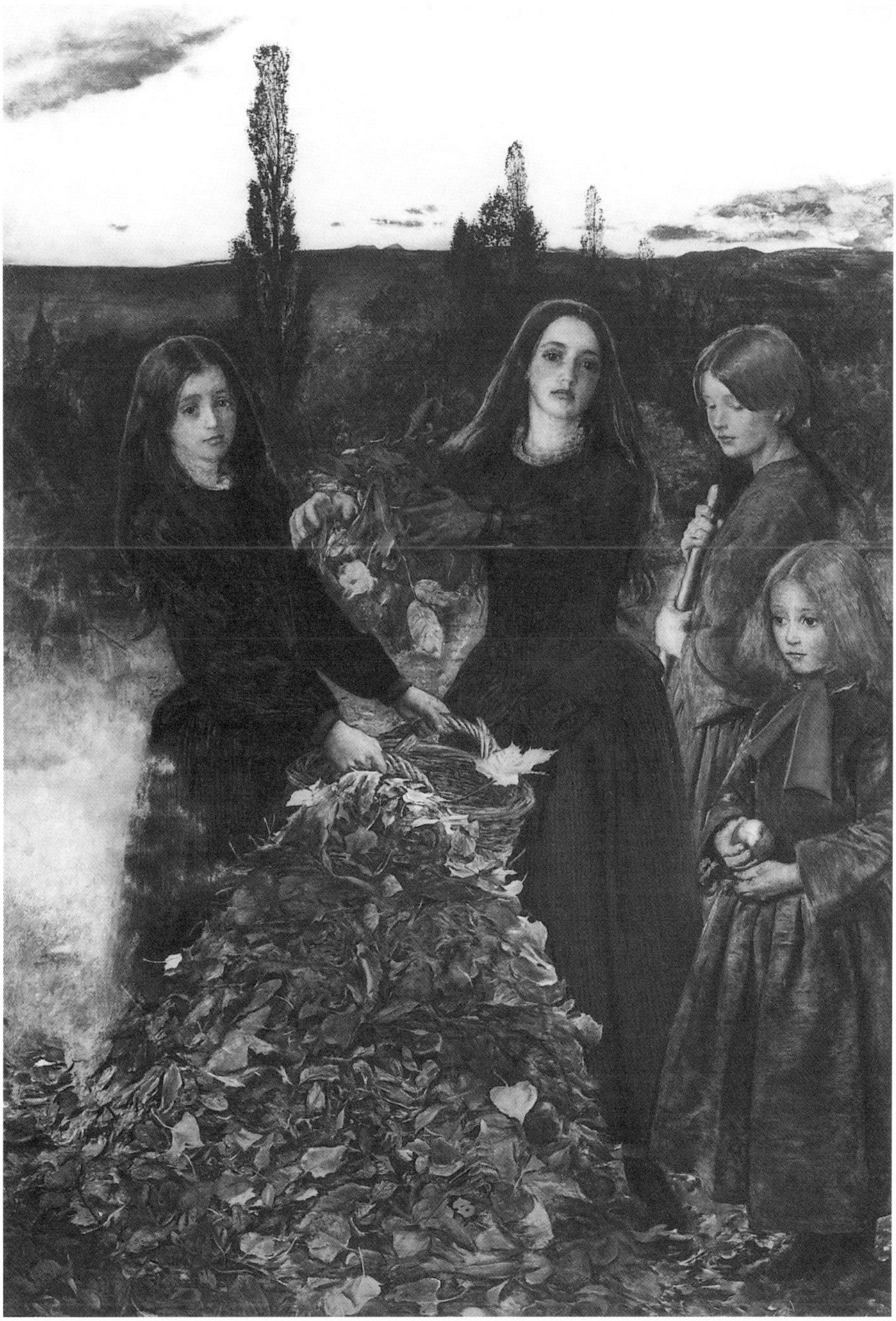

FIGURE 13. John Everett Millais, *Autumn Leaves,* 1855–56

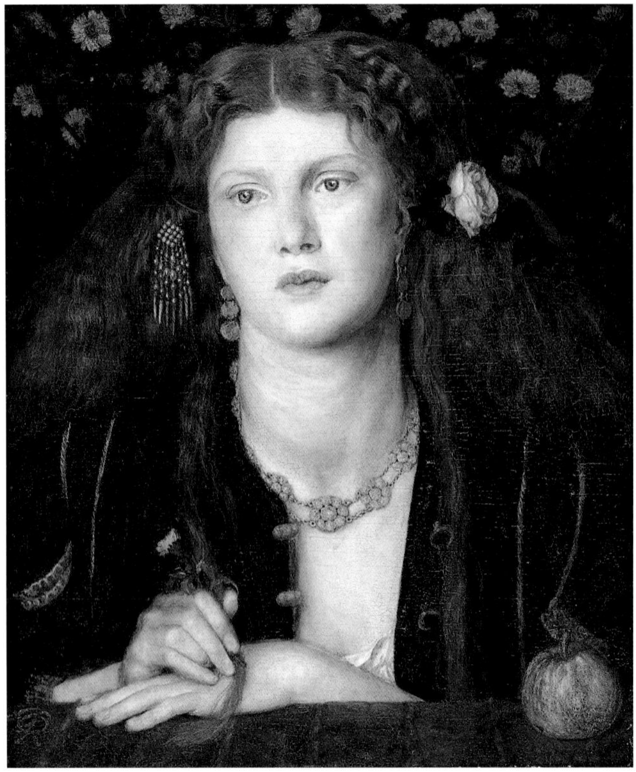

FIGURE 14. Dante Gabriel Rossetti, *Bocca Baciata,* 1859

autonomy, or "art for art's sake." Such ideas provided the grounds for increased attention to the physical nature of the artwork, while the implications of claiming such autonomy tended to draw a strong boundary around the work. This situation expresses itself in part through the appearance and proliferation of metaphors of autonomy in the artworks that Aestheticist artists and their fellow travelers produced. Questions of surface, texture, and independence from other forms of meaning—questions raised and examined through the figuration of autonomy that these works conduct—become the manifest subject of their meditations.

Rossetti's commentators are thus encouraged to identify the emphasis on "visual delight" as central to the long series of works that begins with *Bocca Baciata* in 1859. More complexly (but in a similar spirit), Prettejohn sees these works as pictures that weave together emphatically modern accounts of femininity with images of self-sufficiency and sexual power to achieve metaphors "for art's independence from conventional morality."[64] The turn toward interiority and reflection on the status of the art object expressed in these formulations gave rise to a number of paintings that parallel the skepticism of "St Agnes

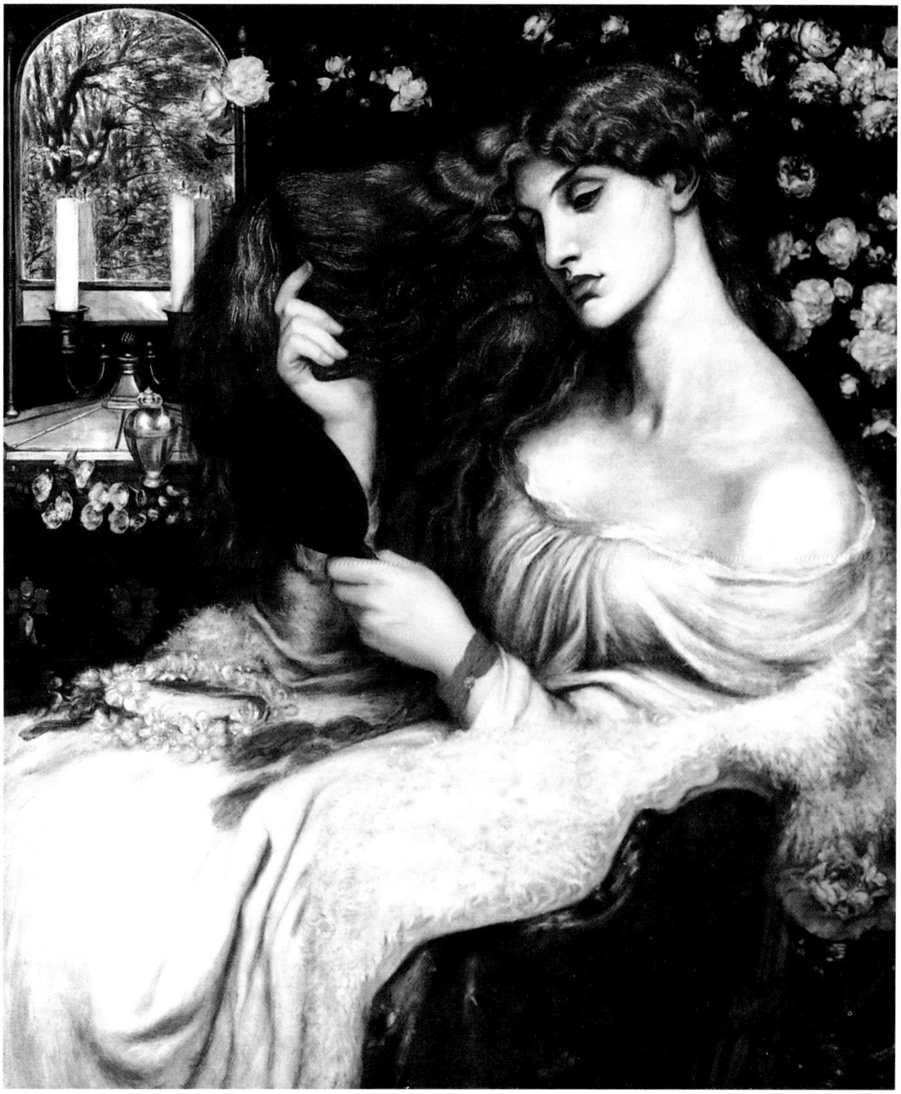

FIGURE 15. Dante Gabriel Rossetti, *Lady Lilith,* 1868–73

of Intercession." They, too, concern themselves with the occlusion of understanding that the visual carries within it, the veiling and blinding of sight and meaning instead of penetration through the material world to truth. For Rossetti the visual artist, though, that occlusion now turns out to have a positive as well as a negative aspect.

Lady Lilith (1868–73, fig. 15) takes as its subject Adam's apocryphal first wife, a sexual demon in Talmudic tradition.[65] Appropriately enough, the painting seemed to Rossetti's early critics to be the apogee of the sensuous evocation of bodily experience for its own sake.[66] "No painter has ever idealized like this the elemental power of carnal loveliness," thought H. C. Marillier; Stephens spoke of "the ardent languor of triumphant luxury and beauty" in the painting, and he went on to associate this sexual glamour with the self-absorption of Lilith's gaze: "she holds the mirror with negligent grace, and, self-absorbed, trains her bewitching locks."[67] Rossetti himself called it "a *Modern Lilith* combing out her abundant golden hair and gazing at herself in the glass with that complete self-absorption by whose fascination such natures draw others within their circle."[68] But Swinburne, reviewing the Royal Academy exhibition in 1868, gave the most developed account in this mode:

Her head leans back half sleepily, superb and satiate with its own beauty; the eyes are languid, without love in them or hate; the sweet luxurious mouth has the patience of pleasure fulfilled and complete, the warm repose of passion sure of its delight. . . . For this serene and sublime sorceress there is no life but of the body; with spirit (if spirit there be) she can dispense. . . . She is indifferent, equable, magnetic; she charms and draws down the souls of men by pure force of absorption, in no wise wilful or malignant; outside herself she cannot live, she cannot even see: and because of this she attracts and subdues all men at once in body and in spirit. Beyond the mirror she cares not to look, and could not.[69]

It is Lilith's literal superficiality that "attracts and subdues." Confined to the surface of the mirror, she is confined as well to the body, to appearance rather than to depth, "dispens[ing]" with "spirit." Her version of interiority is self-absorption, repudiation of the world outside the self, not an uncovering of what lies hidden beneath the surface. Her self-contemplation remains at the level of appearance. Described in Rossetti's paint, which flattens objects onto a single plane and pushes hard up to the point where the picture meets the exterior world, she is contained, poised, surrounded by exemplars of surface; the circuit of her contemplation never penetrates to the interior.

McGann notes the oddity of the mirror set behind the edge of Lilith's hair: although it "functions . . . as a window . . . its allusion to that typical piece of pictorial symbology is negative and ironic, for it does not face (spatially) outward and (temporally) forward, but inward and backward."[70] In fact, this mirror is referential in time *rather* than space. The only point of depth within the painting, it looks back into the history of Pre-Raphaelitism, already distant by the 1860s, and cites the large and ornate mirror behind the couple in *The Awakening*

Conscience (see fig. 5). Hunt's painting, though made after the disintegration of the Brotherhood was underway, stands, as I have already argued, as a centerpiece of its invocation of spiritual and moral values as a means to understand modernity and to serve as its corrective—and of the accompanying conviction that the visual protocols of painting can express and transmit these values. In the web of references and meanings *The Awakening Conscience* holds within its multitude of precisely rendered details, the mirror plays a central role: "nature, seen through the French windows, is presented as a mirror image; it represents the woman's lost innocence, from which she has divorced herself by her present way of life," in the words of one critic.[71]

In *Lady Lilith,* Rossetti quotes this moralizing, spiritualizing mirror of Hunt's, placing his own version in the same segment of the composition but allowing it to carry a different charge.[72] If Hunt's nature is "lost innocence," or something like it, then it is an innocence that is now unwanted and unsought, its place taken by the exfoliation of pigment that describes the roses, commencing with the bloom that touches the glass of the mirror and ending with the flowers filling the picture plane against (rather than "behind") Lilith's head. Like her flowing hair and wristband, these flowers are metaphors for pigment itself, brushed onto the canvas with a movement of the hand that matches Lilith's sweeping motion through her heavy, highly realized hair. But this adjustment in the economy of the painting has a further aspect. Instead of a direct reference from the objects of the physical, material world to the meaning that they signify, Rossetti's circuit, departing from the painted and now alien world of nature seen in the anti-naturalistic reflection of the mirror, doubles back on itself to reaffirm its own inwardness. There is no meaning to the image of nature in the mirror. It is, as McGann notes, a negation, a refusal of any path out of the picture and into the space that Hunt's earlier painting so forthrightly occupies.[73]

Lilith, described as "subtly of herself contemplative" in Rossetti's matching poem, "Body's Beauty," "draws men to watch the bright net she can weave, / Till heart and body and life are in its hold."[74] Trapping the spectator ("watch") within the self-contemplating circuit of the painting, *Lady Lilith* suggests a further version of the veiling medium of "St Agnes of Intercession." We can read the second, invisible, surface of the (hand) mirror Lilith plies as evidence of this. What she sees within it is only an endless replay of her own self, and that image, denied us by the angle of her hand, points toward a blockage of the visual's power to register reality. Self-referring, it signifies only itself, its own character as a medium, as superficial physical substance, rather than the capacity to know and communicate the realities and truths of the world outside its own constitution. In this way, the painting mirrors the shutting down of the visual sense in "St Agnes of Intercession." It renounces the ability of the visual to see beyond itself—"beyond the mirror she cares not to look, and *could not,*" says Swinburne[75]—and the focus on the visual in Aestheticism of Rossetti's type is no more than the acknowledgment that there is now nowhere else to look.

But despite "St Agnes of Intercession," this is not the final word—or at least not the final vision. For it may also be that Rossetti's inability or unwillingness to finish the short story in 1850—and its revision but continued incompletion twenty years later as a skeptical inquiry into the visual—have to do not only with vision's incapacity but also with the evident visual richness and delight of works like these. "St Agnes" questions the ability of the visual to act as the conduit through which a spiritualized understanding and critique of modernity might be made (and made comprehensible). *Lady Lilith* and works like it, such as *The Beloved* (1865–66, fig. 16), *The Blue Bower* (1865, Barber Institute of Fine Arts, University of Birmingham), and *Monna Vanna* (1866, Tate Britain, London), may reinforce that position but also operate in other ways. Each of these paintings asserts a capacity in the visual, material quality of paint, and in the metaphors of paint and medium that it sets going across the surface of its canvas, for pleasure and for the evocation of those things that belong to the surface rather than to depth, to somatic and sensual experience rather than to intellectual penetration into meaning or significance.[76]

Rossetti's circle and the patrons who first bought these paintings clearly understood and consumed them in this way. Arthur Hughes thought that the first owner of *Bocca Baciata,* George Price Boyce, "will kiss the dear things lips away."[77] Discussing this opinion, Barbara Bryant quotes Swinburne's view that the painting was "more stunning than can be decently expressed."[78] Rossetti himself forthrightly remarked that *Monna Vanna* "represents . . . the Venetian ideal of female beauty."[79] A physical sensuousness is central to the impact and reception of these paintings. What is claimed here is that paint offers a sensual experience in its own right and that such an experience somehow appropriately engages with the world. In other words, the very veiling of meaning that "St Agnes" scrutinizes as a characteristic of the visual is the source of its strength. The lack of penetration into significance that painting enacts in its surfaces—its devotion to appearance and to a literal superficiality of experience as its greatest gift and achievement—precisely allows the visual to mean in a truthful way. The parodic surface of the story, with its ironic acknowledgment of Poe and the fictional playfulness of *Tristram Shandy,* is perhaps a device meant to force prose

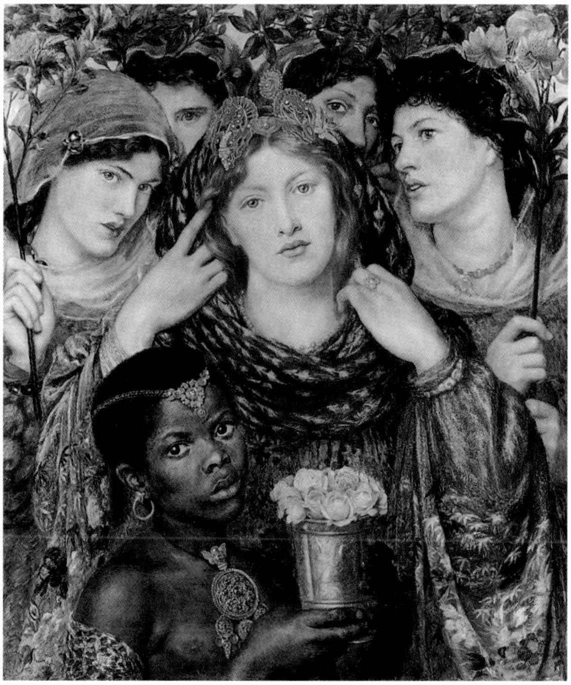

FIGURE 16. Dante Gabriel Rossetti, *The Beloved,* 1865–66

to stay on the surface in an equivalent way. These pictures argue that painting's confinement at the surface, at the sensuous limit of superficiality, allows it to access and communicate a certain category of experience, of truth, or of the world, like no other medium. Indeed, that ability is so developed, so integrated into the nature of the medium itself, that it actually *is* that truth and that experience. The surfaces of *Lady Lilith* and *The Beloved* enact and provoke the swarming, febrile, and sensuous character of somatic experience—and in some genuine sense *are* that experience. The medium here is what it purports to represent; there is no distinction. Painting is what it investigates, makes plain, and opens into understanding for its spectator. It is now an identity of medium and object that guarantees success, not a resonance between the world and the artist's inner self. This makes of these works a version of what I have called "unmediation," a revision of the initial Pre-Raphaelite mechanism connecting art and the world expressed by Stephens and the young Rossetti at the time of *The Germ* and "Hand and Soul."

The literary critic Kathy Alexis Psomiades sees such a refusal of the distinction between "inaccessible psychological depth" and "tangible material surface" in the feminine figures of Aestheticist literature and painting as a metaphor for "the difficult and vexed relation between the categories of the aesthetic and the economic in bourgeois culture." Within the meaning it creates, the interval between the aesthetic and the economic can be "represented and covered over by erotic relations."[80] The doubled signifiers of surface and interiority in femininity equate, for Psomiades, to the effect of the artwork's commodification; the work of art is both privatized and a richly attractive objectified commodity in its own right. This, too, gives a particularly modern character to paintings like *The Beloved,* but one that depends on heedless self-absorption as a sign of surface. *Monna Vanna* or *Lady Lilith* represent feminine beauty as images that both are and refuse to be commodities. They imagine for their first audience what it might be like to think superficiality and surface as critiques of commodity and as its other. Like Swinburne's use of "art for art's sake" in his Blake monograph of 1868, surface and self-absorption work to "assert that, in a thoroughly utilitarian culture, even the seemingly apolitical, disinterested pursuit of art is necessarily oppositional in nature."[81]

This is a type of answer to the problem posed at the moment of Pre-Raphaelitism in 1848–50. Identity of self, world, and representation guarantees the ability of the work to deal adequately and justly with reality. If that adequacy cannot be explained through the mechanism of "Hand and Soul," as the Pre-Raphaelites first proposed—and as the darker possibilities of blindness, delusion, and the deflection of reality in representation rehearsed in "St Agnes of Intercession" skeptically question—then perhaps the superficiality and self-identity of the work of art can do so instead. Its very lack of utility and external significance, its inability to penetrate to meanings held beneath the surface of the material world, might provide the grounds for its relevance and significance. When Rossetti returned to complete "St Agnes" on the basis of the experiments in painting he had begun in the late 1850s, he broached the questions raised by the apparent negativity of the visual and its failure to access the world. The paintings of the 1860s and 1870s amount, in their superficiality and self-regard, to a repudiation of the visual's access to the real and to the most powerful assertion of the identity of representation and reality that he can imagine. In doing so, to recall Edward William Cox's formulation, he provided a vision of painting as, paradoxically, "*material* enough" to be "a soul of the age." That vision, as it turned out, proved a precarious one for other artists in his circle.

Unmediation in Burne-Jones

When the young Edward Burne-Jones contrived to travel to London and to meet his hero, Dante Gabriel Rossetti, in the early months of 1856, he confirmed that a further generation of would-be artists would delve into the heart of these issues. This generation, of which Burne-Jones is by far the most important painter, found itself deeply involved in the set of questions confronted by Rossetti's work after 1859. The potential of the visual was both exemplified in Rossetti's art and at the same time inimitable (and possibly unsustainable). In this section of the chapter, I look at some of the ways in which this situation generated thematic responses in the work of Burne-Jones. I argue that his paintings, feted at the Grosvenor Gallery in the 1870s as successful assertions of the Aestheticist cause, in fact develop an extended meditation on the sustainability of such strong claims. To reassert and maintain the promise of the visual, Burne-Jones's art imagines an unmediated relationship between the world and its representation. His paintings offer an imagery to express that relationship. (Although his example was not taken up by the surviving first-generation Pre-Raphaelites, a similar preoccupation with unmediated representation is central to the work of many of Burne-Jones's Aestheticist peers, as I will go on to show in Chapter 2.)

From the moment of their first meeting in January 1856, Rossetti became a key intellectual mentor for the younger artist. When Burne-Jones left Oxford and settled in London shortly afterwards, he gravitated to Rossetti's studio and there received his most important training—sporadic, unsystematic, but inspiring in the Rossetti manner. "He taught me to have no fear or shame of my own ideas, to design perpetually, to seek no popularity, to be altogether myself," remembered Burne-Jones later, indicating the extent to which Rossetti's example was fundamental to his understanding of his own mission and sense of himself as an artist.[82] Rossetti remained "a vital source of inspiration for everything that followed," a standard by which Burne-Jones judged himself, a constant imaginary companion whose views he would mentally consult to the end of his life whenever he began a new picture.[83] It was Rossetti who introduced him to Ruskin and to the Holland Park circle that revolved around G. F. Watts, and it was Rossetti who formulated the conceptual structure within which Burne-Jones learned to be an artist and began to practice. Among the chief supports of this structure was the awareness of the intersecting relationships that Rossetti imagined for words and images, and Burne-Jones's work thus shared the concerns Rossetti himself was setting out in the paintings and drawings of the 1860s and 1870s.[84]

The position Burne-Jones took up in relation to these concerns could never have been identical with the one adopted by the older artist. As I have suggested, Rossetti's ability to advance superficiality as a solution to the problem of the visual depended on his dual currency in both literature and the visual arts. The issue was simply less acute for Rossetti than for others because he had, in this sense, a foot in both camps, the ability to offer different types of approaches to the world in his own work. If the visual was confined to the surface, he still possessed language as an instrument of depth. Other, less versatile Pre-Raphaelites—and Burne-Jones, the leading painter of the second wave—had no such option. As a result, it became of vital importance to demonstrate painting's capacity to register the fundamentals of reality in a convincing way.[85]

Burne-Jones's art reflects this pressure thematically in two ways. First, he stages a contest between word and image in which language is fantasized as subservient to the visual. Second, he elaborates the trope of unmediation as an imaginary solution to the question of the visual's access to reality. This concept, which is a more thoroughgoing variation on Ruskin's "innocent eye" and on the argument from surface, provides an intensely complex image of the collapse of observing self, object, and medium into a single identity: paint is the world, and the world is paint, without any intervention of agency or mediated knowledge. In these works, visuality stands for this desired identity of world and knowledge.

From his early formation in Rossetti's orbit, Burne-Jones inherited technical concerns and his relationship to the capacity of the visual to signify through its material qualities. Rossetti called Burne-Jones's early drawings "marvels of finish and imaginative detail," and Burne-Jones himself always thought of a painting as a "decorated surface," "every inch . . . so fine that if all but a scrap from one of them were burned or lost, the man who found it might say, whatever this may have represented it is a work of art, beautiful in surface and quality of colour."[86] From the first, his works draw frank attention to their visual character in a number of ways.[87] Commentators such as Henry James saw clearly that Burne-Jones introduced spatial and material oddities into his paintings that were sufficiently striking to demand response. Writing about *Laus Veneris* (1873–78, fig. 17) when it was first exhibited in 1878, James thought that the figures "are too flat, that they exist too exclusively in surface" and were therefore "wanting in relief and in the power to detach themselves."[88] Burne-Jones's studio assistant, T. M. Rooke, remembered for his part the idiosyncratic character of Burne-Jones's medium: "a stiff pigment of the texture of soft cheese."[89] And so heavily worked were his surfaces, according to Graham Robertson, that "he appeared wilfully to ignore the possibilities of his medium and to put it to uses for which it was not intended."[90] In many works, the crust of the paint, applied in dry, multiple touches, is entirely un-mimetic. The sub-

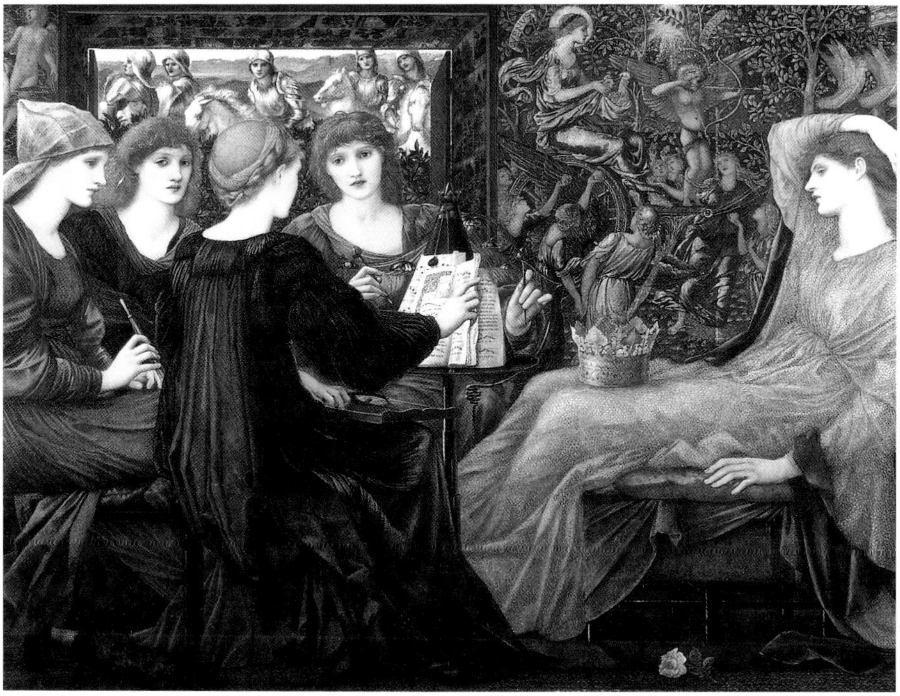

FIGURE 17. Edward Burne-Jones, *Laus Veneris,* 1873–78

stances it describes, no matter how diverse, are rendered through a variation on a single rough plasterwork texture.[91] "You might be looking at a tapestry woven with infinite pains in exile, by a philosopher or a mathematician," wrote Sizeranne.[92]

This cultivation of the materiality of surface and execution finds a parallel in the frequently strange perspectival elements in Burne-Jones's paintings. The recession apparently signaled by the complex space of the interior architecture in *King Cophetua and the Beggar Maid* (1880–84, fig. 18), for instance, is, in viewing the picture, largely canceled by the effect of the flat, decorative shapes of the lance and helmet that lean against the balcony. The form of the helmet presses up against the picture plane almost like an anamorphosis, so acutely angled is it. It becomes a mutating shape or "patch," to use Didi-Huberman's term, spreading its flatness across the surface of the picture plane.[93] All these accumulated devices give the character of the paint surface a peculiar prominence in the experience of viewing Burne-Jones. Its refusal to mime the textures of the world redirects attention toward the painting's own constitution as substance, as matter and flat, fictive surface.[94] "I don't want to pretend this isn't a picture,"

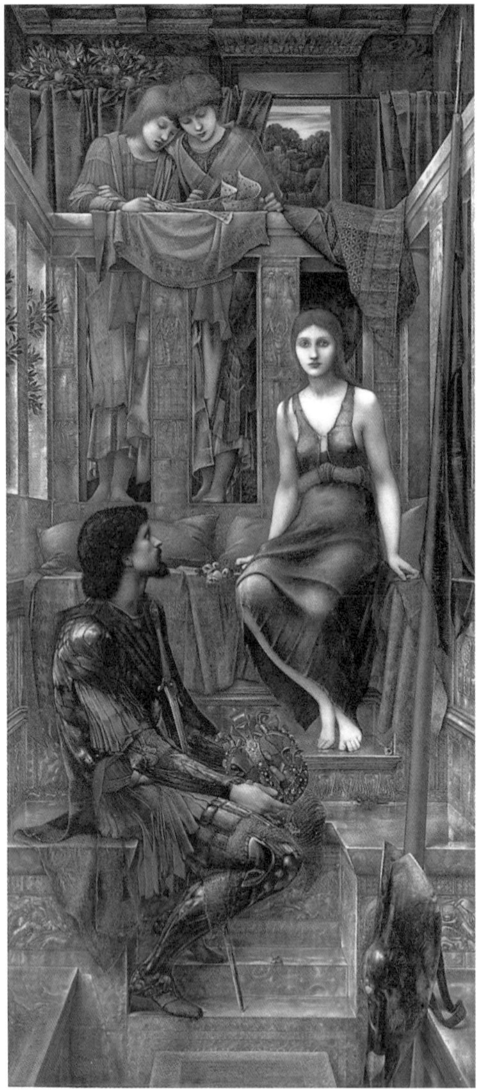

FIGURE 18. Edward Burne-Jones, *King Cophetua and the Beggar Maid*, 1880–84

Burne-Jones declared during a discussion of realism.[95] Surface was one way of emphasizing that conviction—that painting was, above all else, an expressive instance of the visual, "fine," decorative, and concerned with "the beautiful."

It seems to me that, contrary to what might be imagined, this assertiveness represents a moment of anxiety in Burne-Jones's work. Faced with the importance of claims for the visual (and specifically for painting) to serve as a means of knowing and evaluating the contemporary world, Burne-Jones finds himself faced with the problems that, as we have seen, tend to go along with such views. How does paint know the world? How far can it judge the nature of what it represents? And how can it propose or advance alternative values or modes of understanding? His paintings, in their visual elaboration of complexity, their emphasis on surface and on visual fineness, echo the solution Rossetti was proposing during the 1860s and 1870s. But that solution seems vulnerable in Burne-Jones. Without Rossetti's ability to posit paint as superficial and to reserve depth for language, Burne-Jones had to find a way of asserting painting's capacity both to offer the truths of surface and to penetrate into fundamental meaning. Instead of adopting Rossetti's example in its strong form, therefore, he extrapolates from it and imagines an alternative solution, one that operates in a different way to assert the identity of the world and visual representation.

The thematization of an imaginary unmediated relationship between the world and the painting is widely observable in Burne-Jones's works from the 1870s onward. The need to provide an image of this possibility partly accounts for the appeal he found in subjects such as *The Baleful Head* (1885, Southampton City Art Gallery) as well as the *Perseus* series to which it belongs, with its central interest in the thematics of sight, or the set of four paintings known as *Pygmalion and the Image* (1875–78, Birmingham Museums and Art Gallery) that details the translation of the work of art into living flesh. In a major painting of this period, *The Beguiling of Merlin* (1870–74, fig. 19), his choice of subject allows Burne-Jones to show an image of the work of art as passive before the world and, by virtue of that passivity, identical with it, powerfully unmediated.

The painting derives from Arthurian legend. In the version that Burne-Jones drew on, Merlin's lover, Viviane, uses her own magic to betray him, binding him into a hawthorn tree for eternity.[96] Burne-Jones's painting shows the process of weaving the spell, with Merlin rather unconvincingly incorporated into the hawthorn and Viviane chanting from the folio in her hands. Merlin is caught at the moment of powerlessness when the spell begins to work. Apparently enervated and without force, his head and hands loll weakly and he seems entirely supported by the hawthorn tree. The skin of his face is stretched over the bone so that he looks almost at the point of death. Only his eyes, fixed on Viviane, are still active. She, for her part, seems to squirm apprehensively away from him, powerless though he is. Her eyes look back at him anxiously even while she declaims the words from her book. She seems to expect him to break the spell at any moment. Behind and around them, the sinuous rhythms of the tree and its blossoms and the twisting fabric of their clothing mimic the forms of the paint itself.

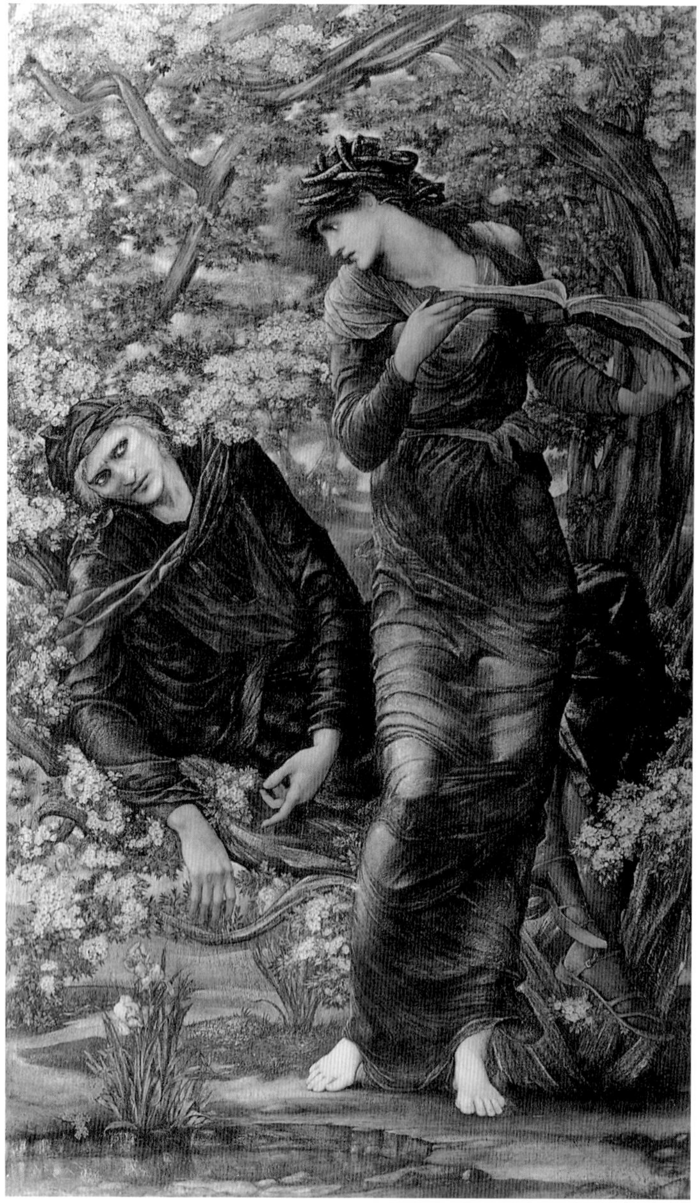

FIGURE 19.
Edward Burne-Jones, *The Beguiling of Merlin*, 1870–74

The Beguiling of Merlin has often been given a biographical interpretation stemming from Burne-Jones's claustrophobic relationship with his own lover, Maria Zambaco.[97] But although the helplessness of desire is clearly a key element in the painting, the relationship between Merlin's lapse from power and force, the book, and the emphatic declaration of paint in the background and in the clothes of the two protagonists suggests another meaning. The painting, I argue, imagines a contest between words and images, Merlin rendered feeble, Viviane herself a mixture of insecurity and determination, as if she is no more than the mouthpiece of an uncertain authority that speaks through her. She shares with Merlin the swirling metaphoric brushstrokes of their clothing that accommodate them to the flattened, decorative two-dimensionality of the hawthorn tree and its blossoms. But unlike him, she stands out from the flowing forms of the branches that continue the metaphor of paint surface and paint application in a thoroughgoing suppression of depth throughout the picture plane. The book Viviane holds emerges as the only three-dimensional object in the painting.[98] As she chants the words that bind Merlin into the magical prison formed from the world that surrounds him, leaching the power and force out of him, they enact the enervation of the visual before the imagined power of words.

But Burne-Jones's picture only appears to present a tableau in which word triumphs over image. The enfeeblement of the visual in fact becomes the moment when it declares its triumph most powerfully. Christine Poulson sees Merlin's pose as the "helpless surrender" associated with mesmeric healing and links it directly with the idea of Burne-Jones's surrender to erotic turmoil in his relationship with Zambaco.[99] But this debility is actually a source of strength, because it stands for the imagined absence of mediation in the relationship of the visual and the world. Merlin's incapacity and powerlessness—as his head lolls weakly and the skin of his face stretches over the bones like parchment—point to and make possible his potency in the direct identity with the world that the visual can achieve. The flowing brushstrokes and flattened, unreal depth of the image enact that possibility: through the material medium of the paint, the visual creates an alternative space, collapsing the distinction between pigment and the objects it claims to describe. Unmediation, like Ruskin's "innocent eye," is both the expression and the metaphor of this situation.[100] The argument of Burne-Jones's picture is that paint *is* the world, its articulation identical with reality, manifesting itself through an exact match to what it purports to know and communicate. Merlin *becomes* the hawthorn, as the flurry of surface description both *is* pigment and *is* the physical world it describes, a languid melting, through the medium, into the stuff of the world itself.

In the same way, the central figure of Venus in the slightly later *Laus Veneris* is also exhausted and helpless. Described in dense, impacted, emphatically material brushwork, Venus sits in a claustrophobically shallow space where extension across the surface of the picture plane stands in for recession into depth. The play of the visual replaces action: color, form, and surface extend across the breadth of the canvas. This is a painting in which narrative has been held in reserve—literally so, because it is relegated to the tapestries in the background—so that the eyes can have their moment. That richness and elaboration is linked to the passivity of the self.[101] Objections to Burne-Jones raised in the face of the painting's exhibition at the Grosvenor Gallery in 1878 largely seized on these qualities as the source of the spectators' unease. Viewers found the personages of the painting unhealthy, morally corrupt, and exemplifying a lapse from "masculine" vigor and energy that sent out worrying messages for late Victorian society.[102] Frederick Wedmore, the most pungent of the painting's critics, thought the figure of Venus the "unpleasant and uncomely" epitome of this disruptive languor and negativity. Like Merlin, she is ill, physically feeble; hers is "a body that has writhed with every impulse of sickness."[103] But in her passivity and languor, Venus is the true centerpiece of the energies of the painting—the image around which everything else, from the seated companions to the armored knights riding past, revolves.[104] She may be motionless like Merlin, without strength or energy, but that enervation guarantees her authority.

In the final and most thoroughgoing versions of this trope, the subjects of *The Briar Rose* series (1870–90, Buscot Park, Oxfordshire, The Faringdon Collection Trust) and *The Last Sleep of Arthur in Avalon* (1881–98, fig. 20) echo the central figures of *The Beguiling of Merlin* and *Laus Veneris,* lapsing toward unconsciousness, sleep, or nonbeing. They are fully abstracted from awareness, giving "definitive pictorial form" to "the isolation and psychological impenetrability of the sleeping figure."[105] Held in a death-like stasis in *The Briar Rose,* or, like Arthur, dead in Avalon, these figures complete Burne-Jones's desiring push toward the abolition of the triad of self, medium, and world that attends the moment of understanding. In *The Prince Enters the Briar Wood* (1870–84, fig. 21), the Prince, the only wakeful figure in the entire series, serves as a primary image of the picture surface. Like the helmet in *King Cophetua,* his body folds out and flattens against the picture plane, an effect reinforced by the visual rhyming of his armor and the shields that are hung against the surface of the picture and by the exfoliation of pigment described through the tangled growth of thorns that acts as painting's principal metaphor.[106] As he looks out into this painted world, the Prince stands for the observer, forming one point of the triangle of perception but at the same time entirely identified with the images of medium and the world described in the paint surface. *The Briar Rose* imagines a world in which observation and what is observed are melded together as expressions of a single medium. The self is able both to observe and to be nothing more than an instance of what is seen.

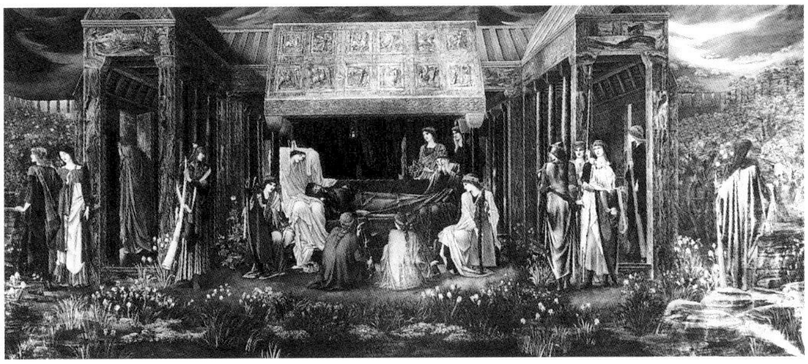

FIGURE 20. Edward Burne-Jones, *The Last Sleep of Arthur in Avalon,* 1881–98

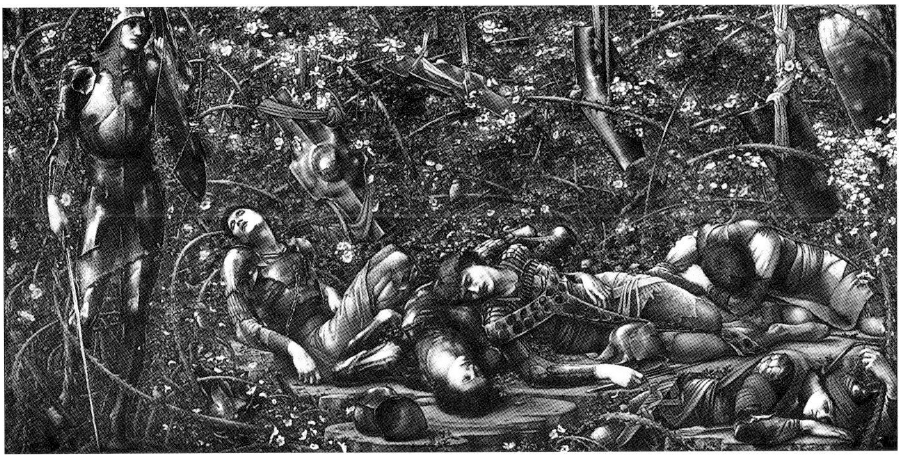

FIGURE 21. Edward Burne-Jones, *The Prince Enters the Briar Wood,* 1870–84

The Cracked Mirror

I began with a painting by Hunt, *The Awakening Conscience* (see fig. 5), that in the mid-1850s embodied one of the most powerful impulses of early Pre-Raphaelite picture making—the desire for a socially realistic account of modernity. It seems appropriate to conclude by looking at the issues raised by one of Hunt's last paintings, *The Lady of Shalott* (1886–1905, fig. 22), which was completed when both Rossetti and Burne-Jones were dead and stood for much of the subsequent history that I have traced. Like *The Briar Rose* series and *Arthur in Avalon, The Lady of Shalott* draws on concerns with representation, and its principal theme is the fate of the self as one term of the triad that constitutes the scene of interpretation and understanding. But in Burne-Jones, the rhetoric of representation collapses the world and the medium of observation into identity, and the observer, too, is imagined as fading out of existence, flattening into nullity like the Prince in the Briar Wood. Hunt's last work, by contrast, imagines the inevitable reemergence of the self.

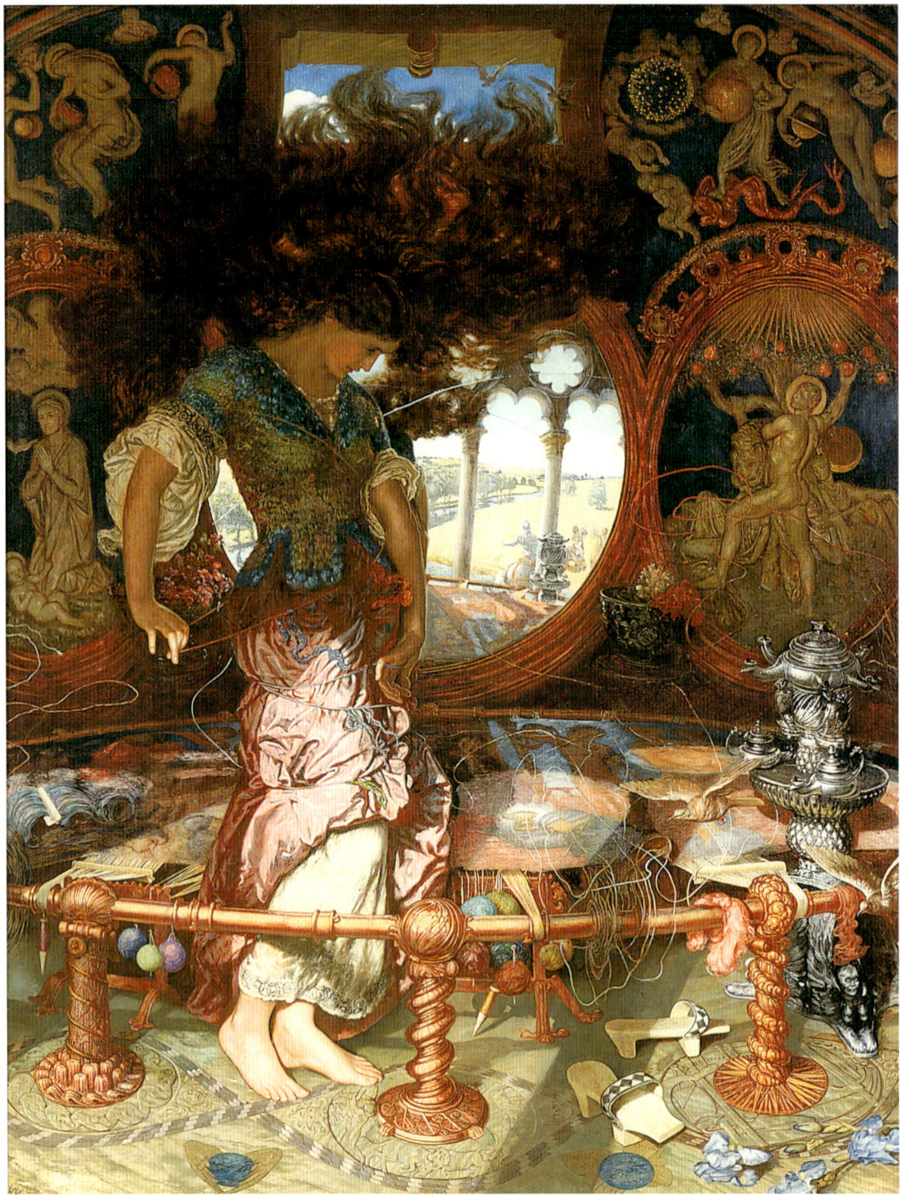

FIGURE 22. William Holman Hunt, *The Lady of Shalott*, 1886–1905

A number of paintings made by the inheritors of the Pre-Raphaelites use the Tennyson poem to take up a corollary of this snuffing out of the observing self.[107] They represent the self as anxious, fraught, and embattled under the pressure that passivity exerts. The well-known version by John William Waterhouse (1888, fig. 23) imagines her setting off in the "boat / beneath a willow left

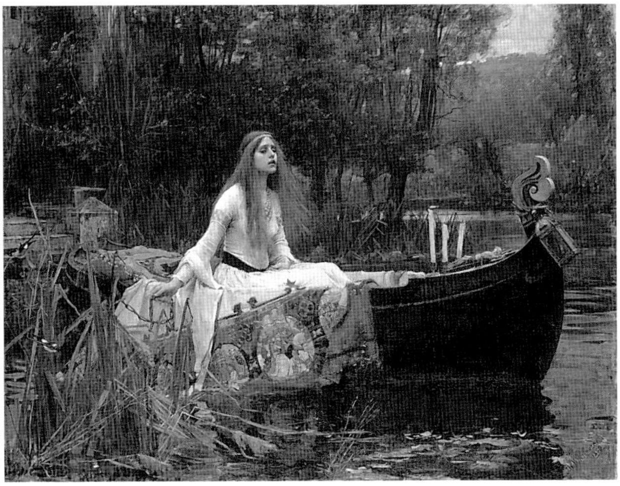

FIGURE 23. John William Waterhouse, *The Lady of Shalott*, 1888

afloat."[108] "Like some bold seer in a trance," the self floats away on her spiritual journey, "singing her last song," anguished in the consciousness of her difference from the world but perpetuating its mediation through the song.[109] Waterhouse's dark image blends this moment of agency into the renunciation of the self that is expressed in the poem by the Lady of Shalott's death. As she casts off the chain that ties the boat to the riverbank, she also casts off the links that bind her to life. Identity with the world is achievable only at the cost of death and the renunciation of selfhood in a languorous drift toward oblivion.

Hunt's *Lady of Shalott* is more robust. It pictures the return of the self that unmediation seeks to imagine as abolished or absent. From the first, Hunt seems to have conceived of the painting as in some way opposed to Rossetti.[110] In his revisionist autobiography, *Pre-Raphaelitism and the Pre-Raphaelite Brotherhood,* first published in 1905 when *The Lady of Shalott* was finally completed (and begun in 1886, at the same time as the painting), Hunt mounts a prolonged effort to modify views of the Pre-Raphaelites that had by then become conventional and to downplay the role of Rossetti, who was assumed to have been the "leader" of the Brotherhood. Rossetti is said to have "never strictly adhered to the original character of our movement."[111] Hunt presents himself as abandoned by his colleagues: "I alone still declared that I worked on the simple principle of Pre-Raphaelitism, which, being the unending study of Nature, is an eternal law" (2:334). In contrast, Rossetti, avoiding "Millais, Woolner and myself to a degree that proved to be more than unstudied" (2:134), took up with the Aesthetes of the Grosvenor Gallery and "completely changed his philosophy . . . leaving stoicism for Epicureanism" (2:143).

This change in Rossetti's art calls forth an extraordinarily intemperate denunciation from Hunt. Having established that Rossetti's painting from the 1860s onward amounted to "a treatment," one that "gradually grew to be overpowering, as is the odour of voluptuous perfumes in a closed room," "mannered" and "exotic" (2:363), and that "the manner he developed showed a settled aversion to the vertebrate principle of Pre-Raphaelitism in its original inception" (ibid.), Hunt goes on to castigate the "busy jackanapes" and "unthinking critics" (2:364) whose "hysteric grimacings . . . would deny the name of poetry to all that was not sickly and morbid" (2:365):

This was no mere passing frivolity, it was the fumes from festering decay; it was the complete distortion of art which is the highest perfecting principle of the human mind, expressed by strenuous labour. The Lord of Misrule had usurped the throne and was caricaturing beauty and wisdom into tawdry over-dressed vanity and folly . . . it was rioting and selfishness masked by pretentious learning and sophistical philosophy alluring weak minds with the sheen of superficial culture. (2:366)

It emerges that Rossetti's betrayal was on the smallest as well as the grandest scale. Extensive revisions in the second edition of the book include, at the very start of the second volume, the addition of a letter from Rossetti dated January 1855. It says, in part, "by the bye, I have long had an idea for illustrating the last verse of 'Lady of Shalott'"—the very subject Hunt had drawn in 1850 and was reworking for the 1857 Moxon Tennyson.[112] Rossetti asks Hunt to relinquish the drawing for the last verse so that he can take over a related subject from the poem.[113] Hunt later gives an account of the episode in which he presents Rossetti as petulant and unreliable, with Hunt himself taking the grown-up role, condescendingly allowing Rossetti his request despite the injustice: "I had determined . . . to illustrate the latter incident in the poem, but that I will give up to you . . . so that you may have no cause for driving old Moxon to desperation."[114]

The illustration Hunt eventually provided for Moxon's edition—once Rossetti had proved himself incurably dilatory, says Hunt—is very close to the oil painting that he completed more than fifty years later, while his autobiography was also being brought to a close.[115] The narrative tells a story of betrayal, honest manliness, and the injustice of later reputations when measured by the facts.[116] In the second edition of *Pre-Raphaelitism,* there is a reading of Tennyson's poem that takes up these themes in the account of the painting. The Lady, Hunt contends, typifies "the Soul," whose duty is "to weave her record, not as one who, mixing in the world, is tempted by egoistic weakness, but . . . charged to see life with a mind supreme and elevated in judgement":[117]

The mirror stands as the immaculate plane of the Lady's own inspired mind, or . . . the unsullied plane upon which Art should reflect Nature as opposed to bald realism, and so far she has obeyed its mandates, but, seeing the happiness of the common children of men denied to her . . . she becomes envious. . . . In this mood she casts aside duty to her spiritual self, and at this ill-fated moment Sir Lancelot comes riding by heedlessly singing on his way. Fascinated by his reflection in the mirror, she turns aside to view him through the forbidden window opening on to the world below. Having forfeited the blessing due to unswerving loyalty, destruction and confusion overtake her . . . her work is ruined; her artistic life has come to an end.[118]

Lancelot, of course, "who brings no offering but lip-service, kissing his fingers," is the "betrayer," and the poem's "parable, as interpreted in this painting, illustrates the failure of a human Soul towards its accepted responsibility."[119]

As a retrospective assessment of the P.R.B. from Hunt's particular perspective, *The Lady of Shalott* links a version of this diagnosis with the appearance of both the embattled self and the mirror that we encountered at an earlier stage of Pre-Raphaelite development.[120] Reality, reflected though the medium of representation, chimes with the mirrors of Pre-Raphaelite history and with the mirror in *The Awakening Conscience* that I have taken to stand at the inception of that history.[121] In his account of the later Rossetti's iniquities, he names the Aesthetes "the alien fringe and reversing mirage of our [founding Pre-Raphaelite] company" (2:365). The painting imagines its tale of betrayal and dishonor through an image of the ruptured Aesthetic moment of unmediation.

Shortly before beginning *The Lady of Shalott*, in *The Triumph of the Innocents* (1876–87, fig. 24), Hunt had interwoven a disturbingly solid account of spiritual beings—the souls of the children massacred by Herod—with the scarcely more material figures of the Holy Family and placed them over a sequence of interpenetrating reflective surfaces, partly mirrored and partly watery that, uniting, extrude the bubbles that float through the syrupy air at the center of the painting.[122] Reflective of and identical to the world itself, both water and mirrors, these bubbles—the spume and surface of appearance—meld representation and reality, the mirror blending into a self-identical and self-aware version of the world in a way that is characteristic of Burne-Jones's work and of Aesthetic painting more generally. Hunt in the 1880s seems content to continue the unmediation of the Aesthetes. But when the mirror reappears in *The Lady of*

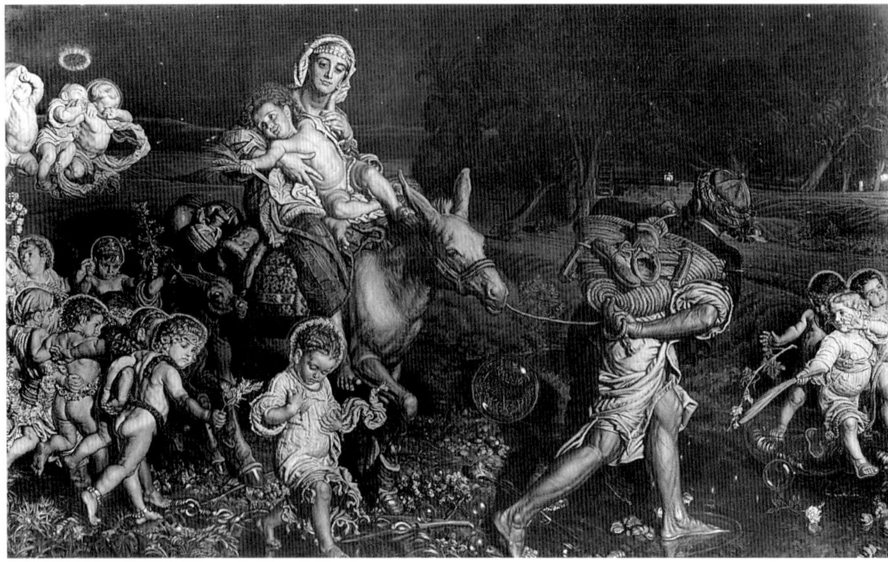

FIGURE 24. William Holman Hunt, *The Triumph of the Innocents,* 1876–87

Shalott, it now declares the separation of the world and representation. The Lady's revulsion, "half sick" of "shadows" as they move in the enchanted mirror before her, provokes the sundering of representation, self, and world.

Tennyson's verse, combining this trio in a single space, describes the scene of identity:

And moving through a mirror clear
That hangs before her all the year,
Shadows of the world appear.
There she sees the highway near
Winding down to Camelot.

But, once Lancelot captures the Lady's attention and she glances away from representation and toward the world to encounter it directly, finally free of "shadows," the fragile identity disintegrates:

She left the web, she left the loom,
She made three paces through the room,
She saw the water-lily bloom,
She saw the helmet and the plume,
She looked down to Camelot.

Out flew the web and floated wide;
The mirror cracked from side to side;
"The curse has come upon me," cried
The Lady of Shalott.[123]

Behind the anguished figure of the Lady shrugging off the unraveling threads of her mirrored world in Hunt's painting, the uncurling warp and woof of representation releases the observing subject, and the three terms of the triad of self, medium, and world spring apart again. As they do so, *The Lady of Shalott* enacts the disintegration of what Burne-Jones's elaborate machines of denial strive to hold together. Unmediation is inherently unstable; the triad of terms dissolved within it constantly threaten to crystallize out into their separate elements.

For artists working in the 1870s, Hunt's painting, with its skepticism about the persuasiveness of representation's marriage with reality, was thirty years into the future. The possibility of the identity of world and medium continued to attract. Hence the trope of unmediation was subjected to further active scrutiny among the Aestheticist artists with whom Burne-Jones shared exhibition space after 1877 in the Grosvenor Gallery and elsewhere. In the next chapter I consider such painting's implications and its limits.

Aestheticism and Unmediation

MOORE, LEIGHTON, WATTS, WHISTLER

Walter Pater's "Conclusion" to *The Renaissance* (1868) begins with the evocation of a physical and material world.[1] From "that which is without," "our physical life," Pater summons up a pure experience: first a "moment . . . of delicious recoil from the flood of water in summer heat," and then an ultimate physicality beyond consciousness, "the passage of the blood, the waste and repairing of the lenses of the eye, the modification of the tissues of the brain under every ray of light and sound." Finally, a vision follows, one that suggests the infinite extension of the material constituents of life: "Like the elements of which we are composed, the action of [such] forces extends beyond us: it rusts iron and ripens corn. Far out on every side of us those elements are broadcast. . . . This at least of flame-like our life has, that it is but the concurrence renewed from moment to moment, of forces parting sooner or later on their ways."[2] "At first sight," says Pater, meditating on this situation, "experience seems to bury us under a flood of external objects, pressing upon us with a sharp and importunate reality." But he sees that this emphatic materiality describes only one aspect of our existence:

> *When reflection begins to play upon these objects they are dissipated under its influence; the cohesive force seems suspended like some trick of magic; each object is loosed into a group of impressions—colour, odour, texture—in the mind of the observer. And if we continue to dwell in thought on this world, not of objects in the solidity with which language invests them, but of impressions, unstable, flickering, inconsistent, which burn and are extinguished with our consciousness of them, it contracts still further: the whole scope of observation is dwarfed into the narrow chamber of the individual mind.*[3]

The world, in our subjective perception of it, is "fleeting," contingent, infinitely "vanishing away" in a "perpetual weaving and unweaving of ourselves."[4] This draws from Pater his famous insistence on living for the transitory moments of intensity allowed us by experience. The ultimate residuum of the process through which the intersection of our subjectivity and the material world "fines itself down" to "the narrow chamber" of mind is "a single sharp impression, with a sense in it, a relic more or less fleeting, of . . . moments gone by."[5] It is the intensification and formalization of these impressions that art offers.

Pater's argument is usually read with an emphasis on its concluding, more plainly Aestheticist stages.[6] But the opening paragraphs I have quoted, with their exposition of a world in which the materiality of objects bounds and defines individual subjectivity—and in which that subjectivity lives in an intense way only through attention to its intersection with the material event—suggest a somewhat different interpretation. This is not only about the Victorian death of belief and the collapse of established faith in the wake of the scientific revelation of a hostile, materialist universe. It is also about the fact that this position, abandoning the validation of experience of the world by transcendental meaning, leaves its exponents with nothing else *but* the material world. Objects and physical sensations—"colour," "texture"—define and circumscribe the experienced world and allow it its promise of a temporary, aesthetic redemption. Art, "proposing frankly to give nothing but the highest quality to your moments as they pass," is an experience of this dominating physical world.[7]

In the previous chapter, I explored issues of surface, vision, and the capacity of paint to act as knowledge about the world in the light of formulations very close to these by first- and second-generation Pre-Raphaelites. In this chapter I shall take up the ways in which an emphasis on the materiality of experience similar to Pater's manifested itself in the work of a broader range of his contemporaries. The link here is Aestheticism and the thought that grew up around it—ideas already in circulation during the decade before Pater published his book. As early as 1867, the critic Sidney Colvin had been able to group Frederic Leighton, Albert Moore, and James McNeill Whistler together under the heading "beauty without realism." He summarized what they stood for in ways that came to epitomize the Aesthetic point of view: "Pictorial art addresses itself directly to the sense of sight; to the emotions and the intellect only indirectly, through the medium of the sense of sight. The only perfection of which we can have distinct cognizance through the sense of sight is the perfection of forms and colours; therefore perfection of forms and colours—beauty, in a word—should be the prime object of pictorial art."[8]

By May 1877, when the Grosvenor Gallery opened its doors in New Bond Street for the first time,[9] these painters and others discussed by the same commentator—including Rossetti, Burne-Jones, and G. F. Watts—had become a recognizable and influential presence on the English art scene.[10] Here, I will continue to argue for a series of developing connections between the attitude toward the visual character of paint and paint surface, thematic metaphors of the visual, and the struggle to think through its promise as a direct access to experience. While Aestheticism is a convenient way to point up certain characteristic tensions and interrelationships, it is nonetheless only a particular focus for a wider history of developments in the art world during the decades after 1860. It allows me to show something of the diversity of solutions imagined by painters in the late 1870s to meet the challenge posed by the trope of unmediation as its pitfalls become clear. I shall need, however, to discuss in this context G. F. Watts, who is not conventionally associated with Aestheticism or its preoccupations. If Pater's fatalistic materialism describes the potentialities of the surface from its own rather abstract perspective, painterly Aestheticism and its fellow travelers push forward that exploration in other, more concrete ways.

Even leaving Watts aside, Aestheticism, like most art-historical "movements," was a broad church. Still, the central preoccupations of the disparate artists, writers, and thinkers who contributed to the climate of opinion it created revolved around the sensual remaking of the environment in which experience took place. The aesthetic embodied difference from the instrumental values that surrounded art in the culture. In what Paula Gillett has called "one of the classic formulations of Aesthetic movement ideology,"[11] Pater wrote that art is not the vehicle for morality or codified verbal knowledge. It promises access to the sensual world at the point at which our experience focuses: "In its primary aspect, a great picture has no more definite message for us than an accidental play of sunlight and shadow for a few moments on the wall or floor: is itself, in truth, a space of such fallen light, caught as the colours are in an Eastern carpet, but refined upon, and dealt with more subtly and exquisitely than by nature itself."[12] By 1877, when Pater published "The School of Giorgione" (the essay from which this comes) in the *Fortnightly Review,* he could explicitly assert "the sensuous element in art" as the principal character of painting, so that the quality of surface, the "mode of handling, should become an end in itself." "This is what all art constantly strives after," he continued—not so much the condition of music as a self-consciousness of its own limitations and materiality as potential vehicles of knowledge about the world.[13] The visual aesthetic for Pater is a self-referential space in which the world itself will be reformulated as immediate sensuous experience through the materiality of paint surface, the "special form" through which the world "is conveyed to us" in the medium of the visual arts.[14]

I consider these ideas to be confronting the consequences of the most uncompromising version of Aestheticism—the proposition, signaled by Pater and developed by others, that only by the means of the material character of paint, its manipulations of color, line, and form, can "pictorial art" speak to its viewers and address their "emotions and intellect." The very wholeheartedness of this stance brings with it an extreme version of unmediation, so extreme indeed as to make evident the inadequacies of its proposed solution to the identity of pigment and the world. I show that Frederic Leighton struggles against the implications of this situation. He sees the risks attached to the belief that pure vision can comprehend the world: such a view brings with it the complete abnegation of analysis or understanding. Leighton attempts to rethink it through a revised version of the role of the artist's personality. G. F. Watts and James McNeill Whistler go further with the reintroduction of agency into painting, although in different ways, as each attempts to imagine how the artist's self might be put back into the process of representation. Both find a solution in the potential of the self to appear in and through the manipulation of paint as a material substance. This signals the emergence of a new version of the claim for the visual, one that, through the line that leads on from Whistler, played an important role in the subsequent history of modern English painting.

Personality and Unmediation

In the 1860s Albert Moore, subsequently thought of as "one of the greatest exponents of pure aestheticism," began to make paintings that largely dispensed with the expectations that his mid-Victorian audience brought to the viewing of pictures.[15] That popular taste for content, story, and anecdote as the principal pleasures of visual art appears in a painting like *The Schulamite* (1864–66, fig. 25) as the vestige of a subject that the picture as a whole abjures. The discoursing Schulamite from the Song of Solomon presents an image of the act of narrative within a canvas that substitutes passivity and the physicality of bodily intimacy for the pleasures of story.[16] The frieze-like arrangement of the figures and the tight tonal range operate to draw the spectator's attention away from narration and toward visual display. For the unfolding of events in time, Moore substitutes the rhythmical sequencing of his figures across the flattened surface of the canvas; for the explicit subject of storytelling, he offers images that, in their lack of affect, their "ideal repose and silent remoteness," as William Michael Rossetti phrased it, are hard to associate with a readable response to the events the Schulamite recounts.[17]

Reviewing the first Grosvenor Gallery show, at which Moore showed *The End of the Story* (1877, fig. 26), *Sapphires* (1877, private collection), and *Marigolds* (1877, private collection), Sidney Colvin summed up this aspect of Moore's work for the Grosvenor audience. He noted that Moore's figures, like Whistler's, were there "simply as the principal element in a pattern," and he described their repudiation of subject and affect: "the subject has no weight at

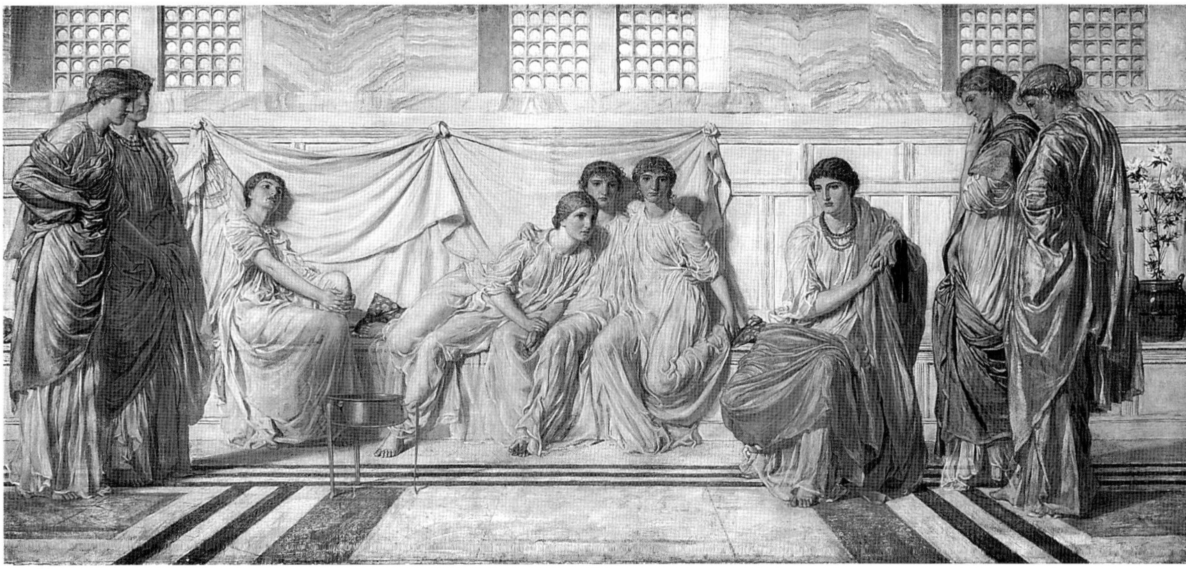

FIGURE 25. Albert Moore, *The Schulamite,* 1864–66

all; their pictures do not invite the mind to consider the thing represented but only the representation."[18] Appropriately, *The End of the Story* continues the self-conscious rejection of narrative that *The Schulamite* expressed a decade earlier. Dropping her hand so that the book she holds swings disregarded by her side, the model gazes away from her reading and out of the picture toward some unknowable scene of contemplation that functions independently of the attractions of narrative pace and rhythm. Like most of Moore's paintings, *The End of the Story* offers a static tableau, inviting the spectator's contemplation and presenting only "the sensuous possibilities of the motives," the seductions of surface, color, and physicality, as the focus of attention.[19] "Such a title naturally excites our interest," complained one reviewer, "but Mr Moore gives us nothing of this. His figure is a graceful woman, charmingly draped, and she holds a book; but that is all he tells us."[20]

In a remarkably pure version of unmediation, Moore and his commentators promote the possibility that the effect of color, line, and form can be a pure instrument of knowledge, one offered uniquely by painting. Moore pursues this ideal, engaged in a project to reduce all distracting elements within the painting. He strives to leave nothing that can signify except the material substance of paint itself, however ascetic that surface may be in his case. This may be one reason why, in the mid-1870s, Moore's figures relax into supine attitudes or even thoroughgoing unconsciousness in series of pictures that are "virtually identical

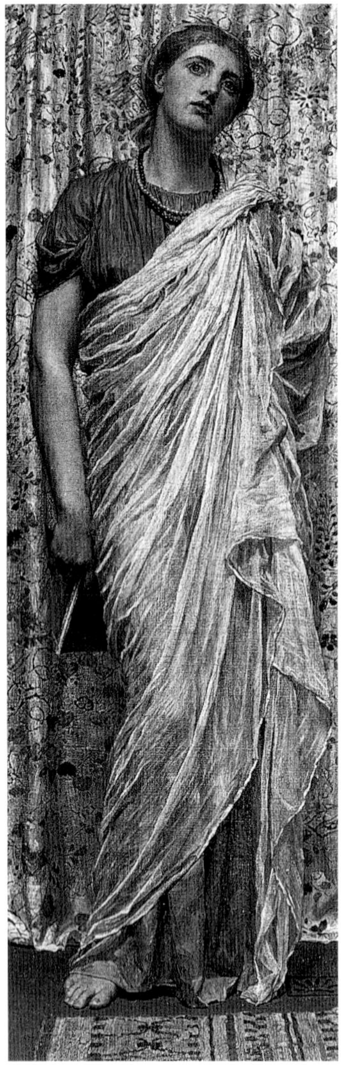

FIGURE 26. Albert Moore, *The End of the Story*, 1877

in all respects except colour scheme"—and hence are flagrant demonstrations of "the irrelevance of 'subject'" in his art.[21] *Beads* (1875, fig. 27), a work from one such series, provides us with an image of surface that deliberately renounces any possibility of meaning beyond itself.[22] This is thematic as well as literal. There is nothing beyond "Moore's fundamentally decorative purpose,"[23] so much so that Cosmo Monkhouse defined the paintings as purely form and color. Each "is a little problem of colour inimitably worked out in lovely forms."[24]

But this fundamentalism brings with it powerful difficulties. An attack written in the late 1870s takes Aestheticism—this time in the person of Moore's

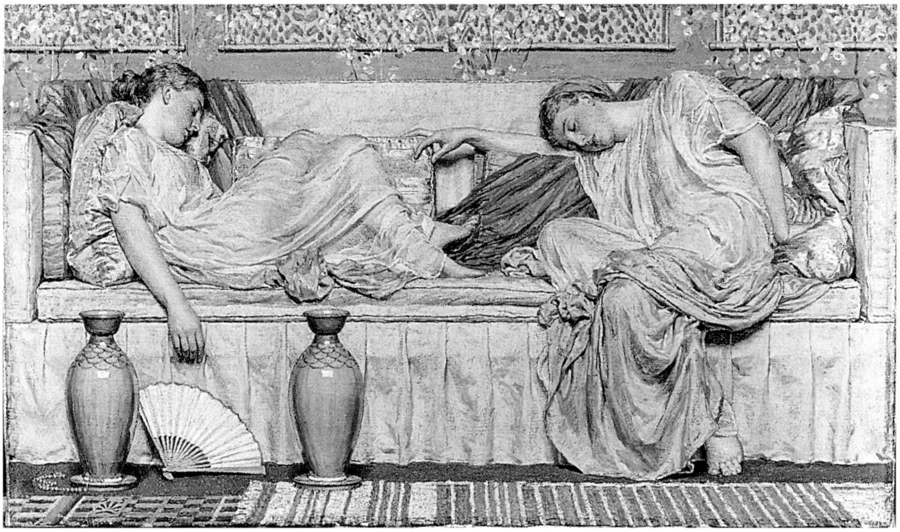

FIGURE 27. Albert Moore, *Beads,* 1875

close collaborator, Whistler—to task for the triviality of its emphasis on color at the expense of subject, commenting on the shortcomings of "a theory which, totally ignoring local qualities and personal characteristics, relies exclusively on the sensuous impressionability and play of fancy of the artist." The author astutely wrote, "It is a muffled, unfledged art, equivocal and deceptive in significance, and unintellectual in aim. The sharp critic who generalized these productions as a superior kind of wall-paper was not far from the truth. Although their fundamental basis reposes on an aesthetic truth, which is imperatively required for the exercise of highest idealism in all art, yet it is so fantastically treated as to be made little, if at all, superior to refined decoration."[25] The fundamental challenge to the valuation of the visual that characterizes Aestheticism (and that Whistler's art summarizes) is that line, color, and form can deliver only a partial, "unintellectual," and insufficient understanding of the world. Against this haunting possibility—as much as anything else—the artists I consider here struggle to assert, if possible, that the visual *is* an adequate way of knowing the world, of understanding experience and illuminating it for its audience. The whole thrust of what I have been calling "unmediation" is geared toward solving the problem that now, with Moore's version of Aestheticism, becomes articulated in a newly acute form.

It is perhaps tempting to imagine a dichotomy, represented by the Grosvenor on the one hand and the Royal Academy on the other, between the "new" and "modern" and the old-fashioned and recidivist. But this would be misleading. Frederic Leighton was already poised to become President of the Royal Academy when he was invited to exhibit at the Grosvenor's opening show in 1877.[26] A strong supporter of Moore, Leighton was the first artist to be identified in English criticism with the slogan "art for art's sake," and he was a major contributor to the creation of Aestheticist painting and theory even while his early relations with the Academy had been far from smooth.[27] Indeed, a recent commentator believes that his paintings of the 1860s "must be seen as a manifestation of a nascent avant-garde rather than part of the artistic mainstream."[28] Although he had an ambivalent relationship with the Grosvenor, for instance, Leighton's recorded opinions make it clear that Aestheticist theory was strong in his thinking and that he, too, was preoccupied with the scale and nature of the claims that could be made on behalf of painting as a living force within contemporary society.[29] The early lectures that form part of Leighton's *Addresses,* delivered to the students at the Royal Academy annually between 1879 and 1893, attempt a systematic presentation of these claims.

In the series, Leighton ruminates on the role of art in the modern world, on how it might be significant, and on how it can communicate the insights that he believes are uniquely available through art to its spectators and audiences. He gives an account of art as clearly problematic within modernity and as opposed to modernity in value, "the whole current of human life setting resolutely in a direction opposed to artistic production": "Everywhere a narrow utilitarianism which does not include the gratification of the artistic sense amongst things useful; the works of artists sought for indeed but too often as a profitable merchandise or a vehicle of speculation, too often on grounds wholly foreign to their intrinsic worth as production of a distinctive form of human genius with laws and conditions of their own."[30]

This is a familiar idiom. The place of art within contemporary society is uncertain, its proper status ravaged by the depredations of modern venality, materialism, and greed. In the *Addresses,* Leighton imagines the situation in antiquity, "when Art . . . was in her prime" (4), as very different. In contrast to the contemporary, when "the questioning spirit" of modernity "asserts itself on all sides, and . . . leaves nothing unassailed, takes nothing for granted, calls every belief to account, casts everything into the balance," the integrity and coherence of culture in these earlier eras allowed art to fulfill its appointed role of expressing experience through its *unconscious* embodiment of accepted norms and beliefs (5). Leighton accordingly speaks of "the gift of artistic production" as "spontaneous and imperative, and . . . in its origin . . . clearly emotional and independent of the action of the intellect" (4). He associates this unconscious, unintellectual expression of the visual arts—its "normal and constant condition" under proper circumstances (ibid.)—with an ideal state that modernity is dragging into conscious, verbal form. Under the negative impact of the "critical intelligence" of the modern age, then, "unconscious work has become and will be henceforth all but impossible" (5):

Those were halcyon days; the questions "Why do I paint?" "Why do I model?" "Why should I build beautifully?" "What—how shall I build, model, paint?" had no existence in the mind of the artist. "Why," he might have answered, "does the lark soar and sing?" (ibid.)

If meaning in the visual arts is a function of its physical and material character, Leighton concludes, appropriately, that "the language of Art is not the appointed vehicle of ethic truths": "the simplest spoken homily, if sincere in spirit and lofty in tone, will have more direct didactic efficacy than all the works of the most pious painters and sculptors from Giotto to Michael Angelo" (55). But Leighton wants to rescue contemporary art from any negative interpretation of this fact and to offer an explanation justifying his claim for its continuing power and authority as a serious pursuit. Once this contrast between modernity and the native value systems of art has been set up, and once he acknowledges that art cannot be available as a vehicle of discursive thought, he claims for the visual arts an "efficacy" equal to language, but in a different mode:

On the other hand, there is a field in which she [Art] has no rival. We have within us the faculty for a range of emotions of vast compass, of exquisite subtlety, and of irresistible force, to which Art and Art alone amongst human forms of expression has a key; these then, and no others, are the chords which it is her appointed duty to strike; and Form, Colour, and the contrasts of Light and Shade are the agents through which it is given to her to set them in motion. Her duty is, therefore, to awaken those sensations directly emotional and indirectly intellectual which can be communicated only through the sense of sight, to the delight of which she has primarily to minister. (55–56)

Leighton provides a mechanism through which these sensuous communications become meaningful: "these sensations . . . are inseparably connected by association of ideas, with a range of perceptions and feelings of infinite variety and scope" so that "lines and forms, colours and combinations of colours have acquired a distinct expressional significance . . . and will convey . . . notions of strength, of repose, of solidity, of flowing motion and of life . . . of joy or of sadness, of heat or of cold, of languor or of health" (56–57).[31] Hence it is "in this power to excite certain sides of our aesthetic sensibility, and not its power of imitation, in which the strength of our Arts regarded as a language, lies" (15–16).

In Moore, one consequence of his absolute type of claim for the visual is an emphasis on the materiality of paint itself as both an analogue and a literal instance of the world.[32] If Leighton's opinions seem to argue for his own similarly active interest in materiality, it comes as a surprise to find how inexpressive his surfaces can be. George Moore memorably thought them "invariably made of soap—not common yellow soap, but cream-pink, fastidiously scented toilette soap," and Prettejohn, who quotes this opinion, speaks of how his canvases' "surface smoothness" and "hygienic polish" were seen by some contemporaries as "lacking the performative mark of the brush."[33] If Leighton's paintings are not always scoured quite so cleanly as this implies—he called himself "a great *cuisinier*" who "tried quite innumerable methods and vehicles"—it is nevertheless true that compared to Moore, or to Burne-Jones, or to Watts or Whistler (whom I discuss below), materiality is of another order here.[34] A painting like *Greek Girls Picking up Pebbles by the Sea* (c. 1871, fig. 28) displays the sort of smoothly accomplished finish that Charles Rosen and Henri Zerner have taught us to think of as the "licked surface" of academic art.[35] Moore's otherwise snide remarks about "toilette soap" have some justice on their side.

But how, then, do Leighton's paintings imagine their relationship to emotion through the "sensations" of his facture and manipulation of paint? Surely the impassive surfaces of these works prohibit any direct address to the feelings of their spectators. In her 1906 two-volume critical biography of Leighton, Mrs. Russell Barrington struggles with this aspect of Leighton's work, what she calls his "one great principle," his devotion to the "thoroughness" of "intense finish."[36] Barrington feels obliged to defend this aspect of Leighton's practice partly because French Impressionism—already prestigious by the early years of the twentieth century—had made the smooth surface of academic painting suspect. She is also strongly aware of the paint surfaces of Watts and Burne-Jones as potential challengers to Leighton's precision and high finish. Barrington fears that Leighton looks shallow and insubstantial in comparison to his peers, and her text contains a substantial excursus to justify his practice within the terms set by Burne-Jones and Watts.[37]

The root cause of Barrington's anxiety is the apparent lack of connection to meaning beneath or behind the surface that is offered to the spectator's gaze in Leighton's painting. No sense of urgency or significance emerges behind the skin of paint, nor any sense of the imminent or possible irruption of some

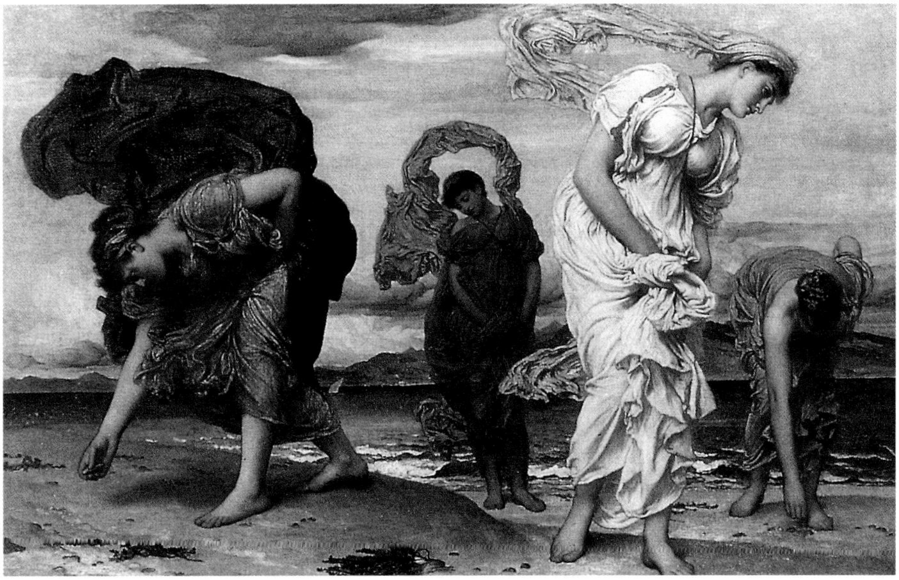

FIGURE 28. Frederic Leighton, *Greek Girls Picking up Pebbles by the Sea,* c. 1871

Freudian symptom into the contrived calmness of their surfaces. They appear sheer, hygienic, affectless—"smooth as a highly-finished bas-relief," as the *Art Journal* commented on *Daedalus and Icarus* (1869, Buscot Park, Oxfordshire, The Faringdon Collection Trust) when it was first exhibited in the 1869 RA show.[38] In this, Leighton's paint is of a piece with his biography, famously without affect or emotional connection. "Mr Leighton's manner is here somewhat cold," commented a critic of *Electra at the Tomb of Agamemnon* (1868–69, Ferens Art Gallery, Hull). Comyns Carr remembered him, in terms many other contemporaries echoed, as "admirably equipped" for "all . . . official duties," though "it was difficult in ordinary converse to feel that he had ever quite thrown off his official garb."[39] Leighton appears all public surface, supremely capable as an administrator, highly skilled socially but without emotional depth, "the public *performer*—the man whose whole personality goes forth in . . . representation and aspect and sonority and phraseology and accomplishment and frontage," as Henry James imagined.[40]

In keeping with this surface blandness, a primary characteristic of the paintings is the restraint of significance. Leighton suppresses the possibility that meaning might be available for excavation or discovery beneath the surface of the paint, and he offers no clues to take us further than the material substance of the pigment itself. In a work like *Music Lesson* (1877, fig. 29), the surface is the descriptive account of fabrics, different textures of flesh or stone, organic and

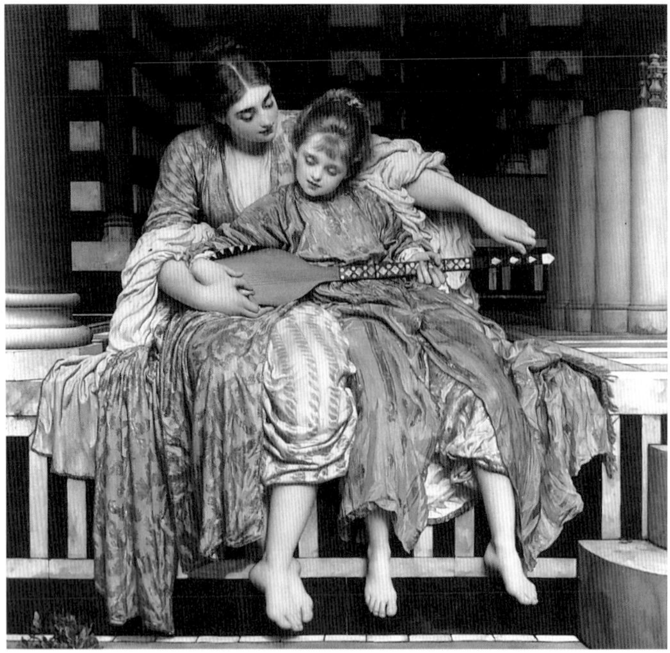

FIGURE 29. Frederic Leighton, *Music Lesson,* 1877

inorganic, the evocation of sensuous emotion through what Barrington calls "nature herself," the "construction of all things that nature builds . . . constantly realised by our sight."[41] There is the same valuation of sensuous experience for its own sake in the earlier *Lieder ohne Worte* (c. 1860–61, Tate Britain, London), which Leighton described as an experiment in the evocation of the senses: "the subject is . . . quite incomplete without colour, as I have endeavoured, both by colour and by flowing delicate forms, to translate to the eye of the spectator something of the pleasure which the child receives through her ears."[42] This may be thought appropriate in pictures that take as their theme the self-sufficiency of bodily experience, but it is arguably as true of a painting like *Hercules Wrestling with Death for the Body of Alcestis* (1869–71, fig. 30), in which the dramatic action takes place beneath a uniformly smooth and finished surface.[43] The polished sheen of Hercules' skin, the pleats and folds of the fabric that covers Alcestis's corpse, and the dresses of the watching chorus all operate independently of the action proceeding within the painting, thus mitigating the initial impression of violent activity on closer inspection and redirecting it as surface and "frontage."

The *Hercules,* with its surreptitious undoing of the core narrative values on which successful subject and history painting were deemed to depend, was painted at the same time that Leighton was making the long series of works

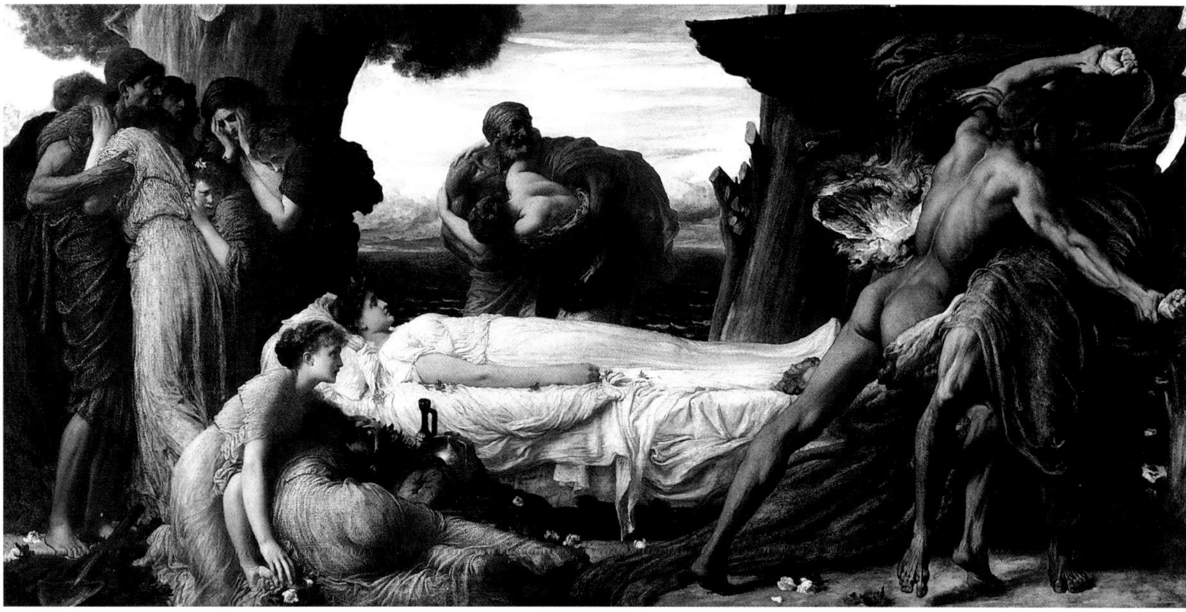

FIGURE 30. Frederic Leighton, *Hercules Wrestling with Death for the Body of Alcestis,* 1869–71

that wholeheartedly repudiate literary, mythological, and in some cases even readily identifiable subjects in order to concentrate on the possibilities of paint itself. *Greek Girls Picking up Pebbles* has been seen as a prime example of this development in his work. The subject, if there is one, has never been ascertained, and the emphasis rests firmly on the possibilities of texture and fabric that form the true "subject" of the painting rather than on any event or meaning.[44] Without the significance provided by narrative or subject, the picture becomes an instance of what William Michael Rossetti had already characterized in 1863 as the essence of Leighton's painting—"the art of luxurious exquisiteness; beauty, for beauty's sake; colour, light, form, choice details, for their own sake, or for beauty's."[45] Sensuousness, the absence of subject, and the offer of a purely surface aesthetic experience to the spectator all contrive to underline the essential concern of Leighton's art with blocking signification and replacing it with a registration of the surface of the world, "those sensations directly emotional and indirectly intellectual," as he said, "which can be communicated only through the sense of sight."

This moment of blockage, resistance to meaning or to any significance below the surface, the insistence on a Paterian cleaving to the appearance and materiality of things, marks the place where Leighton's interests and those of Aestheticism as I have described them in Rossetti, Burne-Jones, or Moore converge. Leighton's smooth and depthless surfaces imply the identity of description and experience, representation and world. The goal of Leighton's practice, as of the theoretical account he gives in the *Addresses,* is to abolish meaning beneath the surface of the paint on the grounds that paint is itself the world. In keeping with this, Barrington's solution to the problem of Leighton's facture is to claim it as inexpressive because it is identical with the world, free of the distorting impress of the medium: "Leighton had no sympathy with the artificial, neither had he any with the shadow put in the place of the substance. The actual was ever sufficient for him, for in nature herself he never failed to find sufficient inspiration."[46] There is no expressive "medium" in Leighton because under these circumstances interpretation literally does not happen. Art sets emotion in train through manipulating the surface of the world itself as embodied in "Form, Colour, and the contrasts of Light and Shade." Paint is the actor and the vehicle, a living slice of the world it describes, sharing with it the sensual realities that it evokes and wields in the service of meaning.

Flaming June (c. 1895, fig. 31) combines a strong version of this claim with the sleeping figure I have identified as elsewhere representing unmediated knowledge about the world.[47] The unconscious woman, her body folded into itself beneath the sliver of light that describes the sea behind her, is one of Leighton's most forthright and absolute assertions of the power of painting, of its ability to conjure meaning through the embodiment of the material world. If the surfaces of Leighton's paintings are inexpressive, metaphors of paint abound. *Flaming June* offers twisting folds and convoluted fabrics as a central feature of its composition.[48] And here, as in *Greek Girls Picking up Pebbles, Daedalus and Icarus,* or *Greek Girls Playing at Ball* (1888–89, Dick Institute, Kilmarnock), the metaphorical dramatization of paint surface through the use of drapery to mime pigment is a way of asserting the authority of paint.[49] Paul Barlow, who sees *Flaming June* as an exploration of "the relationship between specificity and abstraction," argues that the drapery, conveyed in "molten ripples" that "flatten the body over which they play," "acts to transform the body into a carrier of pure colour," with the drapery "*becoming* the content of the image."[50] Surface pervades the whole extension of the picture plane as the fabric, loosely brushed in the passages that describe the darker veils falling on either side of the body and in some episodes of the sitter's dress, helps flatten and abstract the sequenced vertical bands of marble, sea, sky, and awning that rise above her to the top of the picture plane. The symmetry of the composition, culminating with the decorative anthemion pattern of the awning, reinforces this impression.[51] Nor is this mere rhetoric on Leighton's part, for this

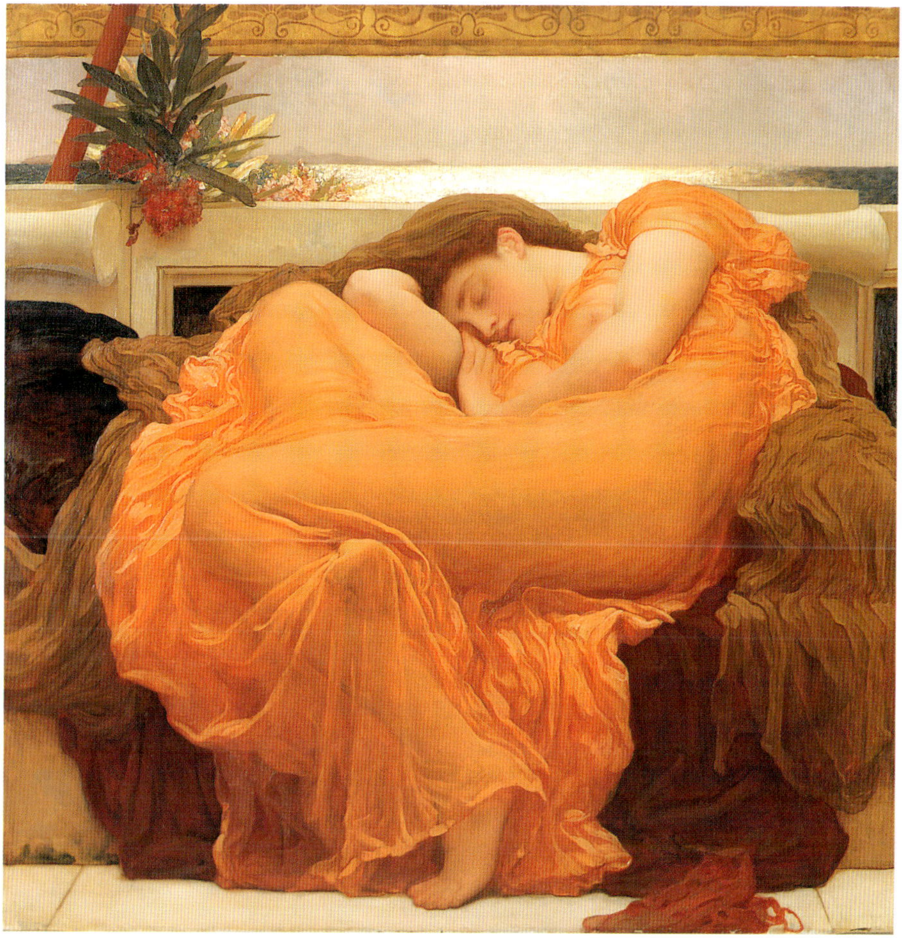

FIGURE 31. Frederic Leighton, *Flaming June*, c. 1895

transformation is not a question of metaphor. Medium and subject are imagined as a singularity, a melding of the image and the world. The creatures stirring in this sleep of consciousness are made of nothing but Pater's "mode of handling," of the senses, color and texture and the mark of the brush. Deriving their power from identity with the tangible visual surface of the world, they abolish awareness to assert identity.

But the very absolutism of this position suggests a further, negative implication: so identical is this painting with the world that it becomes meaningless. For it is not enough merely to reproduce the world. Knowledge must be active if it is to convince as a true account. This must always be the pitfall of such a vigorous assertion of an unmediated identity with what is represented. If the claim is that painting can present the world for knowledge because it can know and convey it to our perception so well, then knowledge is central; but because knowledge requires interpretation, precisely requires the mediation that is imagined away, that is the one thing rendered unavailable where pigment is identical with reality. The scene of understanding, with its trinity of the observing self, the medium, and the world, cannot be so fully abolished without the collapse into identity turning out also to be a collapse of knowledge. Where there is no distinction between the object and its representation, there is no critical distance, no perspective from which reality can be judged and weighed, and thus no means through which the fundamental imperative to evaluate and communicate the nature of experience to the audience can possibly be achieved. The end result of the drive toward imagining the visual as capable of knowledge of the world is to rule out knowledge itself.

The *Addresses* attempt to confront and resolve this problem. There, Leighton draws on Pater's arguments in an effort to connect the capacity of the visual to know the world through its sensuous materiality back to the personality of the artist:

> *Primarily the source of all Art whatsoever . . . is the consciousness of emotion in the presence of the phenomena of Life and Nature. This conscious emotion, this momentary intensification of life it was which, seeking for a vent either through some direct form of personal utterance, ejaculation, or movement of the body, or through the endeavour to imitate the spirit which aroused it, called Art into existence; for Art is based on the desire to express and the power to kindle in others emotions astir in the artist and latent in those to whom he addresses himself.* (13–14)

The artist's personality is, therefore, the conduit through which the world is related to its visual apprehension:

> *Every emotion that reaches us through the channels of an artist's temperament comes to us coloured and determined by the idiosyncrasy of that temperament, and we get the man added to the thing. The impression produced on us is of a sensation of which we recognise the germs within ourselves, but which is modified and controlled by another sensation more or less new to us, but evidently spontaneous in the artist, who communicates it to us, and who is thus himself revealed to us in his work. This is the secret of the fascination of that work; and an ineffable weariness seizes us in the prolonged contemplation of all Art which is devoid of this stamp of personality.* (20–21)

This position allows Leighton to offer direct access to nature while asserting the role of the artist in forming it. "An artist's temperament," interpreting the stained colors on the retina, acts as "the secret of the fascination" of the artwork because it reintroduces understanding to the painting. Leighton, says Barrington,

> *viewed the influence of art as one which should perfect the life of every class; should purify in all directions the debasing elements of materialism and self-interest; should put zest and gratitude into the hearts of all men and women who can see and feel, by awakening a sense of the perfection and beauty of nature, art forming an explanatory and illuminating link between her and mankind—a translation of her perfection transmitted with all reverence by the artificer;—a perfecting beautiful pinnacle in the erection and development of a noble human being.*[52]

It is the "translation . . . by the artificer" that is important here. The central role played by the artist's personality reintroduces a medium and a process of mediation to the representation, and in doing so, it reintroduces the possibility of knowledge. Art can once again form "an explanatory . . . link between [nature] and mankind" and "awaken" an understanding of the oppressive realities of the time.

This effort of recovery leaves two incompatible systems operating in Leighton's art. His works manifest on the one hand a drive toward the abolition of the distinction between self and world in the scene of interpretation, and on the other, a strong reintroduction of the self as a principal element in the functioning of art. The tensions set going by this complex of claims and solutions appear most clearly in the *Elijah in the Wilderness* in Liverpool (c. 1877–78, fig. 32).[53] The prophet driven into the wilderness, on the point of death from starvation and thirst, implores God to release him from his suffering. In response, an angel visits him in his sleep and provides him with food and drink to sustain him until revelation comes. Leighton's painting presents an Elijah whose sleeping head and powerful heroic torso appear to be radically disjunct. Both writhing and still, his face and head peaceful and unmoving while his body from the neck downwards appears agitated and in the midst of some energetic activity, Elijah's heroism is not at all mitigated by his unconsciousness.[54] On the contrary, this unconsciousness, from which he is in the throes of an impossible awakening, is central to the incident Leighton chose to depict. The biblical text describes how Elijah's despair is healed by the angel: "And as he lay and slept . . . an angel touched him, and said unto him, Arise *and* eat. And he looked, and, behold, *there was* a cake baken on the coals and a cruse of water at his head" (1 Kings 19:5–7). Elijah awakes to the material world ("a cake . . . a cruse of

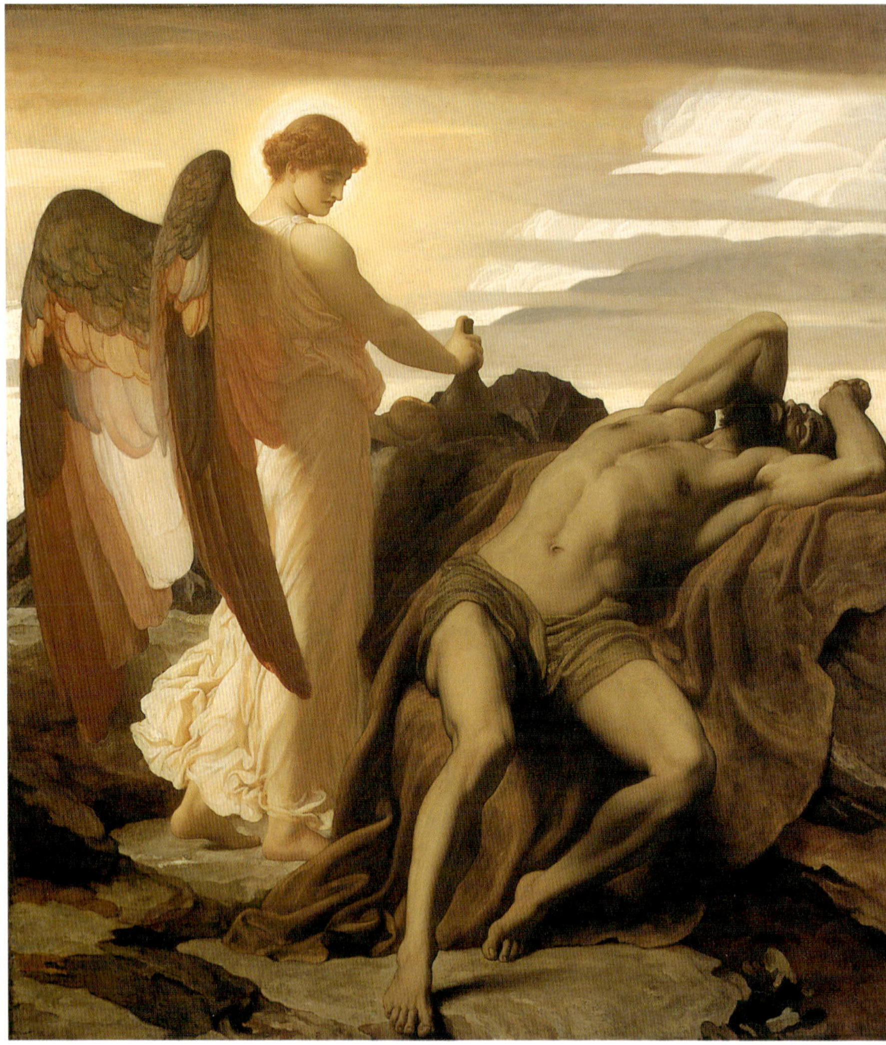

FIGURE 32. Frederic Leighton, *Elijah in the Wilderness*, c. 1877–78

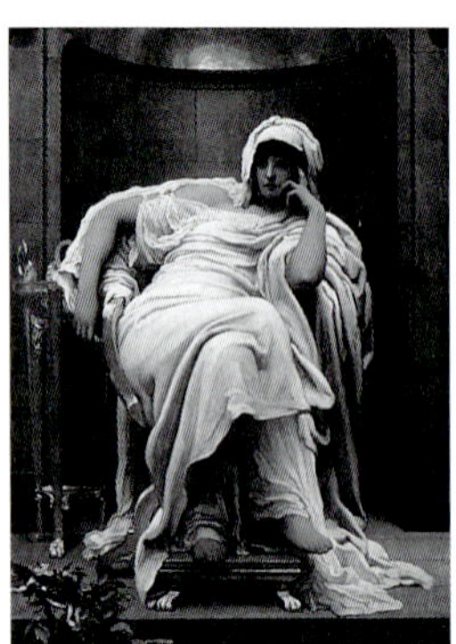

FIGURE 33. Frederic Leighton, *Fatidica*, c. 1893–94

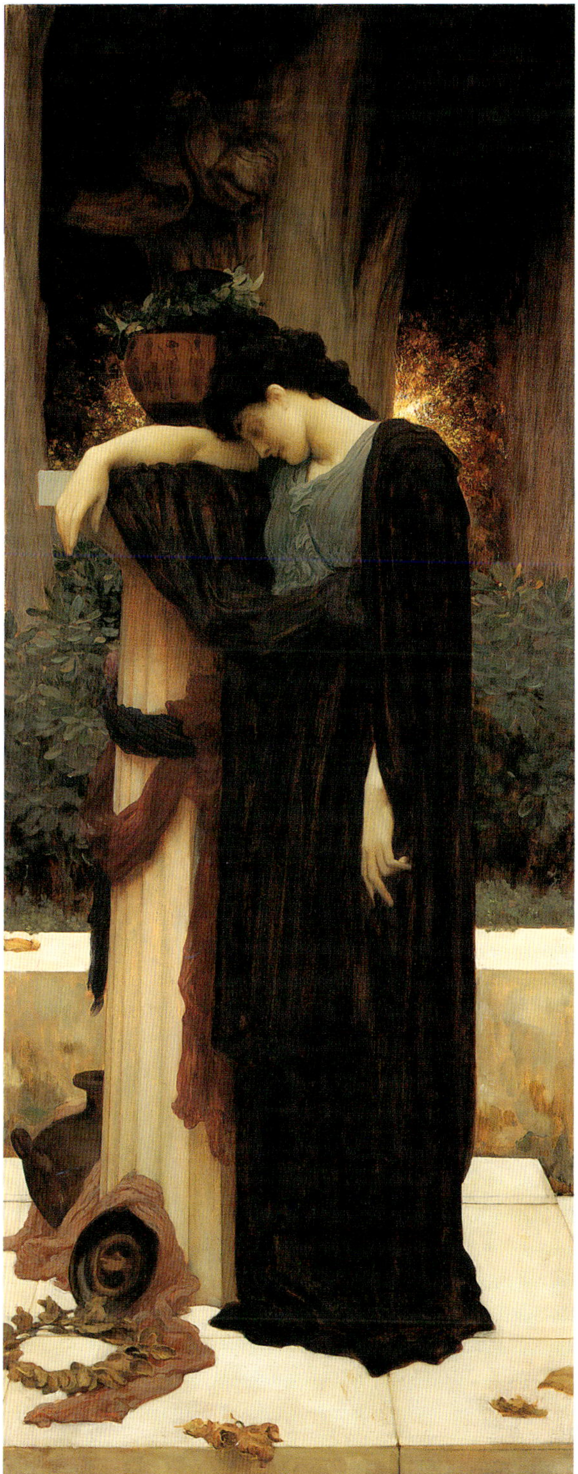

FIGURE 34. Frederic Leighton, *Lachrymae,* c. 1895

Aesthèticism and Unmediation

MOORE, LEIGHTON, WATTS, WHISTLER

water"), and as he does so, he struggles into consciousness ("Arise *and* eat"). The passively sleeping figures of unmediation stir and begin a return to life as the breath of personality hovers over them in this promise of recovery. But Leighton's painting cannot show us wakefulness itself. Personality, however desirable as a solution to the problem of passivity, is too risky. Elijah can only writhe and struggle, promising at any second to awaken to the world and find it present in a material plenitude, but meanwhile—and forever—remaining restlessly locked in the sleep of unmediation.

This dichotomy is never fully healed in Leighton's art or thinking. *Flaming June,* which exemplifies a thoroughgoing version of unmediation, is a late work. It was painted at a period when Leighton was making both paintings that thematize unconsciousness and others that show figures, always female, engaged in conscious—indeed, self-conscious—reflection (see, for example, *Fatidica,* c. 1893–94, fig. 33). Leonée Ormond has suggested that this latter group of paintings, "where women are seen as powerful" because they are engrossed in "thought and personal inspiration," complements those images in which women appear "somnolent and inactive." She goes on to speculate that they could be read as indications that Leighton thought of himself as "in some sense the Apollo figure whose dictates these women, the artist's models, perform."[55] Personality and the release of consciousness engage in a dialectic in these works, although even in the meditative figures—such as *Solitude* (c. 1890, Maryhill Museum, Goldendale, Washington, D.C.), *Fatidica,* or *The Spirit of the Summit* (1894, City Art Gallery, Auckland)—we are still confronted by an "absorptive" state of consciousness. But, even when self-absorbed, intelligence and will in these paintings aim toward comprehension, understanding, and the disentangling of meaning from the world.

If these paintings represent Leighton's own reintroduction of personality into the forceful assertion of identity in *Flaming June,* then *Lachrymae* (c. 1895, fig. 34), with its muted central figure lost in a somber contemplation, aware but abstracted, might stand for them all.[56] *Lachrymae* is the obverse of *Flaming June,* its darkly robed figure a negative projection of the glories of its partner image. Pigment and color flare and burn here, most notably in the impastoed burst of the setting sun that recalls Watts's *After the Deluge: The Forty-First Day* (c. 1885–86, fig. 35) and in the "almost impressionistic effects" allowed to play along the low wall behind the column.[57] The world flashes out in visual intensity, but the central figure ignores it. Consciousness brings with it understanding but also mourning for the unawareness it has lost, as self and the world separate out once again.

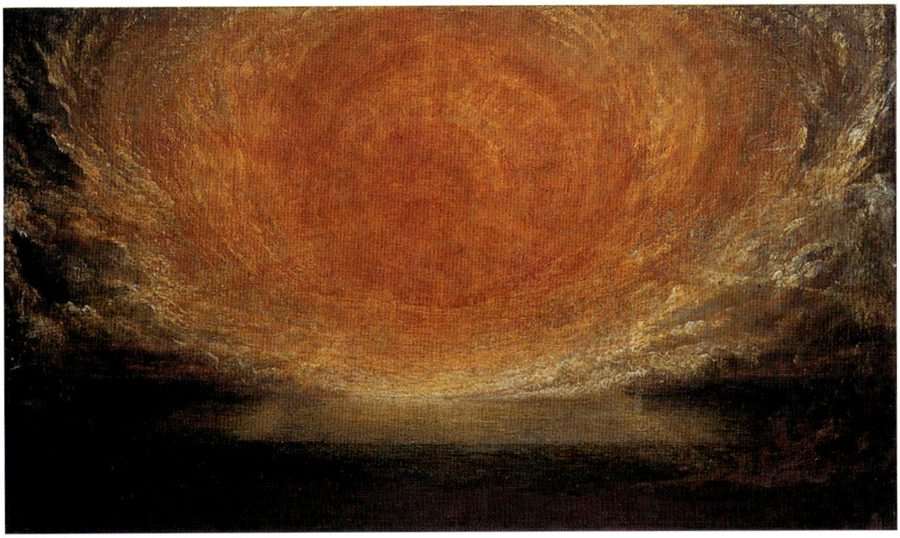

FIGURE 35. George Frederic Watts, *After the Deluge: The Forty-First Day*, c. 1885–86

Watts's Pigment

Leighton wrestled with the most thoroughgoing versions of unmediation. Other artists associated with Aestheticism sought a resolution of the impasse by asserting agency through the medium itself. For those artists whose conception of their own role depended on ideas of the social utility of art or the artist as the vatic interpreter of culture for its citizens, imagining the artwork as passive or powerless—or the self as perpetually denied presence or understanding—was an unattractive prospect. This, at least, was the view of G. F. Watts, an associate and intimate friend of Leighton's from the 1850s until the latter's death.[58] Watts shared Leighton's distaste for the materialism and brutality of contemporary life, but unlike his friend, Watts was impelled to think that his art was capable of making a concrete difference.[59] David Loshak contends that Watts, "for ever nagged by his conscience, entertained an almost bardic conception of the social duties of the artist as a teacher of his people."[60] His hope throughout his life was that painting could speak directly to his culture and actively counter, in some measure, what he saw as the destructive rule of modernity. Watts explained this ambition by explicitly calling his paintings "thoughts, attempts to embody visionary ideas,"[61] writing that "the object in work has been to suggest, in the language of Art, Modern Thought in things ethical and spiritual."[62] A flavor of this ambition can be caught from this note by Watts on his painting *Life's Illusions* (1849, Tate Britain, London): "An allegorical design, typifying the

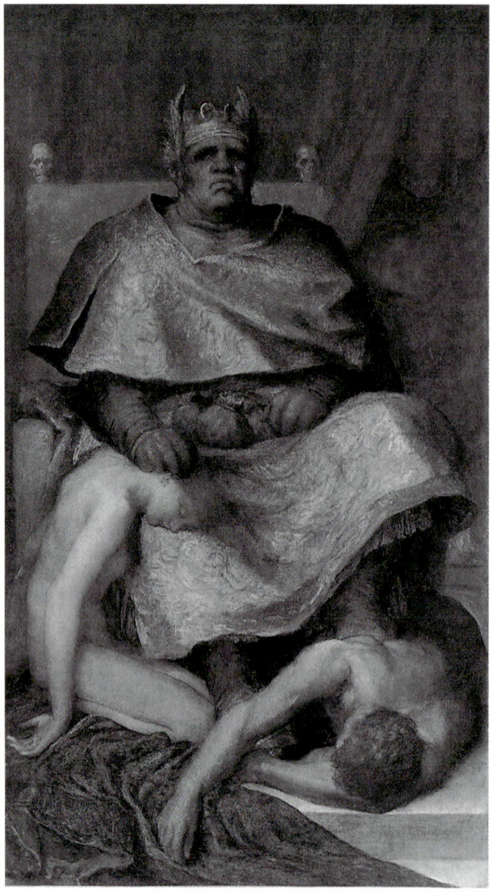

FIGURE 36. George Frederic Watts, *Mammon: Dedicated to His Worshippers,* 1884–85

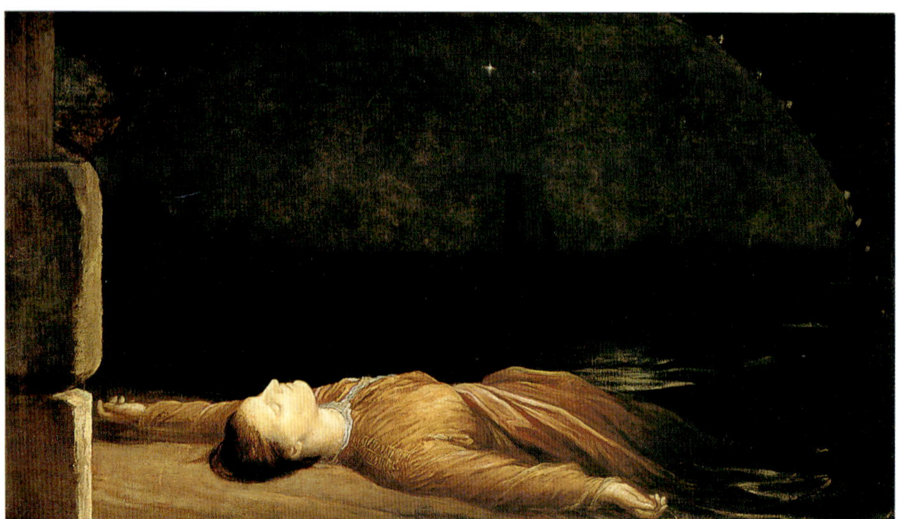

FIGURE 37. George Frederic Watts, *Found Drowned,* 1849–50

march of human life. Fair visions of Beauty, the abstract embodiments of divers forms of Hope and Ambition, hover high in the air above the gulf which stands as the goal of all men's lives. At their feet lie the shattered symbols of human greatness and power, and upon the narrow space of earth that overhangs the deep abyss are figured the brighter forms of illusions that endure through every changing fashion of the world."[63] Such evocative but imprecise figures flock through Watts's allegorical paintings, "impressive symbols of the mysteries that surround human life from its beginning to its close," signs of spiritual and contemporary realities that are often clearly meant as resistance to nineteenth-century values.[64] *Mammon: Dedicated to His Worshippers* (1884–85, fig. 36), a painting that Watts himself described as an exposure of the fact that "material prosperity has become our real god," envisages a forthright relationship between the painter's images and the fundamental concerns of his society.[65] Indeed, Watts made four major canvases in the 1840s that engaged with contemporary social issues: *Found Drowned* (fig. 37), *The Irish Famine, The Song of the Shirt,* and *Under a Dry Arch* (all 1849–50, Watts Gallery, Compton). Perhaps encouraged by the social realist paintings of the 1870s and 1880s, he showed all four pictures for the first time at the Grosvenor in 1882 to considerable notice.[66]

Determined that his painting should be active in the wider social sphere, Watts could not easily adopt the passivity embraced by Leighton or Moore. The concerns this gave rise to loom large in the substantial writings that he produced at intervals throughout his life. Although Watts accepted the account of the "unconscious" reflection of life in art under the ideal conditions that Leighton also put forward, he is more emphatic than Leighton about its unfeasibility: "we cannot return to the state of the unconscious being who found notes within a reed and dimly felt they expressed his joy or pain."[67] His writing is therefore often concerned with how to imagine an active role in the creation of social meaning for painting. In 1879, Watts published in *The Nineteenth Century and After* one of the most significant of these attempts—an essay called "The Present Conditions of Art." Watts's essay, "the result of the accumulated thought of a lifetime," synoptically sets out his ambitions for painting at the end of the nineteenth century.[68]

He begins by asking whether it is possible to create a British school, given modern conditions. Watts's view of what it would mean to do so is instructive. Such a school would be

a group of painters, sculptors and architects, whose work collectively would have a force marking the age in which they live, becoming part of the history of the country to which they belong, and existing in the future as a lasting monument of the best feelings and thoughts of the present time. Will the people, say, of the twenty-third century be able to read what is best in our English history of the nineteenth century, its highest feeling, its purest and subtlest thought, by the light of those monuments of art now being produced or capable of being produced, as we read the history of Egypt, Greece, and Italy in the legacies of art those countries have left behind? (149)

The finest art, bound up with the character of its contemporary culture, expresses that culture in its most developed form. Although what is expressed is always the "highest," it is also understood as the most fundamental and representative. The function of art is to give form and shape to the truthful understanding of experience, so that art is later said to be the only "cure" for social ills (156). But the chance of contemporary art in England achieving this level of expressiveness and response to its local conditions is slim: "our confirmed habit of regarding art and all that belongs to it, all the delights that come to us through the medium of the noblest of all our organs, as necessarily separated from the serious business of life, must be fatal to art" (151). The root of this neglect is said to be the perceived incompatibility of art and contemporary values. "All modern conditions are nearly as unfavourable to art as they can be," says Watts, adding that "our modern art . . . enters into no natural life of the time" (150).

For Watts, the central characteristic of the arts is "beauty," a term that includes the material qualities of color, form, and line. But in "The Present Conditions of Art," its expression depends on the available medium of its time, by which Watts seems to mean the ambient stock of images and visual forms circulating in the culture on which any understanding of meaning in the arts must draw if it is to live up to its ambitions for contemporaneity: "it must be remembered that the artist, no less than the poet, should speak the language of his time, not only because he can only naturally find expression in it, but because of the direct appeal it makes to those whom he addresses" (159). In the case of the late nineteenth century, that medium has been corrupted by the brutal nature of its modernity: "modern civilisation has sadly distorted that aspect of life which is the painter's language" (160). There, "beauty" is confined to trivia, its objects no more than "trifles" or "playthings." It is "not wanted" in those aspects of nineteenth-century life most characteristic of the age, in machinery, finance, or in the "hard-headed" and "practical," so that "utility and charm appear to be intentionally disconnected" (150–51).[69] In effect, "in our modern life the cultivation of the eye is sacrificed to all kinds of meaner considerations" (152). The ambient medium on which the painter can draw is accordingly an inadequate and impoverished resource compared to that enjoyed by earlier ages.

Deprived of a surrounding visual culture that can properly reflect the age, the artist is hamstrung, for "to compel [the painter] to invent his material language is like asking the poet to write in Hebrew or Greek, yet the alternative to the artist in these times is analogous to restricting the poet to slang or words of one syllable" (159). As a result, although "with the language of beauty in full resonance around him, art was not difficult to the painter and sculptor of old as it is with us," the contemporary artist has to deal with a material visual world—including dress, design, and other mundane expressions of taste—that effectively impedes the realization of the essentials of his time (161). Watts declares,

every artist must paint what he sees, rather every artist must paint what is around him, can produce no great work unless he impress the character of his age upon his production, not necessarily taking his subjects from it (better if he can), but taking the impress of its life. The great art of Pheideas did not deal with the history of his time, but compressed into its form the qualities of the most intellectual period the world has seen; nor were any materials to be invented or borrowed, he had them all at hand, expressing himself in a natural language derived from familiarity with natural objects. Beauty is the language of art, and with this at command thoughts as they arise take visible form. (ibid.)

It is the absence of beauty in the material conditions of late-nineteenth-century life that renders it so difficult for a great art to arise and express its time. The mediating term between the conditions of experience and their expression in art—that is, what Watts calls "beauty" in the everyday visual environment—is blocked or absent. Art's ability to articulate and express its time, then, is blocked as well: "the artist is obliged to return to extinct forms of speech if he would speak as the great ones have spoken. Nothing beautiful is seen around him." For Watts, "the world" cares nothing for "beauty" and hence for "the language of great art" (162).

That "beauty"—the quotidian visual character of a culture—is the necessary mediating term between the essential realities of experience and their expression in art on which any modern art must rely, Watts argues. To be convincing, the artist must use this mediating principle in order to develop the specifically visual beauty of his creations. They constitute the fundamental building blocks of his available visual language and are Watts's articulations of the "special form" that Pater describes in "The School of Giorgione," expressive of "that true pictorial charm," the essential and nonverbal character of the medium.[70] They are, too, effects of surface. Faced with the fundamental Victorian difficulty of articulating his age with the materials of this everyday visual culture, Watts turned to the possibilities inherent in the medium itself. Paint's very distance from the means-end values of nineteenth-century society, its resistance to the category of the useful, suggested that it could function as an alternative to the ambient visuality that Watts longed for and missed in his contemporaneity. The result is that for Watts, paint itself comes to occupy a homologous mediating space to this missing visual culture. In the absence of a present stock of images and design on which to draw to define the modernity of his painting, Watts substitutes the paint surface. In an echo of this ambition, G. K. Chesterton believed that Watts's paint technique "almost startlingly correspond[ed] to the structure of his spiritual sense" and that the moral force of Watts's paintings is discernable "from the mere colour and line."[71]

In Watts's mature work, the calculatedly declarative character of his paint, distinguished (in the words of a contemporary commentator) by "perpetual retouching, a scumbling of half dry paint dragged over the surface," draws attention to mediation as a principle of artistic practice.[72] Such surfaces allow an intervention in the relations between the world and its expression in art to be imagined as essential to the processes of making works of art at all, asserting their power to offer a diagnostic and developed critical view of the modern world. By this means, the mediation that is blocked or aborted in Moore and Leighton is reintroduced as an active agent in painting through the materiality of the pigment. What has been passive becomes an active principle.

Although Watts occasionally made it sound as if he despised his medium as "mere painting," he showed a dedicated interest in it throughout his career.[73] His earliest experiments were in fresco, indicative in his case (as in those of other Victorian artists) of the appeal of the midcentury Pre-Raphaelite project to innovate and achieve a public art through paint technique.[74] But this gave way to the development of an elaborate and individualistic oil paint practice that ultimately involved a careful preparation of the paints with the minimum of medium, the colors laid on blotting-paper in order to dry them out before use, and its application with worn, stumpy brushes, "rags . . . nasty old bits of paper, and . . . your thumb," in the words of a contemporary witness, to produce a rough paint surface, created by dragging veils of scumbled pigment across existing layers of paint.[75] The result is an encrusted and articulated surface within which the gradual buildup of competing granulated layers of paint is hard or

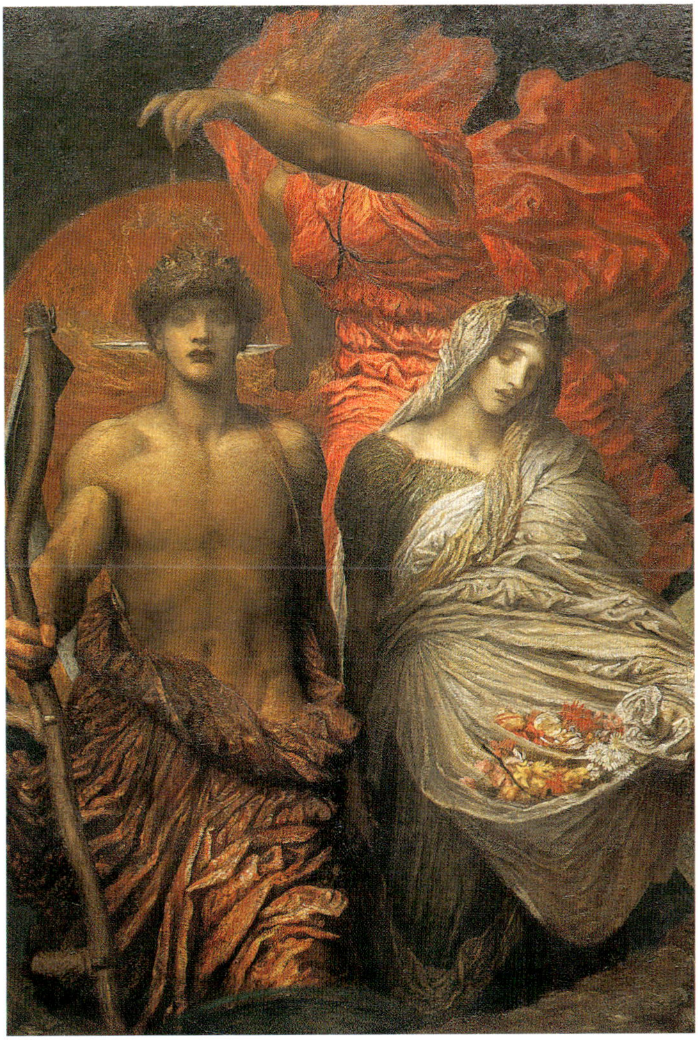

FIGURE 38. George Frederic Watts, *Time, Death and Judgement,* 1880s–1893

impossible to disentangle. This effect is compounded in many of Watts's paintings by their long histories of execution, sometimes extending over decades, during which the paint surface was repeatedly reworked and manipulated, registering "the endless movement and 'evolution' of matter" in a "palimpsest" of overlaid paint layers.[76]

In the version of *Time, Death and Judgement* (1870s–1886) now in the Tate, the creation of a non-naturalistic surface was the work of nearly two decades. Another version of this painting given by Watts to St. Paul's Cathedral in 1897—and now in the Watts Gallery at Compton (1880s–1893, fig. 38)—shows almost no difference between flesh and fabric and combines very solid scumbled layers of pigment with areas of thinner application through which the prepared canvas is clearly visible and contributes to the painting's effect. The evidence of this elaborated mode of application is visible, too, in *Love and Death* (1874–87, fig. 39), which Watts showed at the opening exhibition of the Grosvenor Gallery.[77] Here the impacted nature of the oil paint and the dragged and scumbled marks that articulate the composition are, as Barbara Bryant has noted,[78] conceived as contributing to Watts's major claim for the seriousness of purpose and intention behind his "symbolical pictures," "poems painted on canvas."[79] Of *Love and Death,* Watts told Barrington that "the intention in this picture has been . . . to transmit by form and colour a vision of an idea."[80] For Watts, the very eccentricity and overtness of the paint surface asserted the visual as the medium through which the spectator would be brought into contact with the deep aspirations for moral seriousness and worth that he cherished. Such works aimed "to give the impression of some great truth of nature, something so far too great for expression that finally it must remain indefinite. The infinite looming large behind the finite . . . the impression which great art alone can convey."[81] The tortuous argument of the "Present Conditions of Art" essay is Watts's attempt to articulate this function of the medium and of the mediated nature of oil paint as homologous to the mediated nature of meaning as he believes it must persist under modernity. The very opacity and resistance of pigment to linguistic meaning is its principal virtue in this. "The vague figure may be vaguely called conscience," wrote Watts of *The Dweller in the Innermost* (c. 1885–86, Tate Britain, London), a painting in which the atmospheric effect of ethereal space is created by its "network of feathery brushstrokes."[82] As Loshak notes, "the ultimate justification of the Wattsian type of symbolism is precisely that it cannot be translated into words, yet exercises a powerful effect in purely pictorial terms."[83]

The danger in Watts's approach is that it risks compromising his claims for the visual by forcing paint to live up to an impossible ambition. The aim of social relevance and meaning that Watts claimed for his works is only possible if we believe that the visual in and of itself is capable of sustaining such meanings, that "intellectual" qualities of this sort are not alien to it.[84] This was by no means clear, even to Watts, as the very existence of the convoluted arguments in "The Present Conditions of Art" suggests. Other commentators felt equally uncertain. The critic J. E. Phythian, in a book on Watts published after the artist's death, expressed his anxiety about the viability of paint as a medium for investigating contemporary experience. The terminology Phythian chooses is

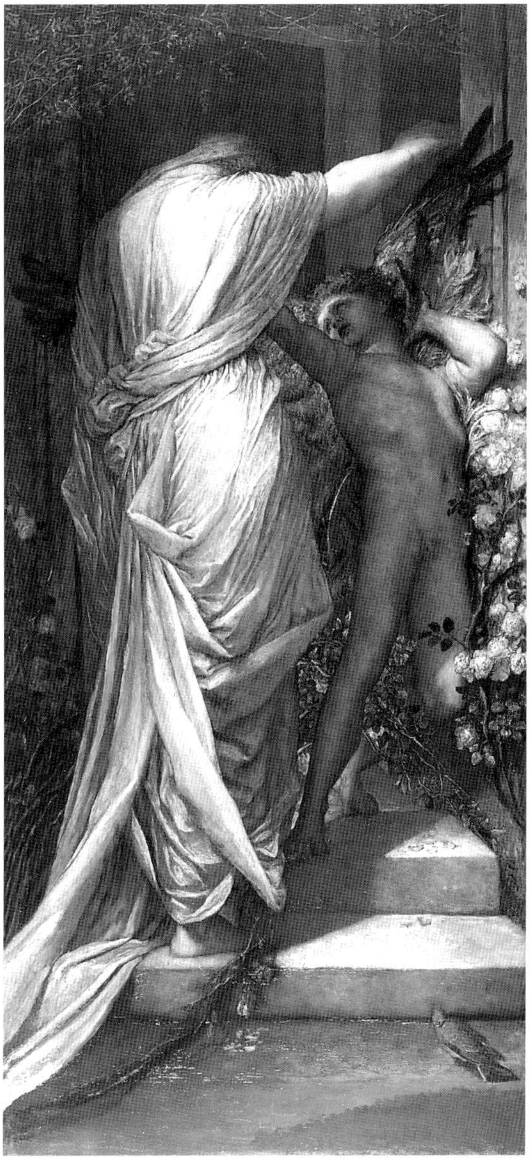

FIGURE 39. George Frederic Watts, *Love and Death*, c. 1874–87, reworked until 1887

his own, but his concern is the capacity of the visual to live up to Watts's ambitions for it. For Phythian, Watts "was concerned . . . with Love," by which he means a force or value opposed to the means-end values of late-nineteenth-century modernity and distinct from its instrumental calculus. Watts "felt deeply the lovelessness that makes possible, that makes inevitable, our existing competitive methods. We do not believe in love as a motive strong enough to ensure steady social activity in the ordinary work of the world."[85] Phythian suggests that Watts's art sets itself through the medium of the visual to provide both a revelation of that situation and some alternative to it. Just as important, Phythian insists that this project was carried out not as a piece of simple didacticism but within the confines and possibilities of the visual itself. Watts's art "was controlled not by thought, but by feeling," and this allowed Watts to be a sort of limit case for the capacity of the visual to deal directly with knowledge and to debate these central social and cultural concerns.[86]

Phythian is anxious about the success of Watts's use of the visual in this way. He worries that the pictures in which Watts deals most directly with social issues, such as *Mammon: Dedicated to His Worshippers,* are "from the art of beauty's standpoint among the worst of Watts's pictures" (though, he quickly adds, "they are far from wanting in aesthetic quality"), and he concludes that "the pictures do not lack beauty; only they insist so on our feeling other than sensuous emotions that those who will have nothing else from art inevitably grow angry with them."[87] Phythian's concerns revolve around the essential impossibility of Watts's ambitions. Determined to see the capacities of the visual as susceptible to mobilization in the service of a new and vivid understanding of contemporary experience, Watts tries to reinvent the connections between paint and social meaning. His attempted substitution of surface for the complex relationship between visual culture and the contemporary in the theorization of "The Present Conditions of Art" defines the difficulty of that position. Rather than any direct assertion of personality, agency becomes the property of paint itself. Knowledge and control flow through the pigment, now literally a medium between the world and understanding, the mark of representation that also forecloses difference. But that desire of the visual to function so purely as itself, a project for a social Aestheticism, proved unconvincing, a noble failure about which contemporaries remained uneasy.

Whistler's Agency

This desire to recover agency in paint was also a major concern in the work of James McNeill Whistler. Although his solution and perspective were different from those of Watts, Whistler, too, takes a central role in the drama of Aestheticism and its coevals. Albert Moore wrote about Whistler as his "most intimate friend and keenest sympathizer."[88] "Partners 'in a joint crusade,'" there is no doubt that the two men were intimate during the 1860s and probably thereafter and that their friendship also involved a shared aesthetic project. Like Moore, Whistler was concerned with the possibilities offered by the visual as a unique medium, and he too exploited the "exact knowledge of the capabilities and limitations of his material" that contemporaries noted in Moore.[89] Parts of an 1871 commentary in *The Times,* according to the authors of the catalogue of Whistler's paintings, "match Whistler's ideas so closely that they might almost have been dictated by him":[90]

[His works] are illustrative of the theory, not confined to this painter, but most conspicuously and ably worked out by him, that painting is so closely akin to music that the colours of the one may, and should be used, like the ordered sounds of the other, as means and influences of vague emotion; that painting should not aim at expressing dramatic emotions, depicting incidents of history, or recording facts of nature, but should be content with moulding our moods and stirring our imaginations, by subtle combinations of colour through which all that painting has to say to us can be said, and beyond which painting has no valuable or true speech whatever.[91]

This is a keynote statement of Aestheticism. But Whistler, like Watts and Leighton, could not accept the passivity such views seem to imply. Whistler envisaged painting as an analysis of the world that was to be dominated and transformed through the mastery of the artist. By controlling pigment, the painter can control understanding, bend experience to his will and thus comprehend it, make it subordinate to desire rather than its nemesis. Whistler therefore develops and exploits in his work the possibilities offered by control of the medium and its meanings.

We can start to see how this is so by considering accounts of Whistler's working practices. The American etcher Otto H. Bacher gave this description of Whistler at work in the early 1880s: "He had many exquisite tints from which to select the proper type or color which the sitter required. . . . With a brushful of paint, he walked to the canvas, made a single stroke much as one would with a rapier, returned, compared his subject and work, and mixed another brushful. Stroke after stroke he applied in his way until the picture satisfied him."[92] Elsewhere, Bacher described Whistler as continually experimenting with "paints" and "color tubes of tints" and as producing his own pigments: "he ground his colors in a special medium of his own upon a large surface of plate glass," so that they were "thinner and easier to spread on the canvas than the usual colors bought in the market."[93]

It would be easy to multiply examples of Whistler's interest in technique as the expression of a masterful self. Other commentators, such as Mortimer Menpes, Whistler's pupil, remembered the "Master's" interest in pigment and medium and his technical flamboyance and individuality. According to Menpes,

Whistler's working practices were both highly ritualized and geared toward innovation: "whenever I was with him," he wrote of Whistler's restless questing for improved techniques in pigment and color, "Whistler and I used to make experiments."[94] Bacher wrote, "His most ambitious desire was to paint a grand concerto-like picture with the title 'Full Palette'—'just as in music,' he explained, 'when they employ all the instruments they make it "Full Band." If I can find the right kind of thing I will produce a harmony in color corresponding to Beethoven's harmonies in sound.'"[95]

Another associate, Arthur Jerome Eddy, recalled that "so susceptible was his color-sense that he could not mix colors to suit him unless canvas and sitter were before him precisely as they would be when he began to paint." Eddy also spoke of "what he called Whistler's 'grand manner,'" achieved only "when everything—sitter, light, weather, spirits, mood, enthusiasm—was just right,—a combination that might come several days in succession or but once in a fortnight."[96] Like the rapier-swift confidence of the autographic brushstroke in Bacher's account of Whistler before the canvas, Whistler's use of pigment seems to be bound up with an effort of mastery or dominance. This passionate investment in the potentialities of color and pigment, the absolutism of his ambition—a "Full Palette . . . corresponding to Beethoven's harmonies," the "grand manner" achievable only "when everything . . . was just right"—produced art that makes considerable demands on the spectator. Like Moore's contemporary pictures, these paintings offered nonrational and nonverbal visual experiences that resisted conventional narrative readings. Audiences, without language to hold on to, found themselves reduced to the world of emotions, of intuitive and instinctual responses of the sort the visual was deemed to call forth. For many, it was an uncomfortable sensation, and contemporary commentary often sneered at Whistler's art. The *Nocturnes* of the 1870s (figs. 40–44), said a critic of the first Grosvenor Gallery show in 1877, suggested "a choice between materialized spirits and figures in a London fog."[97] To others, Whistler indulged in "fantastic tricks" and "the extremest excess of tone-painting."[98] His achievement in color was recognized but deemed to be unpersuasive, the result "not a picture."[99]

From the point of view of Aestheticist thinking about the visual arts, the local value of Whistler's painting lay precisely in this dedication to visual forms that, like those of Moore, resisted the narrative model familiar in British culture. Like Watts, Whistler mobilized color and pigment against dominant values, although in Whistler's case, the suppression of subject in favor of the visual often seemed a direct affront.[100] Flint sees this as "the expression of a particular form of desire: a desire for the plenitude of the visible," but Whistler's paintings can also be read as affirmations of a *strategic* relationship to the modernity they strive to repudiate.[101] Whistler still functioned successfully within the contexts imposed by professionalized modernity. Deanna Marohn Bendix has argued for Whistler's "belief in his powers of manipulating the press" and managing press reactions to his exhibitions.[102] "Art is upon the town," he famously said, and he persistently (if not always successfully) strove to attract media attention to himself and his art.[103] This ambition was imaged partly through Whistler's overt eccentricity and larger-than-life behavior as dandy and designer.[104] Andrew Stephenson has recently shown how Whistler's own careful, invested management of his public persona formed a central aspect of his publicity campaigns and sense of himself as an artist.[105] "The book is really an artistic autobiography," wrote the Pennells, his hagiographers, of Whistler's one large-scale publication, *The Gentle Art of Making Enemies* (1890): "Whistler gave the sub-title *Auto-biographical* to one section, he might have given it to the volume."[106] This assertion of the self was evident to contemporary observers—and seemed suspicious. "The artist's eccentricity is somewhat too premeditated and self-conscious," thought *The Graphic* in 1872, while William Rothenstein remembered him as "almost a legendary figure whom I never thought to meet in the flesh," but who was "generally considered . . . something of a *poseur*" in Paris.[107] And Max Beerbohm reported a similar response in London, accusing Whistler of showmanship in publishing *The Gentle Art of Making Enemies,* a book that the *Saturday Review* not atypically thought was an example of Whistler "acting like a clown."[108]

Like his presentation of self or the famous butterfly with which he signed his paintings, the exhibitions Whistler mounted were carefully constructed to capture press and public interest, in this case by their insistence on a "perfection" of "finish" and a designed quality that fascinated by its unfamiliarity and extreme ambition to control the viewers' environment.[109] His first exhibition in Dowdeswell's Gallery, held in 1884, was famously announced as "Arrangement in Fleshcolour and Grey." Every aspect of the decoration and exhibition space was controlled by Whistler and managed for effect. One review noted:

The walls are of a warm flesh colour, the ceiling toned to correspond, the carpet is grey, the mantelpiece is draped with grey velvet edged with flesh-colour cord, and at the corner of the mantel valance a Japanese butterfly of flesh-coloured velvet and a darker shade of grey is appliqué. . . . In front of the grey velvet curtains, which close up the fireplace, stands a large crater of flesh-coloured earthenware, containing a large plant of marguerite daisies.[110]

Already in 1874, reviewers had been struck by the decor of Whistler's solo exhibition at the Flemish Gallery: "a glaring yellow matting striped in two shades"; "the finely-formed couches and chairs . . . covered with rich light maroon cloth."[111] Bendix believes that by such devices Whistler's exhibitions and private views "became the major means by which he kept his name and ideas alive in the press."[112] His famous intemperateness in language and deportment similarly expressed his sometimes manic determination to keep his name before the public and his career flourishing.

The most notorious of Whistler's skirmishes in this combat was that prolonged over more than a decade with Oscar Wilde. Wilde and Whistler conducted the intimate rivalry of their relationship through the emphatically material means of self-presentation, performance, and clothing as well as in the materialized space of language.[113] The most formalized arena in which they fought this rivalry out was that of the lecture-and-response—Wilde's presence saturating the "Ten O'Clock Lecture" of 1885, in which he is roundly mocked, and Whistler derided in his turn in Wilde's replies published in the *Pall Mall Gazette.*[114] Reading through the various moments in this combat, it is obvious that intellectual antagonism has here become commodified on its own account as professional advantage.[115] Much depended on who most successfully stated his claim to some piece of professional capital, and questions of priority tended to loom largest in the debate. Whistler regularly claimed as his original inventions ideas that Wilde put forward as his own: "what has Oscar in common with Art? . . . Oscar—the amiable, irresponsible . . . Oscar—with no more sense of a picture than of the fit of a coat, has the courage of the opinions—of others!"[116]

But Whistler's aggression was not confined to Wilde, and the careful stage management of the "Ten O'Clock Lecture"—with its finely tuned outrages upon Victorian aesthetic and moral norms—and the Ruskin trial are examples of his self-promotion. The history of the trial has been told many times, and I will not repeat it here.[117] Provoked by Ruskin's adverse comments on *Nocturne in Black and Gold: The Falling Rocket* now in Detroit (1875, fig. 40) when it was shown at the first Grosvenor exhibition, the trial notoriously allowed Whistler to parade his selfhood in public as a sign of his artistic worth. Whistler later reified the trial into the laconic reportage of *The Gentle Art of Making Enemies:* "'You have been told that your pictures exhibit some eccentricities?' 'Yes; often.' *(Laughter).*"[118] Throughout these public events, Whistler's medium was language, not the visual, and its instrumental force in the commodified art world was the dominating characteristic of his activity. "He wrote, in his way, perfectly," said Beerbohm,[119] and words functioned for Whistler, his "pockets

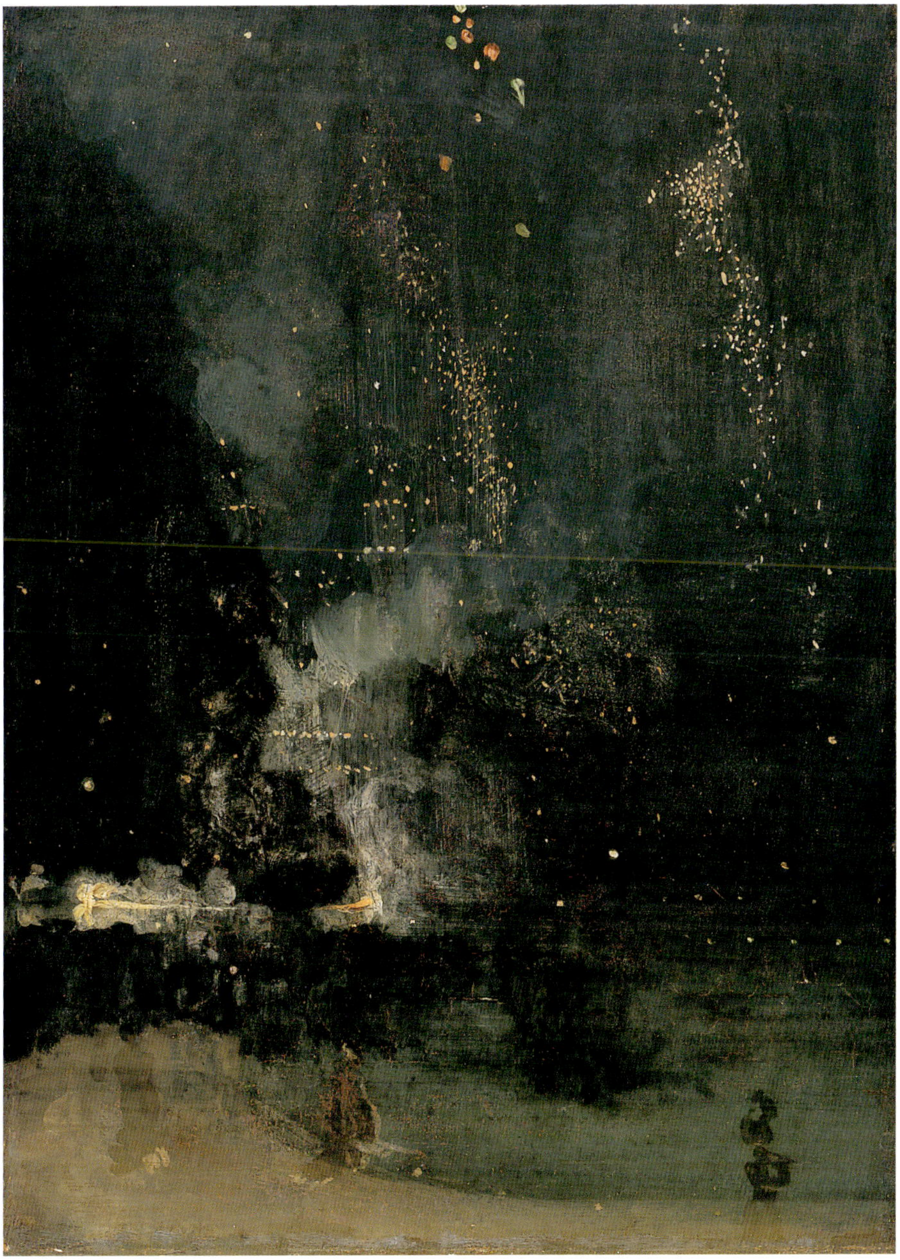

FIGURE 40. James McNeill Whistler, *Nocturne in Black and Gold: The Falling Rocket*, 1875

bulging with newspaper articles," as the vehicle through which the pure meanings of the image could be articulated and rendered functional within the instrumental processes of a capitalized art market.[120]

But this situation also provoked a sharp conflict, "the war . . . between the brush and the pen," as Whistler put it, as a way of denying implication in this modernity and claiming the visual as a space for alternative value.[121] In this combat, visuality itself came to serve as the expression of that opposition to modernity. In contrast to the world of language and commodification, Whistler famously thought of the *Nocturnes* as purely visual: "I wished to indicate an artistic interest alone, divesting the picture of any outside anecdotal interest which might have been otherwise attached to it. A nocturne is an arrangement of line, form, and colour first."[122] Looking at examples such as *Nocturne in Blue and Silver—Chelsea* (1871, fig. 41) or *Nocturne: Blue and Gold—Old Battersea Bridge* (1872–77, fig. 42) bears out this emphasis. Whistler's paintings affirm the material qualities of pigment and color. *Blue and Silver—Chelsea* is composed of very clearly visible horizontal strokes of the brush, using Whistler's famously liquid paint, thinned down so far that he is reported to have been forced to lay some of his canvases flat on the floor while working on them to stop its running.[123] These strokes, which build up the painting by superposition, rising vertically one on top of the other from the base to the top of the canvas, are inflected by the brush marks that describe the lone fisherman and the lights on the far shore. But the paint that makes up these elements, as well as that describing the silhouette of the buildings and the low-lying barge, is so transparent that the initial strokes of the water and sky are clearly visible through it. This same translucence and fluid quality appears in *Old Battersea Bridge,* where the figure and the barge (the subject of debate at the Ruskin trial) are thinly liquid additions to the scene. Whistler composed both paintings from a very restricted range of tones and color: "my whole scheme was only to bring about a certain harmony of color," he later said about *Old Battersea Bridge.*[124] In a related idiom, with the exception of the clock tower known as Morgan's Folly, the *Nocturne: Grey and Silver* in the Philadelphia Museum of Art (1873–75, fig. 43) seems deliberately to renounce all the technical resources of painting except those of color. The depth of field that the image achieves precariously depends on the Folly. Wiping it away would mean wiping away mimesis entirely and surrendering the canvas to the frank and direct appeals of color, to brilliance, pleasure, and visual compulsion, a profound seduction of the materiality of pigment itself.

But as we have already seen, such a thoroughgoing "pure" visuality brings problems with it. It was evident to many contemporary commentators that the impulse to reduce the field of painting to the visual alone was to risk the sort of meaninglessness that I have shown Moore, Leighton, and Watts wrestling with in their own art. Whistler's attempt to seize the initiative and assert agency in the field of a "pure" painting is, like Watts's interest in the visual as a vehicle of knowledge, a response to this uncomfortable challenge. In that project, the very alien-ness and difference of the visual from the instrumentalized world of words proved crucial.

In a complex argument that will help clarify Whistler's response to this challenge, Georges Didi-Huberman opposes the resistant materiality of "the substance paint itself" to the transparent, primary meaning that language seeks to impose upon it.[125] Didi-Huberman describes this resistance through what he calls the "patch" of paint, its nature as substance. The "patch" is a visual moment that exceeds or refuses mimesis, declaring itself as pure matter spread across or marked onto the canvas. It works as "a virtual explosion in the picture"; through "the blazing flash of a substance and a colour without a well-defined limit . . . [it] confronts us with its material opacity" and, "tempted as we may be to plunge through it, opposes any *mimesis* likely to be thought of."[126] The patch is

a way of naming those zones, those moments in the painting where the visible vacillates and spills into the visual. It is a way of naming the "cursed part" of painting, the indexical, nondescriptive, and dissemblant part. In fact paintings often reserve—and this is . . . their gift for disconcerting—a part of themselves for negating or clouding what they affirm in the mimetic order. Something in their aspect collapses at that point and dissemblance, a sort of disturbance, comes to reign there as the omnipotence of strangeness. There is nothing metaphysical about this strangeness in itself: it is only the power, the very symptom of painting.[127]

Didi-Huberman identifies an "otherness" of painting through which materiality and opacity to logical modes of knowledge of the visual declare themselves most explicitly, threatening to overwhelm both the object and the watching spectator. At the time of the Grosvenor Gallery exhibition in 1877 (and when he showed *Nocturnes* later), Whistler's paintings served to declare both the materiality of paint in this sense and its essential resistance to the logical languages of the media of modernity. This, famously, attracted censure from Ruskin and other critics—almost literally "the pot of paint" flung "in the public's face"—and gave to Whistler's art its potential force and resistance to the modernity within which he also functioned.[128]

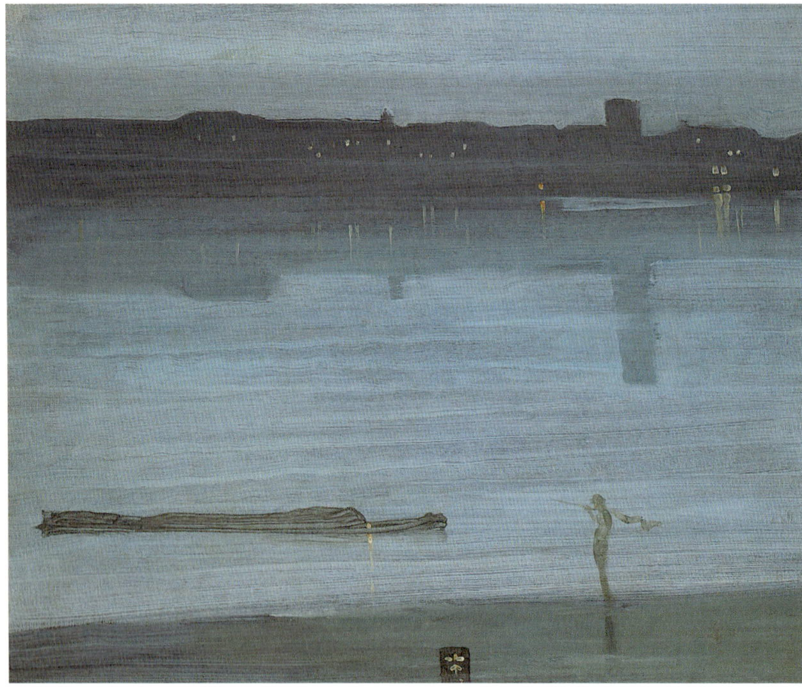

FIGURE 41. James McNeill Whistler, *Nocturne in Blue and Silver—Chelsea,* 1871

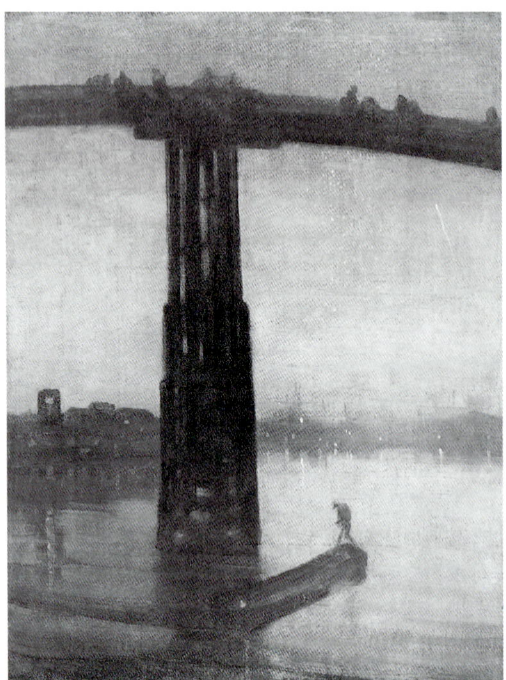

FIGURE 42. James McNeill Whistler, *Nocturne: Blue and Gold—Old Battersea Bridge,* 1872–77

FIGURE 43. James McNeill Whistler, *Nocturne: Grey and Silver,* 1873–75

FIGURE 44. James McNeill Whistler, *Nocturne: Black and Gold—The Fire Wheel,* c. 1872–77

Nocturne: Black and Gold—The Fire Wheel (c. 1872–77, fig. 44) reduces the visible world to almost a single hue, the fluctuating rhythmic brightening and darkening of the night created by insubstantial washes, against which the flare of the display on the Cremorne Gardens fireworks platform spins out in a swirl of dripped and openly brushed pigment. Such a painting, like the better-known *Nocturne in Black and Gold: The Falling Rocket* that served as the proximate cause of the Ruskin trial, seems programmatically to assert Didi-Huberman's sense of the "indexical" materiality of the patch. These paintings strongly affirm pigment and its capacity to provide certain sorts of knowledge about the world. They are essentially visual in the way I have described Rossetti's paintings of the 1860s as visual and as Leighton put forward in his *Addresses*. Occupied with their own status as a certain category of experience, confined at the sensuous limit of the surface, they claim to access and communicate reality like no other medium. The articulate surfaces of the *Nocturnes* enact the sensuous character of experience, claim to *be* it with an unmediated directness that modernity prohibits elsewhere. And they do so in an active sense. Abandoning the passivity of unmediation, Whistler imagined paint and the visual as overtly active participants in the assessment of modernity and did so in a more thoroughgoing, sustainable way than Watts.

If we imagine, however—with many of the contemporary commentators—that this quality of visuality means a lack of effort or control, we would be wrong. The authors of the 1994 Tate Gallery catalogue entry on the *Falling Rocket* suggest that the visual rhythm of "the whole picture . . . imitates the path of the rocket from launch, to explosion and dying fall," and they note that "these effects are achieved not through spattering paint on the canvas, but by carefully painting in each separate fleck of colour."[129] Whistler's effort at mastery and control is evident in this aspect of his canvases. Didi-Huberman's rupture of the "representational system" of the painting through a "negating or clouding" of "the mimetic order," which is often associated for him with a deliberate renunciation of control, is here programmatically manipulated to serve as a repudiation of conventional conceptual orderings through pigment, a repudiation that depends on a precise control and a certainty of brushstroke that Whistler famously cultivated. The extent to which visible pigment of this sort stands *indexically* for the visual's formlessness and resistance to verbal meaning, marking the trace of conceptually opaque materiality, is exactly the extent to which Whistler wants his control to run. This painting is all about controlling the *difference,* the *alien-ness* of the visual as a deliberate claim for its capacity to mean in ways denied by the conventional ascription of truth to modern rationality.

If the *Nocturnes* are radical in this sense—powerful and ambitious manipulations of this quality of paint as *other,* as what is left out of modernity, emotion, pleasure, visual fascination—they direct that controlled transgression toward a specific end. As is now well known, these paintings take as their subject views of London that emblematized the city's modernity when Whistler was painting. The watercolor *Nocturne in Grey and Gold—Piccadilly* (1881–83, fig. 45) proved instantly recognizable to its first audience as "the gas illumined, smoky atmosphere" characteristic of the central metropolis, with its "Hansom cabs and hurrying figures in the roar and activity of this great London thoroughfare."[130] The 1994 Tate Gallery catalogue links the painting to the dense fogs that shrouded London during this period, the consequence of industrial and domestic pollution, and comments, accurately enough, that Piccadilly itself was "a nightmare of noise and dirt."[131] Whistler himself recognized the modernity of the fogs and identified himself with that aspect of their nature, declaring, "I am their painter!"[132] The same modernity of subject features in the riverscapes. The south bank of the Thames across from Whistler's Chelsea home is as much a modern cityscape as Piccadilly, as it raises the silhouettes of industrial buildings up against the sky. The views that the *Nocturnes* describe and allow to resonate with the visuality of color and brushstroke are views toward this urban modernity across a polluted river, one in which fish could no longer live, fetid with sewage and turbulent with the wake of passing boats in the crowded daytime river traffic. Whistler's lone fisherman in *Blue and Silver—Chelsea* stands for a loss or absence rather than for any direct plenitude of experience.

We might be tempted to read this aspect of his works as a sign of Whistler's determination to link up the transgressive power of pigment with the imperative to invent a new, modern art that would evaluate contemporary conditions of modernity. We could say, as I have suggested, that the visual in the *Nocturnes,* with their flagrant demonstration of the meaninglessness of the visual, its difference from language, serves a *critical* function. The references to the city's polluted riverscape would then become radical. But this is partly a question of focus. For Whistler's *Nocturnes* are in this sense about the *transformation* of modernity, and transformation turns out to have its own logic and imperatives. Whistler wrote in the "Ten O'Clock Lecture" of his ambition to take the mundane world of late-nineteenth-century urban modernity and transmute it into visual gold:

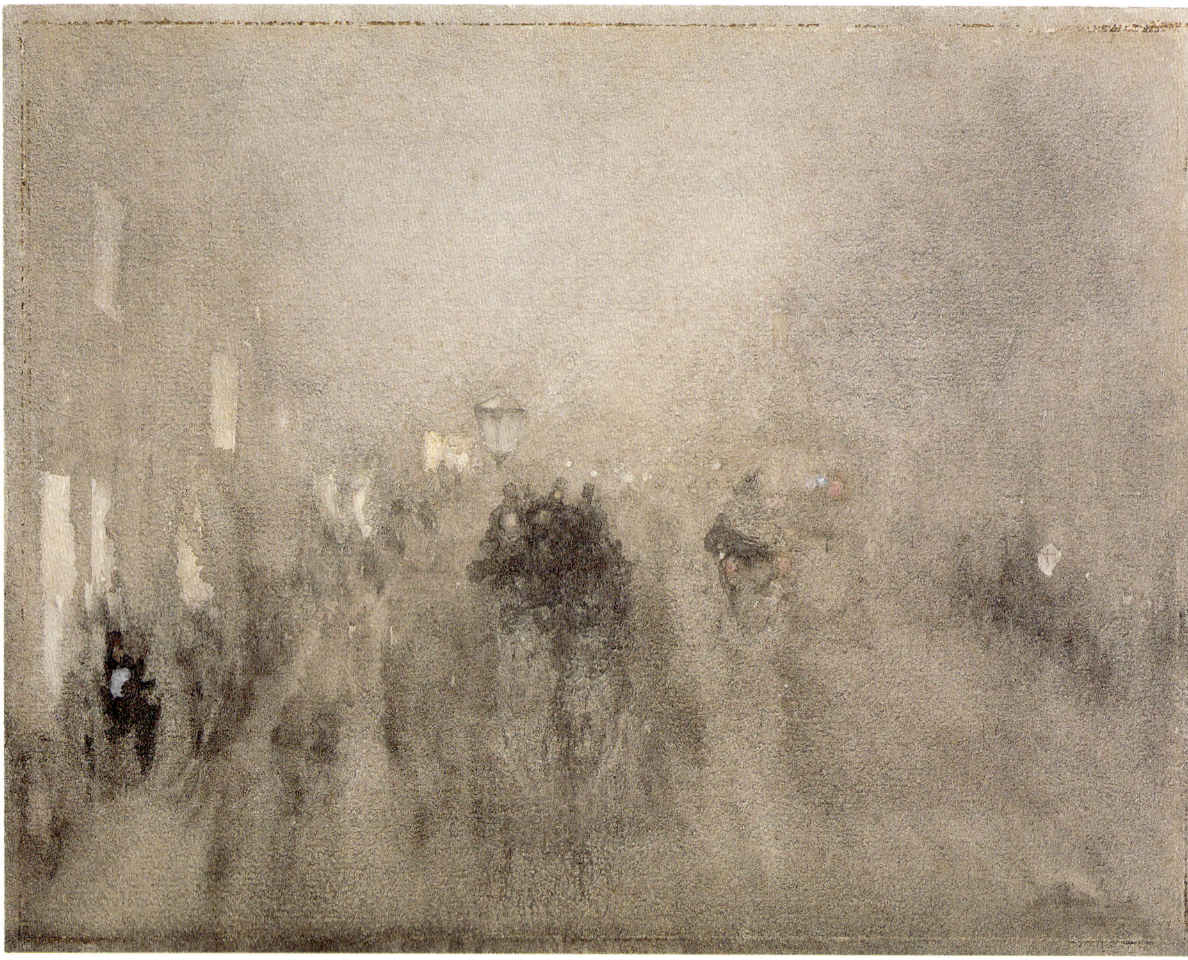

FIGURE 45. James McNeill Whistler, *Nocturne in Grey and Gold—Piccadilly*, 1881–83

The sun blares, the wind blows from the east, the sky is bereft of cloud, and without, all is of iron. The windows of the Crystal Palace are seen from all points of London. The holiday-maker rejoices in the glorious day, and the painter turns aside to shut his eyes. . . . And when the evening mist clothes the riverside with poetry, as with a veil, and the poor buildings lose themselves in the dim sky, and the tall chimneys become campanili, and the warehouses are palaces in the night, and the whole city hangs in the heavens, and fairy-land is before us . . . Nature . . . sings her exquisite song to the artist alone, her son and her master—her son in that he loves her, her master in that he knows her.[133]

This passage asserts that the artist functions not so much to register the nature of modernity as to demonstrate his masterful dominance of the shy femininity of "Nature" by translating what is brutal and repulsive—the goggling masses whose "seeing" is merely "for the sake of seeing" and who consume the ugly "iron" world of the modern city as readily as anything of "beauty"—into the clarification and focus of Nature through his painter's eyes.[134] Transformation here, as a function of control, persistently glances away from the modern toward its own constitution. "He sees," wrote Whistler of the artist, "in [Nature's] choice selection of brilliant tones and delicate tints, suggestions of future harmonies."[135]

Whistler, then, mobilizes the transgressive character of pigment itself, through the device of color and the materiality of pigment, to repudiate the modernity into which he was himself locked, the modernity of the arts within a commodified art world. He affirms the capacity of the visual as a means of engaging with modern experience. But, as the quotations from Bacher suggest, Whistler's affirmation of the nature of color and pigment is bound up with what I have called an *effort* of mastery or dominance—a heavily gendered effort directed at the transformation of the modern into an alternative realm where everything that modernity leaves out is flagrantly allowed to flourish. The irrationality and material opacity of paint detached from mimesis and frankly declared on the surface of the painting serve, in Whistler's work, as a metaphor for the perceived opacity and resistance to understanding of modernity, of modern experience itself. But it is also a means through which that threatening otherness can be ameliorated. Once translated into the metaphorical medium of the pigment, the other can be brought under the painter's compositional control, remade as *pleasure,* as visual and sensual affect at the behest of the artist's controlling and observant eye. I suggest that the desire to imagine art as alternative to the values of modernity functions in Whistler as a means of mitigating the perceived threat of modern experience. The visual itself becomes the means by which modernity can be subjected to an ordered and rationalized system, one provided in the pleasures of the surface, the skein of paint itself.

If this has a critical potential, it appears unrealized, for the realm of visuality is defended and walled about with a realm of words and manipulations of audience, press, and media. Whistler's practice of a "pure painting," in other words, is partly conceived in terms of the modernity that he seems to wish to repudiate. Profoundly involved in the systems of modernity and their expression through language, Whistler's declaration of paint, the patch that Didi-Huberman speaks of writ large as a violent and assertive declaration of the *otherness* of painting, opposed to modernity, is in important ways tied to the impulses that language and capital themselves define. This transformative function of pigment and its promise of control over an objectified modernity, however, were later to have important consequences for English modernism, as I shall go on to show in Chapters 4 and 5.

Conclusion

By 1882, when Lawrence Alma-Tadema received a retrospective exhibition at the Grosvenor Gallery, these concerns with the specificity of paint and the visual—and a concurrent move toward a self-conscious declaration of its capacities in the application and manipulation of paint on the canvas—had become widespread in the English art world. By the late 1870s, partly as a result of his turn away from the polished surfaces of his early work toward a more overtly painterly style, Alma-Tadema was linked in critical discussion with art for art's sake and valued for his "materialism," the evocation of surfaces and haptic, sensual details of objects, fabrics, and flesh in his work.[136] *Tepidarium* (1881, fig. 46) offers precisely this combination of the haptic evoked by the visual and a frank equation of the sensual character of the paint surface and the materiality of the body depicted and its surrounding objects. By the 1880s, the status of the material and the sensual was very different from that of the years after 1848. Art criticism had elaborated a technical account of the surfaces and formal qualities of paint and composition in the making of paintings that had distanced the understanding of increasingly large segments of the potential audience from the concern with narrative and story widespread in the decades after midcentury.[137] At its most extreme, this criticism presented the visual as so alien to language that it was "untranslatable, the mediating word of the commentator redundant."[138] That difference and inaccessibility arose from the very materiality and specificity of paint, itself a powerful exemplification of the difference of the visual. The Aestheticist art of the Grosvenor Gallery and beyond embodies that difference and expresses the particularities of the visual.

Like Pater, then, these artists are left only with the material. But it is that very materiality that they put forward as a means of knowing the new conditions and experiences of the world. The nonverbal, "special forms" of painting (as in Pater's 1888 "School of Giorgione"), the material surfaces and procedures of paintwork itself, serve as the means through which the world can be known. In the most utopian of these versions, that of Watts, the world can be adjusted, made over again into a shape free of modernity's impress. Watts shares with Whistler a desire to recover paint from the passivity of unmediated knowledge embodied in Moore and Leighton. For them, paint becomes something asserted

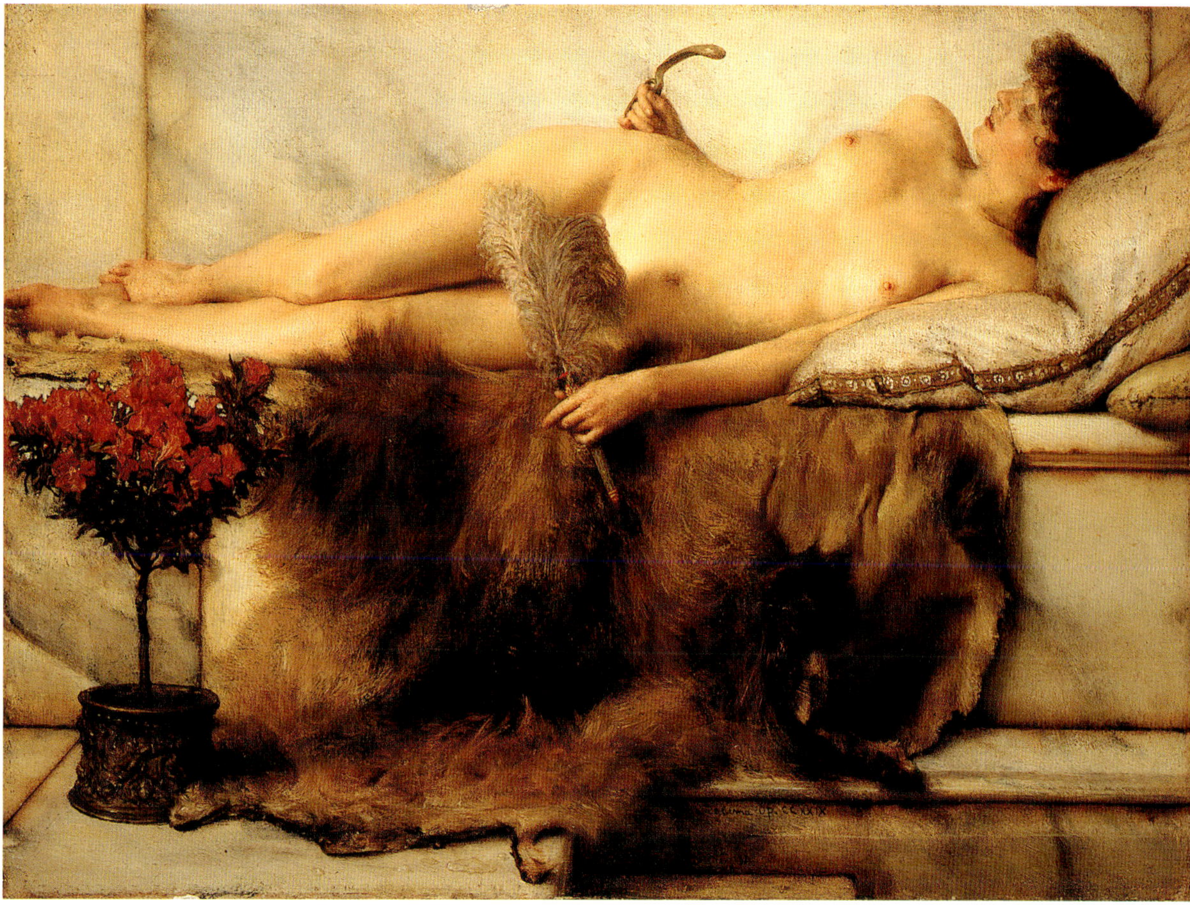

FIGURE 46. Lawrence Alma-Tadema, *Tepidarium*, 1881

but also distant from the possibilities of contemporary meaning. All these artists produce subtle attempts to balance the promise and the difficulties of the power of paint as a modern art form. But for other artists who inherited these possibilities or were working with them in other contexts, the balance proved highly precarious. I now want to consider further some of the ways in which these ideas had a public life in the commercialized forum of the late Victorian art world and how that public debate was conducted in the professional lives of artists and writers as well as in the details of their works.

Personality, Portraiture, and Illustration

CHARLES RICKETTS AND OSCAR WILDE

The entries in Charles Ricketts's diary for December 1900—scored through, altered, and revised as they are—give an intriguing account of his reactions to the death of Oscar Wilde.[1] On 5 December he heard the news, then six days old: "I feel too upset ~~touched~~ to write about it, ~~and the end of that Comedy that was realy Tragedy~~ . . . ~~I know~~ I know that I have not realy [*sic*] felt the fact of his death, I am merely wretched, tearful, stupid, vaguely conscious that something has happened. ~~Oh~~ that stirs up old resentment, and the old sense that one is not sufficiently reconciled to life it~~s vicissitudes + + to~~ death."[2] The effect of these cancellations and revisions—the phrase containing "~~vicissitudes~~" has been added and then subsequently struck through—is to place the emphasis on "life" rather than "death," partly by drawing attention to the difficulties of expression entailed in writing about "life." It is the "life" Ricketts shared with Oscar Wilde, rather than the fact of his death, to which Ricketts cannot "reconcile" himself.[3] The pages for the rest of the week have been cut out from the diary, and the next entry is for 17 December: "I dreamt all last night about Oscar Wilde or what seems so to me, for I woke up and fell asleep again more than once. The interview after all these years was so vivid and the news of his death following on it so keen + likely that I am all upset this morning and must have made up in the night for a certain measure of insensibility or rather non-realization of his death."[4] When he came to write a summing-up entry for the year on 31 December, Ricketts returned to his feelings about Wilde's death, contrasting what he felt to be a gain in his own career with the end of Wilde's: "The year has seen a marked increase of ease in our work . . . an assurance against those inexplicable moments of failure and lack of self-control so disheartening in the past. One sorrow, the death at first hardly felt of poor Oscar Wilde; this affects me at stray moments, when one is off one's guard. . . . Moments with me of introspection, hesitation, or regret."[5] Ricketts's uncertainty about his relationship to Wilde is graphically registered in his diary. Ricketts is "hesitant," unwilling to acknowledge his feelings about Wilde, so much so that they appear frozen, half-conscious, returning only in the form of dreams, portents, and canceled expression.[6]

Ricketts's entries reflect the themes of this chapter. First, there is a strong sense of the interconnectedness of two practitioners—Wilde the writer and

Ricketts the visual artist. Illustration and book design made up an important cultural industry in the closing decades of the nineteenth century, and, with the exception of *Salome* (which Aubrey Beardsley worked on[7]), Ricketts designed and illustrated all of Wilde's books of the 1890s (fig. 47).[8] He and his partner, Charles Shannon, became "almost the official artists to Wilde."[9] Ricketts and Wilde were first acquaintances and then friends for five or six years before the latter's disgrace and trial in 1895. Second, Ricketts is very unwilling to acknowledge that connectedness, an unwillingness that seems to depend in part on issues relating to ambition, or the development of individual careers by distinct artistic personalities, as well as their respective successes and failures. Connectedness between verbal and visual artists, the professional competition of such personalities, and the denial of that connectedness are the chief themes of this section of the chapter, together with the ways in which they are manifested in the practice of collaboration. Practitioners in the 1890s felt intense pressure to present themselves in terms of artistic uniqueness and an autonomous artwork, making collaboration—particularly as it appears in the published illustration and design of a writer's work by an active visual artist—paradoxical and heavily invested with fiercely contested struggles for authority, especially so with two strong and ambitious personalities.

Competition and Collaboration

The economic modernization of artistic practice—and the rise of claims for the artwork's autonomy in response—has already structured the discussion in previous chapters.[10] The processes of modernization involved in this development fascinated and alarmed Ricketts and many of his contemporaries. "The nineteenth century brought a new world," he wrote in 1902, "the upheaval of a new stratum of society."[11] Throughout the 1880s and 1890s and well into the new century, he was preoccupied with the struggle to conceptualize what was occurring and to posit the artwork as a viable alternative and source of value. In the same summary of the year's thoughts on 1900 in which he remembered Wilde's death, Ricketts gave way to a typically anxious formulation of the problem: "The mob is diseased by the mob, we are suffering from the effects of the majority Babel, and intellectual Hooliganism, a state of things so complicated and unimportant that old tests, based on a smaller and more intellectual experience are no longer valid. Soon everything will be equally important, i.e. not important at all. This is the curse of the moment, and the curse of the many."[12] Ricketts's palpable struggle with this issue, his striving for analysis while swept by gusts of instinctive revulsion and fear, stakes out the ground on which, from

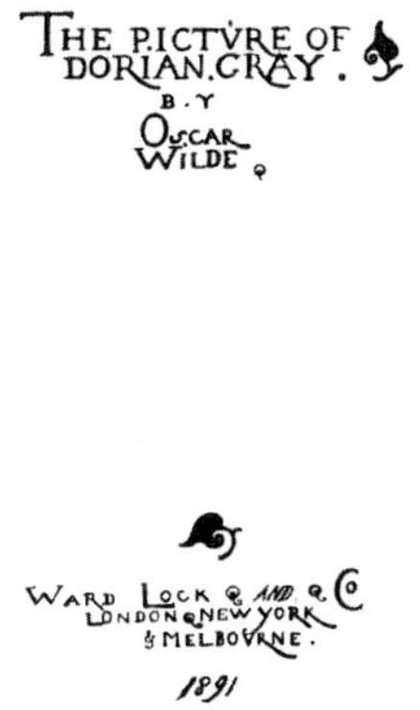
THE PICTVRE OF DORIAN GRAY . BY OSCAR WILDE

WARD LOCK & CO LONDON NEW YORK & MELBOVRNE.

1891

FIGURE 47. Charles Ricketts and Charles Shannon, title page, Oscar Wilde, *The Picture of Dorian Gray* (1891)

the 1880s onward, he opposed a self-consciously elitist connoisseurial and cultured practice to the vast "mob" of the new multiple audience. He developed an elaborate theory of artistic "personality," or "nature," keyed to a repudiation of the new mass reading and viewing publics—replacing them with an ideal of art that expressed a refined sensibility. That personality should play such a large part in this response is not fortuitous. Personality has already figured in my argument as a defining pattern in the art and careers of Watts, Whistler, and Leighton. As the art world came increasingly to resemble other areas of bourgeois culture, the reality of career making within a competitive free market came to be constructed for artists and writers in the identifiable, branded *difference* of their work, a process very clearly observable in the evolution of Whistler's public career. As a result, creative innovation to achieve difference and the promotion of the artist's public personality as a *sign* of difference became tradable commodities and functioned to mark the grounds of artistic success. Ricketts noted this when he wrote of the "century of art" between 1810 and 1910 that "our period might be termed the period of competitive painting, *i.e.* competition to secure attention against other artists, other aims, and other schools."[13] He conceives of competition here not only in terms of the market—competition *against* other art to "secure attention"—but explicitly in terms of personality as well. Although "the modern mind has had little hope, less trust, and no belief in art" and has "hugged other ideals," Ricketts interprets the modern period as "an epoch of hope and endeavour among the artists at least" because of the continuing appearance of "great artists," such as Puvis de Chavannes, G. F. Watts, Rossetti, and Alfred Stevens.[14] In Ricketts's mind, the force of artistic personality plays a major role in promising an alternative to painful and menacing "mob" rule.

Not surprisingly, then, throughout his writings Ricketts demonstrates a preoccupation with his own personality and its gifts as well as with those of the artists he most values. He meditates frequently on his own abilities as a painter and designer, but—and perhaps more unexpectedly—he is just as interested in his critical and evaluative talents.[15] This is partly signaled in the confidence of his judgments—"a priceless work, unimaginably delicate and reticent in its power, insight and profound art, and profound taste" is typical enough of his willingness to ascribe value—but it also surfaces plainly in his aesthetics.[16] Ricketts insists on the role of "genius" in shaping the world: "the fact is that genius moulds circumstances to itself," he writes in *The Prado and Its Masterpieces* (1903). Moreover, he identifies personality and its concomitant intensity of perception as characteristic of all great art.[17] Titian's work is valued because its interpretation of the world is controlled and "coloured by the generous gravity of [his] own temper"; in Velasquez, "we yield to the freshness and delicacy of his vision, the grave and subtle charm of his personality" that allows him to reveal to us "the delicacy, the nobility even, that lies in common things."[18] However compelling the subject matter, Ricketts suggests that the force and subtlety of personality that the artist can command are more important. "The success of an artist" depends on this power of the individual sensibility: "if he has remoulded the world of sensation and event for himself, he has enlarged our experience by the intensity of his own, and we should be satisfied."[19]

The concentration on the artist in this aesthetic should not blind us to the fact that the issue here is also the quality and strength of Ricketts's own sensibility, the way in which this position implicitly translates *him,* too, out of the common run of humanity and asserts his access to intense levels of experience and reality. Personality and individual taste are essential to Ricketts's view of himself and yet the source of a deep anxiety. The diaries are dotted with speculations on the nature of talent and success and on his own reception and appreciation by others. These moments typically mix confidence with apprehension about his own abilities. In 1903, for instance, when he met Rodin, he thought the sculptor clearly in decline. According to Ricketts, Rodin said "nothing fine or even intelligent" and so was "hardly conscious, I think, that I was a rather more than ordinary man, who probably knows and understands his work better than any man in Europe."[20] As a corollary to his detestation of the "mob," Ricketts frequently dwells on what he believes to be an attack by society on the talented individual. In 1900, in the midst of a characteristic train of thought about "that resentment in England . . . one raises unconsciously on one's way through life," he decides that "vanity, jealousy and fear are incalculably developed and widespread."[21] When he tries to define genius, he notices its entanglement in these hostile forces: in 1900 he spoke, according to W. B. Yeats, "as he often does, of the lack of any necessary place for the arts in modern life" and "talked of the disordered and broken lives of modern men of genius . . . no one thinks of them till some misfortune comes—madness or death."[22] Elsewhere, Ricketts repeatedly identifies a "prevailing anarchy in our social ideals, or lack of sense for the finer responsibilities in life."[23] He argues that

> *a sign of our decadence lies in our ready depreciation of genius, our prevailing sense that it is "too good to be true." This at any rate is the habit of the more cultured; and between this caste, once a small one, and the many, there is only an unimportant difference of numbers, hardly of kind. . . . We moderns dislike personalities that require too much room, and the spread of education has made us jealous of our separate good and of our important unimportance.*[24]

The obverse of this is a frequent anxiety about his ability to secure recognition from the art institutions of his day. "South Kensington [the National Art Library] has refused to buy my book on the Prado," he wrote in his diary, "alleging that they had all, or most of the pictures in photography. It is curious that this book, containing more synthetic criticism than perhaps any book on art written in English in the last twenty years is thus closed to students."[25]

This preoccupation with the personality, emerging from the history that I have traced in previous chapters, served as a central conceptual plank on which resistance to the commodification of the art world could be built. The personality of the artist or the connoisseur functions as the guarantee of value and authenticity untouched by the base modernity of the art world and resonant with the truth of experience. The corollary of this emphasis on personality as resistant to the marketplace is an equally strong emphasis on the work of art as detached from the protocols and requirements of the commodity. Value and quality in the artwork are asserted *against* its commodity value through the aesthetic of autonomy that I have discussed in earlier chapters.[26] As a gesture that repudiates the "means-end relationships" of bourgeois life,[27] autonomy conceives of the work as detached from praxis, hermetically self-sufficient, and, as Wilde put it in "The Decay of Lying," "in no case . . . reproduc[ing] its age."[28] But it is also understood as accessible to the judgment of such personalities and as resulting from their creative energies. In fact, the acknowledged authority of such personalities to access the value of autonomous works justifies their asserted status. In a familiar declension of appeals to grounded authority, autonomy rests on the development of an aesthetic of personality that is presented as natural and not susceptible to critique.

This move was not without its problems. In order to formulate a convincing theory of autonomy, practitioners had to repress autonomy's historical specificity and present it as something eternally and invariably true about the constitution of the artwork. This strategy enabled its champions to achieve a partial recovery of artistic value independent of art's commodity value—partial because, in effect, it also served as a powerful instrument of the novelty and differentiation in artistic practice that commodification and exchange value demanded.[29] Wilde's reply to an adverse comment on Ricketts's cover design for *A House of Pomegranates* (1891, fig. 48) exemplifies this. The critic of the *Speaker* denigrated "the Indian club with a house painter's brush on the top which passes muster for a peacock, and the chimney pot hat with a sponge in it, which is meant to represent a basket."[30] Wilde dismissed the criticism as irrelevant and as evidence of judgment by an inferior personality: "There are only two people in the world whom it is absolutely necessary that the cover should please. One is Mr Ricketts, who designed it, the other is myself, whose book it binds. We both admire it immensely!"[31]

Strength of personality is everything here. Wilde's reply manages simultaneously to assert the irrelevance of an audience and to promote the excitement of artistic innovation for that audience. The logic of autonomy meant that its proponents, like Wilde, were obliged continually to deny autonomy's historical and immediate use value even as they mobilized it, introducing a tension at the center of their conception and presentation of the work. The "praxis of life," in Bürger's phrase, intimately bound up with artistic endeavor, thus became an area deliberately and often vigorously pursued—and effectively denied at the level of articulation.[32] In an important way, it was difficult to acknowledge that a competitive art world existed. Personality lies at this intersection of autonomy, commodification, and competition as well as their denial. Perhaps this is why, on hearing of Wilde's death, Ricketts appears to find himself oppressed by

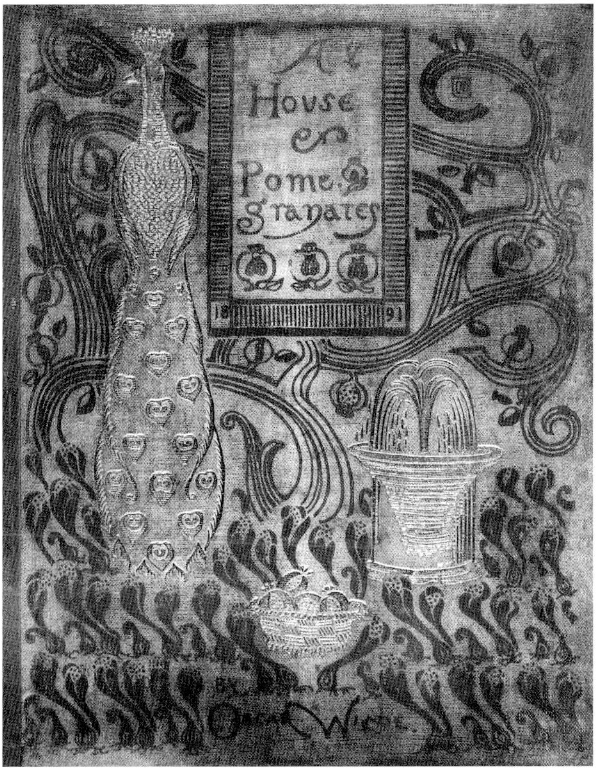

FIGURE 48. Charles Ricketts and Charles Shannon, cover, Oscar Wilde, *A House of Pomegranates* (1891)

the personal consequences of this situation. The issue for him relates to "life" rather than "art," and is mixed up with it, but its articulation in the diaries is choked off, hesitant—in the end, all but impossible.

I suggest that we can understand these things at the level of practice by looking at artistic collaboration, particularly the way in which collaboration brings with it competition between the partners involved. By this I mean that the end product of collaboration—in Ricketts's case, the design and illustration of books—can resist, deflect, and negotiate the meanings bestowed or intended by the senior partner, the writer whose works are designed and illustrated. This is so because the issue of illustration and design embodies, in detail, the paradoxical status of the autonomous work that I have sketched out above. On the one hand, illustration and book design are conceived, at what is really a metaphorical level, as reinforcing the autonomy of the senior work by underwriting its uniqueness as text. The scarcity value of the finely illustrated and designed book reflects and confirms the uniqueness of the text it serves, and its richness signals the independence of the work from the vulgarity of exchange value—even as it contributes to it, of course. But on the other hand, illustration powerfully threatens claims about the autonomy of the work. It explicitly acts as a supplement, adding to the meaning of the parent work, either by claiming to "illustrate it"—that is, to bring into the light what is obscure in its meaning[33]—or by correctly presenting to the reader what the text only "suggests" or "evokes." Moreover, where artist and author are not the same person (as is usually the case), illustration is necessarily a *collaborative* venture and as such trespasses dangerously on the issues of competition and resistance that career making carries with it. It smacks unmistakably of senior and subsidiary work and of questions of priority and status in meaning and professional precedence. In other words, the issues that cluster around commodified practice are in play within the collaborative product itself.

The illustrator finds himself in an invidious position. He has to support a text he may be at odds with—even advance a career he may be at odds with—and yet shore up the mutually beneficial aesthetic of autonomy that it would be in no one's best interests to undermine. In addition, he has to assert himself and his own creative autonomy against the subordinate position of illustrator and designer. In this context, the collaborative work provides an arena in which the problematics of competition (present but largely unconfessed in the actual relationships between collaborators) can be given concrete, if still oblique, expression. This "resistance" operates not so much on the level of a challenge to the overt meanings of the text itself, although it does do that, but rather through a complex negotiation of the whole network of meanings that accrue to the parent work by virtue of its status as a commodity. In raising these issues, artistic collaboration focuses claims for the relative status of language and the visual with particular clarity. The remainder of this chapter explores what it reveals in the light of my themes in the book. I will concentrate on four detailed readings. First, I will consider further the relationship of Ricketts with Wilde and relate this to aesthetic differences between the two men. Second, I will look at the ambitious claims for the visual exemplified by G. F. Watts's mammoth project to record nineteenth-century life in a "Hall of Fame"—a long series of portrait studies of his great contemporaries—and the treatment of such claims in Wilde's *The Picture of Dorian Gray* (1891), the first edition of which was designed by Ricketts, and his short story "The Portrait of Mr W. H." (1889). My third reading will focus on the status of the visual in Ricketts's *The Prado* as in some sense a response to Wilde's criticisms, while my fourth and final section considers the collaborative work *The Sphinx,* written by Wilde and illustrated and designed by Ricketts in 1894 for its first publication. This in-depth return to the issue of collaboration allows me to conclude with a consideration of how

Wilde's novel and short story and Ricketts's designs and art writing contribute to the meditation on the limits of the visual in train at the end of the nineteenth century.

Truth and Personality

Plenty of evidence suggests that the personal relationship between Ricketts and Wilde was, in some ways, a tense one. When they first met in the late 1880s, Wilde was already an established public and artistic personality; Ricketts was still an aspiring engraver and illustrator anxious to make a name for himself. Their subsequent association, mingling indebtedness and confrontation, was complex and difficult. The first contact seems to have come when Ricketts sent a set of drawings to Wilde as editor of *Woman's World*.[34] Wilde responded and, encouraged by the older man's interest, Ricketts set out to court him seriously. In 1889 he sent Wilde a complimentary copy of the first number of *The Dial*, the little magazine he edited with Charles Shannon between 1889 and 1897 (see fig. 2) and to which he had contributed some short prose pieces that in idiom, concerns, and presentation seem to depend on Wilde's *Happy Prince*, published in 1888.[35] Ricketts worked hard to make common cause with Wilde and to interest and attract him. When Wilde then asked Ricketts if he would provide a realistic frontispiece for an edition of Wilde's "The Portrait of Mr W. H.," Ricketts worked quickly and made the result a gift to Wilde, despite his perennial need for ready money.

If Ricketts intended the frontispiece to "Mr W. H." to be a loss leader, it paid off. His biographer, J. G. P. Delaney, argues that Ricketts's friendship with Wilde provided the break into book design that established Ricketts and inaugurated "a new era of prosperity" for him.[36] It would be wrong, however, to see Ricketts's behavior as wholly manipulative: his attention and interest were reciprocated. The publication of the first number of *The Dial* ushered in a three-year period during which, Ricketts later recalled, Wilde's "evening visits were constant, and often lasted well into the night."[37] The aunt-niece partnership "Michael Field," close friends of Ricketts, noted in their journal that for the first year of this period, Ricketts and Shannon were obsessed with Wilde: he became "everything to them."[38] For his part, Wilde seems to have felt the power of Ricketts's personality. He found Ricketts "cultivated and interesting" almost at once and told William Rothenstein that "I am taking you to the one house in London where you will never be bored."[39] At the same time, he began to work to maintain his position of precedence over the ambitious Ricketts, who found it hard to accept subservience. Rothenstein, who knew Ricketts and Shannon well at this time, believed that "Ricketts had a passion for influencing others," that it was his "fatal desire."[40] And Laurence Housman, who counted himself as one of Ricketts's disciples for a while, ultimately could not bear his "strained and restless brilliance . . . ever laying down the law."[41] How far this situation was inflected by the shared sexual identity of the two men is uncertain. Ricketts throughout his life was extremely circumspect about his homosexuality, and Wilde's frank declaration of a queer identity may have called forth mixed feelings in the younger man, unassertive in this area if in no other. The particular edge that this combination of patronage, mutual attraction, and resentment gave to the relationship is well expressed by Charles Holmes, who remembered Wilde's treatment of Ricketts as having "tempered laughing assurance with . . . much friendship and respect."[42]

Ricketts's response to this situation was ambivalent, marked by a combination of personal liking, even identification, and some artistic affinity with resentment about Wilde's status in the art world and an ironic stance toward Wilde as an artist. He later wrote that he had failed to appreciate Wilde properly during his lifetime and that he had been an extraordinary man, "his personality . . . the most remarkable one that I should ever meet . . . in intellect and humanity . . . the largest type I have come across."[43] In both the diaries and the late memoir, *Oscar Wilde: Recollections,* Wilde is presented as the victim of a cowardly philistinism in English culture that Ricketts indicts and that has an entirely unspoken sexual dimension. These positive or sympathetic assessments are yoked to the statement that Wilde was flawed and, above all, that he failed to realize his potential as a man and as an artist.[44] No matter how much "friendship and respect" there may have been, the "laughing assurance" that proclaimed Wilde's superior status and power of patronage (and that was no doubt calculated to do so) continued to rankle. Ricketts frankly stated, "my acquaintance with Oscar Wilde was constantly conditioned by the share I had in building and illustrating his books." That this was a source of both advantage and resentment to him was something with which he seems never to have come to terms (*Recollections,* 27).

The most striking biographical instance of this ambivalence concerns the verbal competition the two men staged between themselves. Wilde's reputation as a brilliant conversationalist was well established by the late 1880s; Ricketts's reputation—later considerable—was just emerging. Verbal competition, though, served to express Ricketts's resentment with comparative safety. Holmes remembered an example: "Ricketts, perched on the edge of the table, engaged Wilde in a long verbal combat. So swiftly came parry and *riposte,* that my slow brain could only follow the tongue-play several sentences behind, and cannot remember a word of what passed, except 'Oh! Nonsense, Oscar' from Ricketts, although it lives in memory as the most dazzling dialogue which I was ever privileged to hear."[45] If "Oh! Nonsense, Oscar" does not sound particularly dazzling, it nevertheless seems extremely likely as the remembered keynote and actual subtext of what was said. But even here Ricketts had reason for anxiety. Delaney cites Graham Robertson and Gordon Bottomley—the latter devoted to Ricketts—to suggest that Ricketts's persona as a conversationalist very explicitly depended on Wilde's example. Robertson thought "Ricketts had modelled himself so much upon Oscar—voice and speech sometimes [were] identical," and Bottomley, although less forcefully, supports the view that Ricketts's delivery, "characteristic cadences and a *portamento* on certain words . . . might have been picked up from Wilde."[46] This possibility gains an added charge from the fact that in what he wrote later, Ricketts is most uneasy with Wilde as "euphuist or rhetorician" (*Recollections,* 35).

The consequences of this complex relationship mark Ricketts's 1932 memoir. *Oscar Wilde: Recollections* is supposedly the work of "Jean Paul Raymond and Charles Ricketts," but "Raymond" was a pseudonym that Ricketts had already used for the publication of his *Beyond the Threshold* in 1929, and its use seems to have reflected a period of "crisis" or reevaluation at the end of his life.[47] Appropriately, the format of the book seems designed to distance anything that Ricketts may say about Wilde. It opens with an account by "Raymond" of meeting "an elderly Englishman who, years ago, had known Oscar Wilde" (9). This, of course, turns out to be Ricketts. The "two" fall into conversation and Ricketts, via a fierce condemnation of English culture for its negative treatment of the artist, gives an account of Wilde as the victim of English philistinism and as important and talented but also flawed as an artist. The second part of the book is made up of a series of letters, supposedly from Ricketts to "Raymond," that describe three meetings with Wilde. In the second of these meetings, Ricketts portrays the constraint that by 1895 had appeared in their relationship.

According to *Recollections,* Wilde—then at the height of his fame—appeared unexpectedly at Ricketts's house in Beaufort Street when Ricketts was laboring late at night on his engraving work: "I had not seen him for many months, months of fantastic success for him and of intensive solitary work for me" (39). Ricketts was by now well advanced with plans for his own Vale Press that would give him complete artistic control over the design, production, and selection of books. He describes how uneasy with each other he and Wilde were: "between us brooded [a] sense of silence and estrangement" (ibid.), and at the end of the conversation, "we had hardly once spoken without effort or constraint, his sallies had seemed forced, we had been like two men separated by a chasm and our words, intended to be friendly, had fallen into a void" (42). This uneasiness is given a concrete form when Wilde, hearing of Ricketts's plans to found his own private publishing venture, enthusiastically asserts, "you must print my 'Portrait of Mr W. H.'" "There was a short silence," says Ricketts, the result of his reluctance to publish "Mr W. H."—indeed, his determination not to do so—and his deep unwillingness to confess this to Wilde: "I dared not say that, if his plays enchanted the public, his books were far from being successful" (41). He eventually improvises a suggestion that he should publish Wilde's piece at some point in the future if the Press proved successful, but Wilde is clearly disconcerted. Ricketts writes: "I felt abashed; he had found me work which I had needed greatly; that was not my sole thought, there are small acts of discourtesy which one regrets more than graver things. I felt he had divined coldness and hesitation in my voice whilst promising to issue 'The Portrait of Mr W. H.' at some distant date" (42). It seems likely that this is the principal source for the "interview" that Ricketts refers to in his diary after Wilde's death as being "after all these years . . . so vivid." It has a probable secondary source—the brief visit that Ricketts made to Wilde in Reading Gaol in 1897 days before he was released. This meeting, too, was full of unacknowledged tension. Wilde seems not to have wanted Ricketts there, and, while Ricketts was waiting, to have argued with Robert Ross and More Adey, who were attempting to make arrangements for him after his release. Perhaps tellingly, the question of Ricketts's printing "The Portrait of Mr W. H." came up again, and once again Ricketts evaded it: "my dear Oscar, of course I will publish a book of yours, but for the moment let it be some other work, your *Sainte Courtisane* for instance."[48] Wilde later wrote to Ross, "I was wrong to have Ricketts present: he meant to be cheering, but I thought him trivial."[49] The whole event seems to have been marked by uneasiness, unexpressed thoughts and feelings and resentments. The cumulative effect of these two encounters leads Ricketts to note in his diary "the old sense that one is not sufficiently reconciled." Ricketts seemingly could not resolve, himself, the mingled hostility, resentment, and indebtedness of these meetings, with their summary of Ricketts's relations with Wilde. Particularly unresolvable are the connections between the relationships necessary to advance a career and the need to assert an independence, both on the level of the personality and that of the work. In consequence, Ricketts has to displace and distance the realities of the situation for the rest of his life.

The biographical tension so evidently a part of Ricketts's relations with Wilde is shadowed by a set of aesthetic differences and similarities. In 1903 Ricketts published *The Prado,* in which he advances a set of beliefs—one that sustains and underpins his other writings about art—about art's function, its relationship to the world, and the importance and character of the artist. In doing so, he describes an aesthetic of autonomy consonant with Wilde's, but he also sets out a connection between what visual art represents and what is represented that is at odds with Wilde's thought.

In a later essay, Ricketts rejects the argument from realism. The "wish to conquer facts for their own sake" in the history of art is inferior to the wish "to express that which lies behind fact."[50] And in *The Prado,* he initially appears to endorse art as an autonomous practice. He celebrates "that intense moment in [sixteenth-century] Venetian life when art and the love of beauty had become sufficient ends in themselves—were looked upon not merely as means to a fuller and intenser life, but, like happiness, as things in themselves desirable."[51] This independence of art and "beauty" from life, of course, has elements in common with Wilde's espousal of autonomy. Realism—in the fact-grubbing sense—is rejected vigorously by both, as is the possibility that there is a straightforward relationship between art and its subject matter. The crucial point of difference between Ricketts and Wilde hangs on their attitudes toward fictionality and the role of the imagination. For Ricketts, the transcendental, "that which lies behind fact," can only be revealed through the translating medium of the artist's personality. Ricketts's touchstone in *The Prado* for greatness in art and the expression of an informing personality is Titian: "Titian's faculties of representation do not spring from some preconceived scheme of things, but from the ordering of certain facts into a sequence colored by the richness of his own nature. It is by his power of marshalling his impressions, and by the nobility of his aim, that he has made a world of his own."[52] This "nature" is not identical with the biographical personality, but is a separate, aesthetic self that inheres in the art and functions through a mode of response to and transformation of the world: "character and life . . . are of secondary importance, for to the world a man's art is the real man."[53] In a familiar move, this infusion of a character into the subject matter of the work provides the mechanism by which art comes to have a relevance to the spectator.[54] The quality of creative invention the artist brings to the transformation of the world is central to its meaning for us: "It is incredible what we owe in the matter of vision and experience to the greatest masters. Without Rembrandt, for instance, a whole range of emotion would have partly failed us . . . and we might not understand those beauties which are the fruits of experience and disillusion. . . . Without Titian other experience might have failed us, and . . . we might have remained insensible . . . to the beautiful and unique significance of outward things."[55] As I have already noted, this insistence on personality is a version of autonomy. Both Ricketts's verbal sparring with Wilde and the cult that Wilde created about himself mirror this emphatic claim: the quality of personality defines the greatness of the work of art. On the other hand, Ricketts's particular version of personality leads directly into a claim that art transforms a reality that is there to be perceived and communicated and can be shared in common. Invention, for Ricketts, is not a question of fiction; he does not recommend the development of an imagined world outside what he conceives to be reality. Invention, for him, is the power of bringing into the field of knowledge aspects of reality that have hitherto been neglected. Rembrandt and Titian teach us to recognize emotions and experiences we already have but cannot define for ourselves. The world is transformed and revealed in great art—not invented there.

This is not the position that Ricketts would have heard from Wilde during the early 1890s. Even Wilde's very first approach to Ricketts raised the issue of a fictionality entirely divorced from reality. When he had written "The Portrait of Mr W. H.," a fiction that vigorously undermines the idea of historical verifiability, Wilde asked for a mock Clouet to illustrate the story. When it arrived, he pretended to be convinced that it was an authentic example Ricketts and Shannon had found.[56] This playful but determined disregard of reality is characteristic of Wilde. He told the Michael Fields, "Fiction—not truth—I could never have any dealings with truth—if truth were to come unto me, to my room, he would say to me, 'You are too wilful.' And I should say to him, 'you are too obvious.' And I should throw him out of the window."[57] In "The Decay of Lying," Wilde explicitly asserts that "Lying, the telling of beautiful untrue things, is the proper aim of Art."[58] What is beautiful is what is untrue; for Ricketts, the beautiful may have to be selected, but it is not untrue in any sense. Wilde rejects the idea that art should reveal reality: "Art is our spirited protest, our gallant attempt to teach Nature her proper place. As for the infinite variety of Nature, that is pure myth. It is not to be found in Nature herself. It resides in the imagination or fancy, or cultivated blindness of the man who looks at her."[59] Ricketts designed the first edition of *Intentions,* in which "The Decay of Lying" appeared in 1891 together with "The Critic as Artist," "Pen, Pencil, and Poison," and "The Truth of Masks," and there is no reason to doubt that he knew what Wilde had written. Moreover, when Wilde wrote to the editor of the *Speaker* to protest against the negative comment on Ricketts's design for *A House of*

Pomegranates, he offered an explicit summary of his position. The critic had objected, in effect, to the lack of realism in Ricketts's design for the book's cover. Wilde responded:

What the gilt notes suggest, what imitative parallel may be found to them in that chaos that is termed Nature, is a matter of no importance. They may suggest, as they do sometimes to me, peacocks and pomegranates and splashing fountains of gold water, or, as they do to your critic, sponges and Indian clubs and chimney-pot hats. Such suggestions and evocations have nothing whatever to do with the aesthetic quality and value of the design. A thing in Nature becomes much lovelier if it reminds us of a thing in Art, but a thing in Art gains no real beauty through reminding us of a thing in Nature. The primary aesthetic impression of a work of art borrows nothing from recognition or resemblance.[60]

Ricketts heard these arguments from Wilde during their acquaintance and collaboration, and they strike directly against his own convictions. Ricketts later criticized Wilde for his tendency to be seduced by the fictions that words build independent of reality.[61] Their conversations and debates must have circled around these questions, as Wilde's did with the Michael Fields, Ricketts's intimate friends—not surprisingly, perhaps, as the question of the capacity of the visual to give a direct account of the world gave them a particular sharpness. As we have seen, personality and the belief in the visual arts as privileged registers of reality went hand in hand in the years before Ricketts and Wilde began to collaborate, and the disagreement between Ricketts and Wilde over fictionality resolves itself at one level into a disagreement over the relative status of language and the visual.

Visuality and Portraiture

I want now to make a connection between the contest of personalities I have discerned in Ricketts's relationship with Wilde and the way in which Wilde himself had already repudiated the capacity of the visual (and painting in particular) to engage adequately with the world. I argue in this section that *The Picture of Dorian Gray*—first published in 1891 in book form and designed by Ricketts—as well as "The Portrait of Mr W. H.," Wilde's 1889 short story, respond to ideas then circulating about visual portraiture and critique them from the position of Wilde's strong belief in the superiority of language.[62] I illustrate these ideas by examining the claims made by G. F. Watts for the long series of portraits he produced of his famous contemporaries, the so-called Hall of Fame. These portraits were deemed to provide access to an authentic sense of personality—one central to the argument.

Portraiture is a genre in which the relationship of visual representation to the objects it claims to describe is clearly evident. The human self that the portrait engages is in some sense the one that we commonly experience in social interaction; like that social self, the self offered to the portrait painter is defensive and dominated by a social or egotistical mask. The essential self that we understand to characterize human beings, "the *real* person," is presented through this social mask with apparent immediacy but also under the cloak of disguise that our anxiety about self-exposure enforces in our dealings with others.[63] Portraiture seems to replay this fundamental social encounter because it reenacts both the ideal of access to identity and the experience of its elusiveness, its blockage or deliberate withholding and dissembling. There are other ways in which portraiture can be thought about—as purely about the social self, or as a fetish or ritual object—but in nineteenth-century culture, the portrait promises to reveal precisely this reality of identity through a visual account of appearance.[64] Its fundamental claim is to relate "a physiognomic likeness . . . to the identity of the . . . person depicted."[65] In this sense, its role in forming rather than recording identity becomes suspect and acts as a synecdoche for the general role of representation in forming rather than identically presenting the world. Indeed, for late-nineteenth-century culture, portraiture was one of the areas in which the question of representation and reality was strongly visible and could be examined.

Within the intellectual context that equated portraiture and identity, Watts conceived in the early 1850s the extraordinary project of creating a gallery of portraits of his important contemporaries that would encapsulate the history of the nineteenth century. He persisted with this aim until his death and produced a large number of works, many of them left to the nation and now in the National Portrait Gallery in London. It has been suggested that Watts turned to portraiture as a way of resolving the tension he perceived between the sellable qualities of his commercial portraiture and his ambitions for himself as educator and diagnostician of the contemporary age.[66] The portraiture project "saved him" by offering him the comfort of what was "almost an act of piety . . . a *public service*."[67] Such a role for his gallery was built on an understanding of the portraits as accessing the essential nature of the selves they depicted and in some way conveying the history that had formed them and to which they had themselves contributed. Watts wrote of the portrait as the "summary of the life of a person" rather than "the record of an accidental position, or arrangement of light and shadow."[68] This concept of the portrait as unveiling a socially hidden reality goes some way toward accounting for the format he eventually hit on for the Hall of Fame, in which the sitter is represented with "something of the monumental," at bust length and without significant background or context.[69] The emphasis rests firmly on the power of the face and head to communicate the personality and history of the sitter, his or her "storms and vicissitudes," as Watts said, so that the portrait "should appear capable of action but performing none."[70]

This understanding of the possibilities of portraiture was widely disseminated in the culture. It was this that G. K. Chesterton meant when he referred to Watts's "intense conviction that there is within the sitter a great reality which has to give up its secret" and that provoked comments like that of Lady Holland, who said that she never knew her friends until she saw Watts's portraits of them.[71] It appears as well in popular literature. In the "sensation" novel *Lady Audley's Secret* (1862), several characters discover a hidden portrait of Lady Audley herself, "unfinished, but wonderfully like," and they are shocked by its "Pre-Raphaelite" and Rossettian qualities that represent her with "something of the aspect of a beautiful fiend."[72] One of them explains this unsuspected and bewildering revelation: "'I think that sometimes a painter is in a manner inspired, and is able to see, through the normal expression of the face, another expression that is equally a part of it, though not to be perceived by common eyes. *We* have never seen my lady look as she does in that picture; but I think that she *could* look so.'"[73] The portrait has access to a set of "truths" about Lady Audley to which her social mask and behavior give no clue. It is possible to know her intimately without knowing these things about her. It is only through the capacity of the painter's "uncommon eyes" that reality can be revealed, and once painted, it is immediately recognized, as it is in Lady Holland's comment on Watts's portraiture.

Paul Barlow has written helpfully on Watts's project, exploring the portraits' relationship to "authenticity" and relating them to contemporary protocols of portraiture and identity. Barlow locates a connection between the aspiration to paint the reality of the self and the declarative paintwork of the portraits in which Watts attempts it. The visualization of the self is conducted in Watts through the materiality of paint, the eruptive and dramatically overworked paint surface of the portraits standing for the "vicissitudes" that he strove to communicate as signifiers of history and the world: "thus the struggle to paint a complex surface, half revealing hidden depths, becomes identified with that 'inner secret of the features' described by Froude [Carlyle's biogra-

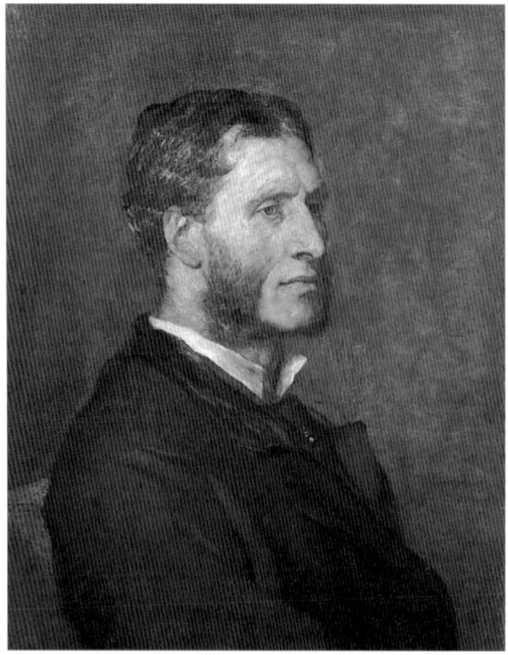

FIGURE 49. George Frederic Watts, *Matthew Arnold,* 1880

pher]."[74] Barlow sees this as a sign of slippage, one essentially unresolved but marking the problematic encounter of paint and its object with the aim of locating and transmitting identity.[75] In Barlow's terms, a portrait like the 1880 *Matthew Arnold* in the National Portrait Gallery (fig. 49) develops a powerfully material skein of paint around the description of the subject's face. Arnold becomes a "monument" to the capacity of paint itself to mime and access the realities of self and identity that lie beneath the surfaces of appearance. Ten years before the *Arnold,* Watts, describing wallpaper behind his sitter, had allowed flowers of white paint to bloom across the frontal portrait he made of William Morris (1870, fig. 50), asserting the presence of the material substance of pigment as a homologue to the act of representing the self that the portrait attempts. This is a symbolist portraiture, delving into depths that stand for reality and doing so by means of the intense physicality of the surface of painting itself.

Watts's project to create his Hall of Fame through portraiture can therefore take its place in the ambitions for painting and the visual that I am describing. Watts's aspirations exemplify the claims made for the visual in the second half of the nineteenth century, opaque depth translated into clearly read surface, the mysteries of identity made transparent. It was to claims of this type that Oscar Wilde, believing in the inferiority of the visual to the word,

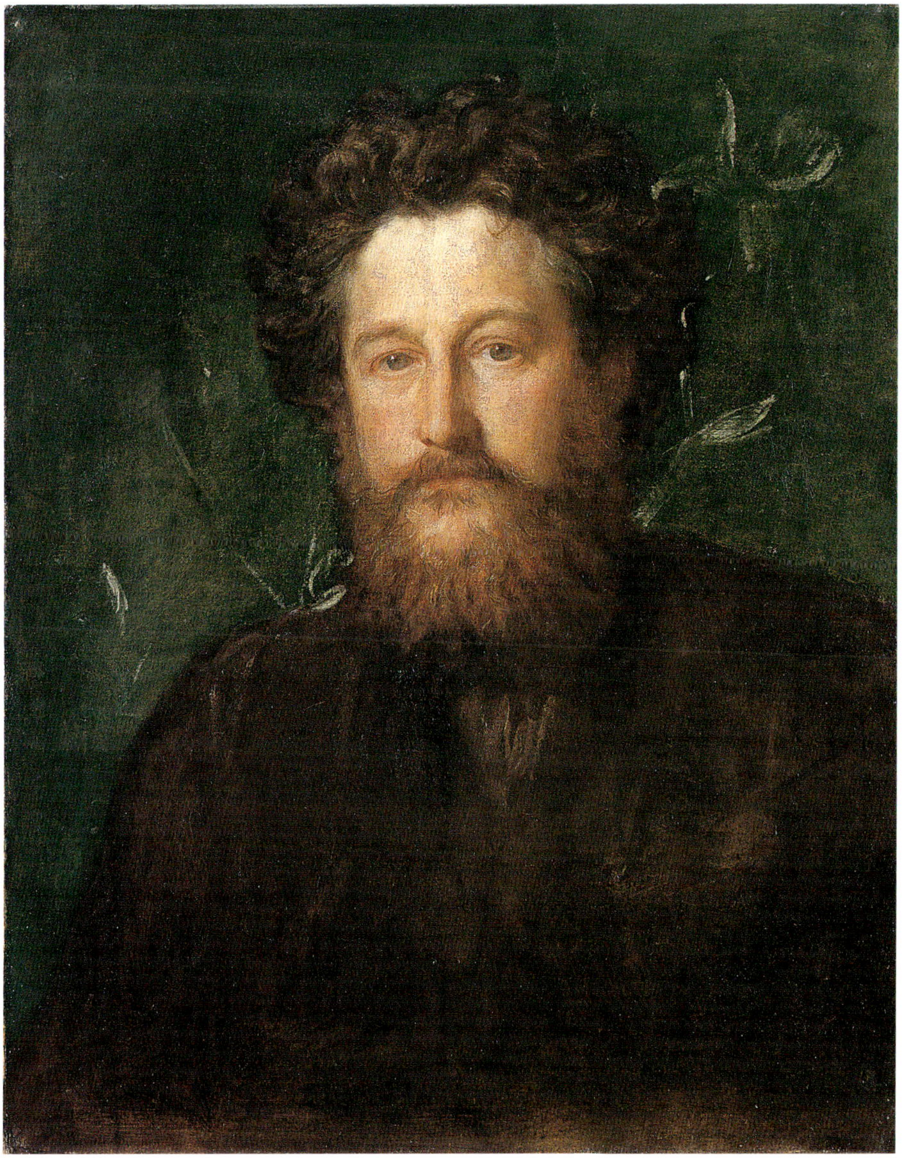

FIGURE 50. George Frederic Watts, *William Morris*, 1870

responded and of which he offered a critique during the 1890s, while he collaborated with Ricketts. Ricketts remembered Wilde's condescending evaluation of his art: "often he had laughingly referred to my 'magic' gift in book designing, 'a little coloured paper smeared with gold'" (*Recollections*, 39). Other comments by Wilde repeat this superior certainty that the visual could never prove a threat or be anything but a minor pleasure.[76] In "The Critic as Artist," Wilde argues for the visual arts' inferiority to literature partly on the grounds that, because the "problem of the visible arts" is their inability to represent time adequately (which "can be truly realised by Literature alone"), an essential aspect of the experience of life is closed to them: "The statue is concentrated to one moment of perfection. The image stained upon the canvas possesses no spiritual element of growth or change. If they know nothing of death, it is because they know little of life, for the secrets of life and death belong to those, and those only, whom the sequence of time affects, and who possess not merely the present but the future, and can rise or fall from a past of glory or of shame."[77]

Wilde's public argument with Whistler had already rehearsed the contest between the visual arts and those of language, and in his 1885 *Pall Mall Gazette* reply to Whistler's attack on him in the "Ten O'Clock Lecture," Wilde emphatically declared that "the poet is the supreme artist, for he is the master of colour and of form, and the real musician besides, and is lord over all life and all arts; and so to the poet beyond all others are these mysteries known."[78] By comparison, the products of visual artists seemed to him insubstantial, narrow and partial in their connection to the breadth of human experience, and necessarily inferior to the inclusive art of the poet. In contrast to the flimsy and subservient nature of visual work, Wilde thought of words as eternal and solid. He told the Michael Fields in the context of a discussion of "colour-words" that "it should be our faith that everything in this world could be expressed in words."[79] Such a view encouraged Wilde to deprecate the claims for the visual that circulated in the late nineteenth century and that emerge in Watts's portrait project.

It is not inappropriate, then, that Ricketts's first real encounter with Wilde should have been through his short story, "The Portrait of Mr W. H." Like *The Picture of Dorian Gray* two years later, the story deals with questions of fictionality and reality. In each case, the visual bears much of the weight of Wilde's suspicions about the possibility of registering the world truthfully. In "Mr W. H.," the portrait of the imagined boy actor, Willie Hughes, occupies a central place in the plot and functions to highlight the uncertainty, unreality, and imagination that form Wilde's themes. And Dorian's portrait in *Dorian Gray* explicitly responds to "reality" in a way that his face and body themselves do not. In both works, Wilde raises and critiques the claims made at the end of the century for the access to reality afforded by visual representation.

The narrative of "Mr W. H." turns on a theory put forward as an explanation of Shakespeare's sonnets. As the story opens, Erskine and the narrator discuss these theories, bequeathed to Erskine when their originator, his friend Cyril Graham, commits suicide in distress at his failure to locate historical proof to support his convictions. Graham's theory posits a boy actor (whom he calls Willie Hughes after punning references in the sonnets) as their recipient and "onlie begetter." As the sequence unfolds, the reading sees Shakespeare seduce Willie onto the stage in the earliest poems, and it chronicles his subsequent, implicitly sexual relationships with Shakespeare, the Dark Lady, and other dramatists in the remainder of the sonnets. The theory is built entirely out of internal evidence derived from the poems themselves and seems enormously consistent and powerful as a tool for construing the sonnets, but it lacks any historical evidence. Driven by Erskine's demands for such proof, Graham has a jobbing painter forge a corroborative portrait of Hughes holding a copy of the first folio edition of the sonnets that "reminded one of François Clouet's later work."[80] Graham commits suicide when Erskine discovers the forgery. Once he has heard the theory, the narrator becomes obsessed by it, working at the nuances and adding much corroborative textual detail—but he, too, cannot find historical evidence. Despite this, he presents his elaboration of the theory to Erskine; he then suffers a very Wildean attack of ambivalence and abandons it himself. Meanwhile, Erskine undergoes a conversion and the story ends with Erskine's death from consumption and the narrator's apparently unresolvable ambivalence. Even the Clouet is now reattributed, and is perhaps an Ouvry.

In *Dorian Gray,* this preoccupation with falsity and with the distinction between what is true within the terms of art and what is true in life is taken further. *Dorian Gray* satirizes the possibility that a visual portrait can, as Watts and others hoped, express the full biography of the individual, reveal the true character that lies beneath the surface, and encapsulate the history of which he is a part. Wilde's novel imagines what it would really mean to impress experience directly onto the canvas in a portrait, and he uses the resulting fantasy to mock and reject the earnest hopes of visual artists. The portrait that registers the experiences of Gray's life is the portrait as it functions in the ideology of the visual. Others are always scrutinizing Gray, fruitlessly interrogating the visual surface of his appearance "with cold searching eyes, as though they were determined to discover his secret."[81] The portrait promises to supply the visual knowledge—the "secret" of personality—that these eyes seek. The painting's power to take on the visible burden of Gray's "sins" initially sets him free to commit them but finally proves unable to hold off the furies that pursue him after his murder of its painter, Basil Hallward: "it was an unjust mirror, this mirror of his soul that he was looking at."[82] When Gray offers Hallward the chance to see the corrupted painting, they both reach for a metaphor of depth and revelation: "'Know you?'" says Hallward, "'I wonder do I know you? Before I could answer that, I should have to see your soul.'"[83] The "soul" is supposed to be the painting, but in Wilde's satirical account, Hallward has succeeded too well in making his portrait penetrate to the heart of reality. When he shows the corrupted canvas to its painter at the climactic moment of the novel, Gray gives way to the temptations of Grand Guignol: "as though it had been suggested to him by the image on the canvas, whispered into his ear by those grinning lips," he kills his friend with a knife, "stabbing again and again" as he is overcome with rage and hatred.[84] In the final scene, Gray, driven to distraction by confusion about the rival claims of art and life, stabs the painting through the heart but dies himself. The servants, of course, discover "a splendid portrait of their master . . . in all the wonder of his exquisite youth and beauty" and "a dead man . . . with a knife in his heart . . . withered, wrinkled and loathsome of visage."[85] As Wilde says in the preface to his novel, "it is the spectator, and not Life, that art really mirrors."[86]

Wilde's play with access to truth about the world connects to his own belief, immediately indebted to Pater, in personality as the key to art. The narrator in "Mr W. H." begins the story by asserting that "all Art" is "to a certain degree a mode of acting, an attempt to realise one's own personality on some imaginative plane out of reach of the trammelling accidents and limitations of real life."[87] And Gray, wandering through "his great house in Nottinghamshire," muses on the same theme: "He used to wonder at the shallow psychology of those who conceive the Ego in man as a thing simple, permanent, reliable, and of one essence. To him, man was a being with myriad lives and myriad sensations, a complex multiform creature that bore within itself strange legacies of thought and passion."[88] This is made concrete for him by a walk through the house's "gaunt cold picture gallery," where he can contemplate the painted portraits of his infamous, corrupt ancestors and imagine some transmission of behavior and fate down the generations.[89]

For Willie Hughes, however, personality is the reason for his inferiority to Shakespeare. Hughes's capacity as an actor "to realise every form and phase of fancy, to embody each dream of the creative imagination," is his utility and attraction for the dramatist; Hughes is the poet's mouthpiece and hence junior collaborator.[90] But that capacity "to have so many personalities" is also what connects him to the inferior art of painting, for acting stands for painting in the economy of "Mr W. H.":

Shakespeare invites us to notice how the truth of acting, the truth of visible presentation on the stage, adds to the wonder of poetry, giving life to its loveliness, and actual reality to its ideal form. And yet, in Sonnet LXVII, *Shakespeare calls upon Willie Hughes to abandon the stage with its artificiality, its unreal life of painted face and mimic costume, its immoral influences and suggestions, its remoteness from the true world of noble action and sincere utterance.*[91]

This sonnet runs, in part, "Why should false painting imitate his cheek / And steal dead seeing of his living hue? / Why should poor beauty indirectly seek / Roses of shadow, since his rose is true?"[92] Personality, finally, merely confirms the superiority of the poet to the visual artist and the writer to his collaborator. Literature is the engagement and revelation of "the true world," with painting no more than the "unreal life" of mimicry and "painted" faces. "Mr W. H.," like *Dorian Gray,* argues out this competition between word and image, and Wilde's two prose works contribute to the late-nineteenth-century meditation on the visual and its limits. For him, visual representation cannot succeed in registering the world directly in the way that much contemporary English visual and literary culture hoped. Portraiture here becomes the limit case, a testing of the claims made for the visual through the contesting medium of language.

Personality and Ekphrasis

The crux of Wilde's repudiation of the visual is his assertion that reality, whether conceived as the heart of personality or more directly, is not available to visual knowledge. Only language can penetrate to the "true rose" beneath the surface of the world; painting, in the end, gives only the surface, however hungrily the eye seeks for meaning in it. Wilde denies the channel connecting the world to the "self-identical" image of the visual work. The blockage of meaning in this process comes about through the insertion of personality between reality and the work of art. Dorian Gray's personality proves in the end to exceed the representation provided by the portrait. The analytical confusion of the novel's denouement asserts the visual representation's inability to absorb all experience and all meaning. Willie Hughes, conversely, is presented as an absent personality around whom a great deal of representation clusters—all of it false. He is only the mouthpiece of the voices—Shakespeare's, Erskine's, the narrator's, Wilde's—who try to speak through him, and he resists as an object of *visual* desire the meanings they wish to find in him. It is, from another perspective, the same point made in *Dorian Gray:* visuality cannot see beneath the personality that blocks its capacity to find meaning.

If these issues were the frequent subtext of debate between Wilde and Ricketts during the years of their intimacy, they also feature in the position Ricketts took up in his own attempt to think through the desire for visual priority active in his own biography and aesthetics. This effort is most clearly visible in his writings on art. In this section, I look at the way in which Ricketts's ekphraseis play out these issues and provide an answer to the challenge to the visual that Wilde had offered in his works of the 1890s. Issues of the personality once again turn out to be central—in this case, to the management of visuality in ekphrasis.

In 1903, Ricketts gave this account of Titian's *Bacchanal* (1523–25, fig. 51) in his book *The Prado:*[93]

On the hill-top we see the grapes crushed beneath the weight of a Polyphemus-like figure: from the grapes issues the rivulet of wine which is the central motive of the work. By this sit two fair Venetians: the fairer one leans towards her companion, and from their hands, a pipe has slipped. Crouched at her feet, with his hands clasping her very ankles, is the brown ardent figure of a man who turns towards the other revellers, who are all absorbed—one in the wine he holds in a crystal flask against the sky; whilst others, wrapped in the mazes of a dance, move at once passionate and listless. . . . Beyond, the vines flash white among the trees at the horizon, and the season and the hour ripen. The love of beauty emanates from the very motive and substance of this work, as the perfume emanates from the flesh of a peach or the cells in a bunch of violets.[94]

This can serve as a good example of the poetic mode of Ricketts's ekphrasis as it appears in his books of art criticism and throughout his journals and diaries.[95] The perspective from which the *Bacchanal* is viewed grows broader, and Ricketts's language more heightened and poetic, as the painting is conducted from its own impenetrability and silence toward his verbal interpretation of it:

Yet regardless of . . . the revel, we have the abstracted figure of the bacchante asleep—white, motionless, and entranced, dominating the design: the blood may seem to mantle to a face, the wine rush into the hollow cavern of a cup: let Silenus gobble his wine, the singer or the dancer continue thus for ever; whilst this canvas lasts the painter and the art-lover will wonder at this master-piece of the heyday of art . . . this symbol of a time when strength and beauty were one, when life and art were one, and time and change themselves were viewed as guests at a revel.[96]

Ricketts, we might say, seems to perceive no gap between the words that he uses to describe the *Bacchanal* and the painting itself. He writes his rapt, poetic conjurations of Titian's works out of a certainty about both the meaning of the

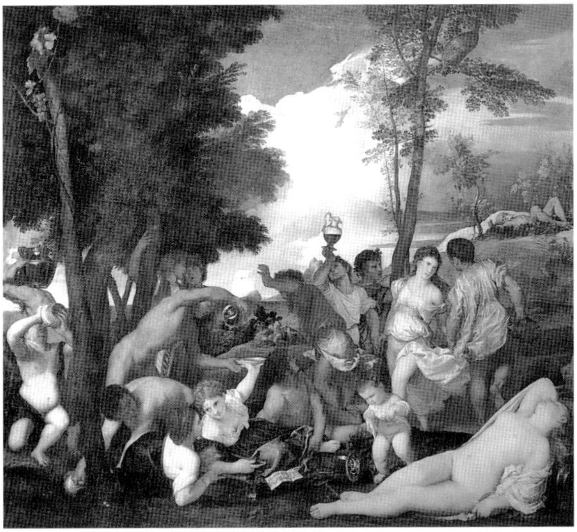

FIGURE 51. Titian, *Bacchanal*, 1523–25

paintings and the status of the sensibility—his own—that translates them into prose. He sees the passion and tenacity of observation that he brings to the work as a straightforward medium through which the painting can be conducted directly to the reader's apprehension. In fact, the case is more complex than this, and we can begin to see how by noticing that most of Ricketts's comments on works of art he sees or considers important in discussing a particular artist are neither ekphrastic nor strictly evaluative in this way.

In contrast to his poetic mode, Ricketts often wields a more prosaic, technical, and connoisseurial scheme of analysis that most commonly amounts to a judgment on the degree to which the painting has been subjected to restoration or neglect and has suffered because of it. This interest is partly the result of Ricketts's painful self-education as a painter—his training as a student was confined to wood engraving and graphic media—but more generally of his belief that modern work should take its place in a tradition, and contemporary artists learn from the painting of the old masters.[97] This technical evaluation is tied to confident, forthright attributions: "the Sitting portrait of Charles V. is almost entirely repainted by Rubens. We [Ricketts and Shannon] had imagined that the landscape was by Rubens but were not prepared for the rest."[98] It is this ability to judge the state of the physical fabric of a picture and to pronounce on its authorship and additions that Ricketts usually refers to when he uses the word "criticism," and he sees it as a central pillar of his task as a commentator and connoisseur. But the image of a painting it conjures up is a strange one: "It is curious that so damaged a work [as this Titian] can still retain a certain splendour from afar off. We think portions of the . . . sky[,] . . . the Virgin, large portions of the robes of the priests are still by T. . . . Some of the damaged male heads look well, but the picture should be viewed only as a map."[99]

Ricketts's descriptions conjure up a schematic outline of the painting, technical and—except in the indignation he often feels against restorers he considers malicious or incompetent—impersonal. His commentaries of this kind are themselves more "maps" of the pictures than evocations of them, descriptions in which value is assumed rather than asserted. Ricketts's remarks on value in the journals—"charming little pictures"; "an adorable picture"; "a marvel of invention"—seem merely to occupy the interstices of these technical maps.[100] This emphasis on technical description elevates connoisseurship, which might be thought to depend on individual sensibility, to the level of a neutral undertaking. It is a question of judgment, but judgment based on impersonal criteria.[101]

This is a familiar situation. Ricketts finds himself still struggling with the issues of reality and representation that have formed the focus of the argument so far. For, operating with both unmediation and personality as central aspects of his thinking, the presence of the mediating personality of the artist-commentator still threatens to undo and disallow the claim for direct access to truth and meaning. The anxiety this continues to generate is clearly signaled in the style and tenor of Ricketts's verbal description in his writings on art. What might seem surprising at first—the widespread evacuation of personality from judgment in Ricketts's commentary—becomes comprehensible when set in the context of his attempt to negotiate a delicate ideological situation. His "technical" mode of criticism means that Ricketts's sensibility is confirmed: it is focused on a practice that is at once susceptible to impersonal corroboration (at least in theory) and intensely individual, because it depends on personal talent for its successful execution. In effect, the problem of personality is mitigated in Ricketts's writing by means of the framework of technical evaluation.

It is only when the mapping of technical information breaks down as a means of plotting value that Ricketts has recourse to evoking the work and its affect through ekphrasis. This is accompanied by a certain degree of resistance. Ricketts knows that as soon as ekphrasis is introduced, the role of the individual sensibility in forming (and not merely reporting) value begins to command attention. The process of recourse and resistance can be observed in his account of the painting by Velasquez now called *Las Hilanderas* or *The Fable of Arachne.*[102] Ricketts begins by introducing and then quickly abandoning his technical criticism: "Recent cleaning has given a certain hardness to the green drapery of the foremost girl . . . recent cleaning and some older restoration have partly deprived the red curtain of its harmony and grain; this is all criticism dare venture, and the lover of pictures may spend minutes or hours in a fascinated study of the work."[103] There then follows, once the claims of criticism have been overtaken by those of the "art lover"—critical analysis, that is, overtaken by the experience of value—a prolonged ekphrastic description of the painting.

The room is full of implied light and the pulsing of it in the shadows themselves. Across the glimpse breaks a shaft of sunlight, blue at its birth, yellow at its contact with the wall, white a little lower down as it catches the floor. To the lover of painting the glimpse itself is a revelation of delicate art; the touches patter upon a surface in spangles of jewel-like paint; here the brush-work pulses continuously, there it sweeps with the sudden movement of a dragon-fly across a space, leaving a trail of glittering colour to thread the neutrals of some spot in which the colour has hitherto brooded.[104]

The revelation here is finally reduced to the intensely personal response, the "spangles of jewel-like paint" and the "glittering" journey of color across the painting's surface that Ricketts's ekphrasis can conjure from the work.

Elsewhere in *The Prado,* Ricketts denies the possibility of fully understanding *The Surrender of Breda*—to which he attributes high value, calling it "one of the finest pictures" in existence, and "the best, perhaps the only, historical picture in the world"—by means of a technical analysis. He writes that "it seems hopeless to explain the science in composition, the invention and resource that this picture reveals; in face of such a result, what does it matter if part of the effect is due to a consummate stage-craft in alternating reposeful or elaborated surfaces."[105] In a parallel moment in *Titian,* Ricketts pushes the argument further by suggesting that formal analysis may be perverted to discredit works that, although they are in theory technically lacking, in fact achieve value in ways not susceptible to such analysis. He repudiates what he takes to be the popular denigration of Titian's *Assunta* on the grounds that its composition is banal:

A subtle and insidious form of attack may be made by analysing the mechanism of the work, since all things may be dissected, and be shown as an aggregate of various quantities of very unequal value. . . . But the fact remains, that with a few obvious elements of design, and a few generalised elements of emotional appeal, and by some indwelling element of rhythm, and a great sincerity in the use of these things, Titian has achieved an effect which he was unable to repeat, and which has baffled imitation.[106]

In this way Ricketts attempts to delay ekphrasis by defining value as a mystery, a force outside the true description of technical analysis. Ekphrasis confesses

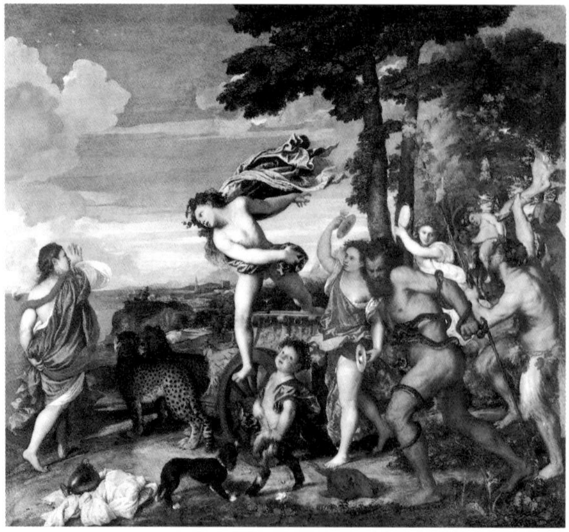

FIGURE 52. Titian, *Bacchus and Ariadne*, 1523–24

the personal interest that technical description displaces, and its introduction is resisted accordingly. But the deferral of value, which is always just out of the reach of technical analysis, ensures that he cannot avoid it. When he does resort to ekphrasis in order to assert value, Ricketts does so unequivocally.

Poetic ekphrasis of Ricketts's type splits the attention of the reader, switching it from the quality of the work to the quality of the description, so that the ability of the writer to see and communicate value becomes the center of attention. This is Ricketts's account of the *Bacchus and Ariadne* (1523–24, fig. 52) in the National Gallery in London, keyed to an interpretation of Titian that sees his work as valuable because it offers an intensification of experience dependent on Titian's personality:

We owe to Titian the vision of the leaping Bacchus with his streaming hair, and the rout of fauns who stamp and chafe in a trance, active, yet held in check by some charm of the god, that rare and ardent Spirit of Delight, who passion has flashed up for Ariadne, who turns fascinated in her flight, though Theseus' ship is still a wing-like speck against the sky. The stars in her crown become lit in the blue where the great clouds roll up and away, and the sea pauses and breaks without foam upon the ground, where shell and moss lie close together. A wild white rose of Sharon creeps among the grass, the iris and the columbine, the wild vine and the jasmine—each brings with its associated beauty an element of intimacy to a scene of splendour and passion at a crisis.[107]

Ricketts arranges the figures of the painting within a verbal equivalent of the pictorial space. His authorial voice assumes the role of director of the painting's action, not just its interpreter; he positions the protagonists and selects and elaborates on their gestures. Elements that are details in the painting—the flowers, the crown of stars—become central in the ekphrasis; elements that loom large in the painting—the elaborate *contrapposto* of Ariadne's body swivelled in torsion between the sea and the land—are signaled in the text only by the slightest of verbal signs. What has occurred here is the replacement of a technical "map," which plots the physical fabric of a painting as a stand-in for value, with an interpretive evocation of the qualities in which that value inheres. But ekphrasis effectively drives a wedge between the value of the work and its evocation in a different medium. The very process of interpretation replaces the work with a simulacrum of itself located between the painting and the experience of it. The space opened up by this strategy is then occupied by the individual sensibility of the writer, whose powers of description and ability to conjure the painting's value become the focus of attention. Ricketts retreats from the possibility of communicating value through criticism in a technical or impersonal way that would grant it—in his terms—a degree of credibility, turning instead to an evocation that depends upon his own powers as a writer, the poetic, heightened language and the ability to conjure a vivid scene. The move is therefore away from value as such and toward the mediation of value through a verbal analogy.

The problem here is that Ricketts is still faced with the usurpation of the place of art by selfhood and personality. This threatens his position and is the source of his anxiety. Ekphrasis declares too openly the function of the individual sensibility and thus impedes its structural purpose in defining a position within the art world. It threatens to reveal, not deny, the implication of the visual in mediation. Once the role of the interpreter in forming value in the work becomes visible through ekphrasis, the possibility of asserting the role of the self as the sensitive reporter of an absolute value collapses. With that possibility goes the art-political role in advancing a career of the self as defined by the fineness of its perception of value (to which it alone has adequate access). To this degree, full-blown ekphrasis in Ricketts is the sign of anxiety about value, not the expression of certainty about it.

In this context I want to return to the ekphrastic description of Titian's *Bacchanal* that I quoted at the start of this section. The most striking thing about this text as a reading of a painting is the degree to which the writing calls attention to itself and replaces the aim of neutrality in description with the assertion of its own qualities of sensibility (quite self-consciously, I think). The passage is full of the declared particularities of language—"the brown ardent figure of a man," "as the perfume emanates from the flesh of a peach," "the blood may seem to mantle to a face." The static tableau of a visual medium is unfolded, piecemeal, in the form of a narrative sequence. A voice emerges and moves very quickly from a rather staid account ("we see the grapes") to an impassioned evocation of the painting, and hence to an exalted moralizing on the good life of sixteenth-century Venice. The effect of all this is to make it seem as if the value of the scene—as an object of "wonder" for "the painter and the art-lover"—in fact applies not to the painting but to the text itself.

This is the essential problematic compressed into a single passage.[108] On the one hand, we have Ricketts describing the power of "this master-piece of the hey-day of art." He is simply the voice, the vehicle, the finely attuned sensibility through which the object itself speaks directly to us. On the other, the vehicle has come to dominate the message. The passage is far more a reworking than an interpretation or description; the distance between image and word has opened up a space into which Titian's *Bacchanal* has fallen and out of which a "Bacchanal" by Ricketts has emerged. This is the *representation* of value with which ekphrasis replaces the value it wishes to promote and through which the voice of the critic rings louder than that of the object. But if the form of Ricketts's text blatantly dramatizes the issue, the content seizes on this crux and disarms it by reading its own deconstruction back into the enacted value of the work.

Ricketts's interpretation describes the painting as a metaphor for the relation between art and the spectator, and in so doing, it blurs the location of value in that pairing. The "dominating" figure in the *Bacchanal* is the sleeping maenad, but Ricketts deals with her only after the remainder of the action has been described. This bacchante, "abstracted . . . and entranced," is the one figure of inaction in the painting, the *passive* center of the surrounding intensity of event, from whose "motionless" image its meaning flows. The bacchante casts the stasis of "beauty" over the scene; she consigns contingency and relativity, "time and change," to the status of "guests at a revel." She is the "symbol" of an identity of self and object—a "truce between nature and the world"—that Ricketts says gives value to the painting. The motionless bacchante governs the silent unity of the painting as it knits together "life and art [as] one."

This amounts to a reassertion of the identity of critic and object. The passive role of the observing spectator allows the meaning of the work to emerge. The spectator here is represented by the bacchante, asleep, "abstracted," "entranced," blind, and hence unable to interfere with the work—simply its channel, merely *reporting* the action of the painting that therefore itself carries the burden of meaning. The critic-spectator is simultaneously full of personality and theorized as an empty vehicle that the values of the work simply use in order to communicate their essential qualities in a different medium. That structuring of meaning is not an assertion but a *denial* of the spectator's role in forming meaning. It is barely a gesture toward interpretation; rather, it is what I have suggested we might think of as the unmediation through which the value of the work passes, granting status both to its origin and to the sensitive channel of which it makes use. The passage asserts its own desired state of things, in which the status of the object is identical to that of the viewer and in which the strength of sensibility of the fine observer guarantees his place as part of the same class of beings as the work of art he evokes.

I am arguing that the passage asserts the opposite of what it enacts, and that by internalizing that contradiction it is able to promote the self and to deny it all at the same time. The identity of self and art, of perception and execution, of "life and art" or of "strength and beauty," in Ricketts's words, reasserts the value of the self and makes it a necessary constituent of art. It promotes a fiction in which the role of the individual interpretive personality is acknowledged but reformulated so as to deny itself rather than the "reality" that is its ideological freight.

The centrality of the idea of the self as a governing principle and its importance in maintaining a position within the art world allow Ricketts to capitalize on what at first seems a disabling position. From this point of view, the distance opened up between the value of the artwork and the representation of that value in art-critical language can become a source of strength. The appropriation of the work in Ricketts's ekphrastic commentary, its transformation into the representation of his own reading of its value, then functions to reinforce his assertion of his own personality as an art-political strategy. It becomes a demonstration of his own sensibility, but one that both he and his audience can connive in ignoring even as it takes effect. That this was clear enough at the time is signaled by Laurence Binyon's reaction to the publication of *The Prado*. He wrote to Ricketts that he had "read it with delight," but the cause of this appreciation is the character of Ricketts's evocation as a writer: "surely a poet was lost in you! On every page there is some phrase that leaps out and is alive and gives one a new sense of the matter in hand. . . . The whole book is so wise and witty." In contrast, his comments on what Ricketts actually says are brief and rather dry: "I liked the bit about Sarto, and what you say of Raphael, and the chapter on Rubens."[109] What is *represented* in Ricketts's ekphrasis is less the value of the work itself than the triumph of sensibility in the critic that allows him to locate, conjure, and communicate that value to his readers. But that sensibility is recuperated and remade to appear as the central demonstration of the strength of art itself and hence the authenticity of the self whose account of value can transmit it, unmediated, to the world.

I think that these ideas were already in play in some form when Ricketts designed and illustrated Wilde's poem *The Sphinx* in 1894. The questions of imagination and fictionality that Wilde used to disparage the visual are directly addressed by his text. Ricketts's aggressive collaboration and his resistance to Wilde's denigration of the visual depend upon a passivity that he later focused more clearly, figuring it as unmediation. That passivity is forced on Ricketts here, however, as clashing artistic personalities—Ricketts, Whistler, Wilde—negotiate status and competition within the abstracted arena of the artwork.

The Sphinx

The Sphinx had a long history for Wilde. He seems to have begun it while he was still a student, returning to it at intervals until its eventual publication in 1894. Even then, he was contemplating changes until the very last moment. He wrote to Ricketts when the text and illustrations were already in proof asking for a set so that he could consider adding more stanzas.[110] This possibility of expansion is not inappropriate, as the character of the text is aggregative rather than clearly argumentative. *The Sphinx* is about the pleasures and terrors of the imagination. It begins with the speaking voice—a student—reflecting on imagination through the central conceit of the sphinx as an embodiment of mystery: "In a corner of my room for longer than my fancy thinks / A beautiful and silent Sphinx has watched me through the shifting gloom."[111] Most of the subsequent poem consists of an attempt by the narrative voice to pin down the mysteriousness of the sphinx by means of a series of speculations about her possible past history. The characteristic phrase is a conditional beginning with a speculative inquiry—"did you?"

> *Or did you while the earthen skiffs dropped down the grey Nilotic flats*
> *At twilight and the flickering bats flew round the temple's triple glyphs*
> *Steal to the border of the bar and swim across the silent lake*
> *And slink into the vault and make the pyramid your lúpanar*

This is declaredly a fiction. The pleasures of the imagination, along with its capacity to realize a world at some distance from what Wilde called "modernity of subject-matter," are played out.[112] The sphinx is solicited and teased by the imaginative speculation she generates in the narrator.

Lift up your large black satin eyes which are like cushions where one sinks!
Fawn at my feet fantastic Sphinx! And sing me all your memories!

After a prolonged immersion in these fictions, the narrator becomes sickened by them. He dismisses the Sphinx as "loathsome mystery!" and enjoins her to "leave me to my crucifix, / Whose pallid burden sick with pain, watches the world with wearied eyes." But he finds this unsatisfactory, too, for his Christ, in the final line, "weeps for every soul that dies, and weeps for every soul in vain."

Richard Ellmann has commented at length on Wilde's capacity to define himself through paradox and apparently opposed positions.[113] This free play with personality provides a way to approach Wilde's poem. Ernest, in "The Critic as Artist," efficiently describes Wilde's own practice as he says, "Gilbert, you treat the world as if it were a crystal ball. You hold it in your hand, and reverse it to please a wilful fancy. You do nothing but rewrite history." Moreover, Ernest employs the very term ("wilfulness") that the Michael Fields reported Wilde using to describe "truth's" probable attitude toward him.[114] The final stanzas of *The Sphinx,* which seem to conduct us away from the now worthless imagination, are in fact only another statement of the power of that imagination to "reverse" the "world" at will. Wilde's gesture toward a Christian solution is a self-consciously fictional one, a paradox that demonstrates the power of "fancy" more than that of Christ.

Wilde's *Sphinx* thus functions as both a demonstration and a consideration of autonomy. Fictionality—the capacity of art to create an alternative world to that of praxis—is its theme and its status as artwork. It is an icon of autonomy and an implicit repudiation by that fact of the possibility of the work's possessing use value within a commodified art world. The problem is that the possibility of an autonomous practice is immediately challenged by the act of design, which brings the previously "abstract" text into existence as a physical object—a book. Every illustration ruptures the autonomy of the text that it supposedly underwrites by demonstrating unequivocally that what claims to be autonomous has become collaborative. The constitution of *The Sphinx* thus mirrors the unresolved difficulty in articulating art-political relationships that Ricketts suffered after Wilde's death and that haunted the constrained silences and embarrassments of their final meetings. Ricketts's design and illustrations for the book respond to this fraught position (and the fine balance of false consciousness that seems required to hold it together) not by an explicit or implicit attack but through a silent struggle *not* to attack, *not* to undercut the autonomy of fiction by the very presence of another hand in the production of the material object—*The Sphinx* as published. The resistance in their collaboration is therefore not simply an attempt to reformulate meanings laid down by the senior partner, though that certainly plays a role, but also an attempt to resist, on behalf of a shared aesthetic, the deconstruction of autonomy that collaboration brings into play as a possibility.[115]

In the arcane system of meaning that this engenders, Ricketts has a number of areas of activity at his disposal. There are ten illustrations, including the title page that occupies an unusual position within the "build" (Ricketts's favored term) of the book.[116] In addition, there are the front and rear covers and the linking spine, the placing of the text on the page and in relation to the arrangement of the illustrations, and the font in which it is printed. Together, all these design decisions create a material form for Wilde's text that must support that text's claims for itself. At first sight, Ricketts's vivid foregrounding of the book as physical object seems to make this difficult, as he declares his design and illustration equal or dominant to the text he is working with. The cover (fig. 53) introduces figures and details (the cowled woman on the reverse) with no place in the text. There is a small "CR" monogram in a cartouche at bottom left of the front, but there is no mention either here or on the spine of Wilde's name or the title. Inside, there is no conventional title page (fig. 54). Instead, a full-page illustration faces the first page of text, and the standard information—author, title, and publication details—is arranged around the illustration without emphasis. The subsequent openings then order the words in such a way that the accepted relationship between text and image is often reversed: design and illustration occupy the reading eye more easily than the poem (fig. 55). Three-color printing, large areas of white space, run-ons, and text apparently arranged to suit large-scale images rather than the other way about all contribute to this reversal.[117]

Ricketts is, we might say, "resisting" the text he is collaborating with in an obvious way and asserting his work's claims to autonomy against those of Wilde's. But this is deceptive. The conflicting understandings of fictionality and the imagination held by Wilde and Ricketts reveal themselves in *The Sphinx* as a complicated relationship of and to fidelity. Wilde conceived of illustration as an underlining and reinforcing of the autonomy and power of the text, and he seems to have been untroubled in doing so because of his very firm conviction that visual art was inferior to literature. This confident attitude about the relative merits of text and image allowed Wilde to encourage a freedom in the illustrations that otherwise seems surprising. The Michael Fields recorded one of Wilde's conversations with them: "He was delicious on the illustrations [to *A*

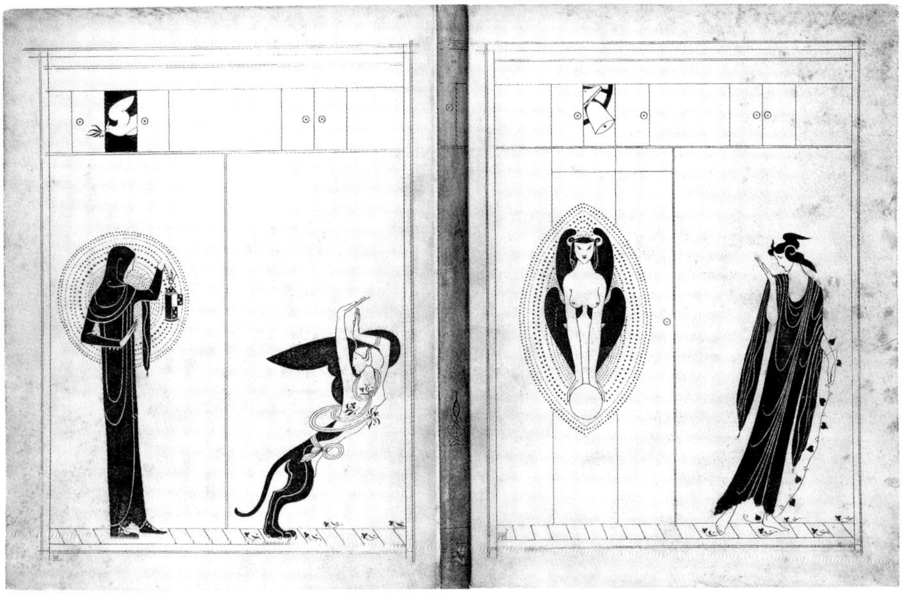

FIGURE 53. Charles Ricketts, cover, Oscar Wilde, *The Sphinx* (1894)

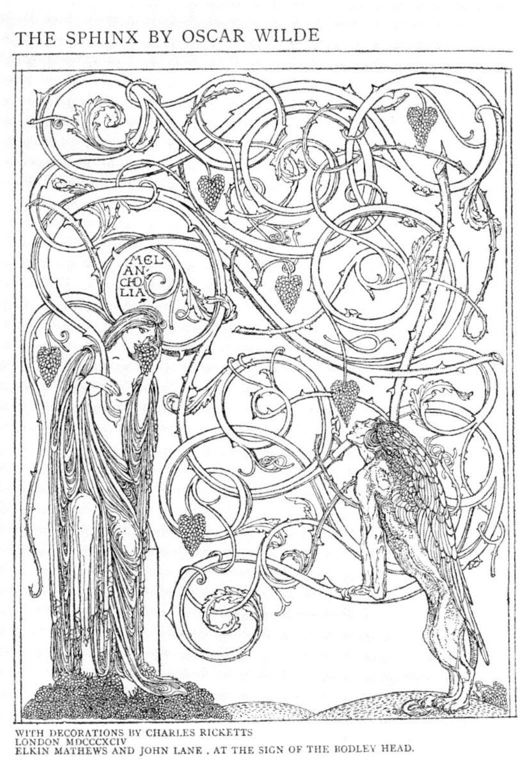

FIGURE 54. Charles Ricketts, title page, Oscar Wilde, *The Sphinx* (1894)

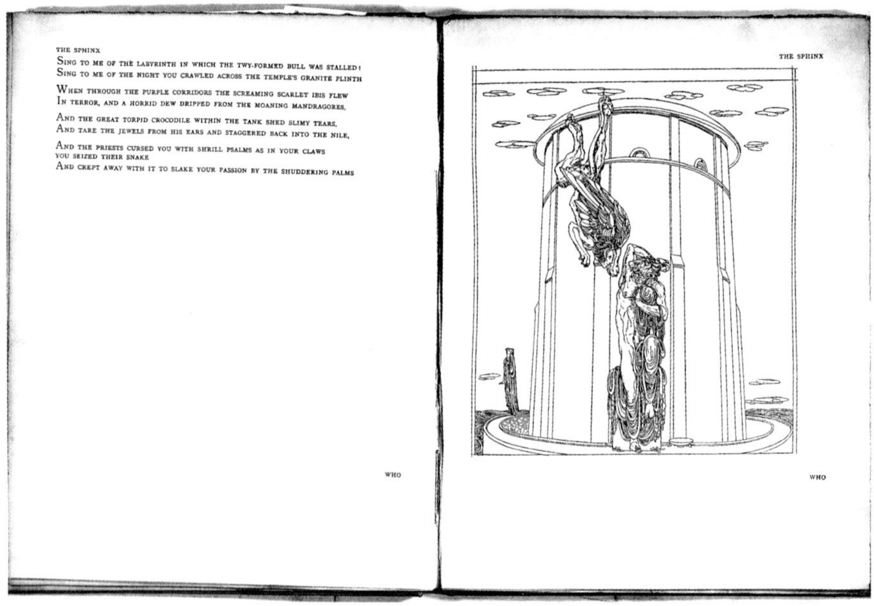
THE SPHINX

SING TO ME OF THE LABYRINTH IN WHICH THE TWY-FORMED BULL WAS STALLED!
SING TO ME OF THE NIGHT YOU CRAWLED ACROSS THE TEMPLE'S GRANITE PLINTH

WHEN THROUGH THE PURPLE CORRIDORS THE SCREAMING SCARLET IBIS FLEW
IN TERROR, AND A HORRID DEW DRIPPED FROM THE MOANING MANDRAGORES,

AND THE GREAT TORPID CROCODILE WITHIN THE TANK SHED SLIMY TEARS,
AND TARE THE JEWELS FROM HIS EARS AND STAGGERED BACK INTO THE NILE,

AND THE PRIESTS CURSED YOU WITH SHRILL PSALMS AS IN YOUR CLAWS
YOU SEIZED THEIR SNAKE
AND CREPT AWAY WITH IT TO SLAKE YOUR PASSION BY THE SHUDDERING PALMS

WHO

THE SPHINX

WHO

FIGURE 55. Charles Ricketts, "Sing to Me of the Labyrinth," Oscar Wilde, *The Sphinx* (1894)

House of Pomegranates], that are not taken from anything in the book, only suggested by it—for he holds that literature is more graphic than art, and should therefore never be illustrated in itself, only by what it evokes."[118] The text of *The Sphinx* is explicitly and programmatically distanced from reality. It states (or implies) that art should concern itself with what "The Decay of Lying" calls "the marvels of art," the "calling forth" of the creatures of its imagination:[119]

Art finds her own perfection within, and not outside of, herself. She is not to be judged by any external standard of resemblance. She is a veil, rather than a mirror. She has flowers that no forests know of, birds that no woodland possesses. She makes and unmakes many worlds, and can draw the moon from heaven with scarlet thread. Hers are the "forms more real than living man," and hers the great archetypes of which things that have existence are but unfinished copies. Nature has, in her eyes, no laws, no uniformity. She can work miracles at her will, and when she calls monsters from the deep they will come.[120]

Wilde displays an antagonistic relationship to fidelity in *The Sphinx*. He explores the "calling forth" by art of the creatures of its imagination. Ricketts, as illustrator, is enjoined by Wilde to depict what is "suggested" by the text—that is, to add to the body of the work a supplement that will *confirm* the text's status as a

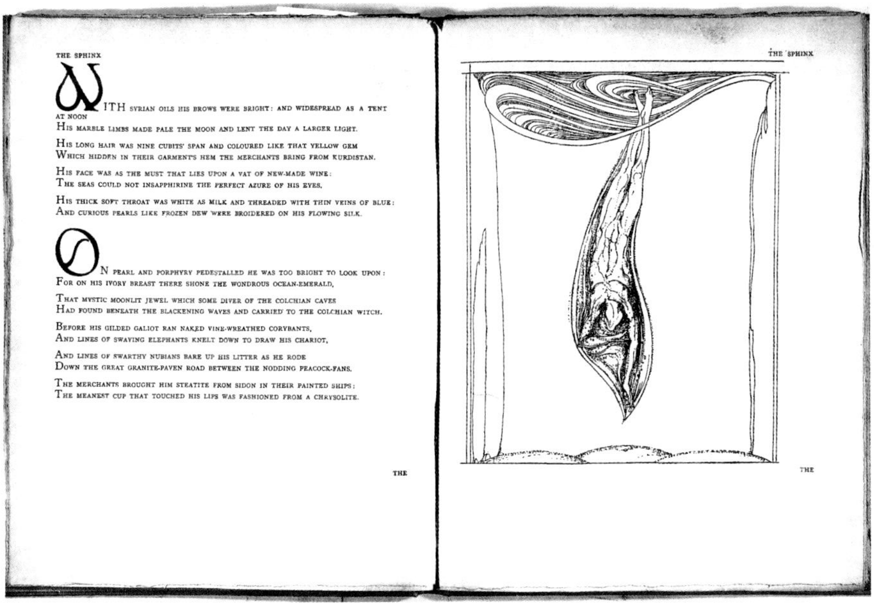

THE SPHINX

WITH SYRIAN OILS HIS BROWS WERE BRIGHT: AND WIDESPREAD AS A TENT AT NOON
HIS MARBLE LIMBS MADE PALE THE MOON AND LENT THE DAY A LARGER LIGHT.

HIS LONG HAIR WAS NINE CUBITS' SPAN AND COLOURED LIKE THAT YELLOW GEM
WHICH HIDDEN IN THEIR GARMENT'S HEM THE MERCHANTS BRING FROM KURDISTAN.

HIS FACE WAS AS THE MUST THAT LIES UPON A VAT OF NEW-MADE WINE:
THE SEAS COULD NOT INSAPPHIRINE THE PERFECT AZURE OF HIS EYES.

HIS THICK SOFT THROAT WAS WHITE AS MILK AND THREADED WITH THIN VEINS OF BLUE:
AND CURIOUS PEARLS LIKE FROZEN DEW WERE BROIDERED ON HIS FLOWING SILK.

ON PEARL AND PORPHYRY PEDESTALLED HE WAS TOO BRIGHT TO LOOK UPON:
FOR ON HIS IVORY BREAST THERE SHONE THE WONDROUS OCEAN-EMERALD,

THAT MYSTIC MOONLIT JEWEL WHICH SOME DIVER OF THE COLCHIAN CAVES
HAD FOUND BENEATH THE BLACKENING WAVES AND CARRIED TO THE COLCHIAN WITCH.

BEFORE HIS GILDED GALIOT RAN NAKED VINE-WREATHED CORYBANTS,
AND LINES OF SWAYING ELEPHANTS KNELT DOWN TO DRAW HIS CHARIOT,

AND LINES OF SWARTHY NUBIANS BARE UP HIS LITTER AS HE RODE
DOWN THE GREAT GRANITE-PAVEN ROAD BETWEEN THE NODDING PEACOCK-FANS.

THE MERCHANTS BROUGHT HIM STEATITE FROM SIDON IN THEIR PAINTED SHIPS:
THE MEANEST CUP THAT TOUCHED HIS LIPS WAS FASHIONED FROM A CHRYSOLITE.

THE

FIGURE 56. Charles Ricketts, "Some Diver of the Colchian Caves," Oscar Wilde, *The Sphinx* (1894)

work of independence because fictional, by demonstrating on its *own* account a freedom from the "external standard" and summoning its own creatures from the "deeps" of the imagination, always with the understanding that the visual supplement is inferior by nature and subordinate in its role. Read like this, the characteristics of the illustrations and design that I have pointed out actually validate Ricketts's fidelity to Wilde's text. The visual work demonstrates and hence confirms the freedom and fictionality of the imagination and the autonomy of artistic practice, although always in a subordinate position.

But Ricketts's apparent independence is not all it seems. In fact, when we read the illustrations together with the text, we notice the connection of images and words. Ricketts does depart from the text in a multitude of minor ways, but the full-page illustration still depends on *The Sphinx,* not on the free play of the imagination but on fidelity to the subject set by the text (fig. 56). By taking seriously his role as illustrator, Ricketts keeps to his position that the function of art is to reveal what is present, not to create what is not. All of the illustrations—once we move beyond the title page—are faithful to the imagination that Wilde sets out for his illustrator, and it is this "resistance" to "suggestion" or "evocation" that was responsible for Wilde's dissatisfaction with the book: "For [*The Sphinx*] I made what I still consider my best work as an illustrator. Wilde's verdict on my . . . designs was different. 'No, my dear Ricketts, your drawings are not of your best. You have seen them through your intellect, not your temperament'" (Ricketts, *Recollections,* 38). According to Wilde, then, Ricketts had worked through an "intellectual" registration of the text in another medium, its illustration—not a dependent but separate "evocation" through Ricketts's personality, his "temperament," the sign of his own supportive autonomy.[121] Paradoxically, the moment of resistance in the collaboration of *The Sphinx* is the moment of greatest fidelity to the text, not the moment of departure from it. It is also the moment of the willed abnegation of Ricketts's personality. Like the unmediation represented by the bacchante asleep in his ekphrasis on Titian's *Bacchanal,* Ricketts's assertion of the visual's power revolves around the denial of the role of the self, the artist's personality. His apparent surrender to Wilde's text in this way marks the moment of his triumph.

Ricketts's illustrations and design, which shuttle between fidelity and independence—which declare on the cover and title page the right to assert the visual over the written, and which maintain, once inside, a faithfulness to the text—register the impasse created when text/image collaboration takes place under the rule of autonomy. The "portrait" of Wilde Ricketts draws is mired in the paradoxes and complexities of autonomy and personality within the commodified art market of the late nineteenth century. Ricketts's biographical and art-political ambivalence toward Wilde, the senior partner, powerfully motivates the visual work. But this resistance is caught in the same net of paradox as the "autonomous" illustrations and design. Ricketts must reinforce the idea of autonomy and creativity against the challenge—the necessary resistance of collaboration. It is in his own interests to do so. This means, though, that he also ends up reinforcing Wilde's position, which he wants to resist, for asserting Ricketts against Wilde explicitly ruptures the claims to autonomous practice and uniqueness that must support that assertion. Ricketts can only win by losing. If he declares himself an "autonomous" practitioner "evoking" what is "suggested" by the text, then by that action he also resigns himself to dependence on and subservience to Wilde and Wilde's aesthetic. His independent position in the art world can only be asserted by denying it. Illustration as artistic practice, like collaboration as artistic politics, is simultaneously attractive and dangerous.

No wonder, then, that in this context, Ricketts cannot focus or articulate his relationship to Wilde by 1900 when he hears of his death (that final confirmation of autonomy), nor even by the late 1920s, when he attempts, in crisis, to reevaluate the key events and relationships of his own long life. I began this chapter with an instance of the negotiation of repressed material in Ricketts's diaries. The paradoxes that cluster around their collaboration have frozen Ricketts's feelings, and they return in 1900 as displacement: "I dreamt all last night about Oscar Wilde," he writes in the diaries. He is only "vaguely conscious that something has happened." Hardly surprising, then, that his memoir of Wilde in *Recollections* comes buried under several layers of distancing fictionality. Ironically, he has to create his memoir partly out of the imagination—the invention of another self in Jean Paul Raymond—to allow the inarticulable to be spoken and simultaneously distanced or denied.

If Ricketts represents a late Romantic response to the issues I examine here, his particular branch of symbolist Aestheticism was not the only option available to English artists and thinkers at the end of the century. In the next chapter, I shall look at the ways in which modernist art emerged out of a complex of different types of art practice and reflected on the power of the visual to deal with its subject matter as it did so. In Chapter 5, I shall return to Ricketts and seek to connect him to English modernism after 1910.

Walter Sickert

SURFACE AND MODERNITY

In this chapter I want to look closely at two key moments in the career of Walter Sickert, who, between the 1880s and the First World War, played a central role in the evolution of a self-consciously modernist art in England. Sickert looked both forward, as a strong influence on the Vorticist group and other English modernists, and back, as an artist for whom tradition and a connection to the art of the nineteenth-century past were essential components of a vital modern painting. In the first section of the chapter, I look at the music-hall subjects that Sickert produced in three series from about 1887 to 1907, and I argue that they carry forward the imperative to depict the realities of modern experience that I have traced in the argument so far. But Sickert was a pupil of Whistler: I also propose that Sickert's work sees the advent of a new type of self-consciousness about the claim that paint can reveal the world to its spectators. His music-hall paintings, then, amount to a meditation on the capacity of paint itself to act as a means of investigating and diagnosing modernity. Sickert confronts the problem of paint's adequacy as a form of knowledge and explores the implications of this question for the registration of contemporary experience.[1] In the process, he confronts as well the role of personality as it had been reintroduced into paint by Whistler and as I have shown it operating in Ricketts and Wilde. Paint continues to serve as the expression of the artist's controlling self, but now under inauspicious circumstances. Responding to this situation, Sickert's paintwork both asserts and questions the grounds of his identity as an artist. In the second part of the chapter, I consider a later phase of Sickert's career and look at the paintings produced during the so-called Camden Town period of 1905–10. I trace a continuing working-through of the issues I have already raised, now complicated by a further reduction of the artist's authority and a troublesome acknowledgment of the insufficiency of the visual as a means to map the realities of modernity, which now threaten to escape from the control that paint—and the strong personality of the painter—promised to exert over it.

The London Impressionists

In 1889, Walter Sickert wrote an introduction to the catalogue of the "London Impressionists" show held at the Goupil Gallery in December of that year.[2] If we expect avant-garde works made during this period to be impelled by a desire to describe modern life explicitly at the level of manifest content, what he said there seems to require explanation.[3] The problem with the London Impressionists catalogue is that Sickert writes about a collection of paintings that appear to depict the contemporary scene as if they were perpetuating the protocols and concerns of Symbolism. In the catalogue, Sickert famously defined his Impressionism in this way:

Essentially and firstly it is not realism. It has no wish to record anything merely because it exists. It is not occupied in a struggle to make intensely real and solid the sordid or superficial details of the subjects it selects. It accepts, as the aim of the picture, what Edgar Allen Poe asserts to be the sole legitimate province of the poem, beauty. . . . It is, on the contrary, strong in the belief that for those who live in the most wonderful and complex city in the world, the most fruitful course of study lies in a persistent effort to render the magic and the poetry which they daily see around them.[4]

Sickert's repudiation of realism has often seemed disconcerting to later readers.[5] In part this is because of its final words, which claim that the means to achieve this rendering of magic and poetry are to be found "in all their perfection, not so much on the canvases that yearly line our official and unofficial shows . . . as on the walls of the National Gallery," an assertion that does not fit well into the conventional understanding of developments in nineteenth-century art.[6] But in part the statement seems odd because of the apparent disjunction between Sickert's language and the perceived subject matter of the show. Sickert's justification for the London Impressionists is not social realism or "the painting of modern life." It is couched in the language of Symbolism—"beauty," "magic," and "poetry"—and in invoking Poe it calls upon one of the arch-Symbolists of the English-language tradition. How are we to reconcile this account with the ambitions that seem to be embodied in works shown at the Goupil like Sidney Starr's *The City Atlas* (1889, fig. 57) or Sickert's *The Butcher's Shop* (1884, York City Art Gallery; Baron, cat. 21), let alone with the music-hall paintings that Sickert also showed? The catalogue introduction with its reminiscence of Whistler's "Ten O'Clock Lecture" seems to suggest a different and inappropriate principle of meaning for images that strike us as plainly about social realism.[7]

It is a mistake, in general, to accept Sickert's written or reported statements at face value. Nevertheless, in this case I think we would be wise to attend closely to what he says. We can understand Sickert's work as expressing a wider dialectic in English painting at the end of the nineteenth century—that

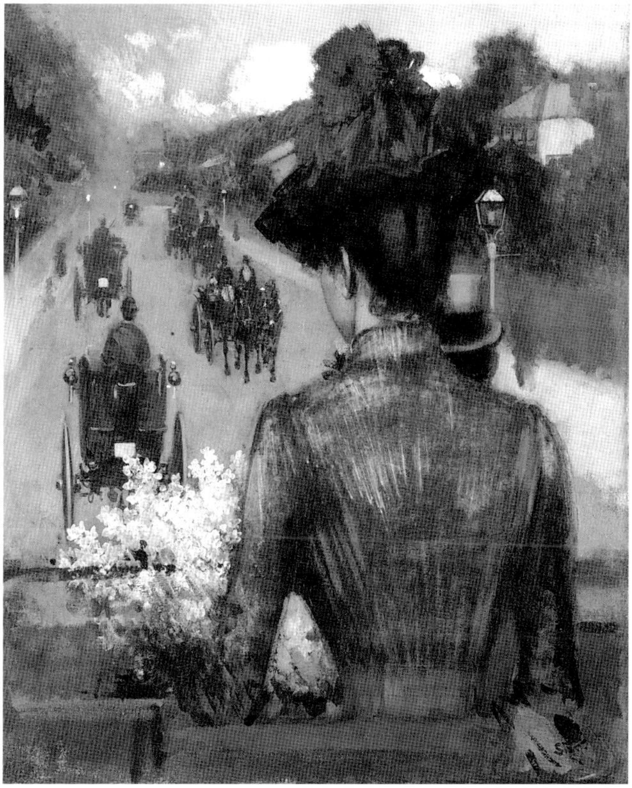

FIGURE 57. Sidney Starr, *The City Atlas*, 1889

between what we might call Symbolist and Realist modes of representation. In Sickert's case, the mutual influences and inheritances from these two intertwined strands in English art provided the material from which he constructed his own confrontation and analysis of modern experience.[8]

Despite recent attempts to subsume a wide range of practice under the portmanteau term "Symbolism," it remains true that English art in the late nineteenth century was a very broad church.[9] The monolithic implications of Symbolism are entirely misleading. By the end of the century, one heterogeneous wing of British painting was composed of artists concerned with the inherent or essential meaning of experience—and hence loosely Symbolist—but a broad array of Realist painters, also working in England, aimed to describe the appearance of the world in their art, whether as plein-air painters, Impressionists, or naturalists.[10] Both groups encompassed a multitude of subgroups, and many artists display characteristics that belong to apparently opposing camps. These options, then, are in fact best understood as points on a continuous range of possibilities. Individual artists frequently had connections to both ends of the spectrum, and many produced work that brought together apparently opposing ambitions and strategies.[11] It is certainly the case, for instance, that Whistler's apparently Symbolist influence is also Realist, feeding into the desire of artists to achieve an optical registration of the motif. Whistler's memory techniques, expressed in the famous nocturnal trips to fix a scene in the mind prior to painting in the studio, reflect a desire to pin down the realities of the subject as well as to transform them within the space of the canvas.[12]

If English art offered a spectrum of positions along the Symbolist-Realist axis (so much so that we might wish to disallow these terms or treat them skeptically), there were also genuinely different approaches to the question of how best to figure the character of reality in the work of art. I suggest that it is possible to use the terms "Symbolism" and "Realism" with some care, in this strictly limited sense, in order to define two influential positions on the question of representation. Both played crucial roles in the development of Sickert's account of modern experience in his art, but as linked positions oriented toward the same goal rather than as opposing forces to be set against each other in an absolute way.

Whistler's *Nocturnes* have been cited as "central statements of the Symbolist position" because of their artificiality and frank distance from reality.[13] But although a painting like *Nocturne in Blue and Silver—Chelsea* (see fig. 41) elides the contemporary elements of the scene in favor of a painterly self-sufficiency and the evocation of what Whistler called "poetry" and "palaces in the night," it nonetheless remains a contemporary, industrial, quintessentially modern scene, recognizable as a view across the Thames toward Chelsea.[14] In a parallel way, G. F. Watts's works certainly exemplify modes of Victorian painting that repudiated the claims of Realism, yet as we have seen, he conceived of his art as directly related to contemporary experience. In the case of a painting like *Mammon: Dedicated to His Worshippers* (see fig. 36), Watts refers to what he saw as the central failure of modern society, the fact that "prosperity has become our real god," that it offers little consolation or spiritual solace.[15] His figure of Death, too, pressing remorselessly across the threshold of a Victorian household in *Love and Death* (see fig. 39), brings questions about the meaning of existence forcefully into the contemporary world. Even his most remote works meant to intervene in the life of his time.

These paintings all derive from a concern with the character of modern experience but deal with it by attempting to find principles through which a more authentic meaning, a deeper truth, can be brought to bear. Symbolism seeks a representation that will access those aspects of existence and reality that it believes the dominant materialism of the nineteenth century covers over. Its most urgent impulses are those that aim to strip away the deceptive surface of experience and suggest or evoke a greater truth beneath. Modernity's surface, an account of its appearance and optical character, is repudiated in favor of the "beauty" that may be found within it. But, as I have argued, this act of revelation remains a way of responding to the contemporary. Watts's symbols of terror and sterility and Whistler's transformation of the London scene equally attribute significance to the contemporary themes and sites from which they begin. Symbolist representation, in the sense I am using it here, is committed to an analysis and understanding of modern experience, but it distrusts a surface account of the visual world as a means of achieving it. Symbolism proposes a deeper investigation and revelation of the conditions of experience than the surface can provide.

In previous chapters, I have discussed some of the ways in which Symbolist art of this type tackled the imperative to register modern experience. The advent of an art explicitly concerned with contemporary life and subjects nevertheless results in part from a shift of emphasis away from this Symbolist ambition—to make sense of the contemporary world by uncovering abstract or generalized truths that can substitute for it—to an ambition to comprehend the modern on its own terms. As previous chapters have shown, both ideas were present and interacted throughout the second half of the century. In the context of that history, artists like Sickert inherited a mode of painting distinct from Symbolism, one that attempted to transcribe and understand the character of modern life precisely by the cultivation of an art of the surface. Realist practice, in all its variety, proposed to pin down experience by replaying visual, often optical, fact rather than by attempting to conjure its essence. Realist attention was directed toward an account of the forms and surfaces of the world, painting modern life through the kind of description the analysis of appearance could offer.[16] A major figure in this tradition, Sickert directly confronts the task of understanding modern life. But, as the London Impressionists catalogue and the works it introduces imply, the character assumed by Sickert's solution, his explicit interest in revealing the essential realities beneath modernity's surface rather than its "sordid and superficial details," is as deeply indebted to the ambitions of English Symbolism to uncover the hidden truths of experience as to the desire of Impressionism and Realism to record and define its surfaces and appearance.[17]

This apparent ambiguity in Sickert's artistic loyalties was the occasion of a great deal of comment in the art press once he began to receive extended reviews.[18] Critics saw Sickert's work as a prime example of modernity in English painting because they recognized a modern kind of puzzle—a very great technical ability and sophistication put to the service of what seems unequivocally sordid and ugly subject matter. On the one hand, for the critics, Sickert is the proponent of an "extremist Realism,"[19] a recorder of the surface of reality, one whose "eye is a purely mechanical contrivance for conveying images" and who "seems to strip his subjects of all the[ir] *aura*."[20] On the other, he is a painter who, "like Mallarmé . . . gives you a fragment here and a fragment there, enough to prove the reality of his vision, but not enough to render it visible to the world,"[21] or who shows "how . . . a subject may be beautified by the touch of mystery that results from a dextrous suggestion of the unseen."[22] The critics understand that Sickert has a visual project, sustained over a number of years and a great many works, but they cannot conceptualize it or articulate it in established terms.[23] They cannot understand the content as anything but evidence of a perplexing desire to be "modern" at all costs, and they cannot see how Sickert's superb technical ability and subtlety of tone and color can be used toward ends that are manifestly not about the "beauty" of subject matter. Thus the critic of the *Observer*, reviewing the New English Art Club show in the autumn of 1909, praised Sickert's "types and music-hall sketches for the cruel truth of their brilliant impressionism," and had this to say about one of his music-hall paintings:

It is in . . . "The New Bedford" that Mr Sickert, who so often devotes his distinguished talent to the cult of the ugly, achieves a degree of sumptuous beauty that only a true artist's eye can discover in the gilt and florid decorations of the hall, when the lights are lowered and only a gleam here and there alights upon some detail. I cannot remember another picture by Mr Sickert that shows so keen a sense of beauty, such absolute knowledge of where to stop, such consistent solidity of handling.[24]

The ambition that leads Sickert to combine both the investigation of interior meanings and the surface appearances of modernity in the halls and elsewhere persistently troubles such commentators, who work, as the *Observer*'s critic has here, to abolish one of the terms, reducing the surface—"the cult of the ugly"—to a known category of "beauty" and technique. In fact, the tension generated by Sickert's collapsing of apparently opposed aesthetic strategies into a single endeavor is already in play in the London Impressionists show, and in this, Sickert and his coexhibitors in 1889 are pivotal figures, engaged in creating

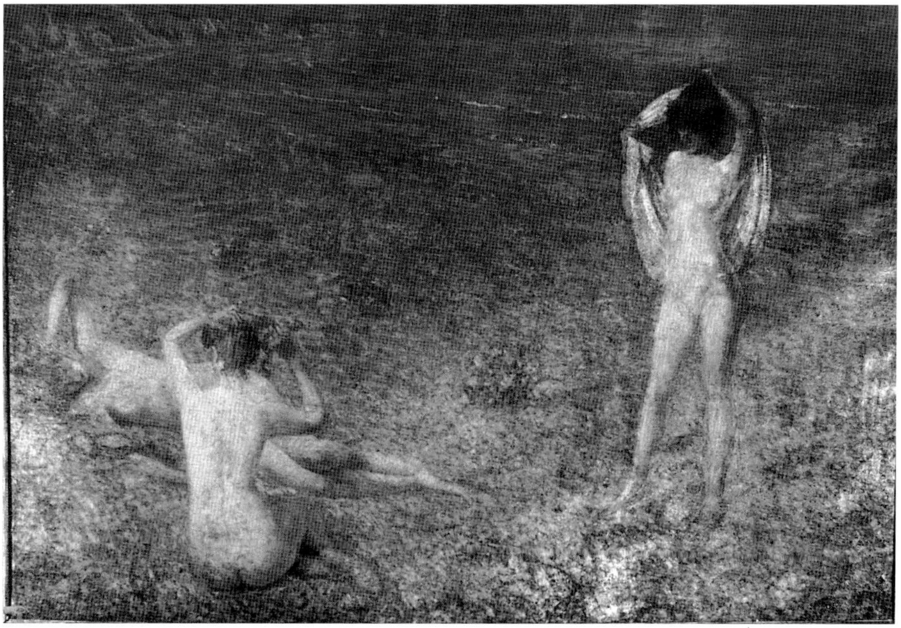

FIGURE 58. Philip Wilson Steer, *A Summer's Evening*, c. 1887–88

out of the inheritances of English painting in the late nineteenth century the grounds and procedures on which a new art that could investigate and register modern experience could be conceived and moved forward.

The perception of the London Impressionists show as centrally concerned with the requirements of representing modern experience is therefore accurate enough. But it is also the "magic and poetry" and the "beauty" of this material in the Symbolist sense that is to be evoked. These works aim to articulate the deep meaning of modernity, an analysis that would truly understand and communicate the character of its manifest subject matter by means of access to its profundities and essences. Leading exhibitors in 1889, such as Philip Wilson Steer, accordingly show a pattern of movement between the recording of surface and this delving for universal truth. *Girls Running, Walberswick Pier* (c. 1889–94, Tate Britain, London), *The Beach at Walberswick* (c. 1889, Tate Britain, London), which was shown in the London Impressionists exhibition, and *A Summer's Evening* (c. 1887–88, fig. 58) combine in their fabric the dual inheritance of Symbolism and Realism. *A Summer's Evening* yokes an overt reference to the universalized Symbolism of Puvis de Chavannes to experimental paint marks that push forward the plein-air and recording ambitions of much English Impressionism.[25] Steer's most interesting works are hybrid, mixing techniques derived from Impressionist attention to the surface with the implication of hidden or indeterminate but significant meaning characteristic of Symbolism. "In painting," wrote D. S. MacColl, Steer's chief critical supporter, "the poetry does not exist if the technique is not sufficient to express it."[26]

Like Steer, Sickert's thinking is saturated with this duality, and he mobilizes the characteristics of paint as a material practice in order to problematize and investigate its competing claims. He can do this because both Symbolism and Realism pursue their project to understand the world through the agency of the visual, although they interpret its character in very different ways. Ideas of the visual underlie both the optical realism of Impressionism and the investigation of the world as deep meaning that supports the project of Symbolist artists. The visual describes both the understanding of the world as surface, as appearance, as what optically registers as its characteristics and organization, as well as the visionary, the province of the seers and prophets so beloved of Symbolism—that which lies beneath the surface and in which reality inheres. Visuality bounces back from the surface, and it penetrates into the depths. It sees the reality of experience because it records what is really there, and it sees the reality of experience because it sees into and beyond what appears on the surface into the depths of meaning.

The question of the surface and of its contrasting meanings thus becomes critical for the representation of the world over which Symbolist and Realist modes of understanding struggle. Ideas about the visual can be understood to describe both an idea of the surface as the only authentic account of the world, and the alternative, the view that perception *beneath* the surface is what counts in the registration of reality. The possibility accordingly arises that paint, the substance of visuality itself, can serve as a vehicle that will accurately register surface reality or will uncover the depths of meaning in a revelatory transcription of essence onto the surface of the canvas. Paint as unquestionably material, a densely physical medium on its own account that inserts its own creation of the world into the ideal space of an unmediated presentation of reality, offers its own dualism that allows it to match the opposition of Symbolism and Realism, depth and surface, with a third set of terms. It can thus act, for Sickert, as a critical tool in opening up the implications of the modes of representation promulgated in Symbolism and Realism. Sickert accesses this possibility by problematizing the signs that paint offers as a route to comprehending the world. On the one hand, there is a neat sequence of connections to be posited that runs from the real (via the visible forms and surfaces of the world) to the surface of the painting that embodies the visual transcription of those forms and surfaces. On the other, there is the surface of the painting itself, a surface that intrudes into the fantasy of an unmediated transcription of reality—a blatantly fictional skin of paint or cluster of marks that constantly threatens to reduce itself to its own materiality and yield up its presumptive rights to *be* the world that it describes. The interplay between fictionality and reality enacted by the painted surface allows the contest between a form of understanding that wishes to see truth in the visible forms and surfaces of the world and one that wishes to see truth only in what is *in*visible, beneath or behind those forms and surfaces, to be articulated and explored within the physical and material constitution of paintings themselves.[27]

Themes of visuality—looking, transcribing, the exigencies of the medium (whether paint or some graphic process)—all take the stage as important actors in Sickert's art because of their relationship to these issues and their power to express and articulate them within his works.[28] The visual seems to Sickert to be both the necessary medium of understanding and one that, by the very fact of its materiality, is compromised or carries within it inherent difficulties of analysis. This gives rise to a critical project within Sickert's oeuvre, one that seeks to use the diagnostic possibilities of the visual to understand and determine the realities of contemporary experience and also attempts, self-reflexively, to understand the limitations and range of those possibilities. In this he inherits and reworks the assertion of control and mastery through the paint surface of Whistler, his mentor. Whistler's transformative visuality continues to live in Sickert's work, often in the same gendered terms that Whistler had used. The agency of the painter as the means of modernity's comprehension and diagnosis is asserted, but it is now understood as compromised, subject to a modernist irony, perpetually under question in the surface of the very painters who promulgate it. These preoccupations emerge in the thematization of visuality and the act of looking that occurs in Sickert's music-hall works. It is not simply "poetry and magic" that these works address, the deep meaning of the modern, but also the adequacy of visuality as a tool for uncovering it—in effect, the adequacy of painting as an investigative instrument for apprehending the realities of modern experience.

The Music Hall

Sickert's music-hall scenes fall into several distinct chronological periods.[29] They first appear in his oeuvre around 1887, and Sickert produced a number of paintings and graphic works of the London halls in the years up to 1889.[30] This first period includes a sequence of paintings in which mirrors play an important compositional role. Returning to the theme from around 1894 to 1898, Sickert produced a number of studies, principally of the Bedford Music Hall in Camden Town, most of which concentrate on descriptions of the audience. This phase of his work seems to have been brought to a close with Sickert's departure for Dieppe at the end of 1898. He was based abroad for seven years, returning to London to live and work only during 1905, a move that may have provoked his next sequence of music-hall subjects. In 1906–7, starting with *Noctes Ambrosianae* (1906, Nottingham Museum and Art Gallery; Baron, cat. 230), Sickert produced studies of the audiences seen in halls in London and Paris.[31] My interest here is in the work produced up to and including the 1906–7 series.[32]

This work uses the scenes of contemporary entertainment in the halls to stand for the character and meaning of the modern, instances of what Andrew Stephenson has called his "preoccupation with the 'modern' as precarious and visually estranged."[33] As elsewhere in Sickert, the very sordidness and déclassé quality of the rough-and-tumble music halls mainly located in outlying London districts suggest an authentic, real modern experience of the sort he wishes to transcribe and reveal.[34] The theatricality of the stage and the performances that take place on it—the literal falsity, dissembling, and preoccupation with surfaces—also allow Sickert to mount the dialectic of essence and reality through the depiction of music-hall scenes. The halls are, by their nature as performance, strong exemplars of surface. The stage and the performance, the involvement of the audience, and the question of its meanings for an art that has as its ambition the desire to transcribe and identify the realities of modern experience are all ideal subjects for Sickert's working-through of the issues of comprehension and knowledge that his paintings take on so directly.

Sickert's music-hall scenes of the 1880s enact the injunction of the London Impressionists catalogue to understand the modern world by revealing its essential meanings, by "rendering" them (to use Sickert's term), and he exhibited several in the London Impressionists show.[35] When he was taken to task by a critic for imitating French Impressionist subject matter in his music-hall scenes, Sickert's reply was framed precisely to drive a wedge between the idea of a socially realistic content in painting and the imperatives that he wished to assert actually powered painting as a medium: "At a given moment I was intensely impressed by the pictorial beauty of the scene, created from the coincidence of a number of fortuitous elements of form and colour . . . the fact that the painter sees in any scene the elements of pictorial beauty is the obvious and sufficient explanation of his motive for painting it."[36] Here, as in the catalogue,

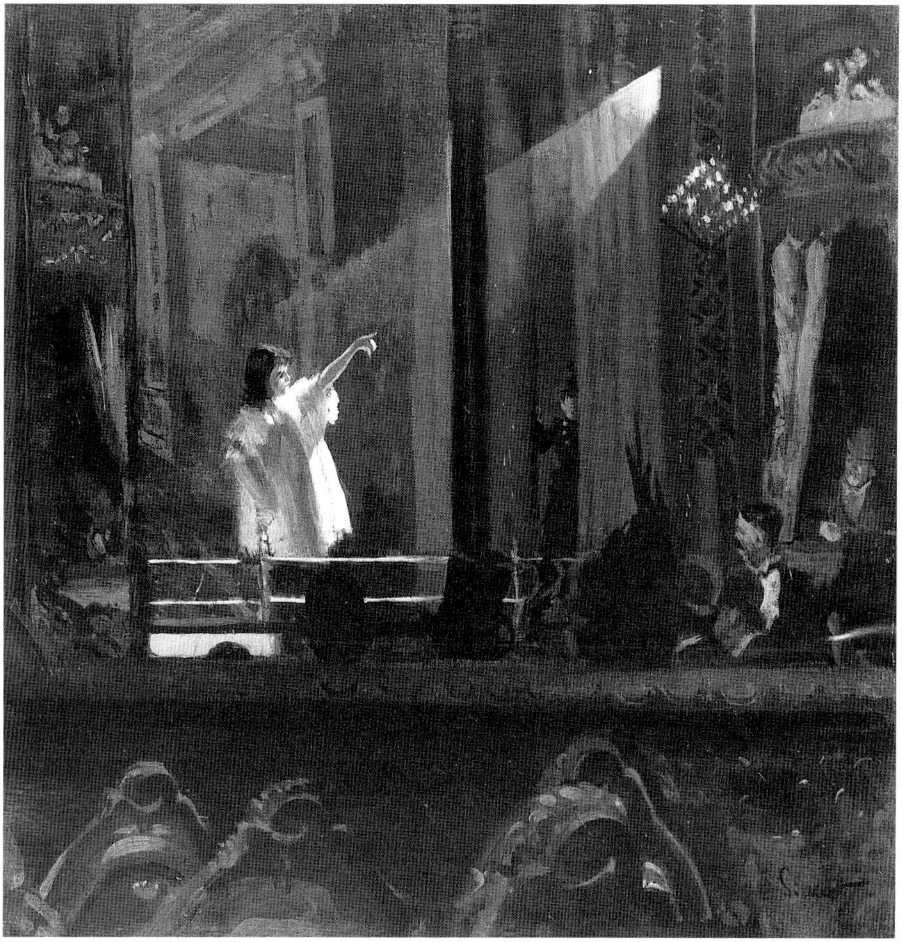

FIGURE 59. Walter Sickert, *Little Dot Hetherington at the Bedford Music Hall,* c. 1888–89

the formal aspects of visual art can stand for the "magic and poetry" of essential realities. As with Whistler's *Nocturnes*, the identification of the "beauty" in modern life defines its deepest truths. The social intentions of representation stand opposed to this. Instead of the depths that define the Symbolist mode in "any scene," realist representation of the social is concerned with surface in the sense that its subject is the strict appearance of the world.[37]

The ramifying visual complexities and nested images of paintings like *Little Dot Hetherington at the Bedford Music Hall* (c. 1888–89, fig. 59) or *Vesta Victoria at the Old Bedford* (c. 1890, fig. 60) are Sickert's meditations on this dialectic between the representation of the material surface of experience and what lies beneath, a dialectic that distills the dual inheritance of Realism's materialist

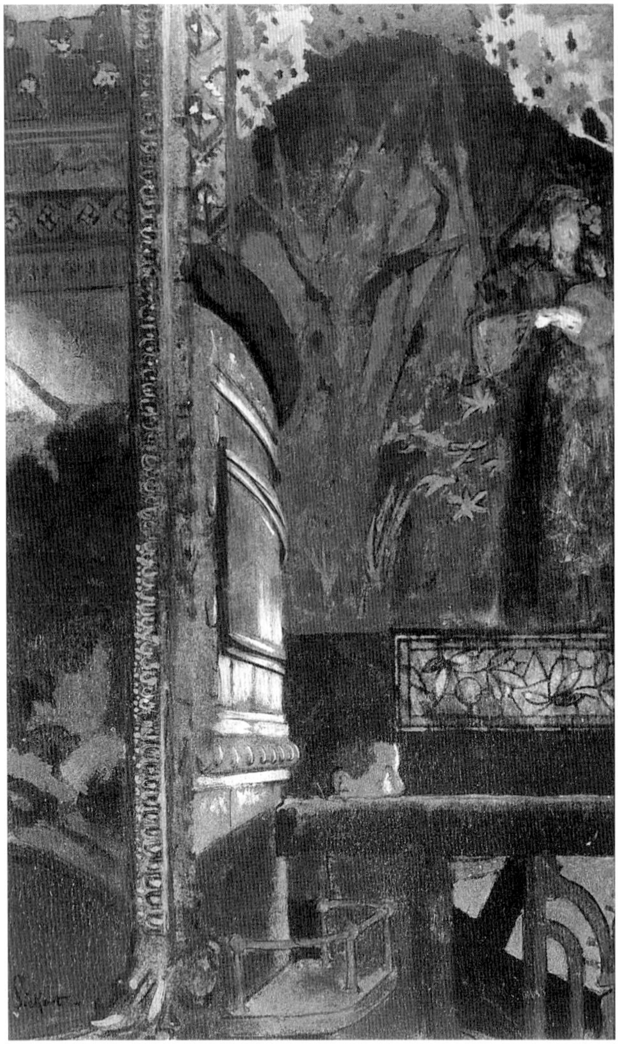

FIGURE 60. Walter Sickert, *Vesta Victoria at the Old Bedford*, c. 1890

observation and of Symbolism's desire to plumb the depths of inner meaning. In these works, the tension between visual appearance and interior essence is thematized across the spatial and representational surfaces of Sickert's canvases by means of a systematic play on the status of representation.

In *Vesta Victoria* and *Little Dot Hetherington,* space is deliberately presented as misleading: what we initially take to be the stage is revealed as a reflection, and the direction and attack of the singer's gestures have to be painfully reconstructed from the reversed information.[38] The first experience of encountering an image like *Vesta Victoria* is often one of pervasive and fundamental puzzlement. What is depicted here? And what are the relationships between the parts that we can make out? The eye persistently attempts to read the left-hand side of the picture as a hollow space that allows us to see into the hemisphere of the box. But the presence of the audience in the gods above therefore becomes inexplicable, a problem compounded by Sickert's abstraction and flattening of the vertical divider between the audience and the stage that here seems flush with the picture plane and parallel to it. Lower down, Sickert offsets the increasing clarity of this vertical element by juxtaposing it with an incoherent passage composed of fields of near-formless color. It is only when we reach the very bottom of the canvas that the vertical element fully crystallizes into the beaded frame of the mirror, at which point the spatial complexities of the painting at last become clear. Sickert, in short, assembles contrasts of represented space and flatness of picture surface in order to confuse and problematize our perceptions of the events he depicts.

Recession, too, challenges our understanding, as in *The Sisters Lloyd* (c. 1888–89, Government Art Collection; Baron, cat. 47) or *Little Dot,* where our perception of the backdrop has to be wrestled clear of the perspective space. The surfaces of appearance are here made problematic for us. What we think we see is rendered uncertain both by the inherent theatricality (and hence unreality) of the performance and by the explicit play on representation and appearance enabled by Sickert's use of mirrors, backdrops, and theatrical devices.[39] *The P. S. Wings in the O. P. Mirror* (c. 1889, fig. 61) shows the performer on the prompt side reflected in the off-prompt mirror behind the watching audience, whose fascinated attention to the stage therefore appears misdirected at first. We see the act of vision, of looking, of surrendered self-consciousness as well as the performance that attracts it, but now the two are disjunctive and ill-matched. Through Sickert's painting, appearance, analysis, and display, the movements of the surface and of its meaning, come to us confused and in an alienated relationship to one another. It is as if the lines of relationship that connect appearance with the meaning of events are disrupted and difficult to access. Surface is revealed as inadequate and deceptive. "Poetry and magic" arise from the observation of this disruption and from the gap between the surface appearance, the act of looking, and the reality of what is seen, imaged in the commercial halls where the essences of modern experience are played out through the surface of entertainment.

This might be regarded as the first stage of Sickert's painted argument. In paintings like *Gatti's Hungerford Palace of Varieties: Second Turn of Katie Lawrence* (c. 1903–4, fig. 62), he advances it further through the extended use of facture and depicted space to problematize visual meaning.[40] In *Gatti's,* Katie Lawrence

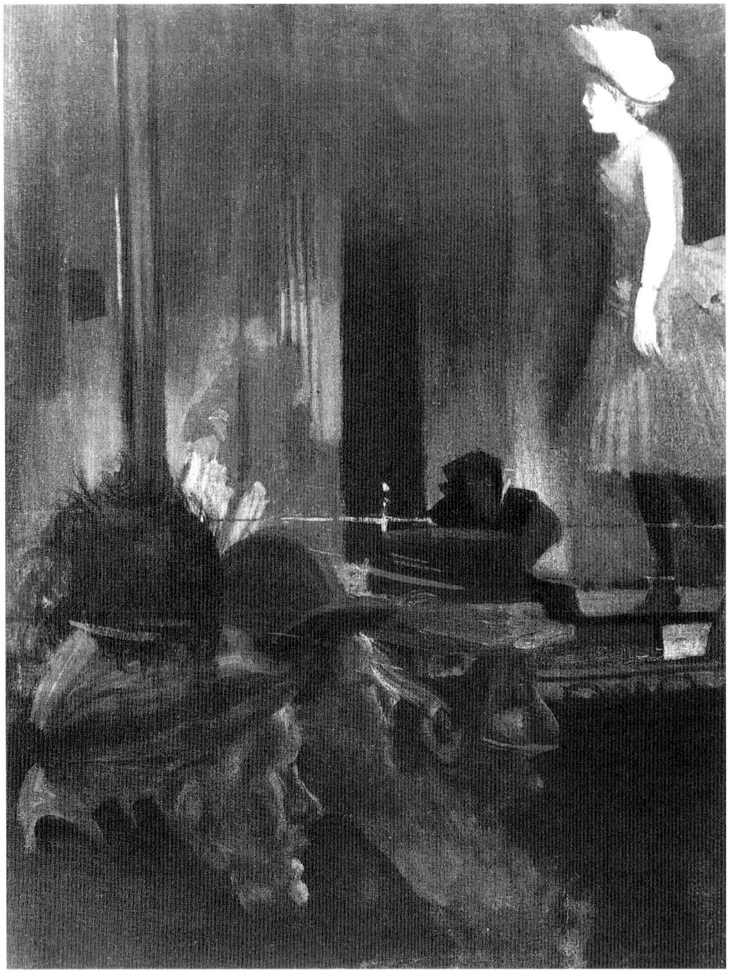

FIGURE 61. Walter Sickert, *The P. S. Wings in the O. P. Mirror,* c. 1889

stands full square in front of a backdrop curtain with an elaborate architectural space painted on it.[41] There is none of the overt spatial obscurity that dominates *Vesta Victoria.* But, having set himself the challenge this poses, Sickert manipulates perception and space, surface and depth, in the picture by exploiting the ambiguities suggested by the backdrop curtain.[42] As in *Little Dot* and *The Sisters Lloyd,* the *trompe l'oeil* effect of the backdrop confuses, because, by the nature of painting itself, it becomes difficult to decide whether what we are looking at is intended to represent real or painted depth. Moreover, it appears that the backdrop is depicted in such a way that the areas between the columns at the "sides" are to be imagined as mirrors.[43] On the right, the distinction between the back-

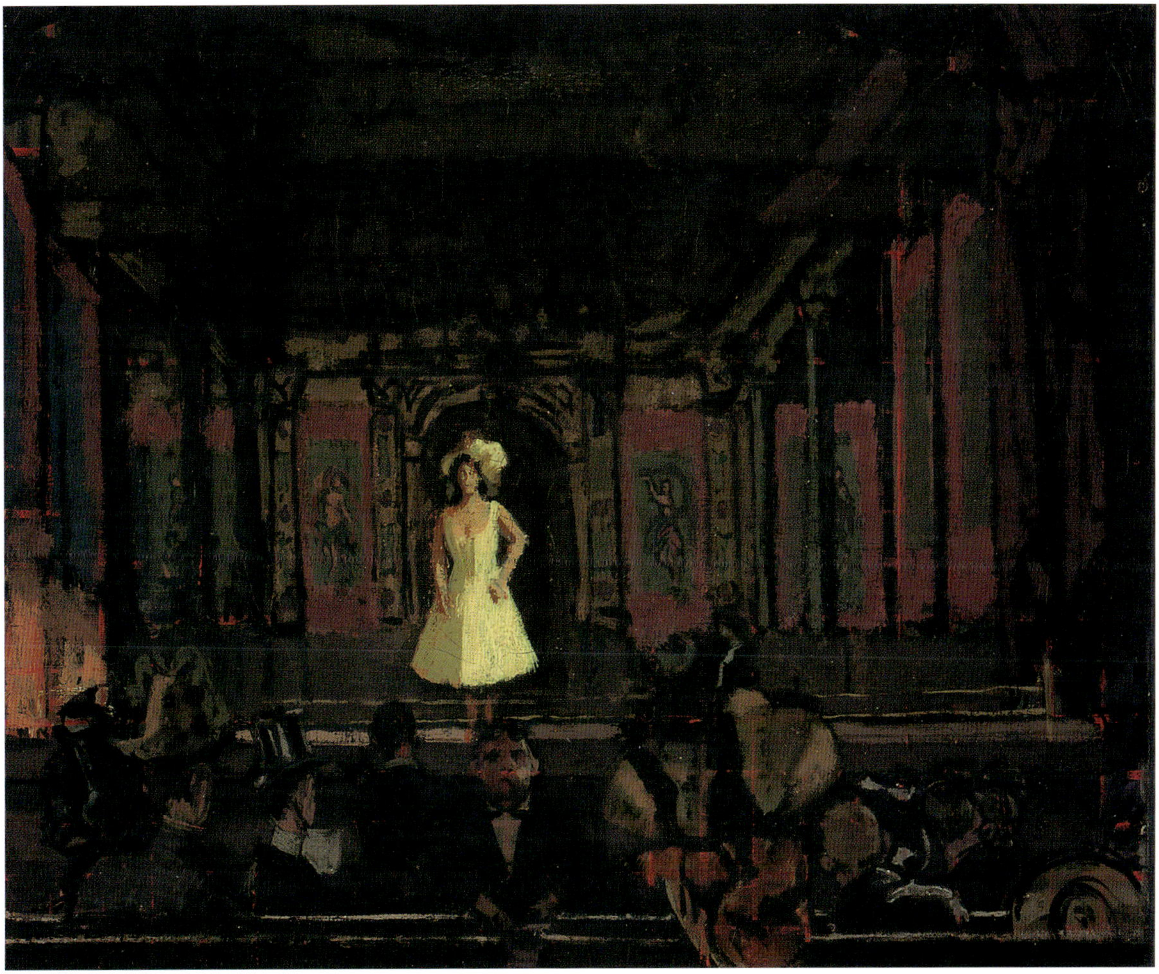

FIGURE 62. Walter Sickert, *Gatti's Hungerford Palace of Varieties: Second Turn of Katie Lawrence*, c. 1903–4

drop and the "real" space is fairly sharply defined by the curtain (although this is only a darker maroon compared to the lighter maroon, plum, and dark pink dominant in much of the backdrop, a similarity that itself suggests more confusion or interblending of real and fictional spaces—perhaps even an identity). Although the pelmet of the curtain is visible across the entire top of the picture, it is much harder to make out what is happening on the left-hand side. The backdrop appears to extend beyond the edge of the canvas, but this does not really make visual sense, as it becomes vertiginously difficult to disentangle real from fictional space. The thin strip of light color at the bottom of the backdrop that marks the gap between it and the floor does not extend beyond the hats of the audience at the far left, so the final section lacks this key marker of difference. Immediately above the space on the left where this gap would be is a strictly illegible patch of paint in light and dark tan colors that has been simply scrubbed onto the surface of the canvas. This patch is strategically placed to allow the design of the backdrop to appear to be real space and to emphasize the effect of the perspective recession painted onto it. With this arrangement, it is almost impossible to read this left-hand section of the backdrop as flat. Only the hint of the swag of the curtain at top left allows us, if we notice it, to key in the proper relationships of depth and reality. At the far right, above the round plate-shaped hat of the watching woman, there is another similar area of illegibility which, although it does not have the same calculatedly disturbing effect as that on the left, also disrupts expectations of clearly differentiated space.

Sickert's technical procedures extend this play on real and fictional into other areas of the canvas. The yellow paint—applied very thin and liquid—that describes the low railings across the front of the stage is very clearly representation rather than mimesis, and it functions as such. It is thin, wavery; it changes width with the pressure of the hand and the fullness of the brush. This is the mark of the medium, the declaration of the materiality of paint that asserts the impact of its physicality on the construction of an account of the world rather than its direct transcription. In a similar spirit, some of the heads at bottom right are outlined in a heavy black line. Sporadically, across the surface (for instance, in the woman's hat and hair in the foreground), there are lines of bright red paint that seem at first to be the remnants of lines at right angles to each other like the grids used for squaring up. Some of the lines are tight and appear to be ruled; others are blotted. This gives a sort of random accent to the surface that provides visual interest, but these grid lines were certainly applied after the main stages of painting.[44] They are visible even where the main body of the paint is wet on wet, and it is clear that in some areas the red paint has been brushed dry over dried wet-on-wet paint.[45] Again, the woman's hat is liquid paint, and the thin red lines can only have been drawn afterwards as overt reminiscences of the constructive capacities of squaring up in transferring the spontaneity of drawings into the more planned and considered arrangements of painting.[46] Like the patches of illegibility that paint itself, paint as material, is allowed to describe at the two sides of the canvas, these dialectical relationships of paint surface and descriptive technique function to draw attention to the character of paint as medium.[47] Paint in Sickert's music-hall scenes is avowedly fictional, a medium of apprehension and understanding rather than a transparent transcription. It is precisely this fictionality, the metaphorical opacity of the medium, that is acknowledged through the literally opaque and declaratively material character of the pigment itself.[48]

These strategies are designed to problematize the scenes' visual surfaces. A mere description of contemporary life will not do. The works explore not only Impressionism's project—to transcribe the surface appearance of modern life—but also the capacity of paint to image a deep, interior reading of the material.[49] The music hall becomes what W. J. T. Mitchell has called a "hypericon," an image that works to raise and inquire into "the act of picturing" or to "imagine the activity of imagination, figure the practice of figuration."[50] It serves as a workshop for Sickert's investigation of how painting might mean in relation to the desire for knowledge about the world. This investigation focuses on the question of the access to reality that paint affords. By exploiting the paradoxes and ambiguities that cluster around the representations the music halls enact, Sickert raises and critically addresses the possibility of a deep understanding of modernity and its communication in paint. Visuality functions as the critical tool of inquiry into this process.

The relationship to visuality also accounts for the interest so many of Sickert's music-hall paintings and drawings take in the audience. The various versions of *The Gallery of the Old Bedford* (c. 1895, fig. 63; see also Baron, cat. 73–76, 78) and the 1906–9 series—which includes *Noctes Ambrosianae, The Old Middlesex* (c. 1906–7, The Beaverbrook Art Gallery, Fredericton, New Brunswick; Baron, cat. 231), with its bird's-eye view down onto the spectators in the stalls, and the two pictures of the *Gaiété Montparnasse* (c. 1907, MOMA, New York, and c. 1907, private collection; Baron, cat. 236, 237) that take the opposite viewpoint, sharply upwards from the stalls into the gods—all dwell on the watching audience. In these works, the loss of the self in the act of spectatorship signals direct involvement with the world, the absence of mediation that Realism might be thought to bring with it. The rapture of the audience members as they watch, craning, leaning, and gawking down, suggests the complete identity and involvement of the spectator with the spectacle through the transparent medium of transcription. But the observation of the audience in these works also allows Sickert to question and explore the adequacy of that account of visuality.

In one of the climactic paintings of the Camden Town period, *The Studio: Painting of a Nude* (1906, fig. 64), Sickert brings the theme of visuality in this sense into the forefront of the canvas.[51] *The Studio* places the nude figure that serves as the center of attention in the Camden Town series into a more complex spatial setting and introduces the explicit figure of the painter observing

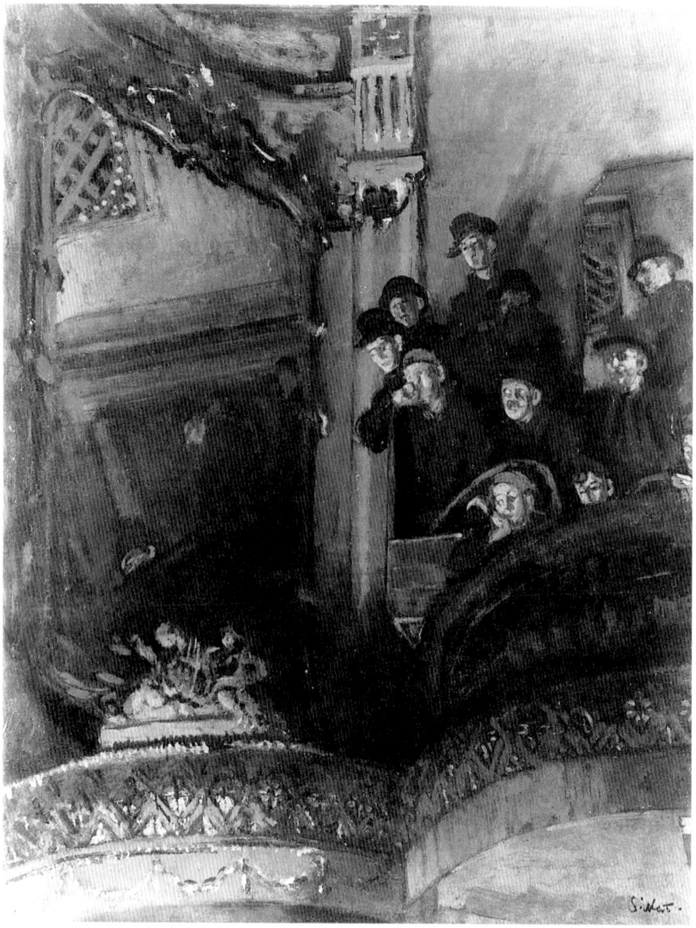

FIGURE 63. Walter Sickert, *The Gallery of the Old Bedford*, c. 1895

his model in a mirror. The multiplication of images of the nude here (both real and implied) and her extreme passivity suggest her function as the object of observation. The important action is the painter's translation of the nude body into the medium of paint. Likewise, the rapture of spectatorship, the loss and dissolution of the self in the parade of tawdry action on the music-hall stage, can be brought back into the realm of comprehension by the pressure of the analysis the painter brings to bear on it. The painter's vision renders the nude and the audience, the music hall and its performers meaningful, exemplary of modernity and reality. The music-hall audience, like the nude, is itself the object of observation by the painter. The meaning of these events seems to be that they *are* observed and therefore brought into the context of knowledge. In both types of subject matter, Sickert's painter's eye can assess, discriminate, classify, and analyze the shifting social practices of modernity.

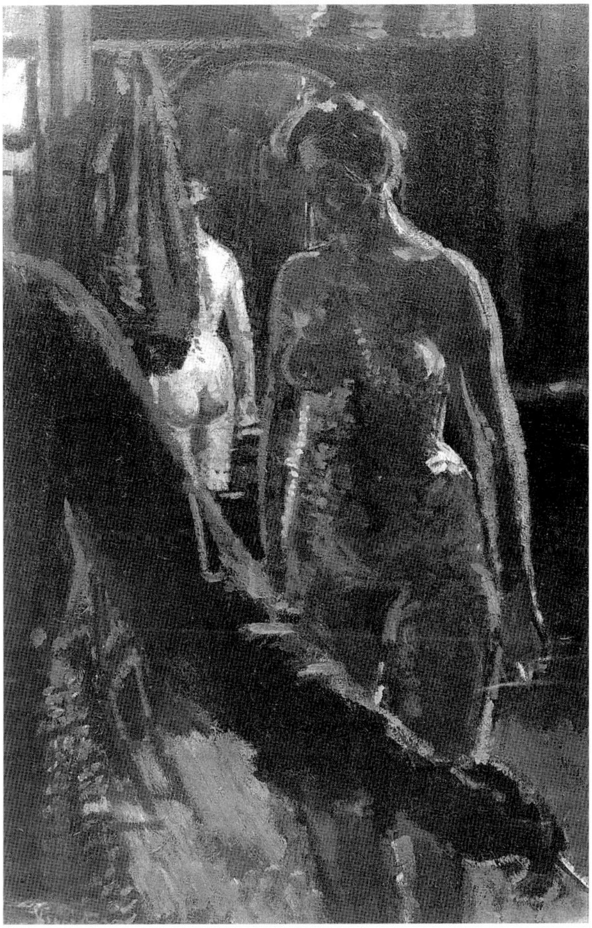

FIGURE 64. Walter Sickert, *The Studio: Painting of a Nude*, 1906

The audience of watchers signals the loss of self-consciousness consequent on the abolition of the medium of understanding that vision is imagined to be, a version of unmediation, in other words, now reified and rejected. But it is also the opportunity for Sickert to create a conceptual laboratory that will allow him to investigate that situation and hence to assess the position of the painter as well as of paint. The painter sees not only the world but also those who look at it; not only reality but its watchers, too. This serves to declare the authority of the painter as the finest example of visuality and its power, the purest vision, and the purest instance of visuality at work. The personality of the artist revivified in Whistler as the locus of authority can now stand opposed to unmediation, represented by the abstracted audiences of the halls. But the fictionality of the music-hall performance acts as a sign of the potential inadequacy of the revelation that visuality, and hence the painter, claims to offer. Sickert's play with mirrors and his insistence on the contested nature of visual knowledge in painting magnify and draw attention to this effect. Thus the audience is the image of direct engagement with the world that visuality claims it can deliver, but the example is located within clearly fictional circumstances. The audience's rapture is provoked not by immediate reality but by theatrical performance, a fiction that deceives them and their fascinated observation. Depth frustrates surface here. The fact of the artist's own observation of the audience and their deception allows space for Sickert to consider the realities of the claims of the visual. The artist as observer still retains some authority, but the critique of visuality allowed by the audience implies that he, too, is compromised.

I have been arguing that Sickert's perception of the mediation of the painter and of paint itself as matter that stands between the reality of the subject and the transcription (that is, the understanding and apprehension of that reality in the picture) motivates his modernism as a painter. It accounts for his highly wrought and self-conscious paint surfaces and for the shifts and stratagems that he employed as a technician and that he constantly changed or altered, experimenting with their possibilities.[52] It accounts as well for his interest in performance and in the audience, in the observers, and in the observation of observers that so many of the music-hall works conduct and contemplate. Sickert's art at this time is an art about the impact of mediation on our understanding of the world. It is thus also a moment at which Sickert pays attention to surface as such and thematizes it as a subject in its own right. Surface in Camden Town–period paintings like *The Studio* stands for the imposition of meaning on the world by the controlling mark of the painter's hand. Even the nugatory or trivial can be brought into meaning once a particular quality of attention is paid to it by the central self of the painter who wields the brush and pencil as instruments of knowledge and definition of the world. The overt presence of the paintwork in Sickert's surfaces functions as a sign of this authorial knowledge. Surface is the site where that process of definition takes place. But it is also the moment when Sickert's own practice, his own use of surface and materiality to render modern life in a form of knowledge, is seen as inadequate, as a reduction of the fullness of the world into a flattened surface, into *representation*. What presents itself as informational—as knowledge, as reportage about the world—is revealed as discourse, as invested or interested. The view of reality that the surface encapsulates and promotes is a partial rather than a full account. It is compromised and bound into the systems it seeks to explicate.

Sickert's works raise fundamental questions about *how* visual art as a practice can understand and communicate knowledge about the realities of experience and the world, whether through the meticulous transcription of the world's appearance and surfaces or through the transmission of an insight into its conditions and essence. In that account, the painter's identity is placed precariously within modernity, but the power to understand the situation arises precisely from that precariousness. The painter *is* a modern identity, contingent and indeterminate. Katie Lawrence or Vesta Victoria are homologues of this situation. They, too, are quintessentially modern identities that Sickert's paint seeks to transcribe and communicate, to see into and beneath to their essence or essential truth. But they are also marks of paint on the surface of the canvas, things observed, seen, watched, subject to the observing presence of the painter and his distillation of knowledge in the physical constitution of the artwork. In the next section, I take this further—both in Sickert's career and in the argument—to show that the Camden Town–period works that Sickert produced in the early 1900s probe these themes in new ways. They now become indices of the collapse of visuality as artistic and gendered power and thus herald some of the preoccupations of formal modernism in Britain. The primary means through which this change can be mapped is Sickert's relationship to the city as a site of modernity and of the relations of gendered artistic power.

The City and Camden Town

Cities have two modes of existence. On the one hand, there is the city we experience in the abstracted and idealizing forms of knowledge: the city spread out for us in the articulation of the map, with streets, trains, and underground stations arrayed for us with all the force that conceptual clarity can give. This is the city as A–Z, what Michel de Certeau has called the "Concept City," an abstracted geometry that declares itself open to planning, formulation, and understanding.[53] On the other hand, there is the city we experience when we glance up from the map and find ourselves confronted by the normal view of streets and our fellow urban dwellers. From this perspective, the city is unknowable, opaque. We cannot be sure of the behavior of other individuals: we do not know what lies behind the closed doors of the houses. This aspect of the city is not susceptible to rational knowledge. Our response to it is not the analytic and abstracting response of the map-maker. Instead, we people the city with the terrors of our imaginations. We deal with the confusions and uncertainties of urban life by elaborating an interior image of that chaos, which we placate with childish or neurotic rituals of propitiation. We don't step on the cracks in the pavement. We stick to familiar circuits in traveling. We impose an order on the city by sheer force of belief. The city as it is *experienced* rather than *conceived* is unknowable, susceptible only, and then precariously, to magic, ritual, and superstition.[54] In an essay on the city and "modern spaces," James Donald sums this up: "urban space . . . is doubly textured. It is concrete, but just as brutally it is fantastic."[55] Both transparent and labyrinthine, as Walter Benjamin described it, the city in this sense is a scene of the imaginary, a "phantasmagoria," modernity's dream.[56]

This division within the city has been an important one for those who have sought to understand the character of modern life. For many commentators, the presence of irrationality alongside the "Concept City" of rational description marks one of the fundamental complexities of the modern.[57] The more the operation of modernity insists on a rationalization of existence, the more it is said to create a fallout, a state beyond its margins where everything is lodged that does not fit within the systematized world. Inside, there is order, system, hierarchy: the world is planned and arrayed, susceptible to our knowledge. Outside there is chaos, violence, randomness, the absence of community or of the means to share experience in a common language. In this sense, the city as distillation of both order and confusion *is* the experience of modernity for us. The shadows, too, are modernity's right, true creation. It follows from this that the conceptual order we impose is a misrecognition of our experience of actually living modernity. When we attempt to bring it within the domain of knowledge, to understand it, to render it comprehensible—whether through the operations of abstracting reason or through the rituals of unreason—we betray it. We involve ourselves in the very terms of knowledge that it refuses.

Between 1905 and 1910, during what Wendy Baron has called his Camden Town period, Sickert's painting is strongly related to these themes of modernity.[58] Sickert, in these years, takes as his subject matter images of London that embody the threatening and random aspects of the modern metropolis as the social and gendered other. In these depictions, Sickert's eye can assess and grant meaning to the urban. The ascription of meaning in paint becomes the means through which the city can be analyzed and known. Because these images are of the female nude above all, recent Sickert scholarship has recognized that the period requires consideration from a gendered perspective. As Anna Gruetzner Robins puts it in her 1996 book on Sickert's drawings, the radical flouting of "received ideas about the representation of the female nude" in Sickert's writing and practice in this period suggests "a deep psycho-sexual anxiety about prostitution, class and female sexuality."[59] If this formulation does not explicitly acknowledge the idea of control through representation, the central preoccupations of gender and the social are nevertheless firmly stated. It seems to me that Robins is right to continue by noting that "many questions" are still to be "asked about the wider meaning of these drawings."[60] But the argument has not been taken far enough, for in Sickert the assumption of authority in the face of the random world and the assertion of order that this carries with it profoundly reveal the pressure of modernity on gendered identities. I suggest that Sickert's work in the Camden Town period simultaneously promotes a controlling idiom of observation and undercuts the idea that modernity can ever be returned to order by the painter's masculine gaze.

In the years between 1905 and the First World War, Sickert produced a large number of works that dealt with contemporary London and the experiences of those who lived in it. These paintings—and, in particular, the so-called Mornington Crescent and Camden Town Murder series—describe the modern city by concentrating on marginal lives in dingy surroundings. His city scenes were conceived as anatomies of modern life, radical insofar as they were explicitly opposed to what Sickert felt was the gentrified and wilfully escapist gaze of established painting. He advanced this argument when, in May 1910, he published a short article on "Idealism" in *The Art News*. In the essay he set himself against the idealization of the world in contemporary painting and recommended an alternative. Sickert's prime target was the highly stylized and flattering portrait images created by John Singer Sargent and those who imitated him, what Sickert called elsewhere "wriggle and chiffon."[61] For Sickert, it was absurd that Sargent's work should be regarded "as the standard in art, the ne plus ultra and high-water mark of modernity," when it was in reality a form of flattery in which the sitters were beautified and rendered as ideal versions, not of what they were, but of what they would have liked to have been: painted by Reynolds in an imaginary and glamorized eighteenth century.[62]

In "Idealism," Sickert argues that any "ideal work" such as this is compromised by its ultimate reliance on the inventiveness of the individual painter. Idealization can be effective only to the degree to which the artist can imagine ideal forms and circumstances, and that—in most cases—is not very far. In contrast, the artist whose "taste" is sufficiently coarse to prepare him to take "the whole field of nature" for his subject is not "limited to the consumption of his poor finite self" but can engage with wider and more meaningful realities. This is an argument for painting as social critique, for the implication of painting in the experience of life, and also for the derivation of its power from attention to social reality rather than from the inner responses of the painter's personality.

Art cannot be defined by what is "nice"—the English sin, according to Sickert—or by the limits of the autonomous self. It can only function properly when it accepts its own constitution as a material practice and seeks to encapsulate the observation of meaning it conducts in the "gross material facts of bulk and shape, and colour," for "such are the conditions of the very existence of plastic art." Art like Sargent's, which is abstractly allegorical or tasteful ("nice"), abrogates its potential for the identification of "observations, and conclusions, that are very serious realities to us": "The more art is serious, the more will it tend to avoid the drawing-room and stick to the kitchen. The plastic arts are gross arts, dealing joyously with gross material facts. They call, in their servants, for a robust stomach and a great power of endurance, and while they will flourish in the scullery, or on the dunghill, they fade at a breath from the drawing-room."[63] Later in the same year, Sickert elaborated on what "the scullery, or . . . the dunghill" might mean by reflecting on the inadequacy of portraiture of this type to capture anything but a false, belittled version of the individual. He imagines the transformation of an ordinary woman—whom he calls Tilly Pullen, an everywoman of the lower classes—into the idealized subject of a modern drawing-room portrait. In that fictional and meretricious context, she cannot be interesting: "But now let us strip Tilly Pullen of her lendings and tell her to put her own things on again. Let her leave the studio and climb the first dirty little staircase in the first shabby little house. Tilly Pullen becomes interesting at once. She is in surroundings that mean something. She becomes stuff for a picture. Follow her into the kitchen, or, better still . . . into her bedroom; and now Tilly Pullen is . . . become a Degas or a Renoir, and stuff for the draughtsman."[64]

Sickert's "gross material facts," then, are the instruments through which a reconstitution of painting will be effected, abolishing the effete and genteel language of commercial portraiture for a roughly authentic account of the intimacies and privacies of contemporary life. Once she reaches a suitably urban setting, Tilly Pullen becomes of interest. This is a characteristically modern ambition, and in the paintings executed during the years between 1905 and around 1910, these subjects are elevated into a diagnosis, an anatomy of modern life, the social critique that Sickert had argued for as painting's role in the "Idealism" essay.[65] Both the 1916 *Queens Road Station, Bayswater* (Courtauld Institute; Baron, cat. 370)—a final flourish of this period of his work—and the c. 1909 *Dawn, Camden Town* (fig. 65) feature this shabby ordinariness.[66] The lassitude and boredom of the city are distilled into succinct images of the everyday, the "serious realities" and material "facts" of contemporary existence in the

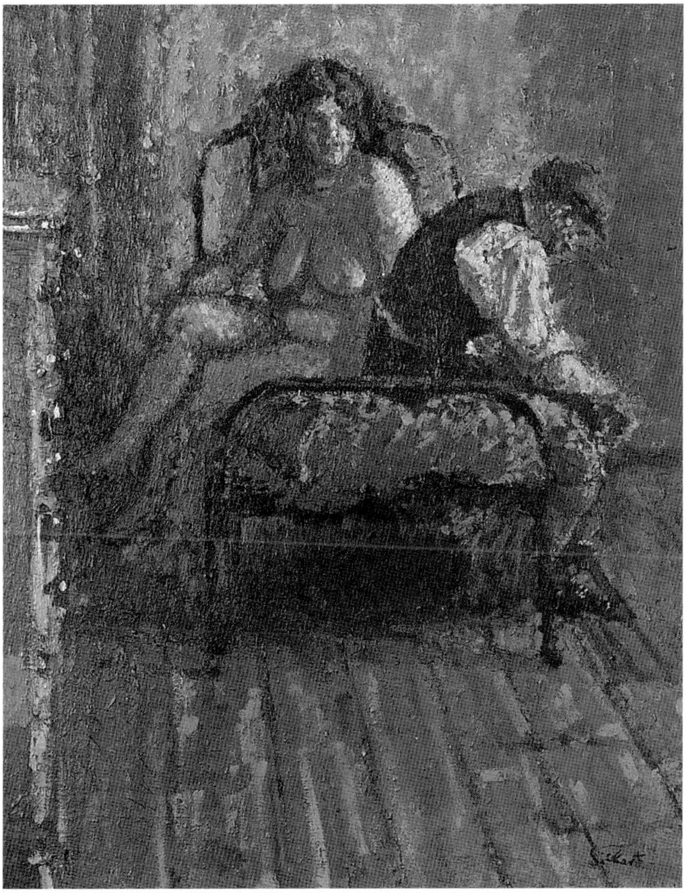

FIGURE 65. Walter Sickert, *Dawn, Camden Town,* c. 1909

first decades of the twentieth century. They address the question of how one could paint the experience of modernity—how one could paint the city as the site of that experience—in such a way as to carry conviction and the possibility of analysis. Sickert's answer was to widen the themes of art. "Anything!" he wrote, "this is the subject matter of modern art," whether sagging nudes in squalid lodging-house rooms or the dwarfed figure of a man surrounded by the luxuriant semiosis of modernity, the spectacle of advertising, transport, and communications.[67] In effect, Sickert conceives of modernity as encapsulated in the intimate, "sordid," and violent working-class histories he chooses as his subjects; shabby nudes, urban anomie, the tensions generated out of marital conflicts.[68] The claustrophobic, enclosed spaces of lodging-house rooms in suburban North London—the London he said he loved for its "evil racy little faces [and] the whiff of leather and stout from the swing-doors of the pubs"[69]—inhabited by the urban working class, minor clerks, railwaymen, laborers, shading off into the criminal and near-criminal, prostitutes, petty thieves, alcoholics, thugs: these become the signs of modern life that Sickert strives to register and describe.[70]

These interests are distilled into a single major motif.[71] From 1905, after his return to London from abroad—a move that may have been prompted by his desire to use what he called London's "drab and sleazy suburbs" as subjects—Sickert explored the possibilities of nude studies in dingy and neglected interiors that he had first broached in Venice in 1903–4.[72] These nude subjects are united by their shared function as the focus of the painter's analytic and ordering eye. Like the eager audiences for the spectacle of popular entertainment in the music-hall pictures, the nude is herself the object of observation by the analytic eye of the painter.[73] In painting a shabby nude on a disordered lodging-house bed, Sickert can mobilize his observation of the classed and gendered other to classify and analyze the city's shifting, irrational social practices.

In a series of works that Sickert began to produce from around 1905, he took up the spatial complexities and mirrors of the music-hall scenes and introduced them into depictions of women in interiors. The paradigmatic women of Aestheticism are present again in these interiors, now transformed from the fantastic creatures of imagination and mythology into the representatives of the modern which that transformation, from Sickert's perspective at this moment, had suppressed. Whistler's *Symphony in White, No 2—The Little White Girl* (1864, fig. 66) must be understood as a stage of the painted argument in which Sickert intervenes. But beyond Whistler lie the abstracted, inward, and sexualized paintings by Rossetti that display women and their mirrors. *Lady Lilith* (see fig. 15) and others, as we have seen, pose their subjects in the process of self-cultivation and invite us to see them as analogues of the contemplative self-absorption of art.[74] Sickert's women are not sirens or distillations of experience; they are simply bodies. They remain models in the shabby bedsits or rooms in which they pose. In works like *La Hollandaise* (c. 1906, fig. 67), the central claims about beauty and display made for them in the Symbolist tradition are challenged. The leonine, mutilated, or simply absent face of the nude on the bed abolishes the subject matter of the *femme—fatale* or otherwise—and replaces it with the circumstances of her existence. The mirrors Sickert paints accordingly reflect not his models but the sordid beds and North London lodging-house rooms that Sickert uses to stand for modern life. *Cocotte de Soho* (1905, private collection; Baron, cat. 207) places the model obliquely next to the glass that is allowed to reflect not her contemplation of herself but the disordered bedclothes. Here, as in *La Hollandaise,* it is the room, modernity itself,

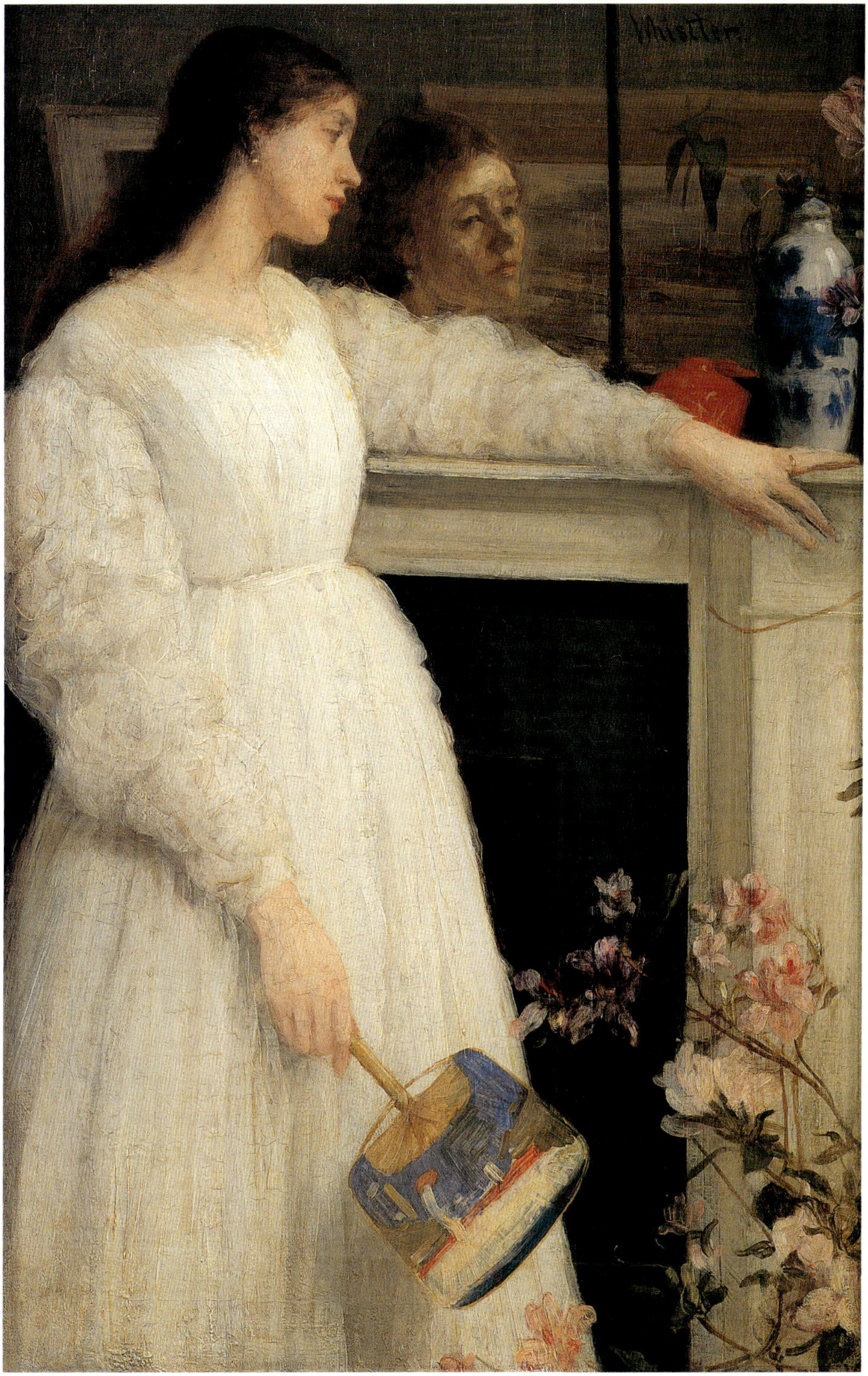

FIGURE 66. James McNeill Whistler, *Symphony in White, No 2—The Little White Girl*, 1864

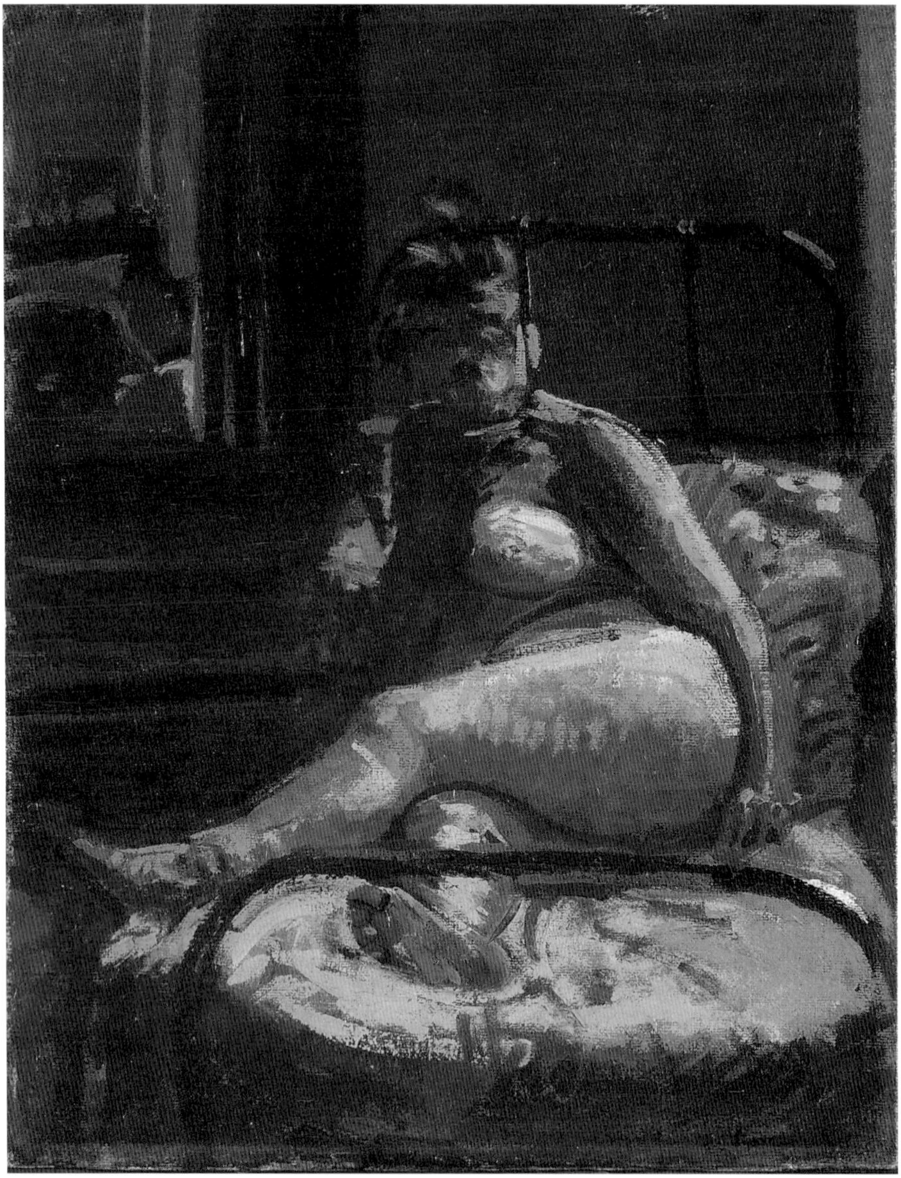

FIGURE 67. Walter Sickert, *La Hollandaise,* c. 1906

that is reflected back to us by the mirror. We watch modern life in these paintings rather than the fantasy of inner meaning and beauty.

In paintings like *Dawn, Camden Town* or *Le Lit de Cuivre* (1906, private collection; Baron, cat. 209), the figures are lounging or feral, displayed on iron bedsteads within rooms of a brutally minimal decoration and cleanliness. The nudes are often fleshy, middle-aged, haggard, relentlessly ordinary and unidealized in ways that seem to guarantee their authenticity as social observation and their freedom from the escapist conventions of "wriggle and chiffon" painting. Sickert's critics responded readily to this quality in the works, and comments like those of the *Observer*—that the artist took a "perverse delight . . . in unsavoury and sordid phases of town life" and "debased types of humanity"—are typical.[75] For *The Star* in 1912, the nude in *Dawn, Camden Town* was "a hideous middle-aged woman in a state of nature," so that it seemed appropriate that "the colour of the picture is a discord in dirty mud."[76] The surface of Sickert's paintings and the wretchedness of his subject matter seemed all of a piece.

These paintings evolve over the period after 1905 through the "Mornington Crescent" series of 1907 to the murder pictures of 1908–9. In these years, Sickert used the theme of the well-publicized sexual killing of 1907 known as the Camden Town Murder as a largely retrospective description for a number of related paintings, etchings, and drawings that explore the psychological implications of a clothed man and nude woman in an interior.[77] This series has some claim to be the definitive expression of the Camden Town period as a whole, based on the appositeness of the critics' response to the two paintings shown at the first Camden Town Group exhibition as *Camden Town Murder Series No 1* and *Camden Town Murder Series No 2*.[78] There, they recognized the paintings as dealing with "the utter depravity of a particularly unsavoury phase of life" and as distillations of the brutality of Sickert's recent themes.[79] Sexual murder seems to have offered a summation of both the grossness and materiality of the city and to have provided Sickert, for a while, with a controlling theme through which to present aspects of his practice that had been developing since 1905.[80] Through the "unsavouriness" of his subject matter, Sickert constructed a narrative from the city by emphasizing categories of experience that, as he later argued in the "Idealism" essay, were elided or inadequately dealt with in standard painting. The materiality of the city is signaled by the brutality, impoverishment, and degradation of the act of murder in a dingy lodging-house room—and more particularly by the violent relationship of a male spectator and the nude figure of woman.

Sickert's nudes serve as the distillation of all that is other in the city, its chaos, its randomness and violence, and its sleazy and repulsive physicality.[81] They depart so brutally from the glamorized ideals of the Victorian tradition precisely because their purpose is to embody the threatening aspects of the city.[82] Lolling in miserable interiors, the nudes function as a stark sign of the uncontrolled modern. Their seediness, dirt, and squalor, their pendulous breasts and middle-aged bodies, stand for a reality that Sickert believed had been omitted from painting and for the ability of an analytic discipline in painting to penetrate that resistance to comprehension and establish it as meaningful. Sickert brings them into the field of comprehension through the device of what Richard Shone has called a "dispassionate observer" who evaluates these lives and events without involvement.[83] Like the rapture of spectatorship, it is the difference of these women that can be made comprehensible through the attention paid by the painter. The important action is the painter's translation of the observed "material facts" of "very serious realities to us" into the medium of paint. This rhetoric of reality guarantees the accuracy of the paintings' transcription of the modern city—and therefore guarantees as well the success of the artist's controlling hand in dominating and ordering the threatening incomprehensibility of modern experience. The grosser and more material these figures are, the more they ultimately confirm Sickert's role as the defining analyst of their meaning. Sickert sees himself as the observer, the transformer of an overweight, vulgar model, sprawled naked on a disordered bed, into an analysis of light and its distribution, the quality and scintillation of a *contre-jour* pose, or into a mysterious and oblique psychological suggestion that the actors themselves would not recognize. Sex, money, violence, the impeded, agonistic silences of sexual couples bound into some intense but unarticulated relationship: these are the circumstances of Sickert's rational sociology of the urban.

This account of the painter's action—the redescription of the world as meaningful in painting—is fully developed in the Camden Town–period paintings. The recuperation of the meanings of the city is not simply effected through the ascription of a taxonomy or the classification of social behavior. The main vehicle for Sickert's assertion of control over the city is the transformations that the painter can effect on the raw material of the life he depicts. The Camden Town paintings and the series of Mornington Crescent nudes that preceded them in 1907—perhaps more than any other period or series in Sickert's career—present a painterly surface to the eye.[84] Sickert rightly described the Mornington Crescent nudes as a "set of Studies of illumination."[85] *Mornington Crescent Nude, Contre-Jour* (1907, fig. 68) positions its subject against the daylight and concentrates sophisticated technical efforts on rendering the resultant dissolution and reintegration of light and form. The Camden Town–period paintings are lushly sensual descriptions of material presence, all dissolved and transfigured by the saturation of the objects of the world in the play of light and the division it enforces of material objects into the brilliantly illuminated and the stygian. It is Sickert's light, "the quivering veil of atmos-

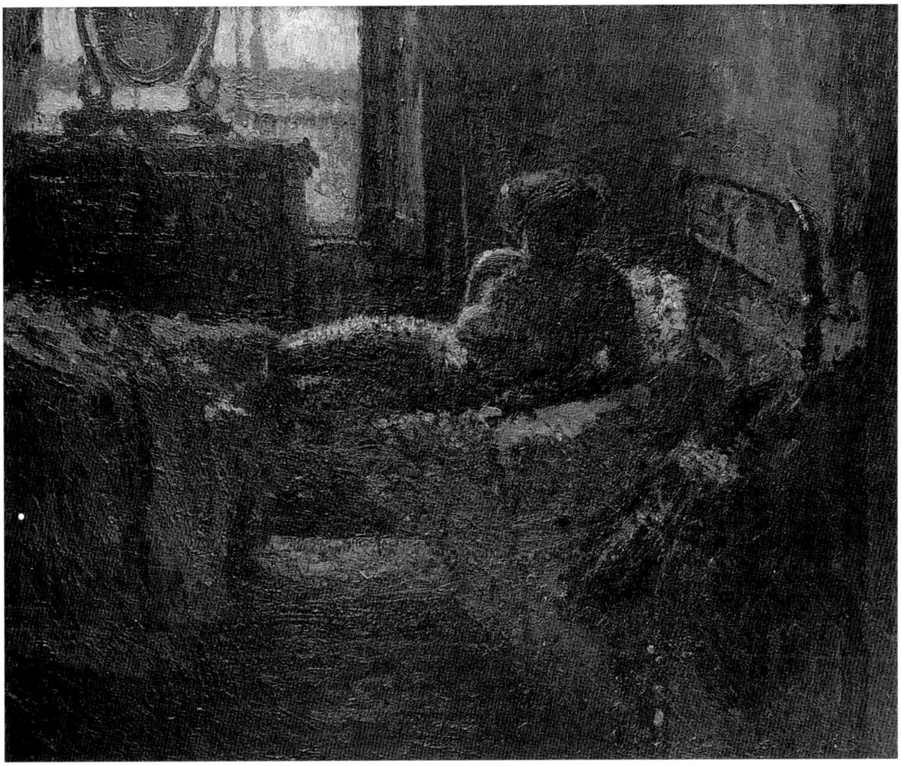

FIGURE 68. Walter Sickert, *Mornington Crescent Nude, Contre-Jour,* 1907

phere" as the *Sunday Times* critic described it, the stroke of the brush, marking the empty canvas and assembling the elements of description, that really defines the capture and rationalization of the world in these paintings.[86] In the end, the moment when the city is rendered knowable is not merely the elaboration of a sociological account of sordid or marginal lives but also the creation of a fluctuating web of color and brushstrokes within which the shifting colors of urban sunlight, dust, and interior gloom are knotted together. The work of the painter is the act that captures the phantasmagoria of the city, its riot of meaning and action, as the play of light and the motes of dust in a London room.

The distillation of the world and its description in meaning, "the prelude or the refrain of movement, the promise of movement to come, or the echo of movement past" that can convey the "pathos," "poetry," or "sentiment" through the "plastic facts" it reproduces: this is the purpose of the gross materiality of Sickert's recommendation.[87] It derives from Whistler's transformative art as I discussed it in Chapter 2. The reintroduction of agency into paint that Whistler promoted, the assertion of control as a means of bringing painting and modernity into analytic conjunction, is taken up by his pupil and pushed forward. In the process, Whistler's transformation of the modern is developed in new and often ironic directions. When he wanted to praise Spencer Gore, Sickert described Gore's ability to evoke the "beautiful" out of the most uncompromisingly "modern" materials. For Gore, he argued,

a scene, the dreariness and hopelessness of which would strike terror into most of us, was to him matter for lyrical and exhilarated improvisation. I have a picture by him of a place that looks like Hell, with a distant iron bridge in the middle distance, and a bad classic façade like the façade of a kinema, and two new municipal trees like brooms, and the stiff curve of a new pavement in front, on which stalks and looms a lout in a lounge suit. The artist is he who can take a piece of flint and wring out of it drops of attar of roses.[88]

The painter can remold the vulgar world in his practice, endowing that world with systems of meaning—the flux of light and its description, the attribution of mystery to everyday conversation, the juxtaposition of figures and attitudes that by themselves would be empty or negligible—that it does not essentially contain by virtue of its own constitution. It is the translation of the world into a different and superior order that is being recommended here rather than fidelity in imitation or social realism. The issues of class contained in Sickert's description of Gore's relation to the municipal, the "bad" classicism of the cinema, and the threatening lout are smoothed away in their transformation into the stuff of fantasy. Whatever he may say about idealism and reality, Sickert's painting is also, in an important way, an idealist practice. Its declaration of realism, apparent in the classed and gendered difference of his subject matter, dissolves on inspection into a dream in which it is the painter's control of his subjects that is real, not the subjects themselves. In this, his debt to Whistler is evident. Despite Sickert's claims, the models and their lives have no status here, except as confirmations of the painter's authority and reality.

Authority and Identity

My argument thus far has been that Sickert's engagement with the city is essentially about knowledge. His description of the life of urban dwellers and of the city environment strives to bring those potentially unknowable things into the field of understanding. Sickert's network of painted light and color amounts to a rationalizing account of the city. Painting itself is the medium through which the city can be understood, but in using it, Sickert invents a fantasy of control, not a realist account of the city itself. And yet, although that is an adequate description of Sickert's own account of the city paintings, it leaves out too much to be satisfactory on its own. In particular, to see Sickert's painting in its own terms as rationalizing evades many of the full implications of his subject matter. Exactly why is it that the project of Shone's "dispassionate observer" to define and understand the city was conducted through the sexualized bodies of working-class women, transformed in the succulent play of Sickert's paint surface into figures of knowledge and control? In what sense is Sickert's social critique an effective analysis of the conditions of modernity it claims to transcend? We can start to consider an answer to these questions by paying attention to some of Sickert's characteristic conversational obsessions.

In the late 1940s, Osbert Sitwell, who had known Sickert well from about 1916, wrote an extended introduction to a collection of Sickert's writings on art. In this introduction Sitwell describes Sickert's conversation—witty, allusive, teasing, but containing "certain invariable strands, immutable monuments that could be invoked for purposes of reference . . . comparison and simile, and [that] also supplied him with an established standard."[89] Two "monuments" that figured particularly were the cases of the Tichbourne claimant and the identity and activities of Jack the Ripper. The Tichbourne claimant refers to a famous trial of the 1860s and 1870s that, like the Ripper case, turned crucially on a question of identity. A man called Arthur Orton—as it turned out, the son of a butcher from Wapping—returned from Australia, where he had been living, claiming to be the long-lost heir to a fortune. The widow apparently recognized Orton as the heir, but during the formal defense of his claim in the courts, Orton suddenly withdrew and found himself arrested and tried for perjury and forgery. He was sentenced to fourteen years' imprisonment. After he was released, Orton appeared, appropriately enough, as a music-hall "turn," "The Claimant," and Sickert likely saw him perform in this role during the 1890s.[90] Fascinated by this tale of identity and misrecognition, Sickert maintained all his life that the claimant had been "the rightful heir," and he was reported at one point to be writing a book on the case.[91]

Sickert's interest in Jack the Ripper, says Sitwell, "apart from the intrinsic and abiding horror of that extraordinary series of crimes," was also because Sickert "thought he knew the identity of the murderer."[92] Sickert told Sitwell (and others) that sometime during the early 1900s he had taken rooms in a London suburb. Engaging the old woman who ran the house in conversation, he learned that his room had had a famous prior occupant—"Jack the Ripper!" This is how the anecdote goes on:

Her story was that [Sickert's] predecessor had been a veterinary student. After he had been a month or two in London, this delicate-looking young man—he was consumptive—took to occasionally staying out all night. His landlord and landlady would hear him come in about six in the morning, and then walk about in his room for an hour or two, until the first edition of the morning paper was on sale, when he would creep lightly downstairs and run to the corner to buy one. Quietly he would return, and go to bed; but an hour later, when the old man called him, he would notice, by the traces in the fireplace, that his lodger had burnt the suit he had been wearing the previous evening. For the rest of the day, the millions of people in London would be discussing the terrible new murder, plainly belonging to the same series, that had been committed in the small hours. Only the student seemed never to mention them: but then he knew no one and talked to no one, though he did not seem lonely.[93]

Eventually, just as the couple were on the verge of going to the police with their suspicions, the student's health declined, and his mother, "a widow who was devoted to him," had "come to fetch him back to Bournemouth, where she lived. . . . From that moment the murders had stopped," and "he died three months later" of his consumption.[94] Like the case of the Tichbourne claimant, matters here turn largely on the issues of identity, its detection, and its ultimate uncertainty.

There is a coda to Sitwell's account that emphasizes the irreducible difficulty of decisions about identity. Sickert supposedly told Sitwell that he had noted down the name of the veterinary student as the old woman told it to him "in pencil on the margin of a French edition of Casanova's *Memoirs*" and had "subsequently . . . given the book away"—to William Rothenstein, Sitwell thought: "Sickert had added, 'And there it will be now, if you want to know the name.'" Sitwell says he inquired of Rothenstein, who knew nothing about it, but was then told by Sickert's wife that the book had actually gone to Rothenstein's brother, confusingly of course named Rutherston (identities are still in question in this riot of names). This proved to be true. Rutherston told Sitwell that "he had only recently lost the book during the bombing of London, and that there had been several pencil notes entered in the margin, in Sickert's handwriting, always so difficult to decipher."[95]

This is all very entertaining, and intentionally so. But even if we regard it, as of course we must, as tainted evidence, and however clear it is that Sickert (and Sitwell) are having a certain sort of complicit fun in which we are invited to join, Sickert's fascination with the Ripper was real, and it is significant that this fascination should have been expressed in terms of the conditions of iden-

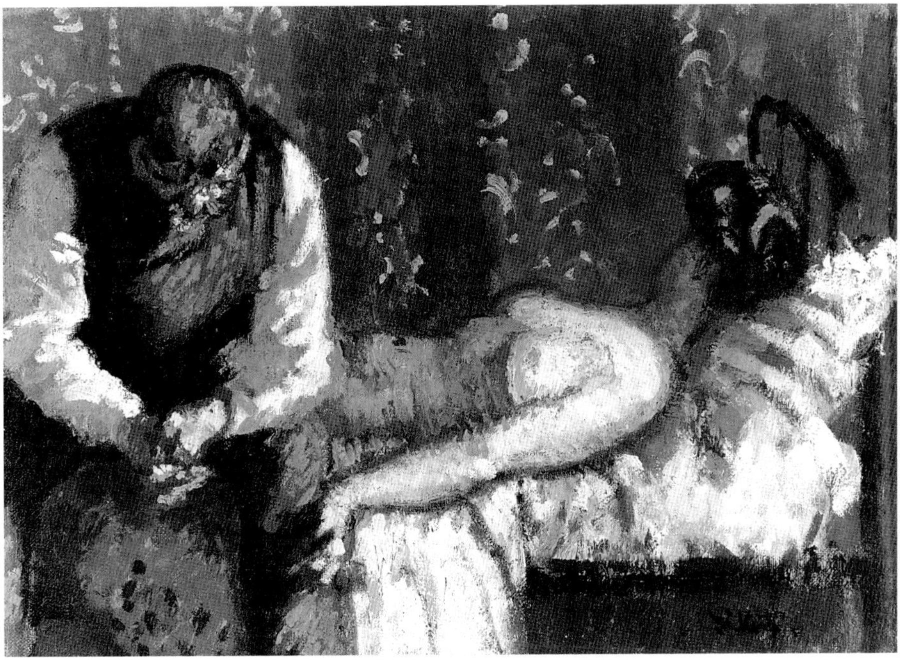

FIGURE 69. Walter Sickert, *The Camden Town Murder*, or, *What Shall We Do for the Rent?*, c. 1908–9

tity and the difficulties of knowledge. Identity and the issues of the susceptibility of knowledge that it raises figure elsewhere in Sickert's biography.[96] Sickert, who began his working life as an actor, was well known for the transformations he effected on his own identity.[97] At a later period, he renounced the use of his first name (Walter) and espoused that of his second, Richard; then he reversed the process, evidence of "a deep desire to change his identity," according to Baron.[98] Beards came and went on his face throughout his life, altering his whole appearance. Moreover, these hairy visual markers of identity were manipulated once grown. Sometimes he sported a pointed beard, sometimes a square-cut one, and sometimes a patriarchal and luxuriant growth foaming over his collar. Periodically he shaved his head or otherwise changed his hairstyle.

The paintings and drawings themselves partake of Sickert's cavalier attitude toward identity and his willingness to put identity into play. Throughout his career Sickert was prepared to change the titles of his works, sometimes apparently simply for change's sake. *Summer in Naples* became *Dawn, Camden Town* (see fig. 65) and *What Shall We Do for the Rent?* is also *The Camden Town Murder* (c. 1908–9, fig. 69). Sickert made repeated reuse of scenes and figures to stand for different meanings, and he repeatedly altered his style, sometimes very drastically, and sometimes from one series of pictures to the next. He moved regularly around the city as well, at some periods maintaining two or more studios in which to work, and a set of rooms besides, all in different parts of London. He was perennially fascinated by disguise, misrecognition, falsity, and pretence.

These characteristics conjure up those of the urban *flâneur,* the male figure who, by virtue of his gender and the privileges conferred by his class status, is able to consume the city and its irrationalism and to subordinate them both to an aesthetic of detached enjoyment. Robins has recently suggested that we see Sickert in this way as an English *flâneur.*[99] But Robins seems to me not to have explored the most interesting historical implications of this identification. Sickert's nudes, lounging in shabby interiors, are the site of a struggle for authority and control, and Sickert's *flânnerie,* I shall argue, is implicated in a losing battle to maintain the *flâneur*'s status and its gains.

Recent work in cultural geography has argued that the authority of social groupings is partly made possible through the spatial settings in which it is exercised and that a social attribute like sexual identity is partly a function of choice, facilitated by locations and spaces that "give permission" for that identity to be assumed and acted out."[100] Sickert's identity as the "dispassionate observer," the male figure of sexual and social authority whose consumption of the degraded markers of the city's chaos can reformulate it into meaning and order, has its own spatial locations. The studio, the bedroom, the painter's presence (however ironic) within the gross materiality of working-class urban space: all are locations where the performance of authoritative masculinity can come into being spatially rather than as essence. These are the places where social meaning supports the assumption of a generic role by the individual. Sickert's choice of nude figures within shabby North London interiors exploits the spatial character of social meaning in the city to underwrite his assertion of the knowability of the modern. The virtue of the *flâneur*—for those who could adopt the role—was that the city and its threatening irrationalities could be subjected to the control of a unified and integral self, such as the dispassionate artist. The identity of the masculine artist and the comprehensibility of the city are linked in a mutually reinforcing circuit in which the connection is made through the "gross materiality" of the social and gendered other.[101]

This is why identity is connected to sexual rapacity in Sickert's interest in Jack the Ripper and the Camden Town Murder. The male spectator's sense of self is confirmed by his right of access to the bodies of working-class women.

But the *flâneur*'s consumption of the city in Sickert—the apparent rationale of analysis and taxonomy and the endless play to which it is subject—suggests an attitude toward the city and its susceptibility to knowledge that is much more open to anxiety than I have acknowledged so far. The constant translation of identity, as if to put it permanently under question, serves to undermine the clarity of effect that the figure of the "dispassionate observer" would otherwise carry with it. Sickert's undoing of the skein of identity proceeds at exactly the same time as identity is functioning in his painting to underpin the representation of the formlessness and violent otherness of the city, the chaos that is susceptible to painting as a form of knowledge. There is a tension between the role of the painter as definer of the city, the clear-sighted observer of modernity in all its variety who can remodel the forms of painting to produce a practice entirely suited to the description of contemporary life, and the persistent undermining of the stable identity on which it depends. These systems of control seem to collapse under the realization that urban existence is not in fact clear or available for rational knowledge.

The material presented in Judith Walkowitz's book *City of Dreadful Night: Narratives of Sexual Danger in Late Victorian London* (1992) offers a way of grounding the systems of anxiety and control that I have identified in Sickert in the early decades of the twentieth century. Walkowitz argues that the freedom of privileged males to roam through urban spaces during the Victorian period as *flâneurs,* "to see the city whole, and thereby to construct their own identity in relation to that diversity," was seriously challenged at the end of the century by a range of cultural developments that threatened the exclusive elite male possession of the city.[102] Walkowitz demonstrates that by the 1890s, the formerly male spaces of the city had been colonized by a variety of "new social actors," many of them women, whose assertion of the right to urban space forced a revision of the cultural mapping of the city that had supported elite male identity: "In fact and fantasy, London had become a contested terrain: new commercial spaces and journalistic practices, expanding networks of female philanthropy, and a range of public spectacles . . . enabled workingmen and women of many classes to challenge the traditional privileges of elite male spectators and to assert their presence in the public domain."[103] The geographical and cultural divisions that had been available for the *flâneur* to consume as the markers that signaled his own stability shattered, and these "protesting workers, platform women, girls in business, and Glorified Spinsters [all categories of the "new social actors"] appeared as telling and disturbing signs of modernity."[104] The response, according to Walkowitz, was the rise of narratives of sexual danger that functioned to both "incite" and "discipline" the threat to male order that the new conditions carried with them.

I think that Sickert's interests as I have begun to recount them here—in the urban working class as an object of study, in the bodies of working-class women, in sexual murder, and in the elaborated and dramatic paint surface of the Camden Town–period paintings—have a place within this history. Inheriting both the effective resolution of identity and the city that the *flâneur* provided, and the challenge to that effectiveness, Sickert's works address the revision of male identity through a catalogue of its own sexual dangers. Because, in reality, the male *flâneur* can hold authority over the bodies of working-class women, once that relationship breaks down in the social sphere, the metaphysical possibility of representing order suffers erosion along with it. Tension is generated from Sickert's continuing attempts to recoup the gains of the *flâneur* and to make those systems of control and enjoyment function again in commanding the dissolute and threatening city of modernity to order. The subject matter of the paintings provides the material for an attempted thematic resolution of this tension.

This goes some way toward explaining why the Camden Town Murder appealed to Sickert as a controlling category for his paintings around 1908–9. Murder in the Camden Town paintings is the medium through which the labile nature of knowledge is given substance. The mysteries of identity and the impenetrability of action in the city find a home there. Murder is the distillation of everything that runs counter to the imposition of knowledge onto the city—it stands for what lacks system, for what is unmotivated, unpredictable, violent, and intense in a way that the rationalized systems of the city, smoothly running, can never be. It is the embodiment of the city as opaque, of the terrors and phantasms that crawl out of the uncertainties of city spaces and haunt the streets. Murder for Sickert—and particularly sexual murder—stands as the impulse through which the irrational aspects of modernity can be explored and subordinated to control. The apparent paradox through which the irrationality and violence of murder stands for the imposition of order only signals the degree to which knowing modernity had come to seem a desperate ambition. But then again, in Sickert's paintings, under the pressure of the revision of this methodology for understanding the city, it is not even clear that murder has taken place.

Sickert is working with material that carries meanings of male authority. The power attributed to the *flâneur* is Sickert's cultural inheritance; the *flâneur*'s possible resolution of uncertainty into order colors his work. But Sickert also

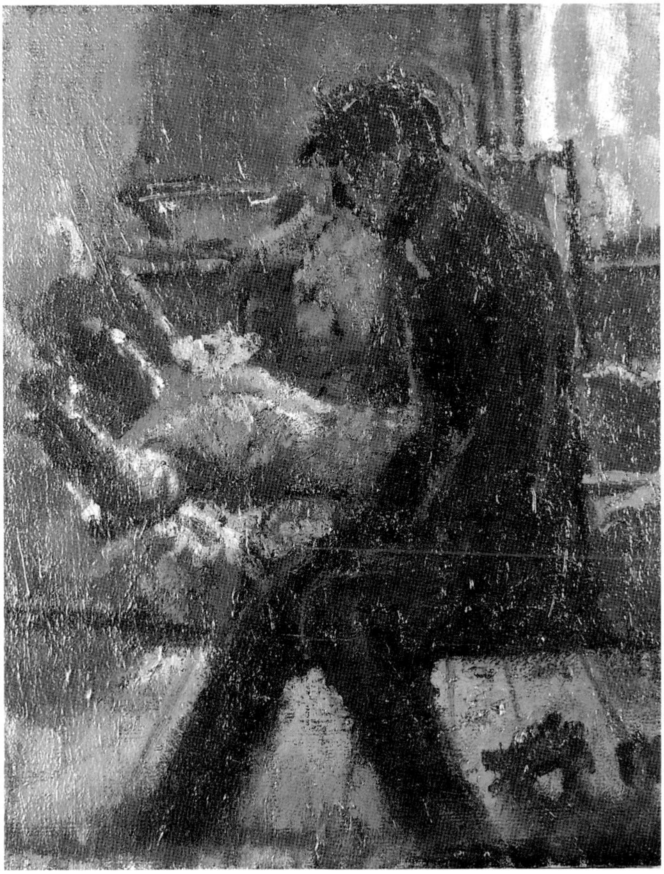

FIGURE 70. Walter Sickert, *Summer Afternoon,* or, *What Shall We Do for the Rent?,* c. 1908

articulates a characteristically modernist response to this fact. The authority of the *flâneur* can no longer convince, and the consequence is an irony, a self-consciousness, before the material. Control through the gendered paint surface—as in Whistler—is not sustainable. Sickert cannot release himself from the promise of the dispassionate *flâneur's* gaze on the working-class bodies of his female models, but neither can he believe in it. Sickert cultivates the gift of identity that the *flâneur* provides, yet also manifests sufficient uncertainty about its success to take risks with it and to push hard at its limits.

The three Camden Town Murder paintings that seem to me central are *Summer Afternoon,* or, *What Shall We Do for the Rent?* (c. 1908, fig. 70), *The Camden Town Murder,* or, *What Shall We Do for the Rent?* (see fig. 69), and *L'Affaire de Camden Town* (c. 1909, fig. 71). All of these titles quite explicitly have non-murderous alternatives written into them; not one of them has an unequivocal corpse. The relations between the clothed male figures and their nude female

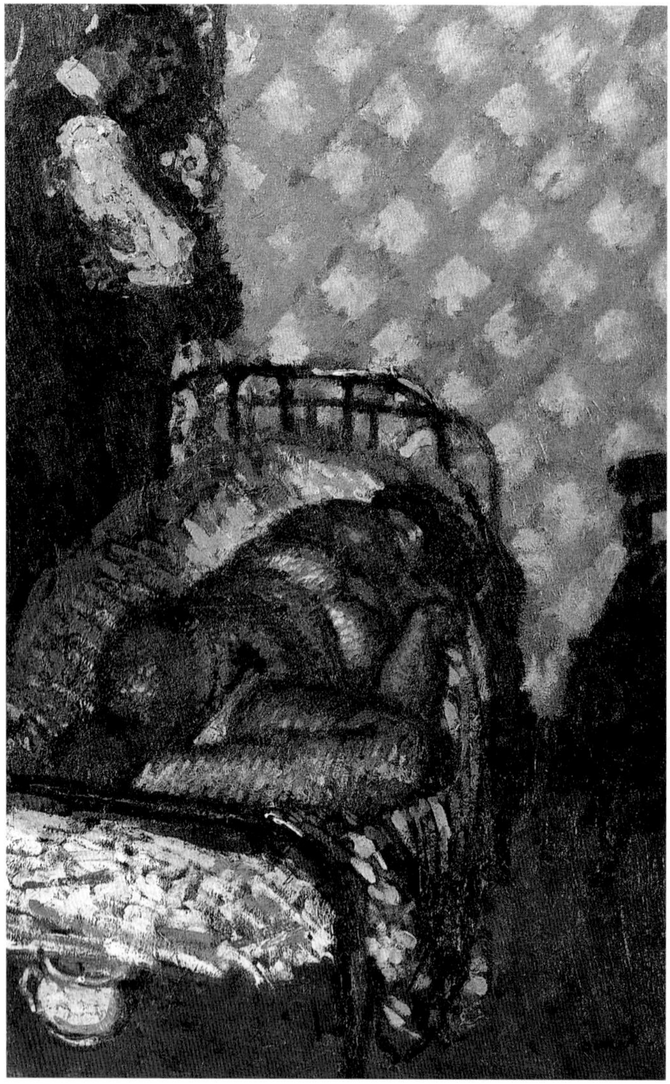

FIGURE 71. Walter Sickert, *L'Affaire de Camden Town*, c. 1909

companions are clearly ambiguous. The slumped, despairing stance of the man in *The Camden Town Murder* may be the result of worrying about the rent, or it may be the consequence of having just cut the throat of the woman behind him. She may be dead, but she is just as credible as a representation of weary resignation. This may be read as a pre- or post-coital moment, as tension generated from any number of causes. What we have here is murder without a corpse, crime without a consequence, signs without fixed meaning. This uncertainty signals the possibility of knowledge while acknowledging that the reknitting of the strands of meaning is essentially a comforting gesture—apotropaic, like the neurotic rituals of propitiation we use to order the chaotic city. Against the stream of light, illumination washing over the body of the nude on the bed in *Summer Afternoon,* the figure of the man, black with the effect of the *contre-jour,* strains to impose his will to meaning on the subject matter, the irrational and unresolved as it sprawls out before him. It is he, however, who is insubstantial, shadowy, atomized by the impact of the world. The nude, that sink of chaos and the unformed that needs to be pulled and bullied into being by the painter's will, lies there, bathed by contrast in the clarity of an illumination that reveals nothing. Her high-heeled shoes, kicked off across the floor, are more substantial than he is.

The role of murder in these paintings, then, is to provide the justification for a solution. It represents the phantasmagoric city and allows itself to be captured for knowledge—but not effectively. Within Sickert's paintings, executed at a moment when the confident seizure of meaning in the city by the *flâneur* was under question, the irrational fights back. The passive, represented body of the nude—the body to which violence is done to wrench its threatening otherness into meaning—stubbornly insists on its materiality and presence, its own "grossness." The observer, whose visual acuity, dispassionate gaze, and transformation of the world into description seemed to support Sickert's rationalizing anatomy of the city, is represented as powerless in the very paintings that assert his power. The observing male figures in all these works stand in for the painter but represent him as a figure of no authority, one whose observation, far from being the guarantee of control, is no more than witness. The irrational in the form of the nude, passive but uncapturable, dominates him nonetheless. The impenetrability of action and relationship in these paintings and drawings stands exactly for the impossibility of achieving knowledge about the world. The nude and her relationships mean precisely nothing within the terms of comprehension the observer sets out. The male figure looking down on the nude in *L'Affaire de Camden Town* might as well be contemplating his powerlessness against her body—whether dead or alive. His cogitations will get him nowhere.

I began this part of the chapter by arguing that the modern city is subject to two competing definitions. On the one hand, there is a rational understanding of the city as a complex but comprehensible collection of systems. On the other, our *experience* of the city is opposed to the rational *concept* we have of it, because our experience is of randomness, resistance to comprehension, and therefore of a city potentially or actually threatening and disquieting. Sickert's painting in the years between 1905 and 1910, so clearly attending to metropolitan experience by its preoccupation with interiors, the minutiae of dull or sordid urban lives, has something to say about that dualism in the city. At first, this painting seems to attempt to cope with the description of modernity through the city by subjecting everything that is disquieting or random to the rule of a rationalizing, dispassionate observer. Painting itself becomes the tool of analysis that can render the city knowable through its material manipulations of the gross facts of urban life. The transformation of the subject matter is, I suggested, no less a fiction than the pleasant fantasies of "wriggle and chiffon" portrait painting. But the harder we look at Sickert's work, the more the attempt to round up and tame the unknowableness of the city, to bring it within knowledge, comes to seem unsustainable. There is, in the contrasted descriptions of clothed male and nude female figures in the Camden Town period, an insidious undermining of the figure of the observer as dispassionate analyst of the urban. The analyst looks strangely powerless before the object of his contemplation. I have suggested that this collapse of the spectator may be referred to the shift in cultural circumstances that wrenched possession of the city away from the male *flâneur* and redistributed it amongst a contending variety of potential claimants, among them the working class and women, both of whom had previously stood for the chaos that the observing *flâneur* was able to bring under control.

Sickert stands at the point of tension between authority and its collapse. He inherits a ready and effective structure of authority in the *flâneur* and through the idea of paint as agency that he learns from Whistler. The otherness of modernity can be mastered through the male painter's conceptual power, his definition of the "realities" of differently classed and gendered lives in the analytical practice of his painting. But he finds as well that this assertion of control is undermined by experience. The material "facts" of these lives will no longer serve to demonstrate the *flâneur*'s successful understanding of the world. The solution to the problem of unmediation that Whistler had imagined no longer functions. Sickert's ironic stance before both the world and male identity that I described flows from this, as does his occasional willingness to interest himself in the other side of experience.

When Sickert painted *Girl at a Window: Little Rachel* in 1907 (fig. 72) near the start of this period of his work, he questioned in advance some of the central terms of the series and produced a work in which the themes of observer and object, contrasted male and female, and reason and irrationality are subjected to a severe scrutiny.[105] The scene is set in the rooms Sickert took in 1905 at 6 Mornington Crescent. The view looks out across Mornington Crescent

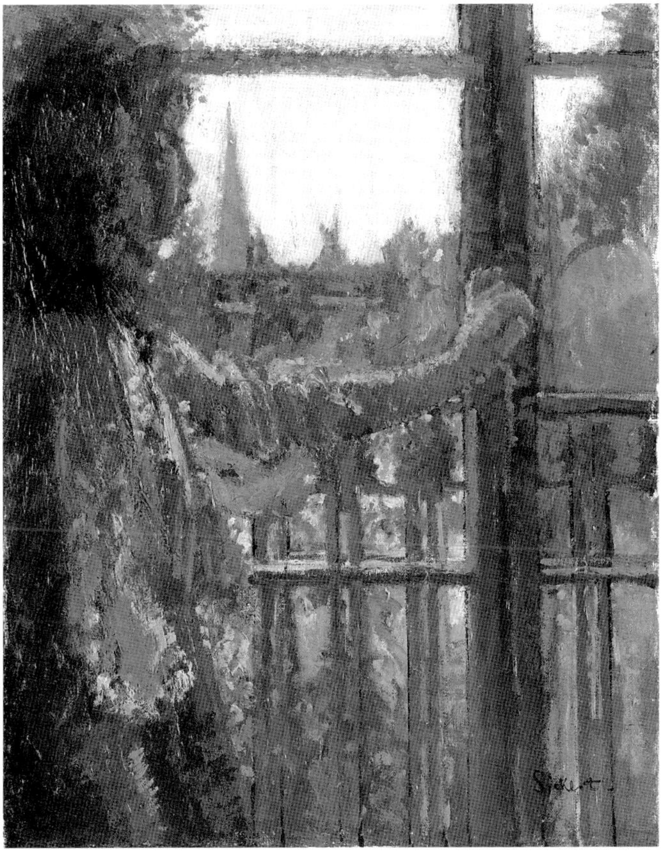

FIGURE 72. Walter Sickert, *Girl at a Window: Little Rachel,* 1907

Gardens toward the Tube station and the steeple of Old St. Pancras. A girl—"a little Jewish girl of 13 or so with red hair," Sickert recalled—gazes out at the view from the interior toward the city.[106] Her gesture, arm out to touch the frame of the window, head turned to the exterior light, is both hesitant and authoritative, extroverted and withdrawn. The paint surface is thick with the lush, sensual impasto of Sickert's Camden Town period, built up into ridges and cavities of paint to describe the interior and dragged dry over the canvas in the sky to allow the color of the primer to show through. It is a technically assertive painting, dandified and self-conscious in a way that might carry the meaning of control and definition that I have attributed to the paint surface of *Mornington Crescent Nude* or *The Studio.* But the normal terms of the Camden Town and Mornington Crescent series are reversed elsewhere in the painting. The observer here is a clothed female figure. It is she who looks out onto modernity, now described as the cityscape that is visible *from* the interior, rather than as *experience* compressed into the interior itself.

The view from the interior through a window onto the outside world is a strong topos in early modernist painting. Looking out of the window is looking out from the shell of the self onto the ranged symbols of modernity. It figures the engagement with the world that Sickert's painting attempts at this time.[107] The girl is a credible stand-in for the painter, with her arm, the only part of her in full illumination, stretching out to touch a framework of vertical and horizontal elements, mostly of wood, that apes the arrangement of the stretcher that supports a canvas. Here the model becomes the observing painter, the raw material of the modern city becomes the painting that pretends to encapsulate and know it. Agency is reversed and the world of modernity seems to take precedence, to dominate and surpass its representation in the painting. *Girl at a Window* is a virtual surrender of the possibility of knowledge by the male "dispassionate observer." Instead, knowledge is given over to the new inheritors of the city. The girl looks out onto the city, and what she sees there she keeps to herself. Her "painting" is the city itself rather than its representation. The illusory integrity that the figure of the *flâneur* provides is revealed as empty. The acknowledgment of the relationship to the city that the girl embodies is of a modernity that is complex, nuanced, and open in ways that make the imposition of order look vapid and hollow.

Sickert's painting itself, then, embodies the dichotomy or duality of modernity with which I began. It is not a practice to which ideas of the "dispassionate observer" or the *flâneur* can be straightforwardly applied. In much of Sickert's work and life, the authoritative male spectator can be seen in the process of collapse. His modernity resides in this. Hence, what we see in *Girl at a Window* is an early acknowledgment of the authority of modernity itself to subvert the claims of the male observer, however "dispassionate" he asserts himself to be. But this provides no resolution; Sickert continues to operate with the materials he inherits and their meanings. His hesitancy before the imposition of authority, coupled with a very clear desire to impose it, defines a particular historical moment. His work allows us to understand the ways in which the ambition for painting to be a social critique—and to understand the conditions of modernity—can be compromised by its involvement in those conditions. But from the tension between the rational and the phantasmagoric aspects of the works emerges a delineation of modernity far more appropriate than the rational analysis it seems to offer at first glance. Behind the apparent reading lies an embodiment of the tensions and confusions attendant upon modernity: the urge to categorize and decipher is negated and extended by the unreadability of the material. I have argued that Sickert's works of the 1890s investigate the status of the visual as a form of knowledge of modernity and, through the dialectic between Symbolist "depth" and Realist "surface," offer a complication of the visual's claims to know. Later, the "gross material facts" of modernity prove to be inadequate as a diagnosis. The modern city turns out to be grossly material—and no longer definable by facts. In the next chapter, I will look at how this situation played out in the years around 1910, when sections of English modernism sought to pull away from Sickert's inheritance.

The Aesthetics of Materiality

ENGLISH MODERNISM BEFORE 1914

At the beginning of April 1914, Walter Sickert published his obituary of Spencer Frederick Gore in the *New Age,* calling him "one of our greatest modern painters" and "a perfect modern."[1] In his account Sickert presents Gore's "perfection" as bound up with an acknowledgment of his medium, "his chosen instrument," the "material paraphernalia of painting," that "truculent and hard-mouthed beast" (354). Gore "accepted the instrument as he found it handed down to us by Monet and Pisarro [*sic*]," an "opaque mosaic" of paint (ibid.). And this determination to "ride" the "beast" was a labor to achieve through his mastery of the medium a meditative understanding of the world beyond the self: "he drilled himself to be the passive and enchanted conduit for whatever of loveliness his eyes might rest upon" (ibid.). This "was Gore's secret," an achievement that he had "wrung . . . seemingly twenty-four hours a day from the exercise of the purest, the serenest, and the most exhilarated reflection. But it was brush in hand that he reflected" (ibid.).

Mornington Crescent (1911, fig. 73), one of a large number of paintings of the motif Gore executed around that time, takes up the urban theme of Sickert's own Camden Town pictures.[2] The canvas evokes the London summer, the markers of the urban facades rising seductively above dense foliage. But it is not the lure of dusty pavements that predominates. The multiple greens of the trees clustering round the grass of the central area built up out of Sickert's "mosaic" of touches make up the major part of the canvas. In "A Perfect Modern," Sickert, who painted his own views of the Crescent, remembered these trees as the principal actors in Gore's canvases:

There was a month of June a few years ago which Gore verily seems to have used as if he had known that it was to be for him the last of its particularly fresh and sumptuous kind. He used it to look down on the garden of Mornington Crescent. The trained trees rise and droop in fringes, like fountains, over the little well of greenness and shade where little parties of young people are playing at tennis. The back-cloth of this scene is formed by the tops of the brown houses of the Hampstead Road, and the liver-coloured tiles of the Tube Station. (355)

Like Sickert, Gore reimagines the view, smoothing away any hint of urban brutality to substitute a gentle fantasia, a meditative reworking of the scene trans-

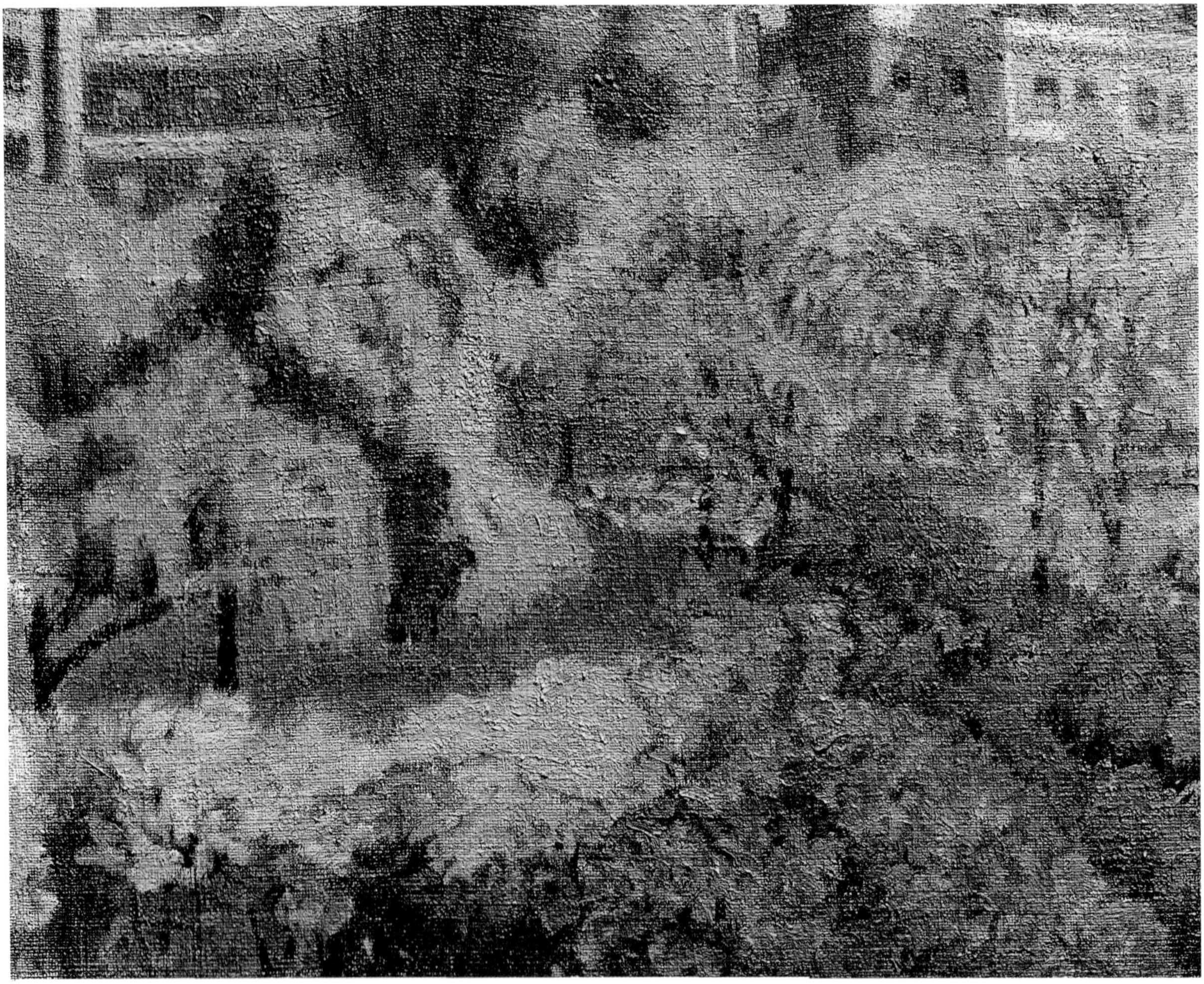

FIGURE 73. Spencer Gore, *Mornington Crescent,* 1911

formed from "a place that looks like hell"—"liver-coloured" London Tube and all—to a scene of pleasure (ibid.). The "opaque mosaic" of Gore's paint, miming the susurration of leaves and the brick and plaster surfaces of the facades beyond them, offers the city as visual seduction: "it is not only out of scenes obviously beautiful in themselves, and of delightful suggestion," wrote Sickert, "that the modern painter can conjure a panel of encrusted enamel" (ibid.). Gore's "passive and enchanted conduit" channels through itself an inner "loveliness" that plain sight can hardly perceive.

For Sickert, Gore's relationship to tradition is allied to this transformative and meditative function. Unlike "the young men who sit in the Café Royal waiting to be crowned on the strength of their own post-dated stumers on futurity" (ibid.), by which Sickert chiefly means the Vorticist group around Wyndham Lewis, Gore both acknowledged and celebrated his commitment to tradition: "it was curious, in these days, and distinctly unfashionable to hear a young man, who was already influencing a whole generation, willingly allude with gratitude and appreciation to the authority of men under whom he studied" (353–54). In Sickert's hands, Gore becomes an exemplum of a "modern" whose "perfection" is in part the result of his refusal of modernist strategies of repudiation. The past is not brutalized and rejected as it is for the Vorticists, whose little magazine, *Blast* (1914), wrote of "years 1837 to 1900" as "abysmal inexcusable," the "GLOOMY VICTORIAN CIRCUS" of the past.[3] Rather, as for Sickert himself, continuity with the technical priorities and modes of understanding of significant precursors is vital to a proper modernity.[4]

The themes of Sickert's obituary are the themes of this chapter. I deal with the continuing role of facture as it found a central place in the appearance and development of a modernist art in England; with the rivalry among modernists in those years; and with the expression of this rivalry in the use of paint and paint surface to accommodate the modern to visual pleasure or its repudiation. Camden Town, Vorticism, and Bloomsbury inherited the diagnosis and amelioration of the threatening disorder of modern experience through the pleasure offered by pigment and its application that I have traced in previous chapters. For the Vorticists, that transcendence is undone and reconstituted in a thoroughgoing and sometimes violent reformulation of the spectator's experience. For the Camden Town and Bloomsbury painters, however, the material quality of the paint continues to stand for transcendence through pleasure. The possibilities of pleasure are central to the themes I have raised. They provide a continuity with the earlier concerns of the painters I have discussed so far that gives to these central strands of English modernism an important role in the "tradition" I have been examining. If the Vorticists manipulated facture to repudiate this recourse to pleasure, they were no less a part of that tradition and acted, in choosing their paint surfaces as their weapons in the internecine warfare of English modernism, as its inheritors. In the second part of the chapter, I take up the wider issues of the book and consider the role of continuity in the work and thought of the competing "perfect moderns" of 1910–14. I suggest some of the ways in which our received periodization of the history of English painting distorts our understanding of its actual relationships, and I end by suggesting how they may be reimagined in the light of my arguments in the book as a whole.

The Politics of Modernism

Modernism has its myths, as we now all know. Among them is the myth of the *tabula rasa,* the cleared ground, whereby modernity requires for its expression the erasure of all pasts, even those of the modernist self, and their replacement with a single point of initiation, a clean, focused clarity of understanding within which the confusion of history has finally been stilled. This is why modernism is also a culture of fictions—myths of origin and of the "voyage out." The journey to truth and understanding is endemic, seductive even when parodied, as it is in a whole series of modernist novels. Tales of blocked self-realization, these fictions express a yearning for an integration and achievement of knowledge that modernity itself is understood to frustrate. Dependent on the imagined absence of the past, they are histories that make themselves out of nothing.

English modernism is no different from any other in this way. The London art world before 1914 was a scene of psychic combat where competing factions struggled to assert their own erasure of history, to suppress others who were striving to suppress them in their turn, and to write out of the account the achievements and solutions offered by their peers and rivals. It was a textual world, one in which triumph and defeat depended on the assertions of rhetoric and explication rather than on action. In this sense, it was still Whistler's world, the one he shared with Ricketts and Wilde, a world made out of words, out of the din of language used to persuade, bully, and betray. But it was also a world made from the visual, one in which the surfaces of paintings also operated a semiotics of modernist display. On these surfaces, the *tabula rasa* was initiated, rivals were repudiated and dismissed, and claims for radical priority were asserted and maintained.

The story of the competitive English art world before the outbreak of war has been told many times.[5] We know about Roger Fry's Post-Impressionist exhibitions in 1910 and 1914 and their "epochal" impact.[6] We know about the currents of connection and animosity that lay behind the grouping and regrouping of Fitzroy into Camden Town and then into the London Group. And we know about the appearance of Futurism on the scene in 1912 and how it introduced another, more radical Continental modernism that threatened Fry's bid to make of Post-Impressionism the definitive modern English art. Finally, we know how Wyndham Lewis and his colleagues threw off their connections successively to Camden Town, Bloomsbury, and Continental modernism in order to found Vorticism. Despite the brevity of its flowering (between June and August 1914), Vorticism remains the principal contender for an indigenous English "avant-garde movement."

I do not see any reason to repeat this story again in detail here. But I do want to trace one example of the myth: the fiction of origin without generation or parentage, "modernist originality" and the journey to knowledge that forms a part of it.[7] In doing so, I shall show something of the complex history of the politics and changing rivalries and relationships of English painters in these years, when a number of separate contenders for the role of interpreter of the culture's modernity in paint staked their claims and had to fight their corner against equally convinced opponents.[8] This shifting landscape of rivalry and factionalism will prove to be important, partly because it has hitherto been interpreted very largely from the perspective of the winning side, the "radicals," the "advanced," and the modernists whose histories commentary has concentrated on elucidating—accepting, in order to do so, their vocabulary of "progress" and the out-of-date, the cleared ground of modernist fantasy. I shall take the career of Wyndham Lewis, a central modernist figure, and trace it through from the mid-1900s to 1914. By doing so, I shall provide a structure for a rather different reading in subsequent sections of the argument.

Lewis's modernism includes a cult of personality, and his progress through the political minefield of English art after his return from the Continent in 1908 is a history of relentless self-promotion as the new genius of modern English painting. When he returned to London in that year, he encountered an art world he later spoke of as in "an unusually somnolent condition," as the culmination of the "miniature Dark Ages for the Fine Arts" of the nineteenth century.[9] These descriptions are appropriate to Lewis's later insistence that Vorticism appeared unheralded to transform a moribund order with its own, vital, modern art, but they are accurate only from the perspective of modernism's self-image. The story Lewis tells about himself presents the dynamic young painter illuminating a modernity that has hitherto been ignored or suppressed, without support and against the obfuscation and dishonesties of the past. "Our vortex is not afraid of the Past: it has forgotten its existence," declared *Blast,* adding "Our Vortex insists on water-tight compartments. There is no Present—there is Past and Future, and there is Art."[10] Such blatant attempts to imagine away the past (represented, as we shall see, by Fry and Sickert) and the future (represented by Futurism) have all the hallmarks of fantasy. These years saw Lewis slowly working his way up the ladder of success through careful association with these other groups and artists.

Lewis had been at the Slade with Gore and Harold Gilman and had remained in contact with them. And when, in the winter of 1910–11, the members of Sickert's informal Fitzroy Street Circle formed themselves into the

Camden Town Group, with sixteen invited members, Lewis was one.[11] Beyond its central core, the group was diverse in its aims and methods. Charles Ginner observed that Lewis's election "caused much opposition in certain quarters" because of the "advanced" nature of his art.[12] And while Lewis had support for his interests from within Camden Town in the form of Ginner, Gore, and Gilman, the latter of whom "was determined that . . . Lewis should be one of the select few," it was not always a comfortable situation.[13] Despite this lack of fit, in 1911 his opportunities for showing were sufficiently rare to make it worthwhile to pursue any opportunity that presented itself. He would try to make his own career while clinging to Camden Town. Its political support was too valuable for him to give up merely because of artistic differences. As he himself remembered, "though not interested I was there."[14]

When the first Camden Town exhibition was held at the Carfax Gallery in June 1911, Lewis, seeking to establish himself through the "advanced" character of his art, exhibited what seemed to commentators a brutally simplified pair of drawings that abjured the Impressionist aesthetic of his Camden Town colleagues (fig. 74).[15] Aware that the advanced nature of his art was likely to be an issue, he chose to exploit it rather than to play it down. He wrote to Sturge Moore, a close friend, after the Carfax show had closed:

the drawings which I showed at the Carfax Galleries which I supposed, naturally, would go unnoticed, caused widespread indignation. The criticism would begin: "Despite the alarming announcements of the character of this 'Group', we find that amongst this band of honest, hard working & interesting young men (with one exception) that good old English conservatism has saved them from excesses" etc. Then the next paragraph would begin: "That one exception is Mr Wyndham Lewis, *whose blackguardly, preposterous, putrid" etc. But invariably! Every notice that came along to our President followed, roughly, this itinerary.*[16]

Lewis exaggerates, of course, but it is clear that he was testing the effect of encouraging negative comment, "almost as if he wanted to be resented," as Richard Cork has noted.[17] Lewis is playing the modernist, one who "values his practice in terms of its power to generate the sense of a need for progress, where progress is measured by the victory of one 'paradigm' of practice, one 'hypothesis,' one 'concept of art,' one manner over another less novel."[18] Responses like that of *The Times,* which saw only "three geometrical experiments which many people will take for bad practical jokes" at the second Camden Town Group show in December 1911, were exactly what was wanted,

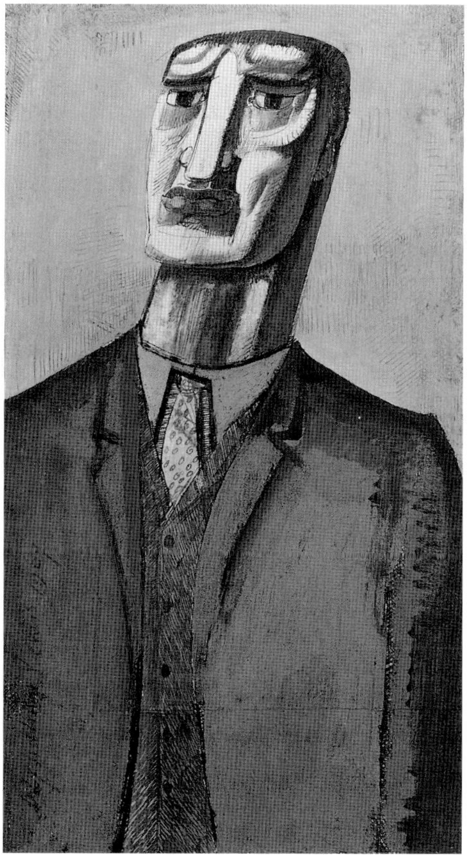

FIGURE 74. Wyndham Lewis, *Architect with a Green Tie*, 1909

especially when they were matched by Frank Rutter's opinion that Lewis was now "the extremist" and Post-Impressionism's "most downright and uncompromising exponent."[19]

Lewis continued to associate with Camden Town, although he was by now very far from the original tenets of the group. But he was also approaching young artists who were part of the "creative ferment" then in progress at the Slade, establishing contact with C. R. W. Nevinson, William Roberts, Edward Wadsworth, Frederick Etchells, and Cuthbert Hamilton—all of whom were to be involved with Vorticism—as well as more independent spirits, such as David Bomberg and Jacob Epstein.[20] From the perspective of such a potential new formation of colleagues in sympathy with Lewis's art, the Camden Town Group now began to seem attractive in a new way. Camden Town's unauthoritative nature had originally provided Lewis with prestigious support from a group that, if sometimes disapproving, did not demand full compliance with its own artistic norms as the price of admission. By 1913 enough artists expressed sympathy with the new art and the group was sufficiently loosely structured to allow Lewis to attempt a coup and to take command of a functioning unit without the risk of courting overwhelming opposition. "Fancy people joining with the idea of forming a teetotaller society," Pissarro wrote at this time, "and coming to the conclusion that in order not to be narrow-minded they must admit some drunkards!"[21]

During this period of reconstruction, the group held an exhibition at the Public Art Galleries, Brighton, although not under its old name. The "Exhibition of the Work of Post-Impressionists, Cubists and Others" ran from December 1913 to January 1914 and signaled the severity of the internal divisions. The various factions were parceled out into separate rooms. Lewis showed six paintings in "the Cubist Room," all of which are now lost, and wrote one of the two forewords to the catalogue. (The other, representing the conservative wing of the group, was written by J. B. Manson.) There is much of the tone of *Blast* in this foreword. The radical painters—Lewis, Etchells, Hamilton, Wadsworth, and Nevinson—are presented as part of an implacable historical force. Lewis wrote: "These painters are not accidentally associated here, but form a vertiginous, but not exotic, island in the placid and respectable archipelago of English art. This formation is undeniably of volcanic matter and even origin; for it appeared suddenly above the waves following certain seismic shakings beneath the surface. It is very closely knit and admirably adapted to withstand the imperturbable Britannic breakers which roll pleasantly against its sides."[22] No attempt is made to distinguish the components of the art Lewis's radicalism is intended to replace; they are all lumped together and dismissed, "placid," "respectable," and "imperturbable," as Lewis celebrates the new art he is promoting. But this rhetoric is also defensive. The sense of isolation is unmistakable. However violent the eruption, this new art remains an "island," one that needs to "withstand" the attentions of its elders. Lewis's ambition has still to defend itself, on its separate "island," from too-close encounters with his colleagues and rivals.

Although Sickert and Manson were diplomatic in public, conciliation was in vain. The irreconcilable nature of the two factions shows through the diplomacy, as does Sickert's bad temper, which, kept in check at the show, was soon to be let off its leash.[23] He confessed in private that "at Brighton the Epstein-Lewis-Etchells room made me sick" and said that he "publically disengaged my responsibility."[24] By February 1914, when the first show of the "London Group" was being discussed, Sickert had ceased to turn up to Fitzroy Street meetings. Nor did he exhibit at the "First Exhibition of Works by Members of the London

Group" held in March 1914, public attention to which was firmly concentrated on the radical wing.[25] Manson and Pissarro resigned at the end of March to hold a secessionist show, and Sickert withdrew to a lordly eminence and began to criticize the radicals in print.[26]

In *Blast* 2 (1915), Lewis discusses Sickert among other precursors and influences whom he assesses, bundles up, and confidently stows away in the dusty museum of the past, giving a potted history of English art from the time when he entered the Slade to the War. Sickert, in this history, becomes an artist exclusively of the days "fifteen or sixteen years ago" when the New English Art Club was "THE revolutionary society."[27] Sickert was then, in company with the likes of Wilson Steer, a "horrifying personage" to the public, although "it is difficult to understand, at this distance, the offence that these admirable gentlemen (and often quite good painters) could have caused" (80). Lewis attributes Sickert's foundation of the Camden Town Group to conservatism: "Now new forces were stirring in Paris, which site Mr Sickert had vacated, and his idea no doubt was to retreat fighting to England, and gather and intench [*sic*] in these slow-moving climes an Impressionist legion of his own" (ibid.). But in doing this, Sickert fulfilled one stage in the progress of English art toward its apogee in Vorticism: "a much more real and lively person than his New English colleagues . . . for a few years he controlled the most sensible and serious body of painters in England" (81). The Camden Town Group, however, has now "served it's [*sic*] purpose," Sickert is "in retirement," and Lewis can afford to be magnanimous in victory: "With the two or three best of my Camden Town colleagues, I have no particular mental feud, though not agreeing with them. And if they would only allow me to alter their pictures a little, and would undergo a brief course of training prescribed by me, I would even AGREE with them" (ibid.). "Mr Sickert is better than a Pompier, though inferior to a Vorticist" (ibid.), and he is now an outmoded forerunner of the radical fulfillment of Vorticism.[28]

While he was working his way through the possibilities offered by Camden Town, Lewis had been developing his connections with another group of important artists and thinkers. Bloomsbury's "Post-Impressionist" aesthetics posed a far more thoroughgoing challenge to Lewis's quest for the laurels of modernism than Sickert and Camden Town. Partly this difficulty arose because, unlike the tolerant attitude of Camden Town, Bloomsbury demanded absolute identity; one was either with it entirely or one was outside it. Moreover, unlike that offered by Sickert, Roger Fry's patronage was inseparable from a strong personal influence. While Lewis needed at all costs to preserve his individuality, Bloomsbury sought to subsume him within the group. During his intimacy with Bloomsbury, Lewis tried to avoid the consequences of these facts, exploiting the relationship but resisting incorporation. He declined to exhibit with either the Friday Club or the Grafton Group, the two Bloomsbury showcases, and he always continued to associate with the other factions. Fry, in the midst of promoting his own version of Post-Impressionism as the definitive English modernism, needed Lewis's innovativeness and intelligence as a painter. He was, however, unwilling to allow him to compromise or walk a middle line.

Although Lewis had met Duncan Grant as early as 1907, it is likely to have been Fry's "Manet and the Post-Impressionists" exhibition that ran at the Grafton Gallery from November 1910 to January 1911 that drew him to the Group.[29] I will return to the significance of the exhibition below in the context of its historiography. Here I want to note its importance in promoting Post-Impressionist art both to the public at large—through the *succès de scandale* of the exhibition that hundreds attended in order to be shocked—and to artists.[30] Ginner and Gore were not alone in going to Paris under its influence to see "everything that could be seen" in Post-Impressionist art.[31] It was, in Charles Harrison's words, "upon the issue of Post-Impressionism that the generations divided" in the English art world into radicals and conservatives, with Sickert and the NEAC unequivocally counted among the latter.[32] For Lewis the success of the Post-Impressionist show in combining a public challenge to received opinion with magnificent publicity and the establishment of a "new movement" in the forefront of English art must have seemed an exemplary demonstration of modernist politics. Fry was a figure from whom Lewis knew he must gain advantage to pursue his career if he were to be numbered among the radicals.

For his part, Fry was not unaware of Lewis and his interest seems to have become intense in the summer of 1912 with the exhibition of Lewis's *Kermesse* at the Allied Artists' Association (lost).[33] The picture provoked a number of comments along the lines of the "boiled lobster legs, each two yards long" of the *New Age* critic, but it also garnered a significant number of favorable reactions.[34] The picture was an index of Lewis's ambition, a semi-abstract design, innovative and successful enough as a painting to attract wide attention. The most favorable reviews of all came from Fry and Clive Bell, writing, respectively, in the *Nation* and the *Athenaeum*. Fry had very clearly formulated ambitions of his own, attempting to set English painting on a line of development that would take the innovations and practice of Cézanne as a touchstone, rejecting both the NEAC, whose place in the art world it sought to usurp, and the modernist extremism of the Futurists, who had appeared in London in 1912. In this attempt, the aesthetics that became known as "significant form" were central: "lines and colours continued in a particular way, certain forms and relations of forms" that "stir our aesthetic emotions."[35] It is clear from the two reviews of *Kermesse* that Lewis seemed to Bell and Fry to be producing art that was compatible with the promulgation of such an aesthetics; both describe him as already operating within its "tradition." Fry felt that "except for Mr Wyndham Lewis's design, there is not much Post-Impressionist work of importance," and he praised *Kermesse* as "a really expressive art of design" and " a rhythmic disposition of abstract units of form" that were "expressive of a particular mood."[36] Bell took his cue very closely from Fry and, after Fry's review, he assumed that "the visitor will probably turn first to the large picture by Mr Wyndham Lewis." Having done so, he must "shed all irrelevant prejudices in favour of representation" and will then "be able to contemplate it as a piece of pure design. He will be able to judge it as he would music—that is to say, as pure formal expression."[37]

The same terms that defined *Kermesse* in 1912 were used to declare the triumph of Fry's new art at the Second Post-Impressionist Exhibition held the same year. In the introduction to the catalogue, Bell claims outright victory and celebrates the "English group" who now figured in the Post-Impressionist pantheon: "The battle is won."[38] He repeats the musical metaphor that he and Fry had used in their reviews of *Kermesse:* "we expect a work of plastic art to have more in common with a piece of music than a coloured photograph."[39] Lewis was invited to exhibit at the second show as part of the English Group, and his *Creation* (c. 1912, lost) was reproduced in the catalogue.[40]

Inevitably this association did not work. Lewis was too concerned with achieving his own ambition and asserting his own more geometric and abstracting art as the true English modernism to sustain a close relationship with Fry and the Bloomsbury Group for very long. To be included by Fry in "my little group of English artists" or by others among his "many young disciples," however temporarily useful, was intensely irksome and ultimately proved disastrous.[41] After a brief period with Fry's Omega Workshops, founded in July 1913 in Fitzroy Square to promote a decorative version of English Post-Impressionism, Lewis seceded in October 1913, taking Etchells, Hamilton, and Wadsworth with him. He almost immediately founded "The Rebel Art Centre," a short-lived rival institution in Great Ormond Street.[42] It was at this period that Lewis seemed to observers to have assumed "all the airs of a maître d'école without being one,"[43] and the secession from the Omega launched Lewis into independence in the few months before the appearance of *Blast* and the formation of Vorticism.

Lewis's subsequent comments focus on the character of Bloomsbury's visuality. He attacks the Omega and the Bloomsbury painters as a group for their formalism and fascination with the "decorative," which he calls an emasculated and frivolous "Prettiness."[44] Omega aesthetics are said to be derivative and only superficially modern: "the Idol is still Prettiness, with its mid-Victorian languish of the neck, and its skin is 'greenery-yallery,' despite the Post-What-Not fashionableness of its draperies."[45] The shared interest in a "pure" visuality in Aestheticism and Bloomsbury is denigrated as superficial and without force or capacity for diagnosis and understanding. In *Blast* 1, Fry and Bloomsbury are not even acknowledged, and the Omega's existence (as well as its significance) is denied by omission. There is a substantial attempt to tackle Bloomsbury in *Blast* 2, which I will deal with below. But whether by ignoring it or confronting it, Lewis refuses Bloomsbury the leadership of the modern movement that Fry claimed for it. The versions of Sickert and Camden Town that Lewis included in *Blast* acknowledge them as precursors of Vorticist art. There is no such attempt to transform influence into retrospective discipleship in the case of Fry. Lewis will not allow a suggestion of contemporary relevance. By denying Bloomsbury's art any presence in modernity, Lewis seeks to defuse the threat of an alternative version of modernism to his own and to reinforce his own claims for leadership accordingly. The exclusion of Fry and the Omega from the legitimate history of modern art in *Blast* seems to indicate the abiding threat that other modernisms posed for Lewis and Vorticism. The categories of exclusion and legitimation that *Blast* wields dismiss the past of Vorticism, projecting Lewis and his "movement" into the forefront of modernist achievement. As part of this strategy, the rejection of Bloomsbury's aesthetics becomes the rejection of the passive, ineffectual, and old-fashioned that Vorticism aims to displace.

But this is also the rejection of a capacity of the visual to mean entirely on its own terms. In a sense, the promise of the visual comes to a rather sorry end in Vorticist avant-garde modernism. Language, still the instrument of modernity, once again making the work of visual art an adjunct to the "rhetorical din" of the time, has the whip hand in the years before 1914.[46] Lewis conducts his career through rhetoric and the word fully as much as Whistler. *Blast* embodies that ambition, wielding its categories of exclusion and inclusion for art-political purposes and subordinating the art itself to a rhetorical imaginary in which the world is recast into forms that suit Lewis's modernist desire. But what is suppressed in this textualization of the world is the possibility that visuality might itself function to achieve knowledge. Vorticism's world is a discursive one. Its painting, as we shall see, is *about* something, and it often contains a programmatic analysis susceptible to linguistic expression. This is an important moment in the history I am discussing, and the time has come to consider how visuality itself operates under these conditions.

Modernist Visuality

It is possible to read Fry's important statement, "An Essay in Aesthetics" (1909), as taking place intellectually within the context of resistance to the instrumental character of modernity, which has been the theme of earlier chapters.[47] In the essay, Fry describes a difference between the world of "the imaginative life" and "the actual life."[48] In the former "we get . . . a different set of values" (79). Consciousness is "focused" wholly "upon the perceptive and emotional aspects of experience" (ibid.), and its expression is art. Art orders and evolves models for the observation of our actual life and does so precisely by virtue of its freedom from morality, use value, means-end rationality, or any of the other values promoted by modernity. Its "unity" (84) is the unity of a fictional construct devoted to the modeling and examination of experience in ways that subject it to evaluations that are not dependent on the everyday, evaluations characterized by "that intense disinterested contemplation that belongs to the imaginative life" (86).

Although Fry offers this argument as a counter to the demand for mimesis, this is a tactic designed to deflect what presented itself as the immediate problem for his contemporary audience, an audience used to defining artistic success in terms of likeness. In fact, the tenor of the position he puts forward in this essay, setting up the arguments for the 1910 exhibition of "Manet and the Post-Impressionists," is deeply anchored in the mid- and late Victorian quest for visual art as the repository of alternative values to those of modernity. Prettejohn has shown how deeply Fry was enmeshed in the art criticism that developed in the last quarter of the nineteenth century to meet the demands of painterly Aestheticism, sharing its "fascination for the sensuous traces of the work's making" as the vehicle for significance.[49] For Fry, the medium's own qualities carried meaning, as this comment on Titian, published in 1904, suggests: "With Titian the idea is inextricably interwoven with the material considerations of pigment, and depends on the subtlest variations of impasto, on the liquidity or fatness of the touch, and, above all, on the infinite modulations, the unanalyzable combinations of colour."[50] The language and concepts here are those of Aestheticism, Whistler, and the Symbolists as I have described them. The medium through which painting signifies operates outside and

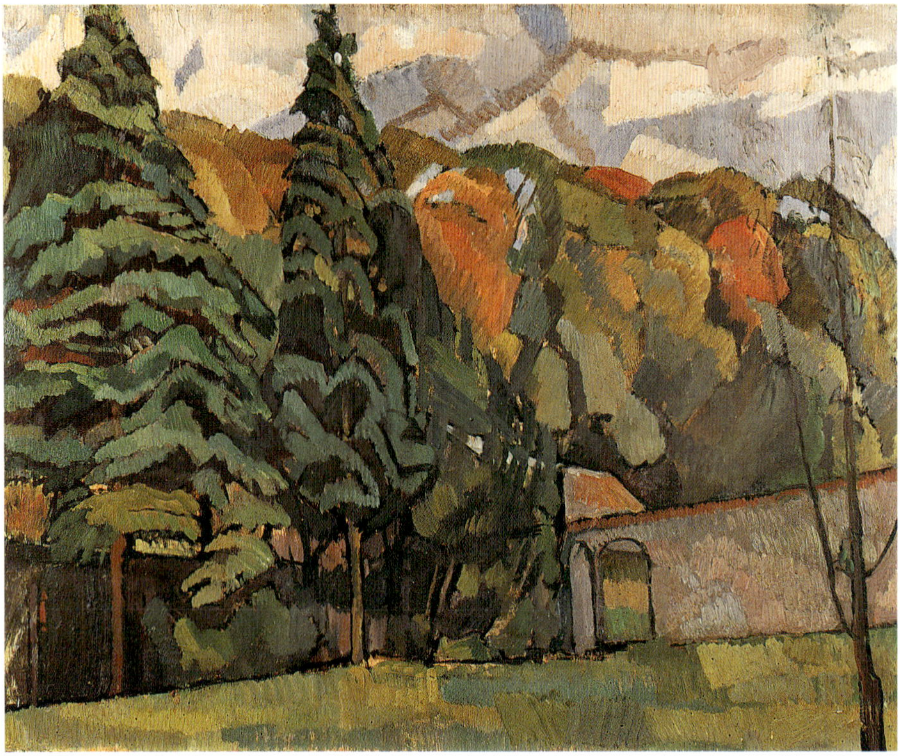

FIGURE 75. Roger Fry, *Landscape at Asheham,* c. 1912

beyond conventional linguistic meaning in a realm of "unanalyzable" but powerful alternative values that can be communicated through its "material considerations."

Fry's own paintings, such as *South Downs* of 1913–14 (private collection) or *Landscape at Asheham,* c. 1912 (fig. 75), pursue their interest in compositional unity and rhythm as homologues of that quest for alternative values. It is precisely the distance between these works and the idea of use or of purposeful and instrumental relationship that is important in the artistic project Fry was working out in the years before the First World War. For him and the other Bloomsbury artists, color, application, brushstroke, and paint surface become the actors through which art's alterity, its difference from the principal values of modernity, are deliberately dramatized. Bloomsbury has accordingly seemed to represent, in English terms and more widely, the moment when the modernist pursuit of formal innovation became most purely visual and was most divorced from the quest for telling accounts of the social nature of modernity. Vanessa Bell's *Still Life on Corner of a Mantelpiece* (1914, fig. 76) and *Omega Paper Flowers on*

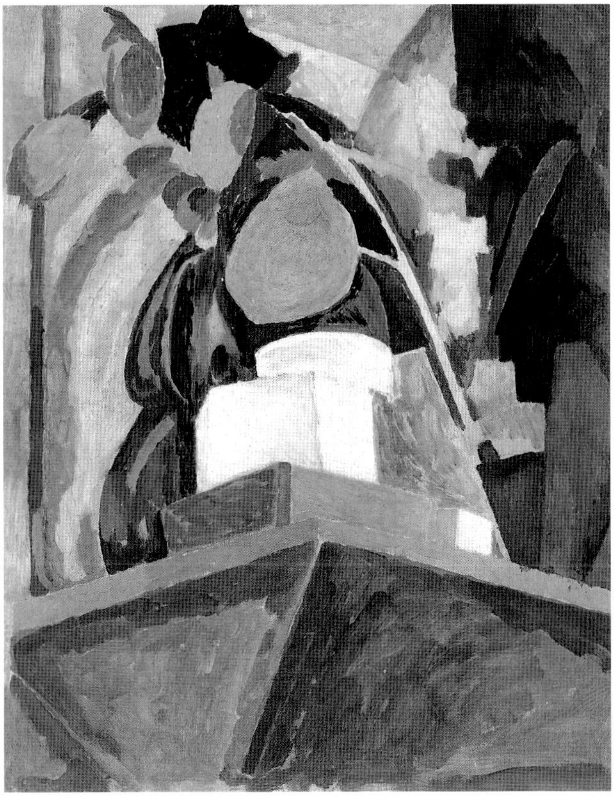

FIGURE 76. Vanessa Bell, *Still Life on Corner of a Mantelpiece*, 1914

the Mantelpiece, 46 Gordon Square (c. 1914–15, Mellon Bank, Pittsburgh) by Duncan Grant were made at a moment when the attention of the Bloomsbury painters was intently focused on the visuality of their painting. These two images are preoccupied with the idea of the visual as the primary emphasis of the picture—"what one thinks beautiful," in Bell's phrase.[51] In both paintings, the surface is marked by emphatically declared pigment. Grant evokes Matisse's decorative order, and Bell exerts pressure to break down linear form into articulations of color—"considering the picture as patches each of which has to be filled by the definite space of colour," as she said of another painting executed around this time, describing her attempt "to paint as if I were mosaicing."[52]

The increasingly simplified idiom of Bell and Grant between 1912 and 1914 traces the consequences of similar desires. In all these paintings, surface and the application of pigment in its overt and declared particularity play a central role. The fascination with the facture of the picture and with the possibilities of line, color, form, volume, and recession, conceived as entities within the composition, is a fascination that arises from the impulse to achieve access to a system of values opposed to the purely instrumental. This connects with the line of thought I have traced from Whistler through Sickert to the Camden Town Group, in which the desire to imagine art as alternative to the values of modernity functions as a means of ameliorating the perceived threat of modern experience. The visual itself becomes the means by which modernity can be subjected to understanding through the pleasures offered by the surfaces of paint. This assertion of the power of paint as a sensuous pleasure occurs throughout Grant's work. *The Modelling Stand,* c. 1914 (fig. 77), offers a paint surface and a concentration on the visual circumstances of the still life that emphasize the degree of pleasure available from paint and its fluent application. The early portrait of *James Strachey* (c. 1909–10, Tate Britain, London), with its carefully rhythmic composition, and *The Queen of Sheba* of 1912 (Tate Britain, London), scattering color and brush marks across the surface of the canvas, take part just as fully in such an assertive claim. Each of these works, cycling through the formal opportunities offered by Continental modernism, presents the picture surface as a field of optical enjoyment, refined, playful, dynamic, and insistent by turns. Bell, even when she tends toward the Symbolist composition of emotional affect, as in *Studland Beach,* c. 1912 (fig. 78), operates with the paint surface and its application as a principal actor in the canvas. The *Lytton Strachey* of 1913 (fig. 79) transforms that leading role into a display of modernist pyrotechnics, hammering home the power of the artist's perception in the declared speed and gestural assertiveness of the execution.

With very few exceptions (such as *Studland Beach*), though, it could be argued that the power of visuality to offset modernity's values is rendered in these works in a weakened version.[53] Do not Bell and Grant again and again represent a comfortable and pleasant interior world, one locked away from the violence of the outside but also locking out its vigor? Bell's *By the Estuary* of 1915 (fig. 80) or Grant's 1913 *Tents* (private collection), set up at Brandon in Suffolk for a "summer camp," surely offer us only "comfort," an enclosed and stable world? *By the Estuary* manipulates paint application and texture in the surface of sensuous and formal "contemplation" (Fry's word for Bell's painting). But paint here is nothing but comfortable, excluding both threat and any consideration of its resolution. The brief excursus into abstraction in works such as Bell's *Abstract Painting* (c. 1914, Tate Britain, London) or *Composition* (c. 1914, MOMA, New York) or Grant's *Abstract Composition* (1915, Hoffmann Collection, Berlin) asserts only color, pigment and composition within a decorative order. This is surely the realization of the meaningless world that Aestheticism's contemporaries objected to in the "pure" visuality of its paintings. Taking the glowing

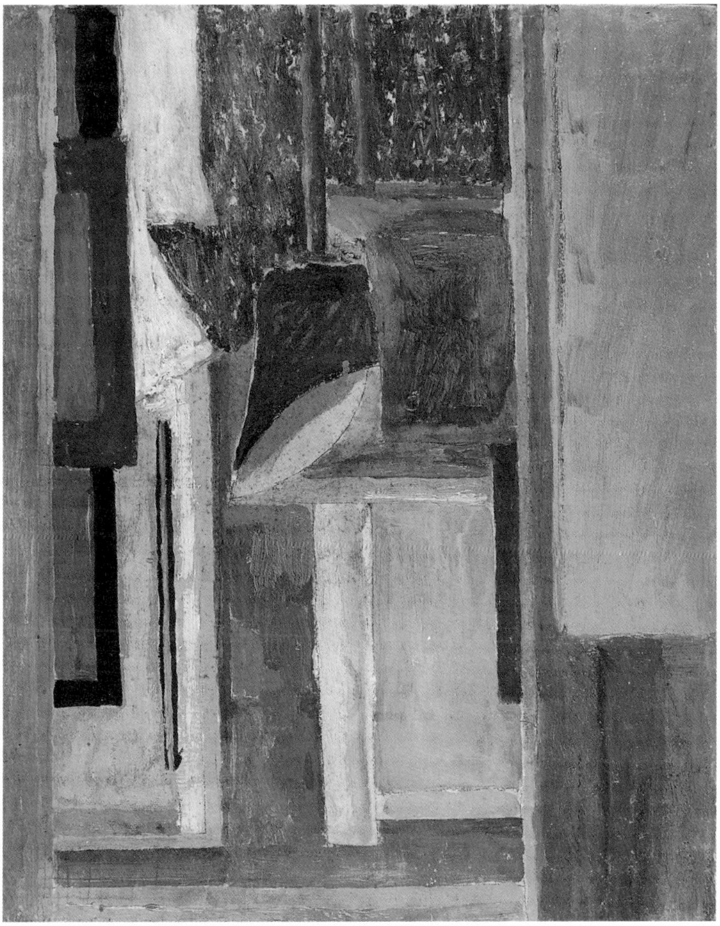

FIGURE 77.
Duncan Grant,
The Modelling Stand, c. 1914

colors and flowing lines and forms of pigment as justifiable by themselves, for their own sake, they abandon the discursive possibility, the chance to make painting *about* something, capable of speaking in a meaningful way to the major themes of society and the responsibilities of its citizens.[54] The world Bloomsbury describes remains a hermetic world, interior, civilized, ordered, and sterile—one very different from those worlds other modernists wished to paint.

Richard Shone has observed that the "falling out" of Fry and Wyndham Lewis in 1913 was "a quarrel which became the fault line of English modernism." The result, he claims, was that "in later years, anyone sympathetic to Lewis's account of events was almost certain to take his side against Bloomsbury."[55] Regardless of whether this is entirely so, it is certainly the case that one can build a critique of Bloomsbury on the back of a comparison with

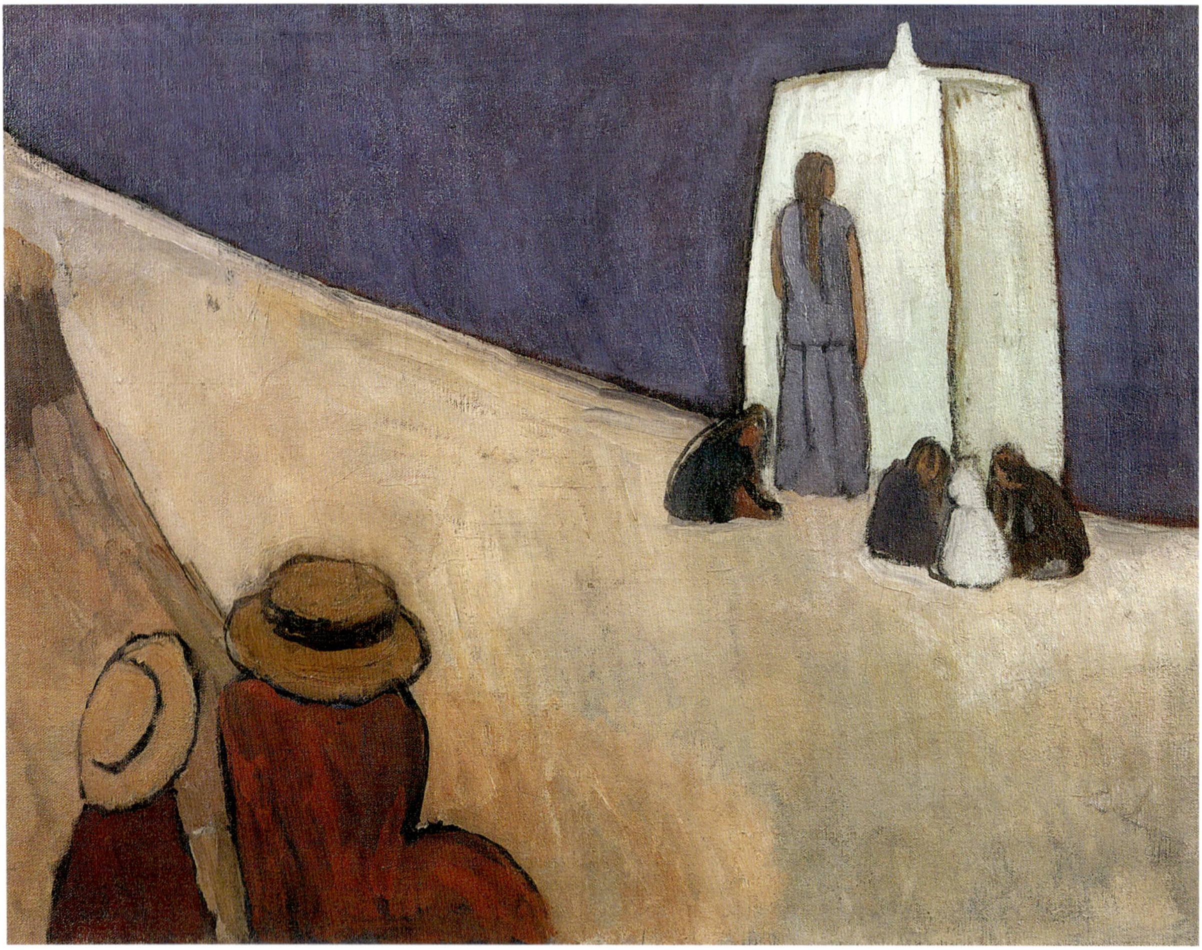

FIGURE 78. Vanessa Bell, *Studland Beach*, c. 1912

Lewis and that such a critique would inevitably reproduce the fault lines within English modernism itself. On the face of it, these oppositions seem workable. Lewis and the Vorticists might stand for a socially aware "avant-garde" modern movement occupied with the idea of modernist art as a "painting of modern life"; Bloomsbury becomes an example merely of "modernism"—and I am using the distinctions proposed by Bürger here, in which avant-garde names an active principle, anxious to "negate" the values promoted in modernity, and modernism exemplifies the pure development of visual innovation for visual pleasure as an end in itself.[56] These distinctions resonate far beyond the small world of English painting and its history. In this formulation, Vorticism represents—perhaps surprisingly, given the political associations Lewis is deemed to

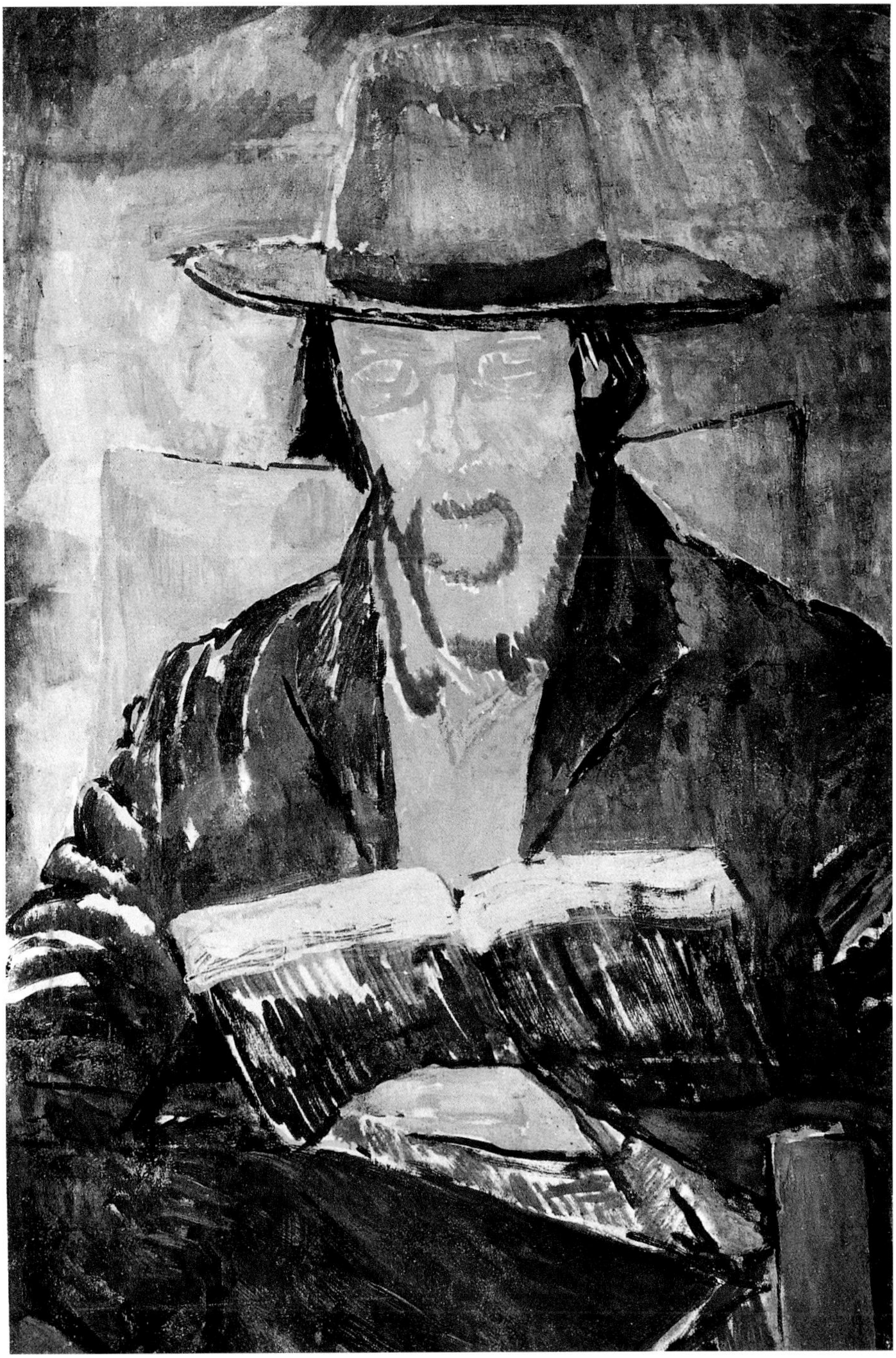

FIGURE 79. Vanessa Bell, *Lytton Strachey*, 1913

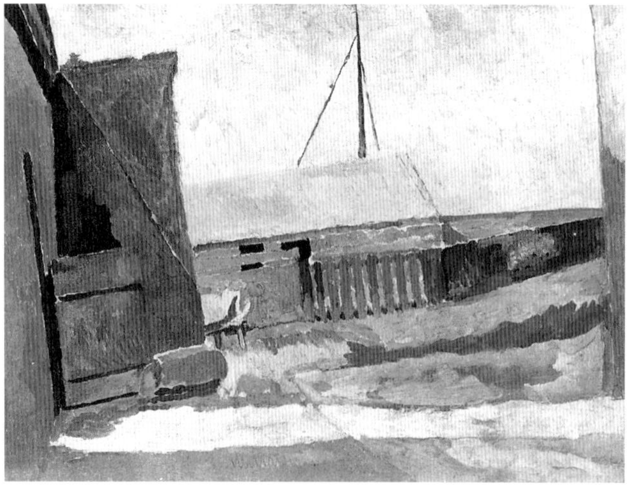

FIGURE 80. Vanessa Bell, *By the Estuary,* 1915

bring with him—the acceptable face of modernism after the social history of art, and Bloomsbury its abnegation, its art based on a complacent and self-serving misrecognition of social privilege for social relevance.[57] This, or something like it, seems to have been the view of the Vorticists: Vorticist painting explicitly sets itself against the representation of modernity that seeks to reformulate it as comfort and visual pleasure, just as Vorticism, as an art-political entity, set itself against its competitor modernist groupings. The reformulation of modernity that takes place in Vorticist facture is aggressive, intended to upset the established viewpoint of the spectator and enforce a new and unfamiliar alternative. Vorticism both repudiates the use of the visual to describe a comforting version of modernity and seeks to mobilize its own rebarbative and aggressive surfaces as critique.

In the lower-right-hand area of Lewis's *Workshop* (1914–15, fig. 81), a band of maroon paint undergoes across its breadth a transformation from geometrical element to painterly brushwork. This movement in the picture is perhaps reminiscent of Roy Lichtenstein's satires on the macho facture of American Abstract Expressionism: carefully drawn or silkscreened imitations of curling brushstrokes, heavy with the artist's autographic weight, sitting forlornly amidst empty spaces of blank paper. Lewis's frayed maroon edge here serves a similar function, poking fun at the overtly painterly surfaces of his modernist competitors. The "workshop" is, of course, a number of different things in this picture—industrial, technological, cerebral—but it is also the atelier, the crucible of representation.[58] Lewis's point is that modernity requires a colder imaging than he believes the overheated paintwork of other modernisms can

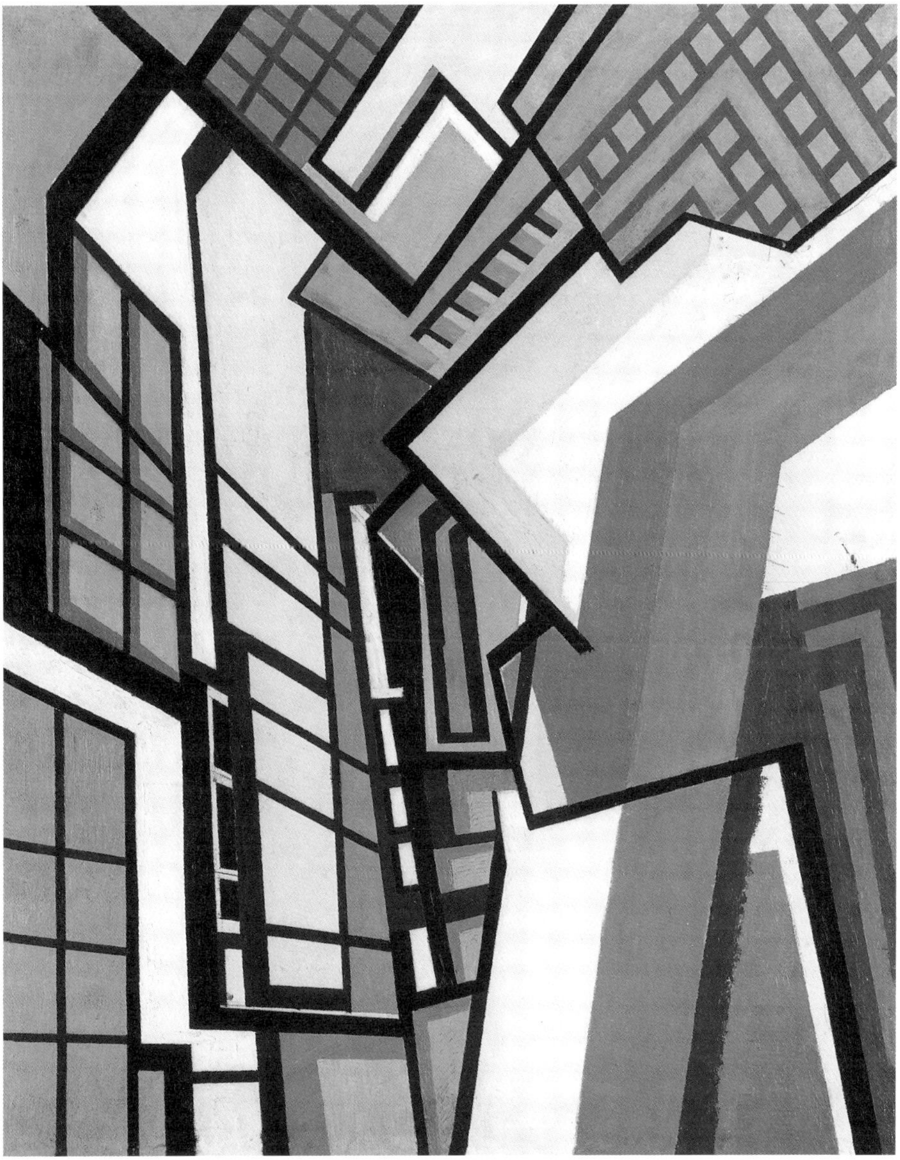

FIGURE 81. Wyndham Lewis, *Workshop*, 1914–15

provide. For Lewis, the problem with modern facture is that it has acquired the *wrong* meanings since its emergence as a live agent in advanced English painting. He associates surface with the blurring of the representation of modernity through its reformulation as pleasure, and to this he objects. The patch (to invoke Didi-Huberman's term) of ragged paint in Lewis is, in response, decoupled from its function as comfort and recuperation and rein-

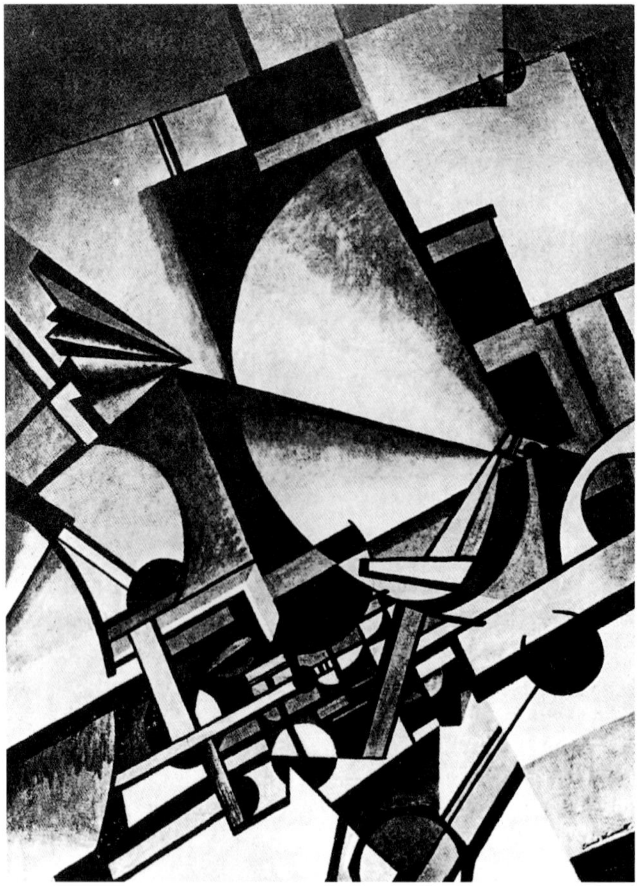

FIGURE 82. Edward Wadsworth, *A Short Flight*, c. 1914

stated as a "symptom," an anomaly within the carefully defined systems of Vorticist representation.

This position is congruent with the Vorticist diagnosis of modernity. *Blast* makes its claim for "an Art . . . organic with its time" by asserting the mechanical nature of contemporary culture. "Machinery, trains, steam-ships" are what "distinguishes externally our time," so that "the forms of machinery, Factories, new and vaster buildings, bridges and works," are "naturally, around us."[59] Hence the injunction to "BLESS England, Industrial island machine."[60] The Vorticist paintings reproduced in *Blast* seem designed to match this rhetoric. Wadsworth's lost painting *A Short Flight* (c. 1914, fig. 82) is very much the sort of image one would expect. In the surviving photograph, at least, the surface of the painting appears divided into an irregular pattern, describing smoothly inhuman shapes with little sense of either mimesis or figure on ground.[61] Clearly visible are simplified versions of mechanical forms reminiscent of compass, T-square, and ruler as well as, more faintly, industrial forms and objects. But there seems nothing precise enough to identify with any certainty. The firmest impression is of a sort of mechanical clutter not necessarily incompatible with smooth operation.

When we look more closely at the image, however, we begin to see that it is not without representational elements and that, like many Vorticist works, *A Short Flight* adopts a bird's-eye perspective, straight down onto the object beneath, so that the subject matter of the image becomes a schematic plan or map of itself.[62] In this case, the view is down from above the airborne plane onto the angular shapes of fields most clearly visible at top and top right. In the center of the painting, the flight, described by both mechanical forms and by the arrowhead shape of the prow, forces its way across the landscape below. There is no sign of the pilot unless we read the T-square shape as a sitting figure. That absence points toward a central plank of Vorticism's understanding of modern experience. *A Short Flight* presents a summary of the Vorticists' preoccupations with the industrialization of the "island" and of the place of the individual subject within it.[63] The absence of the pilot figures the Vorticist diagnosis of the reduction of the individual to an industrial helot, functioning—and hence understandable—only within the context of the mechanical world of modernity in which he or she subsists. As such, it opens up into contemporary works by Wadsworth and the other Vorticists in *Blast* and elsewhere. Wadsworth's "Newcastle-Upon-Tyne" (1913, reproduced in *Blast* 1), Lewis's *Plan of War* (lost, fig. 83) and *Slow Attack* (lost, reproduced in *Blast* 1), and Etchells's "Dieppe" (lost, reproduced in *Blast* 1), all c. 1913–14, deal in the same coin of mechanism, dehumanization, and the abolition of the individual that *A Short Flight* conveys so eloquently.

That diagnosis of modernity as mechanical and rebarbative finds its expression in the optical violence of much Vorticist painting. David Wragg has written interestingly in these terms of the cultivation of ugliness in much Vorticist painting as a way of registering modernity while evading the self-regarding pleasures of Bloomsbury "formalism."[64] In the work of his colleagues, Lewis's satirical refusal of the meanings of the patch of paint in *Workshop* is taken up as part of the project to convey the experiential qualities of the modern in an innovative visual idiom. In this process of representation, the facture of Vorticist paintings continues to stand for modernity, as it had done for Whistler and Sickert. But now, as in *Workshop,* the paint surface becomes the site of a refusal of the accommodation to pleasure as evasion. Vorticist work is designed with the repudiation of the spectator's pleasure in mind, so the acid

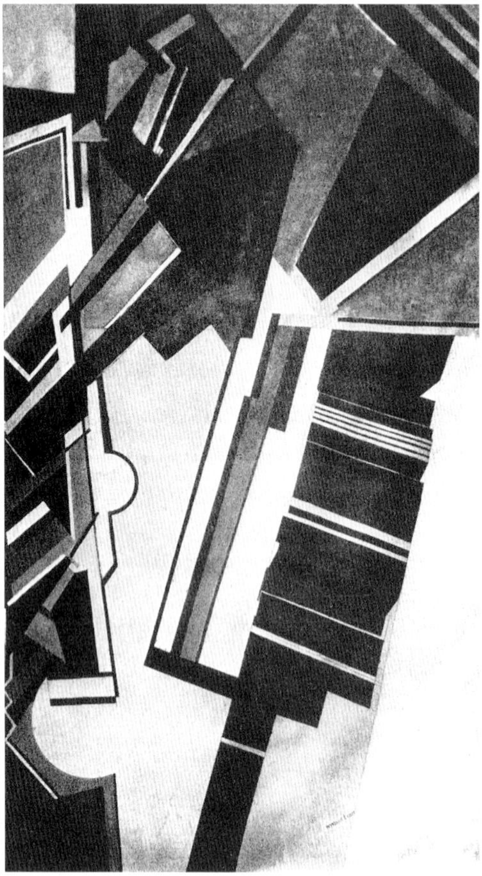

FIGURE 83. Wyndham Lewis, *Plan of War*, reproduced from *Blast* 1 (1914)

colorings and unfamiliar forms of Vorticist painting are deliberately intended to frustrate the spectator. There is often plenty of facture in Vorticist painting, but it is uninflected, *detached* from signification because the visible facture and overt presence of the paint are made over as *random*, so that the effect of the abstract geometric structures is to deprive the paint surface of coherence, making it appear undirected and meaningless. The mismatch between structure and surface obliterates the pleasures it can offer, a refusal reinforced by the often deliberately thick and clumsy character of the paint, parodic in its mimicry of other modernist factures. Indeed, the work of painting here is both declared and obliterated. But it is still present. The "patch"-work of paint is a "symptom," in a sense—the return of what Vorticism feels it has had to repress in order to undertake its representation of modernity successfully. The consequence of this refusal of pleasure in Vorticist painting is both to acknowledge and to repress the painterliness of their practice. The appearance of Didi-Huberman's

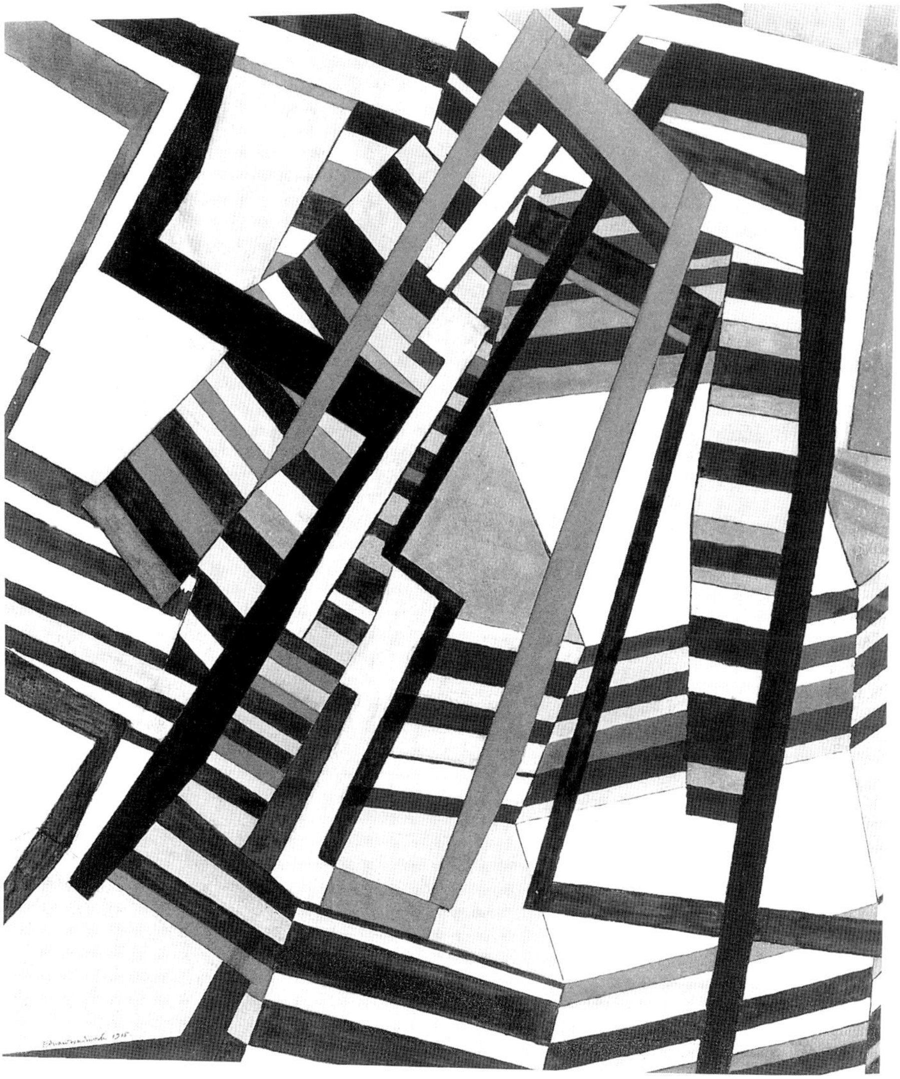

FIGURE 84. Edward Wadsworth, *Enclosure,* 1915

"patch" of paint is cultivated at the core of Vorticist pictorial organization—its "abstraction"—and reconstituted as a pleasure that cannot be taken. A Vorticist work like Wadsworth's 1915 gouache, *Enclosure* (fig. 84), has so little that is identifiable as direct representation of the world that the optical movement of colored form against the shifting, faceted background assumes the role of principal protagonist in the painting. We are obliged to look at the patches of paint—there is little else to see. But that opticality is linked to a determinedly uninflected surface, so that the spectator's eye is solicited and then confronted with a facture that cannot be consumed straightforwardly as pleasure.

It is from this perspective that Lewis attacks Fry and Bloomsbury in *Blast* 2. The preoccupation with the visual in their art is said to be "decorative," a poor, thin-blooded substitute for true art.[65] Lewis separates "the slop of Cambridge Post Aestheticism" from its own professed tradition: "Post-Impressionism is an insult to Manet and Cézanne."[66]

What is known as "Decorative Art" is rightly despised . . . the "Decorative" artist (as examples, the sort of spirit that animates the Jugend, Rhythm, Mr Roger Fry's little belated Morris movement) is he who substitutes a banal and obvious human logic for the co-ordination and architecture that the infinite forces of Nature bring about. . . . The only people who have nothing to do with Nature and who as artists are most definitely inept and in the same box as the Romantic—who is half-way between the Vegetable and the God—are these between-men, with that most odious product of man, modern DECORATION.[67]

Bloomsbury's claim to modernity is slighted.[68] Its artists make no engagement with contemporary life: "This family party of strayed and Dissenting Aesthetes, however, were compelled to call in as much modern talent as they could find, to do the rough and masculine work without which they knew their efforts would not rise above the level of a pleasant tea-party, or command more attention."[69] Decoration signals a lack of positive involvement with the modern world, a weak, old-fashioned, passive aesthetic. It merely provides a gentrified pleasure for the connoisseur's eye.

The gendered reading of "decorative," confining Bloomsbury to a feminized passivity and ineffectualness, hardly needs pointing out.[70] Lisa Tickner observes that many radical male artists before 1914 conjured a masculinity ostentatiously "phallic in its flamboyance, its sexuality, and its studied neglect of . . . the constraints of duty, decency, and social decorum" as a way of defining and confirming their status as modern artists.[71] Once magicked into social being, such a masculinity served as the sign of a serious modernist ambition for these artists, standing for the intensity, relevance, and creativity of their art and its capacity to be modern. When the Vorticists insisted on their own status as the painters best suited to describe the character of contemporary experience, power, masculinity, and the ability to pronounce with authority on the nature of modernity were all connected in a gendered system of signs. This recalls Whistler's assertion of "mastery" over feminized nature and Sickert's own subsequent version of that gambit. As in the case of these precursors, it is the medium, visuality itself, that functions as the dominating "masculine" means through which control is asserted and maintained. But Vorticism seeks to shift this inheritance from the claims of paint and surface to a new diagnosis, a penetration into the realities of modernity and its realization through a new visual language that necessarily has to abjure the tradition that lies behind it. Whistler, Sickert, Camden Town, Bloomsbury, Aestheticism—all belong to a history that is now to be cleared away, erased to make room for the triumphant modernism of the Vortex. But its surfaces, negatives of the history it seeks to replace, depend on what it rejects. In repudiating visual pleasure, Vorticism abandons as well the richness of possibility that earlier conceptualizations had envisaged in the paint surface.

This goes to the heart of the issue. For what are the implications of objecting to pleasure in this way? It is surely willful, even perverse, to assert aggression and confrontation of the spectator over the provision of a sensuous and comforting pleasure. Is this not precisely one of the things painting does well? The material constituents of paint are creatures of surface and of somatic experience, as they were acknowledged to be by the tradition I am examining. A. S. Byatt, in one of her short stories, has a brief exchange between two characters about Matisse's famous—or notorious—comment that his art was "something analogous to a good armchair, which relaxes the businessman as much as the literary artist from his bodily weariness." One of the characters quotes Matisse's aphorism, and there is a familiar curl of the lip. The other asks what is wrong with comfort: "a man who has bone-cancer, or a man who has been tortured, he can recognise a good armchair."[72] Modernity, like life, surely demands comfort and is more than sufficient to justify some amelioration. This a version of the arguments I have suggested one might make about what appears to be "escapism" or a willful or complacent neglect of the subject matter of modern life. Principally, one might argue that such comfort encapsulates a system of values that is directly opposed to the instrumental values cultivated by modernity itself. Comfort, moreover, is not only low on use value but also on its macho opposite, the flaunting shock tactics of the avant-garde.

From this perspective, Bloomsbury and Camden Town might seem more likely modernists than Lewis and the Vorticists. Their visuality is more varied and richer than that of Vorticism, which programmatically abjures such possibilities, but it connects just as clearly to the desire for art to function outside modern rationality. In this sense, perhaps, its radical potential is greater because its discursive aspects are less strong. But to say this is not to make the final judg-

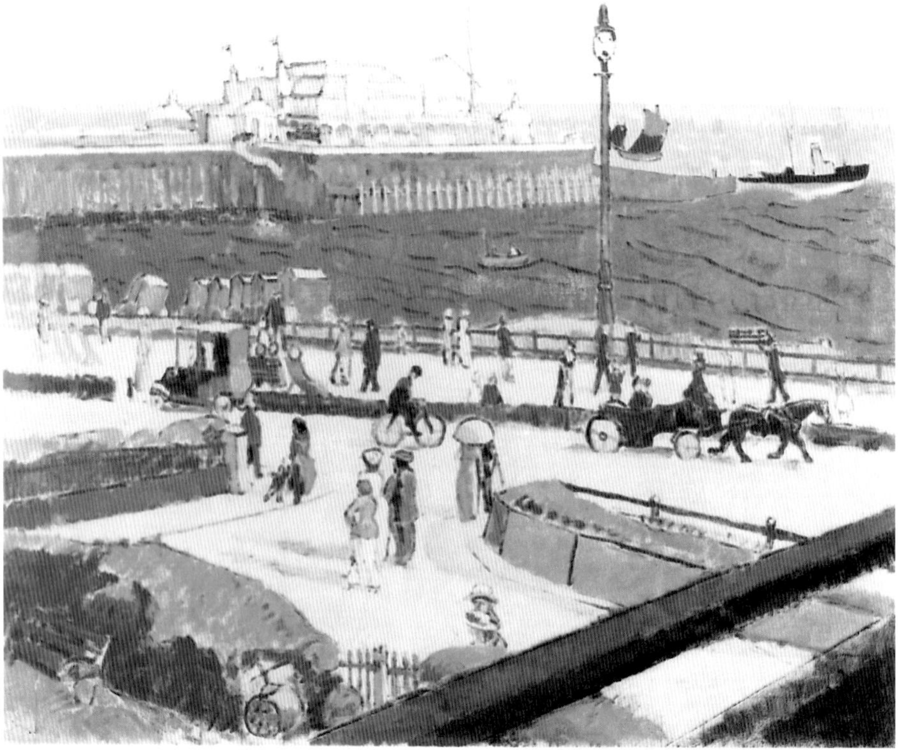

FIGURE 85. Spencer Gore, *Brighton Pier*, 1913

ment. The connections between Vorticism and its rivals are closer than this and less clear-cut. Lewis reproduced a number of Camden Town works by Spencer Gore in the first number of *Blast*. On the face of it, Gore's presence might be deemed a piety on the part of Lewis, whom we can imagine to have been honoring his dead friend and at the same time demonstrating by example how the Vorticists had superseded their precursors.[73] But the fact is that Gore's subject matter is also theirs, the modern as it physically manifested itself in the environment of Britain's landscapes and cityscapes. Gore inserts the balustrade and shadowy interior across the visual field of one of the paintings reproduced in *Blast, Brighton Pier* (1913, fig. 85), as a way of acknowledging the presence of modernity within the Edwardian landscape. In Gore's work, modernity invades the scene, transforming the idiom of past representations as it infiltrates the material culture of transport, leisure, and the built environment. As Ysanne Holt has shown, this is especially true of the paintings Gore made of the suburbs and the rural scene, the suburban and sub-rural world that lay immediately outside the metropolis, forming its hinterland, and encompassed the pleasure-grounds of the South Coast, such as Brighton.[74] Gore's meditative transformation of the urban, suburban, and sub-rural scene, conjuring his "panel of encrusted enamel," as Sickert said, from the "loveliness" others cannot see, is also an analytic procedure, one that switches the world into a new vision.

Gore contended with the demand for representation that these loaded subjects made. The critic Frank Rutter, a strong supporter of modern art in England, agreed with Sickert's analysis when he wrote in his obituary of Gore in 1914 that his sensibility had "enabled him to find beauty in the commonplace and romance in the familiar. Seen through his poetic temperament even a red-brick suburban villa was transfigured, the streets of Camden Town were touched with loveliness and music-halls were turned into visions of paradisiac refinement." As in Sickert's interpretation, for Rutter it is this capacity to translate the brute facts of everyday modernity into the "paradisiac" that had given Gore "his place in modern British art."[75] Lewis's own obituary of Gore, published in *Blast,* also runs on similar lines. For him, Gore's achievement was to have taken a metropolitan summer, arrayed "in trivial crescents with tall trees and toy trains . . . heavy dull sunlight" and "exquisite, respectable and stodgy houses," and, in such "favourite themes," forced together both nature and the modern urban scene.[76] In doing so, his paintings altered the meanings of both. But it was exactly this forcing of the natural and the mechanical into an impacted unity through a painter's vision that seemed to the Vorticists, like their precursors, to be the necessary task of an art determined to define and communicate the nature of modern experience. In *Blast,* it is the dialectic set buzzing by the tense relationship between the mechanisms of modernity and the persisting icons of earlier representational solutions that powers and sustains the character of the issues they confront.

Camden Town Group painting develops a visual analysis of the modern city—Sickert's capital, "the most wonderful and complex city in the world"—that draws on elements of earlier attempts to focus modernity in this way.[77] In the vision of modernity evoked in Camden Town paintings, Sickert's "opaque mosaic" of paint, built up in touches and dashes of color, plays a central role. Gore followed Sickert into the music halls of the capital, painting in a brilliant palette derived from Gauguin and Van Gogh (and intermittently highly offensive to Sickert) glowing scenes of popular entertainment. *The Alhambra* (1908, fig. 86) replaces the dour intensities of Sickert's music-hall interiors with a scintillating "mosaic" of color and light. For his part, Harold Gilman reworked Sickert's example in another direction, transforming the near monochrome,

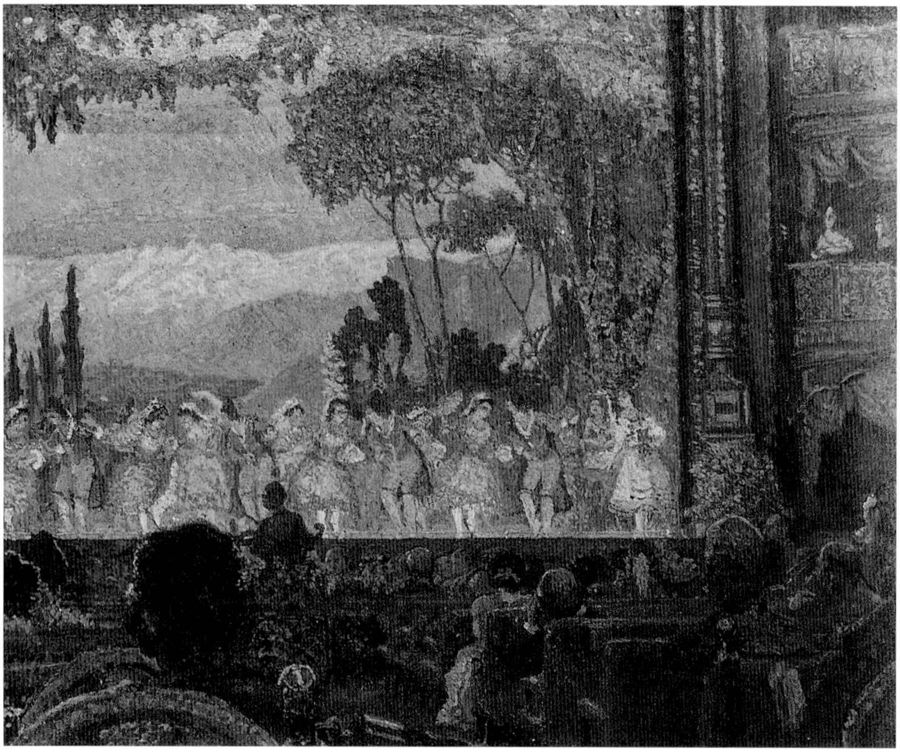

FIGURE 86. Spencer Gore, *The Alhambra,* 1908

subdued tones, and occasional virtual tonal impenetrability of Sickert's bedsitter nudes into his own highly keyed versions (1911–12, fig. 87) and the matrimonial antagonisms of *Off to the Pub* (c. 1912, Tate Britain, London) into the brilliant display of *An Eating House* (c. 1914, fig. 88) or *The Café Royal* (1912, private collection).

Charles Ginner might seem to paint outside this program. *Piccadilly Circus* (1912, fig. 89), with its sweeping taxi and motor bus (the latter advertising Gore's favorite music hall, the Alhambra), is both static and in movement at the same time, the traffic swirling around the flower seller who stolidly clings to a now dangerously outmoded form of commerce.[78] The picture, wrote the *Pall Mall Gazette,* "both in its crude tones and jumbled composition, happily suggests the noise and confusion of that busy thoroughfare."[79] *Piccadilly Circus* and *Sunlit Square, Victoria Station* (1913, Bootle Collection of Paintings, Atkinson Art Gallery, Southport) remake the bustle and energy of the city as static pattern, reducing social action to the function of elements in the overall design. It is as if modernity has been translated from the social to the application of paint.

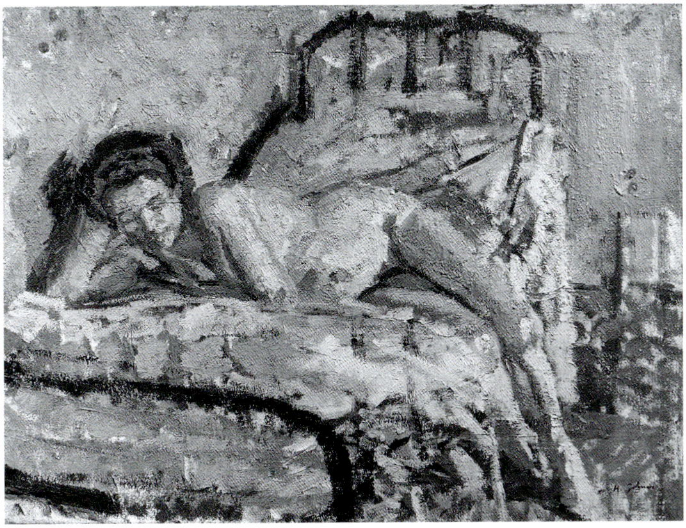

FIGURE 87. Harold Gilman, *The Model Reclining Nude,* 1911–12

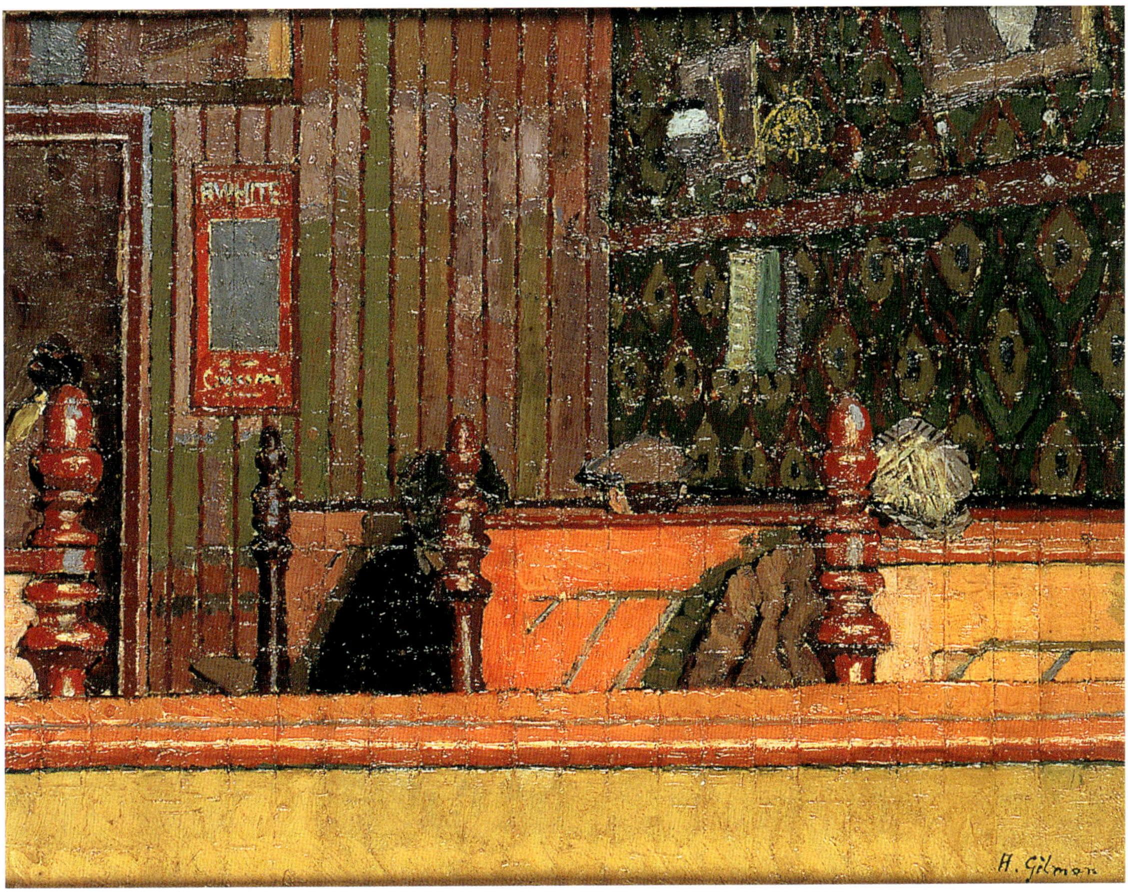

FIGURE 88. Harold Gilman, *An Eating House,* c. 1914

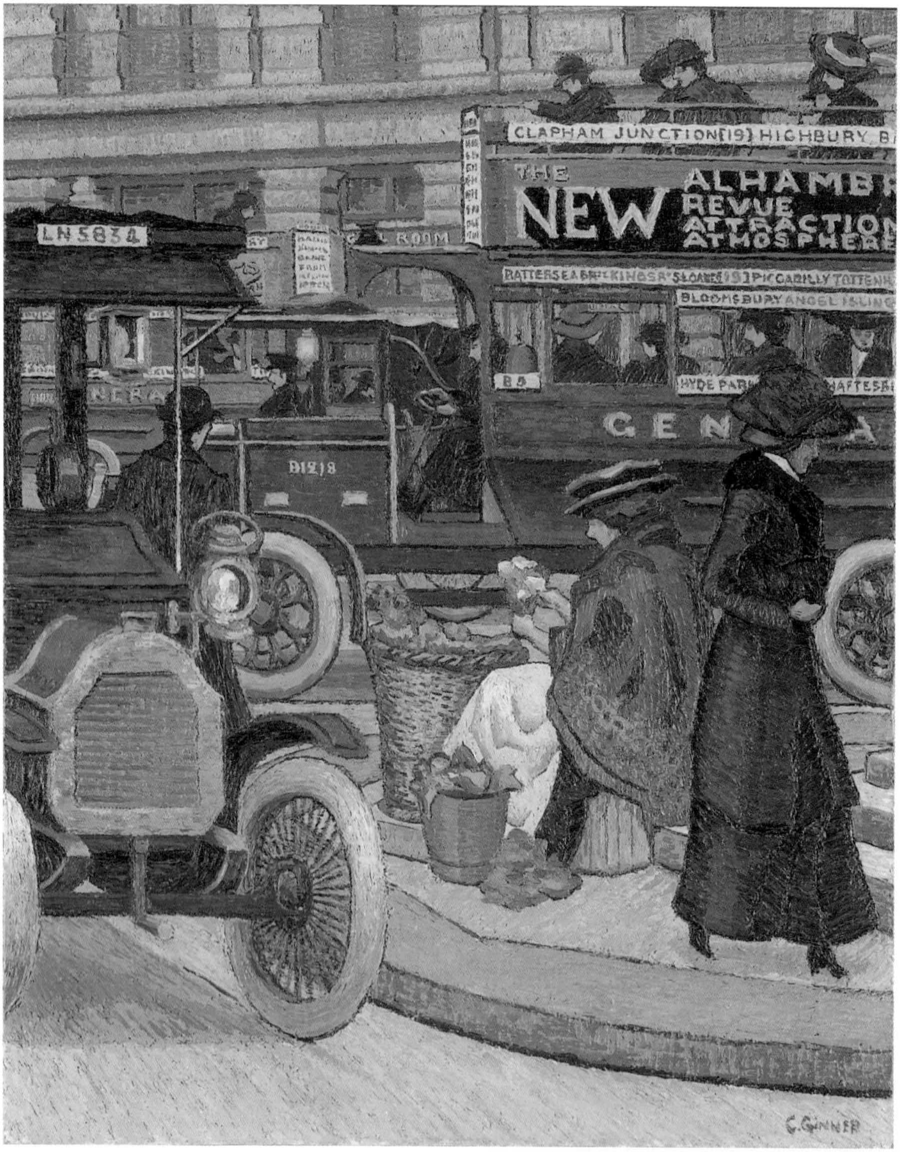

FIGURE 89. Charles Ginner, *Piccadilly Circus*, 1912

Gore's railway engine on its way to Euston Station, puffing through the cuttings that had sliced up the original social landscape of Camden Town and precipitated the area's decline, is a frank celebration of its subject, concerned to evoke the dust of a London summer through its chalky, active paint surface (1911, fig. 90) and to transform modernity and its machines into vital facture.

I have traced in previous chapters the history that supported such a development. If in the Camden Town Group painters, as in Sickert, and before him in Whistler, the materiality of the paint surface comes to stand for the resistant and impenetrable quality of the modern world, for them it is also a way in which the difficulty and unknowableness of that world can be ameliorated. It becomes a pleasurable visual field in which the disquieting aspects of new social experience are displaced and made comfortable in the technique of representation itself.

Wadsworth's Vorticist painting, *Blackpool* (c. 1915, lost), evoked from Lewis a discussion very much in these terms.[80] Asserting that the painting is "one of the finest . . . he has done," Lewis praised Wadsworth for its association of "the quality of 'LIFE'" with the "striped ascending blocks" and harsh colors that describe the "elements of a seaside scene, condensed into the simplest form possible for the retaining of its vivacity." Lewis continues, "It's [*sic*] theme is that of five variegated cliffs. The striped awnings of Cafés and shops, the stripes of bathing tents, the stripes of bathing-machines, of toy trumpets, of dresses, are marshalled into a dense essence of the scene. The harsh jarring and sunny yellows, yellow-greens and reds are especially well used, with the series of commercial blues."[81] This is a description that, despite the acid and attacking nature of Wadsworth's color, resonates with the subject of *Brighton Pier* and Lewis's account of Gore as the poet of nature infiltrating "London back-yards."[82]

Gore's subjects are not so very different from those of the Vorticists. His experimentation with the styles of the European avant-garde in 1913–14 was embarked on as a quest to find an idiom properly suited to the task of bringing the suburban and sub-rural modernity of Richmond or Welwyn Garden City into understanding.[83] *Blast* also reproduced Gore's *Richmond Houses* (now known as *From a Window in Cambrian Road, Richmond,* 1913, fig. 91), which, with its Cézannist faceting and summary, scrubbed paintwork, might also help adjust that reading. If *Brighton Pier* represents in an Impressionist style the encroachment of the sense of modernity onto what Lewis once called "the last days of the Victorian world of artificial peacefulness," then *Richmond Houses* picks up that invasion of the psychic energies of the new and presents it in an idiom much more like that of the Vorticists.[84] In these and similar works of the same period, Gore experiments with the application to modern life of advanced technical representation.[85] Like the Vorticist works in *Blast,* this is a plan, a schematic image and summation that aims to encompass, from some intellectual vantage point poised above the mêlée of contemporary life, its characteristic forms and meanings. The fact is that Gore is an entirely appropriate presence within the pages of Britain's most advanced modernist periodical. His engagement with

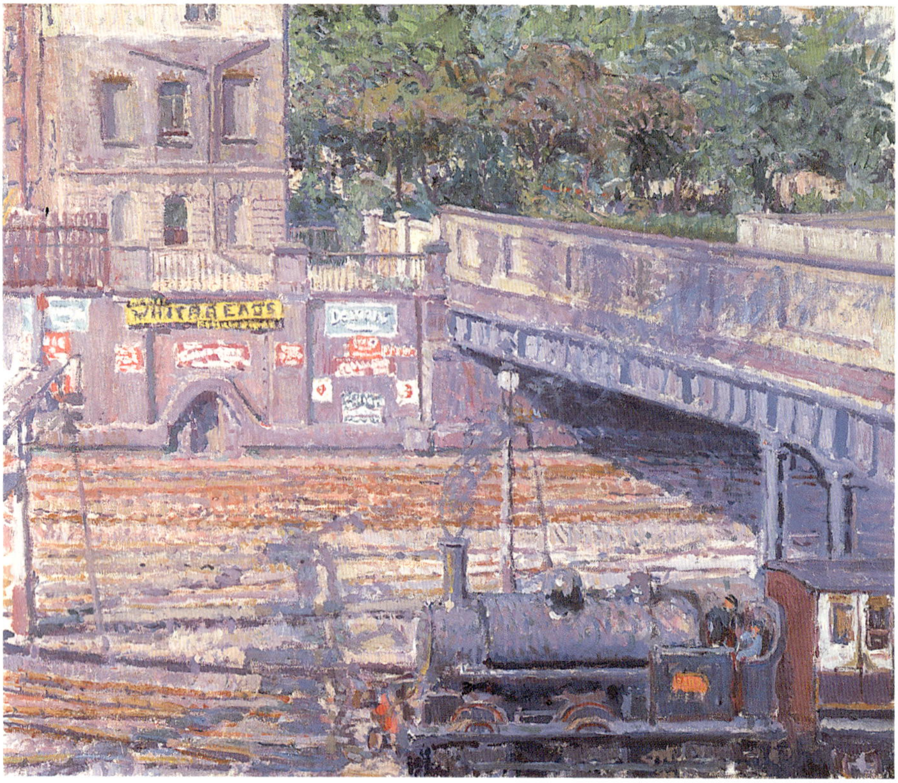

FIGURE 90. Spencer Gore, *Nearing Euston Station*, 1911

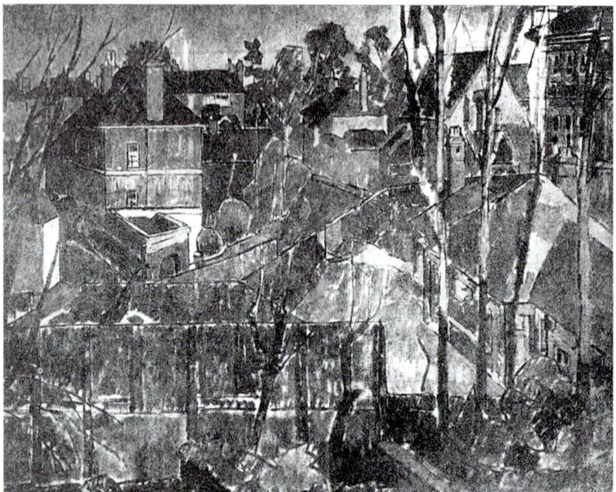

FIGURE 91. Spencer Gore, *From a Window in Cambrian Road, Richmond*, 1913

the problems of representing the close relationship of the metropolis and the landscape within modernity makes his presence in *Blast* so apposite to its Vorticist concerns.[86]

Lewis's 1914 mixed media watercolor *New York* (fig. 92) takes up these themes. Here we have the geometries of the industrial city that feature in comparable Vorticist works like *The Crowd* (1913–14, Tate Britain, London) and *Workshop* (see fig. 81) combined with a highly worked facture as Lewis mixes watercolor, gouache, pen and ink, and crayon to produce a varied and mobile picture surface.[87] The "symptom of painting" is very strong here, and we are constantly reminded in observing it that we are viewing a technical practice—in the built-up gouache over crayon that describes the central section in multiple blues; in the overlaying of the red geometries of the streets and the single, ladder-like architectural bay that strikes up from the bottom of the picture; in the self-conscious shading of the pen-and-ink rectangle on the left. In its way, *New York* is as declarative and as dandified in its surface as anything by Sickert or Whistler. Like Didi-Huberman's reading of the irruption of the patch of painting's opaque materiality into the rationalized detail of the picture, facture in *New York* carries with it meanings contrary to those Lewis is trying to promote. The effect is to obliterate the possibility of any "univocal meaning" in Lewis's image. Painting here is allowed to execute a return of the repressed so that what we see in the dramatic surface of the work is the negotiation of the meanings of facture and their relationship to the representation of modernity. Lewis wants to rescue facture for new meanings, but that proves hard to do. We cannot understand these visual qualities in Vorticist works of the period without understanding the art-political semiology of their surfaces. These works function partly as refusals of Camden Town or Bloomsbury answers. Visuality is of great importance even to Vorticism, then, but the Vorticists rework its contemporary implications, moving visuality toward critique and evaluation in the project to represent contemporary modernity.

I draw the following conclusions from all this. English modernism can be reinserted into a wider historical context than is usually acknowledged to be the case. There are deeper connections between Vorticists and their modernist peers than normally appear, for all conduct their business through the visual surfaces of paint. The acknowledgment of paint and the exploration of its possibilities derive from a self-conscious and powerful tradition. But this context also has implications for our understanding of modernism more generally. We cannot go on refusing the importance of visuality and the visual in modernist painting, however embarrassing a topic the visual may seem to us now in the

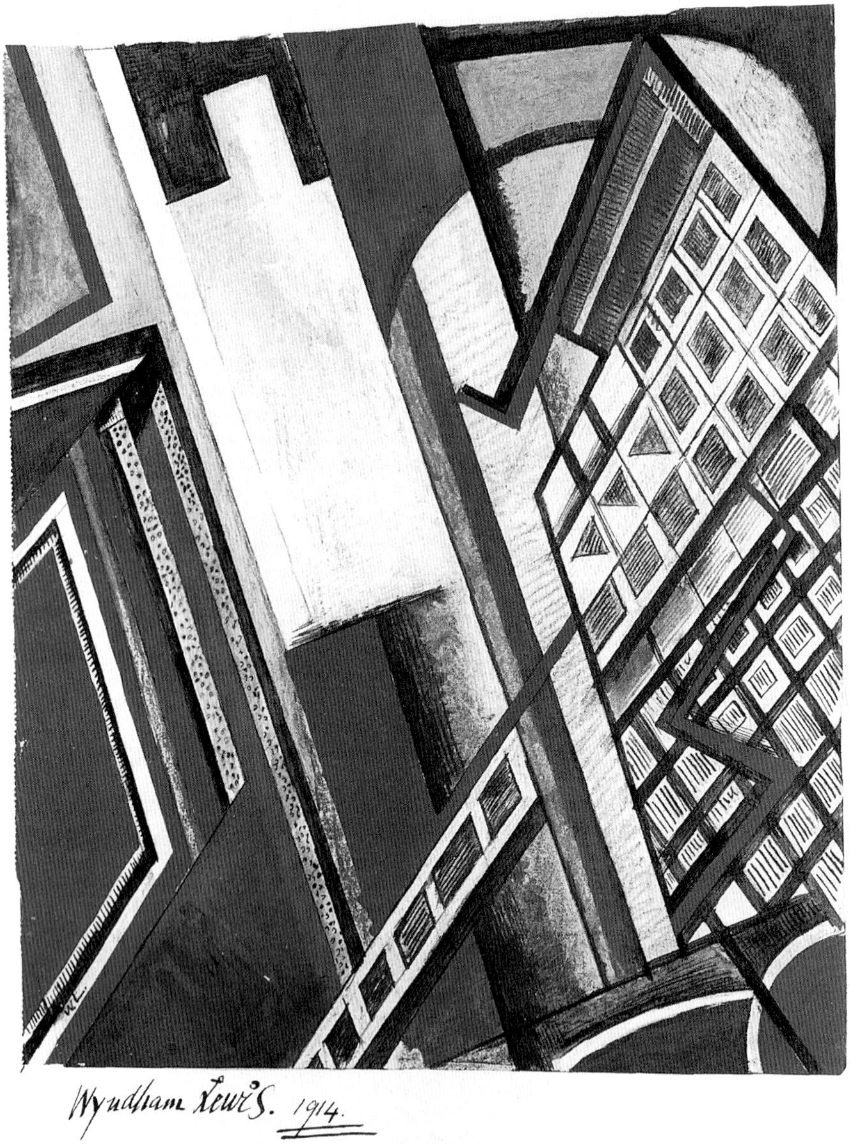

FIGURE 92. Wyndham Lewis, *New York*, 1914

wake of the social history of art. Partly, then, this book attempts to suggest that visuality itself plays a key role in the "painting of modern life" and that, in the English context, that role helps clarify the development of a specifically modernist art. In the final section of this chapter, and to conclude the book, I want to consider some of the ways in which that perception changes our views of English art and its meanings between the Pre-Raphaelites and 1914.

Periodization and English Art

It may be that we no longer periodize. Perhaps one of the things art historians are not currently interested in doing is arranging their subject matter by historical moment.[88] Brief reflection on the nature of much contemporary practice in the discipline might support this view. Robert S. Nelson and Richard Shiff's 1996 edited anthology, *Critical Terms for Art History,* contains no entry for "periodization." According to them, we are concerned to understand "ritual," "fetish," "gaze," and "gender" in art objects (to take a series of terms from Nelson and Shiff's book). It even seems that we might want to inquire into "value," although only to historicize it away as they do. We do not want, however, to make once popular and compelling types of discrimination along period lines.[89]

That seems reasonable enough if we choose to take one cut into the body of contemporary art history. After all, the most innovative and illuminating work of the last two decades has dedicated itself to exploring interdisciplinary and novel perspectives on art-historical material. But it will not do if we adopt other current perspectives. Publishers' lists, the formulations of job advertisements, the chronological scope of monographs, and the "postmodernism" craze of the 1980s and 1990s all suggest that periodization is alive and with us still, even if we do not consider it to be in itself a subject of much theoretical or reflective interest. And the truth is that much of the new work I have referred to depends upon an unexamined inheritance of periodization put in place by earlier art-historical activity. I want to use this section of the chapter to explore some of the implications of this subterranean life of periodization in relation to the concerns of the book—particularly because a revisionist argument about periodization has been implicit in my discussion. I want to consider the importance of periodization for the rewriting of the history of English painting in the late nineteenth and early twentieth centuries and whether we need to reinstate it in different forms, moving the borderlines around the history of art or applying them in different ways.

Postmodern historians tell us that there is no historical account without conceptual tools that allow us to build constructs, intellectual views of what might have happened in the past dependent on the often providential survival of documents, both visual and verbal. Periodization is one of these concepts—and an important one. If we are told that things change in 1905 or 1910 or 1914, then our reading of the art on either side of a given divide is inclined to change to meet our expectations. This is the situation Nietzsche imagined, in which "historiography itself impedes our view of the past."[90] Both modernism and its relationship to the nineteenth-century past assume their definitions under the pressure of the divisions that periods enforce. But periodizations, too, have their histories: often they are the reflections of the political interests of the winning side, the artists or groups of artists whose viewpoints got to the historians first, whose paintings populate the museums and whose art is in the canon.

Conceptual tools like periods define the possibilities of meaning for us but are contingent, tied into the histories they describe, and it is surely uncontentious to suggest therefore that we should keep them constantly in play, constantly provisional and susceptible to change rather than as the unquestioned grounds of all our judgments. English art in the late nineteenth and early twentieth centuries suffers from an inherited rigidity about the ways in which periods can be drawn through the material. That rigidity needs to be dissolved and our understanding refocused if we are to make much progress with the project to define the history of that art in these years. We do need periods, but we need them to be mobile, specific, contingent in the most positive sense of that word.[91]

There is hardly a historiography on English art from either side of 1900 that deals directly with these wider questions. Although there are monographs on individuals or on groups like Camden Town, studies that attempt to clarify our view of the connections and divisions within English art as a whole between, say, 1880 and 1914 are at a premium. Charles Harrison's book *English Art and Modernism,* published in 1981 and now more than twenty years old, still seems current and provides a useful challenge to the standard line on the periodization of English painting around 1900. In that book, Harrison devotes a brief introductory section to the "turn of the century" in which he argues that the nineteenth-century inheritance contributed a view of art as socially engaged that continued to color the "modernism" that arose after 1910. He thus takes on the then dominant understanding of modernism as concerned entirely with visual purity and to qualify it in relation to the art produced in England. Harrison's position opens up the possibility of defining modernism as the art that seeks to confront and evaluate modern life, rather than as a formalist subdivision of the twentieth century, a position most influentially propounded in England by the Bloomsbury theoreticians Fry and Bell. But this remains a sketch of a set of possibilities. Harrison himself accepts, for practical purposes, the idea that 1910 marks a change in period. A lot has happened since Harrison wrote his book. But even if we have now arrived at the point where the social history of modernism threatens to obscure modernism's involvement with the visual, there remains much to be worked through that is hinted at in Harrison's original project for a reconceptualization of the history of British art. Quite how much can be gathered by looking at a more recent book, published in 1996, that deals with the advent of modernism in Britain.

Peter Stansky's *On or About December 1910: Early Bloomsbury and Its Intimate World* presents a history that is essentially unaffected by the kinds of issues that Harrison was signaling fifteen years before. Stansky's view of modernism and of periodization at this moment is straightforward. He takes Virginia Woolf's famous attribution of significance to Fry's Post-Impressionist exhibition—that "on or about December 1910 human character changed"—absolutely for granted.[92] And he accepts the account of what "modernism" is and how it might be related to its past that derives from the art-political needs of Bloomsbury and from its later triumphalist redaction of these events and relationships. "Unexpectedly and perhaps belatedly," he writes, "England in 1910 entered the story of a modernism that since the turn of the century had had a number of its major events occur on the Continent."[93] This striking sentence gives the game away from the start. Stansky's modernism depends unproblematically on the heroic endeavors of the Bloomsbury members. The Post-Impressionist exhibition in 1910 "proved explosive" and "helped propel these writers and artists into a new, fresh, different, indeed a changed world of human character," something that was at the same time crucial "for the history of the modern movement in the twentieth century."[94] It is, in other words, a compendium of assertions that seem to rest on an unexamined periodization that defines (as readymades) "modernism," relevance, and our interest in these things in advance of our encounter with the history itself. For Stansky, the inauguration of a new period in 1910 is a given: what lies on one side is "modernism," by definition "fresh," "changed," and explicitly in touch with canonical developments on the Continent (but "belatedly," of course, as this is England); on the other side lies the rejected nineteenth century, divided from modernity by an unbridgeable gulf. This is, in all essentials, Fry and Bell's account in 1910 and later.

Both Harrison's and Stansky's books are periodizing in this way and both locate the junction at the moment in 1910 when Post-Impressionism crossed the Channel. Harrison's subtlety and appreciation of the issues is much greater than Stansky's, but the questions he proposed to disrupt the thrust of the periodization in 1981 were unrealized in his book and still remain unresolved. We are still struggling to focus the historical account of English art in the years around the "turn of the century" through a lens that insists on Stansky's inalienable periodizations and that has not succeeded in proposing convincing new discriminations. I want to spend some time, now, in drawing out in relation to my discussion so far how inadequate this account must be. I will discuss only one example, but, as I hope the body of the book has made clear, there are many more.

During his consideration of the reception of the 1910 exhibition, Stansky, like his predecessors in this historical reading, attributes a "profound sense of break" to the event.[95] In support of this, he quotes from none other than Charles Ricketts, who wrote to the *Morning Post* about the show during the prolonged public attack that followed the opening. Ricketts was patronizing about Cézanne, noting that "he would leave his paintings in the fields, not deeming them worthy to take home, thereby proving that, if a poor painter, he was an astute critic." Ricketts forthrightly consigned the Post-Impressionists' pictures to the pathological: "they might interest the doctors of the body and the students of the sickness of the soul."[96] The point of this, for Stansky, is to show, yet again, the utter incomprehension of the survivors from the late nineteenth century in the face of the new art, their resistance to its novelty and change. Ricketts is just another example of old-fogeydom for Stansky, but he does provide some contextualization, and it is this (and what Stansky says about it) that I want to consider here.

I have already discussed in the Introduction to this volume Ricketts's catalogue of his exhibition "A Century of Art, 1810–1910" as an answer to Fry's Post-Impressionist Exhibition held the year before.[97] In another essay of the time, written as a review of Fry's first Post-Impressionism show, Ricketts expanded his thoughts on the new art. Stansky quotes the following passage, commenting that "it was the novelty, the lack of tradition, that [Ricketts] particularly disliked":[98] "Art [in the Post-Impressionist view]," wrote Ricketts, "is to become young again, but the slate must be cleaned for a new message to appear in the form of a subconscious ecstasy, from which our past and present must be erased, so that we may attain to the synthetic outlook of childhood . . . novelty itself is valueless. The spirit of beauty and power, of which art is the expression, has centuries behind it; it is as old as thought."[99] I think Stansky misunderstands Ricketts's views here. He objects less to the need for a new art than to a view of novelty that involved, as he saw it, the sweeping clean of the slate of tradition and the past. In the introduction to "A Century of Art," Ricketts is explicit about this: "Between the years 1810–1910 . . . lies more than a century of continuous effort to renew the language of painting and to find for it the acceptance which in former centuries had been achieved by a closer contact between art and the business of life."[100] This is an art that Ricketts approves of and conceives himself to be part of, and it is an art of "renewal," of the recasting of the nature of the tradition while continuing to work within it. Indeed, its emphasis on repairing the gap perceived between "art and the business of life" puts it, as I have argued in the Introduction, squarely within the concerns defined by commentators like Bürger as quintessentially avant-garde. Bürger argues for avant-garde art as intent upon a "sublation" of art and life, that is, the reintegration into life of aesthetics.[101] Ricketts, I have suggested, is a significant figure in the process that unfolded during the last half of the nineteenth century and saw the aesthetic realm increasingly sundered from relevance to lived experience. In his essay, as I have shown, he posits the redemption of art, its return to life. His call—a repeated one—for that alienation to be healed by the evolution of a "renewal of the language of painting" is a founding moment of a strictly avant-garde modernism in Britain.

Ricketts's close friend and colleague, Laurence Binyon, whom Stansky also quotes dismissing the Post-Impressionist exhibition—this time as "childish rubbish"—put this view even more explicitly:[102]

There are always those who cry that to be honestly ourselves we should accept the tendencies of our time, that we are the products of our age and should reflect its current ideas and nothing more. The voice of experience rejects this shallowness. We are made up not only of what circumstances force upon us, but of wants, desires, rebellions; and it is these which are the most vital and motive parts of ourselves. . . . We cannot discard the past; we cannot throw away our heritage, but we must remould it in the fire of our necessities, we must make it new and our own. . . . What is needed now is the fusion of one imaginative effort that shall make art again a single language expressing the whole of modern man, the depth of his spiritual desire as well as the changing lights and colours of his material existence.[103]

This is part of an extended argument put forward by Binyon in his 1913 monograph, *The Art of Botticelli,* and elsewhere that relates the appearance of modernity in the Renaissance to the loss of a spiritual dimension to Western life.[104] The evacuation of meaning from the visual, which Binyon sees stemming from this in the Western tradition, lies at the heart of his desire for a new art:

For the Renaissance, by its want of inner soul, helped to create by reaction . . . Puritanism. . . . The spirituality which might have clothed itself in the gracious forms and hues of art and found in beauty its natural mode of speech, withdrew as to a naked prison-house. . . . Art is the natural language of imagination; but Puritanism murdered imagination. . . . In our own country the long reign of Puritanism left art without the sustenance of those ideas which had most power and vitality in the best minds of the nation. While literature responded to those ideas . . . painting and sculpture remained inert, an appanage of the drawing rooms of the rich. . . . So it was that the advent of the commercial spirit in all its dull insensitiveness and arrogant stupidity found no strength in art to resist it, as it settled blighting on our cities and made hideous our daily existence.[105]

Botticelli, in contrast, possesses just "this power of spirituality," and "it is this which is of import to us, now and today."[106] Ruskin and Morris, "part of our present lives, part also of our future," are said to have striven for "the recovery of that continuity . . . which the Renaissance had interrupted" and which it is now the duty of modern art and painting to take up and pursue, making form and color once again function as meaningful paths to knowledge and experience.[107]

The argument, mounted by both Ricketts and Binyon, is that art needs to be expressive of modern experience and that it needs to change and develop, to be made new, in order to achieve that aim. They differ from the modernists and from later art-historical apologists for modernism in saying that making new must entail *re*making within a tradition of experience and execution, but the impulse to rework artistic endeavor in order to express modern realities—to bring art back into the praxis of life, in avant-garde terms—is a powerful link to the ambitions of advanced modernism, especially when these are understood as about confronting modernity (in the way Harrison hints at) rather than as purely formal developments.

This throws Stansky's claims into a new context, I think. He notes that Fry had been "a regular visitor" to Ricketts in the 1890s and 1900s, but denies that there could have been any considerable influence on the grounds that "Ricketts was an ultimate connoisseur, and in its way Post-Impressionism was an assault on tradition, an attempt to 'make it new,' a change in character."[108] It seems strange to assert that Fry, so recently a consultant to major collectors and museums, would not have responded to connoisseurship, and the espousal of "an attempt to 'make it new'" is something he could have heard from Ricketts any night of the week when he went so regularly to visit him in Chelsea. Ricketts would not have agreed with Wilde's provocative suggestion that "the two things that every artist should avoid are modernity of form and modernity of subject-matter."[109] It seems to me that the possibility of influence flowing from Ricketts to the modernists is being impeded here by the heavy weight of periodization more than anything else. Stansky, taking his cue from Bloomsbury, is determined that 1910 marks an absolute line, a division over which no one could step, and that the formation of attitudes and viewpoints could not, therefore, have been indebted to earlier thinking. Put like that, this is clearly an illegitimate conclusion: history is more continuous than it allows. The indebtedness exists, and it marks an important point at which English modernism derived itself from earlier formations and did so in ways that were heavily involved in the positions laid down by their predecessors. It is no coincidence that two of the founders of modernism, Lewis and Ezra Pound, were closely involved biographically and in intellectual indebtedness with Ricketts and Binyon.

Lewis remembered the years around 1910 in his own (revisionist) autobiography, *Blasting and Bombardiering,* in terms that initially evoke the radical ground-clearing of "advanced" modernism, but he then takes a more surprising turn:

I was an idle student, nursing dreams of obstreperous intervention in a farce or two that was going on upon the stage where the painters acted, and where the aesthetes blinked and blahed. I had written an essay, a story, and an article, about something or other, and had started one or two paintings. . . . Outwardly, I have been told, I looked like a moujik; *but if so it was a moujik who bought his clothes in Saville Row or Brook Street and his most eccentric shirts in the Burlington Arcade. . . . I had the tarnished polish of the English Public School, of the most gilded cafés of five or six continental capitals. And meanwhile I would lunch with an entertaining group of people who were mostly drawn from the official ranks of the great neighbouring Museum. With some afterwards I would dine in Old Compton Street. Mostly they were middle-aged scholars.*[110]

The surprise here is the appearance of a collection of "middle-aged scholars" in the context of a different life entirely. These men, the British Museum Group, provide the clinching evidence in *Blasting and Bombardiering*'s own consignment of Lewis's younger self to complicity with the "official" culture that he claimed, as "the Vorticist," to be deconstructing. The Group, which included Binyon as a major figure, provided an intellectual and professional home for both Lewis and Pound at an early stage of their careers.[111] I have argued elsewhere that the passage I cited from Binyon, with its injunction to "make [art] new and our own," is a source for Pound's celebrated call to "make it new," a call that follows Binyon's formulation by a number of years.[112] The aesthetics and art politics of Vorticism in 1914 owe a considerable debt to those of Binyon, Ricketts, and their colleagues who aim to confront the modern. The art Ricketts and Binyon argue for is an art that can transform itself to deal with new conditions and new exigencies. Its ambitions are modern in a sense that the modernists of 1914 fully recognized: "to bring back art into touch with life," as Lewis wrote later, echoing these earlier formulations.[113]

But it is not my purpose here to explore this history in any greater detail than the foregoing chapters provide. Uncovering the modernity of this phase of English painting cannot be a matter of simply transposing the rules of modernism as they are derived from French examples, or from the history of formal modernism, and finding them exemplified in the Pre-Raphaelites, Leighton, or Sickert.[114] "Though most of us would acknowledge the continuities between Romanticism and Modernism," writes Sanford Schwartz in his study of early literary modernism in England, "few of us would actually confuse a Romantic and a Modernist poem."[115] There is no question of confusing Burne-Jones and Lewis, or Rossetti and Bell. They look different. But what is needed is analysis more subtle than that and more nuanced, an analysis that does not find that observation conclusive enough to forestall further inquiry. That is what I have attempted here. Enough has been said to show that periodization, value, what we mean by modernism, and the question of the canon are all bound up together at this moment. It is the presence of a period division—one ultimately derived from the art-political interests of 1910, in this case—that enforces a selective historical blindness, driving "modernists" and "traditionalists" into historically incredible opposing camps and obscuring the realities of their relationships. Once we begin to open up the question of the periods with which we work, periods we have inherited often uncritically from earlier historians and from the political priorities of artists themselves, the whole conception of our history begins to need recasting.

But do we just abandon periods, we revisionist historians of English art? I have argued that the existing periodization of English art around the supposed 1910 watershed in fact ignores certain connections and linkages that are of crucial importance if we are to understand the history of art in Britain during these years. Is the implication finally that we should declare periodization unnecessary and imagine a steady flow of history in which all things blend into each other instead? There is something to be said for this when we are doing micro-history, trying to untangle the circumstances of particular moments or events. At that level of attention, periods always will dissolve. But we do need as well to answer legitimate questions about the wider differences we perceive. There is certainly a difference around 1910 *for some artists*. But to elevate that to a periodization that rules what we can and cannot notice is to misuse a potentially useful intellectual tool. Great swathes of material of considerable historical and artistic importance thereby get ignored, as I have tried to show.[116]

This book has dealt with the role and importance of the visual as it affected the work painters made in England between 1848 and the First World War. As a major theme, I have discussed the way in which the chimera of adequacy of visual representation and of vision itself pressed particularly heavily on the idea of modern experience and the need to represent what was novel and characteristic in the time. This underlying theme, the perceived need (from at least the Pre-Raphaelite moment of 1848–51 on) to generate or imagine a visual art that could do justice to the modern, makes the answer to the question of the adequacy of visual representation especially acute. The capacity of vision—and of visual art as a particular, self-conscious, highly wrought subcategory of vision—to deal successfully with the world, experience, and meaning was so pressing an issue in the face of the new modernity that it generated resonances and tensions throughout the more general assessments of both language and the visual in circulation within the culture.

In the very last stages of this book, colleagues began to talk to me about an art-historical "return to the object." This may make some of the position-taking of the Introduction redundant—a welcome development. Nonetheless, I want to end the text by revisiting some of the things I said there and that seem central to the aims of the book. First, works of visual art are physical objects, and art history as a discipline neglects that materiality at its peril. Perhaps we really are now coming to the end of a phase when that foundational fact has seemed less compelling than a variety of other things—social, historical, cultural—that one can say about art. But, as I have argued, if the work of painting has historical or social meaning, then those meanings can only arise from the signifying potentialities of its material substance. Any analysis that refuses to engage with that signification and its processes, that neglects to develop an account of the historical resonance of the physical manipulation of material in painting, must be inadequate as an account. Such a project does not necessarily or desirably take place outside history, but if we are to make of the "return to the object" anything worthwhile, we will need to develop ways of speaking about materiality and objectness that can track the making of meaning in nonverbal, visual forms. I find it hard to imagine a credible art history that does not have that aspiration at its core.

Second, what follows from this acknowledgment continues to be uncomfortable for art history. Too often the response to mark-making, the physical manipulation of paint, or surface is edited out of professional dialogue and confined to personal experience, as if the encounter with the object is somehow not a part of what art history is about. An embarrassment about issues of materiality because they seem to bring with them the unresolved questions of the aesthetic, of pleasure, or of usefulness simply leaves art history unable to mount any justification for its own existence that is not a better argument for a history of visual culture. Because we have been unwilling to tackle these issues, there is no existing consensual agreement among art historians to explain why there should be a discipline devoted to this particular category of objects or what the value of studying them actually is. This is a position of enormous weakness, and as long as it obtains, there will be nothing convincing to say to those who want to subsume the study of works of art within an expanded field. If we wish to continue to work with these objects and grant them value, then we need to confront and debate within the public forum of the discipline the nature of that value.

Third and last, it has been a principal claim of this book that English painting between the late 1840s and the First World War is engaged with these issues in ways that are sophisticated, complex, and meditative. It functions to evaluate, understand, and measure the world of experience on which it draws, and it does this through the agency of its materiality, so that paint and the manipulations to which it is subject are central to intellectual meanings based on inquiry and assessment of the sort that I have sought to recover in my discussions. These paintings, through their attention to the capacity of the visual to mean, constitute a cumulative contribution to the understanding of its nature.

Continuities extend beyond my chronological limits at each end. I am not proposing that 1848 marked some absolute upheaval: the Pre-Raphaelites came from somewhere and drew on many precursors, Grub Street was the invention of the eighteenth century (not the nineteenth), and English modernism did not disappear in 1914, although it sustained a major, transforming wound.[117] And yet, throughout these decades, the visual promised to make sense of the new world coming into being. Building from the years around 1840, this process reaches a pivotal moment with the foundation and subsequent evolution of Pre-Raphaelitism, reaches another such moment with the appearance of the ideas associated with Aestheticism, and continues to develop, as I show, into the early twentieth century, reaching a further crux with the appearance of English modernism. Between the moments marked by these rough dates, English painters sought to express their reactions to a perception of their own modernity. In doing so they tested the possibility that the sensuous, material surfaces of their paint could, through those very qualities, understand and explicate the world. They are sophisticated, argumentative, and meaningful in ways that only the visual can be.

Notes

Introduction

1. Ricketts was in Spain to amass material for his book *The Prado and Its Masterpieces* (London, 1903). See Chapter 3 for a discussion of the use he made of it.

2. Thomas Sturge Moore, "Lines on Titian's 'Bacchanal' in the Prado at Madrid," in *The Gazelles and Other Poems* (London, 1904), xix. For the critical reception of the poem, see Frederick L. Gwynn, *Sturge Moore and the Life of Art* (Lawrence, Kans., 1951), 44, and Yvor Winters, "T. Sturge Moore," in *Uncollected Essays and Reviews* (London, 1974), 145. The bacchante figure also fascinated Ricketts, and the interpretations of the bacchante in Ricketts's analysis (in *The Prado*) and in Moore's poem are quite similar. Given the master/pupil element in their relationship, I suggest that Ricketts is likely to have originated the reading.

3. *The Gazelles,* xix–xx.

4. Ibid., xx.

5. As well as his intellectual and biographical connections with the English Symbolism of Ricketts and Shannon and *The Dial,* Moore fulfills the requirements of the definition of Symbolism offered by René Wellek: "the Symbolist symbol has its special character: simple replacement [of the proper term by a metaphor] *and* the suggestion of mystery." See Wellek's "What Is Symbolism?" in *The Symbolist Movement in the Literature of European Languages,* ed. Anna Balakian (Budapest, 1984), 27.

6. Frank Kermode, *Romantic Image* (London, 1976), 13.

7. The phrase comes from the title of Stephen Calloway and Paul Delaney's *Charles Ricketts and Charles Shannon: An Aesthetic Partnership,* exh. cat., Orleans House Gallery, Twickenham (London, 1979). The influence continued until the end of Moore's life and has an enduring monument in his compilation, *Self-Portrait Taken from the Letters and Journals of Charles Ricketts, R.A.,* ed. Cecil Lewis (London, 1939).

8. Stephen Calloway, *Charles Ricketts: Subtle and Fantastic Decorator* (London, 1979), 8.

9. Said of Whistler in J. Comyns Carr, *Some Eminent Victorians: Personal Recollections in the World of Art and Letters* (London, 1908), 135.

10. Cited without attribution in Joseph Darracott, *The World of Charles Ricketts* (New York, 1980), 22–23.

11. J. G. P. Delaney, "Ricketts, Shannon, and Their Circle," in *The Last Romantics: The Romantic Tradition in British Art, Burne-Jones to Stanley Spencer,* exh. cat., Barbican Art Gallery (London, 1989), 45.

12. Charles Ricketts, "Post-Impressionism at the Grafton Gallery," in *Pages on Art* (London, 1913), 150.

13. Charles Ricketts, "A Century of Art, 1810–1910," in *Pages on Art,* 50.

14. Ibid., 47–48.

15. On *The Dial,* see David Peters Corbett and Andrew Thacker, "Raymond Williams and Cultural Formations: Movements and Magazines," *Prose Studies* 16, no. 2 (1993): 84–106.

16. See Peter Bürger, *Theory of the Avant-Garde,* trans. Michael Shaw (Manchester, 1984).

17. Ricketts, "Century of Art," 47.

18. Ibid., 47, 50.

19. Ibid., 52.

20. Charles Ricketts, "Puvis de Chavannes," in *Pages on Art,* 68–69.

21. Charles Ricketts, "G. F. Watts," in *Pages on Art,* 103–4.

22. Ibid., 110.

23. Ibid., 112.

24. See Charles Baudelaire, "The Painter of Modern Life," in *The Painter of Modern Life and Other Essays,* trans. Jonathan Mayne (Oxford, 1964), 13. See also J. M. Bernstein, *The Fate of*

Art: Aesthetic Alienation from Kant to Derrida and Adorno (Cambridge, 1992).

25. See David Peters Corbett, *The Modernity of English Art, 1914–30* (Manchester, 1997), 27. On Symbolism and modernism, see Peter Nicholls, *Modernisms: A Literary Guide* (Basingstoke, U.K., 1995), chapters 2 and 3, and my discussion in Chapter 4 below.

26. Darracott, *The World of Charles Ricketts,* 7.

27. This fascination with the visual aesthetic is, too, a common feature of the artists and intellectuals who orbited around Ricketts—a loose grouping of writers, artists, and critics that included not only Sturge Moore (the author of books on Altdorfer, Correggio, and Dürer), John Rothenstein, the aunt-niece partnership "Michael Field," and Oscar Wilde but also Laurence Binyon, the important curator and historian of British and oriental art. See J. G. P. Delaney, *Charles Ricketts: A Biography* (Oxford, 1990); John Hatcher, *Laurence Binyon: Poet, Scholar of East and West* (Oxford, 1995); and, for an account of Ricketts's circle from a core member, Charles Holmes, *Self and Partners (Mostly Self): Being the Reminiscences of Sir Charles Holmes* (London, 1936). See also Howard Clark, "The British Museum Group, 1885–1920" (master's thesis, University of York, 1998).

28. T. Sturge Moore, notes on Charles Shannon, n.d. [1938], Sturge Moore Papers, University of London, box 9, item 16, fols. ii–iii.

29. This position has a considerable history in the development of ideas of the poetic image. See W. J. T. Mitchell, *Iconology: Image, Text, Ideology* (Chicago, 1986), 19–31, for a useful summary account.

30. T. Sturge Moore, fragment of a lecture, n.d., Sturge Moore Papers, University of London, box 9, item 25B.

31. Jonathan Crary, *Techniques of the Observer: On Vision and Modernity in the Nineteenth Century* (Cambridge, Mass., 1990), 2–3. Subsequent references to this work will appear parenthetically in the text.

32. The most powerful formulation of this view is to be found in T. J. Clark, *The Painting of Modern Life: Paris in the Art of Manet and His Followers* (London, 1984).

33. Ibid., 147. See also T. J. Clark, *Farewell to an Idea: Episodes from a History of Modernism* (New Haven, Conn., 1999), 165, where Clark develops this idea.

34. G. F. Watts, "The Aims of Art" (1888), in *George Frederic Watts: The Annals of an Artist's Life,* by Mary S. Watts (New York, n.d.), 3:230.

35. I do not mean by this that such a project is not viable in other visual media as well. I do not pursue such an argument, though, given the constraints of space in a single book and my particular interest in tracing painting's unfolding project.

36. Gillian Beer, *Darwin's Plots: Evolutionary Narrative in Darwin, George Eliot, and Nineteenth-Century Fiction* (London, 1983), 4.

37. Gillian Beer, "'The Death of the Sun': Victorian Solar Physics and Solar Myth," in *The Sun Is God: Painting, Literature, and Mythology in the Nineteenth Century,* ed. J. B. Bullen (Oxford, 1989), 167, and reprinted in Beer's *Open Fields: Science in Cultural Encounter* (Oxford, 1996), 228.

38. See, for this concept, Harold Bloom, *The Anxiety of Influence* (New York, 1973).

39. The comment is cited in Robyn Asleson, *Albert Moore* (London, 2000), 154.

40. I do not mean to suggest that painting *can* actually know the world through its materiality. My argument is historical. The artists I examine here were concerned with the question of whether visual media could operate as knowledge—and they believed that it might. It is a noble dream.

41. See Nigel Whiteley, "Readers of the Lost Art: Visuality and Particularity in Art Criticism," in *Interpreting Visual Culture: Explorations in the Hermeneutics of the Visual*, ed. Ian Heywood and Barry Sandywell (London, 1999).

42. Clement Greenberg, "Modernist Painting" (1961), reprinted in *Art in Theory, 1900–1939: An Anthology of Changing Ideas,* ed. Charles Harrison and Paul Wood (Oxford, 1992), 755; see also Greenberg's "Avant-Garde and Kitsch" (1939) in the same collection (529–41).

43. Greenberg, "Modernist Painting," 756.

44. Elizabeth Prettejohn justly observes that Greenberg is selective in the physical conditions he identifies; the flatness of the canvas is not necessarily the principal constraint. See her

"Out of the Nineteenth Century: Roger Fry's Early Art Criticism, 1900–1906," in *Art Made Modern: Roger Fry's Vision of Art,* ed. Christopher Green (London, 1999), 43.

45. Semioticians like Norman Bryson and Mieke Bal have also identified the need to interpret the material character of the visual sign. See James Elkins, *On Pictures and the Words That Fail Them* (Cambridge, 1998), chapter 1. A version of Elkins's argument originally appeared as "Marks, Traces, *Traits,* Contours, *Orli,* and *Splendores:* Nonsemiotic Elements in Pictures," *Critical Inquiry* 21 (1995): 822–60, and it called forth Mieke Bal's reply, "What Do We Want Pictures to Be?" *Critical Inquiry* 22 (1996): 590–602. See also W. J. T. Mitchell, *Picture Theory* (Chicago, 1994), chapter 3. Bryson observed in his *Vision and Painting* that "painting is itself a locus of mobility in the field of signification, a process . . . which in the first place is a work on and through material signs." He concluded that "to understand the painting as a sign," we have to attend "to the body whose activity—for the painter as for the viewer—is always and only a transformation of material signs." See Bryson's *Vision and Painting: The Logic of the Gaze* (Basingstoke, U.K., 1983), 170–71. See also Bryson's *Word and Image: French Painting of the Ancien Régime* (Cambridge, 1981), chapter 1, and his "Semiology and Visual Interpretation," in *Visual Theory: Painting and Interpretation,* ed. Norman Bryson, Michael Ann Holly, and Keith Moxey (Cambridge, 1988), as well as Mieke Bal and Norman Bryson, "Semiotics and Art History," *Art Bulletin* 73, no. 2 (1991): 174–208. In *Reading "Rembrandt,"* the most fully developed version of her ideas on the visual, Bal argues for a method that "will let visual texts be read without sacrificing their visuality," and she sees this quality as located in the material "density" of visual signs. See Mieke Bal, *Reading "Rembrandt": Beyond the Word-Image Opposition* (Cambridge, 1991), 19.

46. A number of art historians, such as James Elkins, have attempted recently to rectify this situation. For Elkins, the meaning that inheres in paint depends on the material constituents of the work as a physical object, so that a painting is a materialist way of thinking about the world that is distinct from the verbal but as effective. See James Elkins, *What Painting Is: How to Think About Oil Painting, Using the Language of Alchemy* (New York, 2000); see also Elkins, *On Pictures and the Words That Fail Them.* For an interesting discussion in the English context, see Sam Smiles, "'Splashers,' 'Scrawlers,' and 'Plasterers': British Landscape Painting and the Language of Criticism, 1800–1840," *Turner Studies* 10, no. 1 (1990): 5–11. If it is the case that the material aspects of painting are the most fundamental and specific characteristics of the medium, then it is the physical substance out of which painting is made that must carry meaning if paintings are to serve as vehicles of knowledge about the world. Historical or social meaning can only arise from the signifying potentialities of the material substance that forms this irreducible or ineluctable condition of existence. Any analysis that refuses to engage with that signification and its processes—that neglects, in other words, to develop an account of the historical resonance of the physical manipulation of material in painting—must be inadequate as an account (see Yves-Alain Bois, *Painting as Model* [Cambridge, Mass., 1993]). For a very welcome recent general introduction to the physical constitution of paintings, see Andrea Kirsh and Rustin S. Levenson, *Seeing Through Paintings: Physical Examination in Art Historical Studies* (New Haven, Conn., 2000).

47. Georges Didi-Huberman, "The Art of Not Describing: Vermeer—The Detail and the Patch," *History of the Human Sciences* 2, no. 2 (1989): 162. I owe my introduction to Didi-Huberman to Michael Ann Holly, *Past Looking* (Ithaca, N.Y., 1996). See other discussions of this subject in Charles Harrison, "On the Surface of Painting," *Critical Inquiry* 15, no. 2 (1989): 292–336, and David Joselit, "Notes on Surface: Toward a Genealogy of Flatness," *Art History* 23, no. 1 (2000): 19–34.

48. For the concept of the "innocent" discipline that is not, see Terry Eagleton, *Criticism and Ideology: A Study of Marxist Literary Theory* (London, 1977), especially 11 and 17.

49. Michael Baxandall had drawn this contrast earlier without using the term. See his *Painting and Experience in Fifteenth-Century Italy: A Primer in the Social History of Pictorial Style* (Oxford, 1972), which, with its central assertion and elegant demonstration that a painting "is

the deposit of a social relationship" (1), was an important initial moment in broaching the question of how the visual functions as a form of knowledge in societies.

50. Hal Foster, ed., *Vision and Visuality* (Seattle, Wash., 1988), ix.

51. Nicholas Mirzoeff, *An Introduction to Visual Culture* (London, 1998), 13; see 13–22 and chapter 1.

52. In Georges Didi-Huberman, whose work I cite throughout the book, "visuality" has this meaning. See his *Fra Angelico: Dissemblance and Figuration,* trans. Jane Marie Todd (Chicago, 1995), 57, 66.

53. For a fuller account of the arguments around modernity and modernism, see the introduction to my *Modernity of English Art.* See also David Peters Corbett and Lara Perry, eds., *English Art, 1860–1914: Modern Artists and Identity* (Manchester, 2000). For a very helpful and focused account of the issues relating to art in Britain, see David Solkin, "The British and the Modern," in *Towards a Modern Art World,* ed. Brian Allen (New Haven, Conn., 1995), 1–6. I draw on these arguments in the current book.

54. *Walter Sickert: The Complete Writings on Art,* ed. Anna Gruetzner Robins (Oxford, 2000), 229.

55. For an extended example of such a reading of modernism and its avatars, see Malcolm Bradbury and James McFarlane, eds., *Modernism* (Harmondsworth, U.K., 1976).

56. See Isobel Armstrong, "Transparency: Towards a Poetics of Glass in the Nineteenth Century," in *Cultural Babbage: Technology, Time, and Invention,* ed. Francis Spufford and Jenny Uglow (London, 1996). Armstrong makes large claims for glass as "*the* innovative material of the nineteenth century" that by the 1830s was already "beginning to make possible new meanings and opening up cognitive space, transforming consciousness" (124–25); quotations in text from 125 and 131.

57. Ibid., 131, 312.

58. Ibid., 125.

59. The work of Michael Fried has been an important influence on my formulation of this idea. See, in particular, *Absorption and Theatricality: Painting and Beholder in the Age of Diderot* (Chicago, 1980).

60. Dorothy Ross, ed., *Modernist Impulses in the Human Sciences, 1870–1930* (Baltimore, 1994), 1.

61. Sanford Schwartz, *The Matrix of Modernism: Pound, Eliot, and Early Twentieth-Century Thought* (Princeton, N.J., 1985), 4.

62. W. David Shaw, *The Lucid Veil: Poetic Truth in the Victorian Age* (London, 1987), 3; see also Linda Dowling, *Language and Decadence in the Victorian Fin de Siècle* (Princeton, N.J., 1986), xiii.

63. Shaw, *The Lucid Veil,* 3–4.

64. Sally Shuttleworth, *George Eliot and Nineteenth-Century Science: The Make-Believe of a Beginning* (Cambridge, 1984), 1. Shuttleworth points out this development at work in the opening epigraph to George Eliot's *Daniel Deronda* (1876): "Men can do nothing without the make-believe of a beginning. Even Science, the strict measurer, is obliged to start with a make-believe unit, and must fix on a point in the stars' unceasing journey when his sidereal clock shall pretend that time is at Nought."

65. Dowling, *Language and Decadence,* xv, xii. See also Gillian Beer, "Darwin and the Growth of Language Theory," in *Nature Transfigured: Science and Literature, 1700–1900,* ed. John Christie and Sally Shuttleworth (Manchester, 1989).

66. Max Müller, *Lectures on the Science of Language, Delivered at the Royal Institution of Great Britain in February, March, and April 1863,* 2d ser. (London, 1864), 43, 526, 580.

67. See, on the general topic of optics and the importance of Helmholtz and Tyndall in Britain, Gillian Beer, "Helmholtz, Tyndall, Gerard Manley Hopkins: Leaps of the Prepared Imagination," in *Open Fields.* On Helmholtz in detail, see David Cahan, ed., *Hermann von Helmholtz and the Foundations of Nineteenth-Century Science* (Berkeley and Los Angeles, 1993), and on optics in the period immediately prior to Helmholtz, see G. N. Cantor, *Optics After Newton: Theories of Light in Britain and Ireland, 1704–1840* (Manchester, 1983).

68. Beer, "Helmholtz, Tyndall, Gerard Manley Hopkins," 245.

69. In the most successful of his books, Tyndall announced that he aimed "to extend sympathy for science beyond the limits of the

scientific public." See John Tyndall, preface to *Fragments of Science for Unscientific People: A Series of Detached Essays, Lectures, and Reviews* (London, 1871).

70. Hermann von Helmholtz, "Opinions of an Eminent Scientist," in *Advancement of Science: The Inaugural Address of Prof. John Tyndall, DCL, LLD, FRS, Delivered Before the British Association for the Advancement of Science at Belfast, August 19, 1874,* by John Tyndall (New York, 1874), 11–12.

71. Tyndall, *Fragments of Science,* 100, 101.

72. A number of scholars have seen the consequence of nineteenth-century skepticism about the nature of language and scientific understanding of the world as central to the development of modernist poetics in the work of Ezra Pound and others who were closely connected to English modernism in the visual arts before the First World War. See Ian F. A. Bell, *Critic as Scientist: The Modernist Poetics of Ezra Pound* (London, 1981); Schwartz, *The Matrix of Modernism;* and Martin A. Kayman, *The Modernism of Ezra Pound: The Science of Poetry* (Basingstoke, U.K., 1986). Kayman argues for the relativism of modernist thought and concludes that "Pound's poetics are modernist . . . not inasmuch as they reflect a real scientific world, but inasmuch as they reflect historically specific discourses about that world" (108).

73. Griselda Pollock, *Avant-Garde Gambits, 1888–1893: Gender and the Colour of Art History* (London, 1992), 15. See also Regenia Gagnier, *Idylls of the Marketplace: Oscar Wilde and the Victorian Public* (Aldershot, U.K., 1987), and her *Insatiability of Human Wants: Economics and Aesthetics in Market Society* (Chicago, 2000), especially chapters 2 and 4, as well as Jonathan Freedman, *Professions of Taste: Henry James, British Aestheticism, and Commodity Culture* (Stanford, 1990).

74. George Gissing, *New Grub Street: A Novel* (London, 1891; reprint, Oxford, 1993), 8–9.

75. Ibid., 13–14.

76. See George Gissing, *Will Warburton: A Romance of Real Life* (London, 1905), for a novel in which it is the painter, Norbert Franks, who allows himself to become "consciously debased" (77) and court popular success—and who, as a result, is miserable in a dishonesty he will not acknowledge.

77. Gagnier, *The Insatiability of Human Wants,* 123.

78. On these developments, see Kate Flint, *The Victorians and the Visual Imagination* (Cambridge, 2000), chapters 7 and 8. Flint argues that critics, the wielders of words about art, were perceived from the 1860s on as arch-representatives of the commercialization of the art world. See, on professionalization in late Victorian culture, T. W. Heyck, *The Transformation of Intellectual Life in Victorian England* (London, 1982); Gagnier, *Idylls of the Marketplace;* N. N. Feltes, *Literary Capital and the Late Victorian Novel* (Madison, Wisc., 1993); Freedman, *Professions of Taste;* Andrew H. Miller, *Novels Behind Glass: Commodity Culture and Victorian Narrative* (Cambridge, 1995); Kathy Alexis Psomiades, *Beauty's Body: Femininity and Representation in British Aestheticism* (Stanford, 1997); Laurel Brake, *Subjugated Knowledges: Journalism, Gender, and Literature in the Nineteenth Century* (London, 1994); and Gagnier, "Productive Bodies, Pleasured Bodies: On Victorian Aesthetics," in *Women and British Aestheticism,* ed. Talia Schaffer and Kathy Alexis Psomiades (Charlottesville, Va., 1999), 270–89. On Ricketts in particular in this context, see Corbett and Thacker, "Raymond Williams and Cultural Formations."

79. On the influence of new print media in the latter half of the century, see Laurel Brake, Bill Bell, and David Finkelstein, *Nineteenth-Century Media and the Construction of Identities* (Basingstoke, U.K., 2000), and Gerard Curtis, *Visual Words: Art and the Material Book in Victorian England* (Aldershot, U.K., 2002).

80. Flint, *The Victorians and the Visual Imagination,* 173. See also Flint's "Moral Judgement and the Language of English Art Criticism, 1870–1910," *Oxford Art Journal* 6, no. 2 (1983): 59–66.

81. Ross, ed., *Modernist Impulses,* 2, 1.

82. Ben Knights, *The Idea of the Clerisy in the Nineteenth Century* (Cambridge, 1978), 7. See John Holloway, *The Victorian Sage: Studies in Argument* (London, 1953), for a discussion of the specifically literary manifestations.

83. Thomas Carlyle, "Signs of the Times," *Edinburgh Review* (1829), in *Complete Works of Thomas Carlyle* (New York, 1901), 21:465.

84. Cited in Michael H. Levenson, *A Genealogy of Modernism: A Study of English Literary Doctrine, 1908–1922* (Cambridge, 1984), 13.

85. George Steiner, *In Bluebeard's Castle: Some Notes Towards the Re-definition of Culture* (London, 1971), 25.

86. Since Lessing, at least, the visual had been conceived as the natural opposition to the word. See G. E. Lessing, *Laocoön: An Essay on the Limits of Painting and Poetry,* trans., intro., and notes by Edward Allen McCormick (Baltimore, 1984).

87. Ruskin also offers a contradictory view, as he often does: "Painting, or art generally, as such, with all its technicalities, difficulties, and particular end, is nothing but a noble and expressive language, invaluable as the vehicle of thought, but by itself nothing. . . . It is not by the mode of representing and saying, but by what is represented and said, that the respective greatness either of the painter or the writer is to be finally determined" (John Ruskin, *Modern Painters,* in *The Works of John Ruskin,* ed. E. T. Cork and Alexander Wedderburn [London, 1903–12], 3:87–88). I owe to Elizabeth Prettejohn, in correspondence, the observation that it is this passage that Walter Pater argues against in the very first paragraph of "The School of Giorgione," which begins: "It is the mistake of much popular criticism to regard poetry, music, and painting . . . as but translations into different languages of one and the same fixed quantity of imaginative thought, supplemented by certain technical qualities" (*The Renaissance: Studies in Art and Poetry: The 1893 Text,* ed. Donald L. Hill [Berkeley and Los Angeles, 1980], 102).

88. Ruskin, *Mornings in Florence,* in *Works,* ed. Cook and Wedderburn, 23:329. Compare *Modern Painters,* 5:333: "the more I think of it I find this conclusion more impressed upon me,—that the greatest thing a human soul ever does in this world is to *see* something, and tell what it *saw* in a plain way. Hundreds of people can talk for one who can think, but thousands can think for one who can see. To see clearly is poetry, prophecy, and religion,—all in one."

89. Ruskin, *The Elements of Drawing,* in *Works,* ed. Cook and Wedderburn, footnote to 15:27.

90. Jay Fellows, *The Failing Distance: The Autobiographical Impulse in John Ruskin* (Baltimore, 1975), ix, 68.

91. Lindsay Smith, *Victorian Photography, Painting, and Poetry: The Enigma of Visibility in Ruskin, Morris, and the Pre-Raphaelites* (Cambridge, 1995), 28, 25.

92. Ibid., 29–30.

93. On Ruskin and modernity, see Dinah Birch, ed., *Ruskin and the Dawn of the Modern* (Oxford, 1999), and Giovanni Cianci and Peter Nicholls, eds., *Ruskin and Modernism* (Basingstoke, U.K., 2001).

94. Bernstein, *The Fate of Art,* 4. According to Bernstein, this shows how in modernity, ruled by rationalized and "means-end" categories of value as reason, art claims to be justified as "more truthful than empirical truth . . . more rational than methodical reason . . . more valuable than principled morality"—that is, it claims to lie outside the values of modernity and to be able to define and comment on them accordingly. But, as so often in the history of modern art, this claim seemed to be both intensely desirable and at the same time unsustainable (1–2). See also Russell A. Berman, *Modern Culture and Critical Theory: Art, Politics, and the Legacy of the Frankfurt School* (Madison, Wisc., 1989).

95. M. Watts, *George Frederick Watts: Annals,* 3:161.

96. Cited in Malcolm Warner, "Signs of the Times," in *The Victorians: British Painting, 1837–1901,* exh. cat., National Gallery of Art (Washington, D.C., 1997), 20. The passage, which is echoed in Frederic Leighton's *Addresses, Delivered to Students at the Royal Academy* (London, 1896), is from his notebook. I discuss the argument of the *Addresses* in Chapter 2.

97. Cited in *Burne-Jones,* exh. cat., Mappin Art Gallery (Sheffield, U.K., 1971), 4–5.

98. See Stephen Wildman and John Christian, "Birmingham and Oxford," in *Burne-Jones: Victorian Artist-Dreamer,* exh. cat., Metropolitan Museum of Art (New York, 1998), 45.

99. Mary Lago, ed., *Burne-Jones Talking: His Conversations, 1895–1898, Preserved by His Studio Assistant Thomas Rooke* (London, 1982), 56; Georgiana Burne-Jones [G. B.-J., pseud.], *Memorials of*

Edward Burne-Jones (London, 1904), 2:261. The full text runs as follows: "One of the hardest things in the world is to determine how much realism is allowable in any particular picture. It is of so many different kinds, too. For instance, I want a shield or a crown or a pair of wings or what not, to look real. Well, I make what I want, or a model of it, and then make studies from that. So that what eventually gets on to the canvas is a reflection of a reflection of something purely imaginary. The three Magi never had crowns like that . . . but the effect is realistic because the crown from which the studies were made is real—and so on" (261). The "escapism" here is misattributed; the comment refers to technique. For examples of "escapism" used in this way, see William Waters, *Burne-Jones: An Illustrated Life of Sir Edward Burne-Jones, 1833–1898* (Princes Risborough, U.K., 1989), 5, and *Burne-Jones,* Mappin Art Gallery, 7 and passim. Also see Paula Gillett, *Worlds of Art: Painters in Victorian Society* (New Brunswick, N.J., 1990), 67.

100. Cited in *Burne-Jones,* Mappin Art Gallery, 5.

101. Julia Cartwright, "Sir Edward Burne-Jones, Bart: His Life and Work," *The Art Annual,* "Christmas Number" (1894): 1, 1–2.

102. J. E. Phythian, *Burne-Jones* (London, 1908), 64.

103. Robert de la Sizeranne, *English Contemporary Art,* trans. H. M. Poynter (Westminster, U.K., 1898), 239–40.

104. Ibid., 240.

105. Fortunée de Lisle, *Burne-Jones,* 2d ed. (London, 1906), 4.

106. G. Burne-Jones, *Memorials,* 2:208.

107. Gillian Beer, "Authentic Tidings of Invisible Things," in *Vision in Context: Historical and Contemporary Perspectives on Sight,* ed. Teresa Brennan and Martin Jay (New York, 1996), 85.

108. Ibid. On scientific materialism, see David M. Knight, *Atoms and Elements: A Study of Theories of Matter in England in the Nineteenth Century* (London, 1967).

109. Robert Browning, "Mr Sludge, 'The Medium,'" cited in Beer, "Authentic Tidings," 87.

110. Beer, "Authentic Tidings," 88.

111. See Cantor, *Optics After Newton,* for an account of the institutional triumph of wave theories of light by the 1830s as well as "the emphasis on hypothesis" (185) and abstract and relativizing criteria for the utility of scientific theories that accompanied it.

112. See also, on this topic, Crary, *Techniques of the Observer,* and his *Suspensions of Perception: Attention, Spectacle, and Modern Culture* (Cambridge, Mass., 1999).

113. Timothy Lenoir, "The Eye as Mathematician: Clinical Practice, Instrumentation, and Helmholtz's Construction of an Empiricist Theory of Vision," in *Hermann von Helmholtz,* ed. Cahan, 110. In the same volume, see R. Steven Turner, "Consensus and Controversy: Helmholtz on the Visual Perception of Space," on empiricism and Helmholtz's popularization of his approaches.

114. Robert Brudenell Carter, *Eyesight, Good and Bad: A Treatise on the Exercise and Preservation of Vision* (London, 1880), 3.

115. Cited in Beer, "Authentic Tidings," 90. The passage was inserted in the final edition of *The Origin of Species* that Darwin prepared, but Beer notes that Helmholtz's work in fact predates the first publication of Darwin's book in 1859. See also, on this general topic, James Krasner, *The Entangled Eye: Visual Representation and the Representation of Nature in Post-Darwinian Narrative* (Oxford, 1992).

116. Flint, *The Victorians and the Visual Imagination,* 25, 311.

117. Gagnier, *Idylls of the Marketplace,* 52.

118. See Lynda Nead, *Victorian Babylon: People, Streets, and Images in Nineteenth-Century London* (New Haven, Conn., 2000).

119. Sizeranne, *English Contemporary Art,* 277.

120. Ibid., 282–83.

121. Ibid., 287.

122. The phrase about "a linear view of change" is taken from Stella Tillyard, who also makes the point about distortion; see *The Impact of Modernism, 1900–1920: Early Modernism and the Arts and Crafts Movement in Edwardian England* (London, 1988), xv–xvi.

123. Lisa Tickner, "Messing About in Boats: E. J. Gregory's *Boulter's Lock: Sunday Afternoon* (R.A., 1897)," *Oxford Art Journal* 25, no. 2 (2002): 18.

Chapter 1

1. Ruskin, *Modern Painters,* 3:624. On the painting, see Susan Casteras, *Images of Victorian Womanhood in English Art* (London, 1987), 142.

2. Elizabeth Prettejohn, *The Art of the Pre-Raphaelites* (London, 2000), 94. Hunt "rented a room in a 'maison de convenance' in order to ensure the correctness of every detail," according to Tim Barringer, *The Pre-Raphaelites: Reading the Image* (London, 1988), 94.

3. Ruskin, letter to *The Times,* 25 May 1854, in *Works,* ed. Cook and Wedderburn, 12:333–34, 335. A part of the lyric to "Oft in the Stilly Night" is printed in Barringer, *The Pre-Raphaelites,* 95.

4. The core P.R.B. group involved in *The Germ* comprised Dante Gabriel and William Michael Rossetti, William Holman Hunt, John Everett Millais, Frederic George Stephens, Thomas Woolner, and James Collinson. For an important account, see the introduction William Michael Rossetti wrote to the facsimile reprint of *The Germ: Thoughts Towards Nature in Poetry, Literature, and Art* (London, 1901). After the first two numbers, the title of *The Germ* was changed to *Art and Poetry: Being Thoughts Towards Nature Conducted Principally by Artists.* For general accounts, see Barringer, *The Pre-Raphaelites;* Leslie Parris, ed., *The Pre-Raphaelites,* exh. cat., Tate Gallery (London, 1984); and Prettejohn, *The Art of the Pre-Raphaelites.*

5. *The Critic* 9 (February 15, 1850): 94–95. Cox endeavored to allay any suspicions his readers might feel on discovering that *The Germ* was "the production of a party of young persons," claiming that "an affected title and an unpromising theme really hides a great deal of genius" (ibid.).

6. *The Critic* 9 (June 1, 1850): 278.

7. *The Guardian,* August 28, 1850, 623.

8. On the Pre-Raphaelites and the avant-garde, see Dianne Sachko MacLeod, "The Dialectics of Modernism and English Art," *British Journal of Aesthetics* 35 (1995): 1–14. Prettejohn, *The Art of the Pre-Raphaelites,* makes the more general argument that Pre-Raphaelitism is one "of the greatest achievements of modernity" (262).

9. See William Michael Rossetti's introduction to *The Germ* (6). See also 8: "there was a league of unquiet and ambitious young spirits, bent upon making a fresh start of their own, and a clean sweep of some effete respectabilities." W. M. Rossetti noted, too, that "you cannot have a youthful rebel . . . who is also a model head-boy in a school" (7).

10. According to Peter Bürger, such an attempt characterizes avant-garde practice—and, in this quite specific sense, the P.R.B. arguably marked the arrival of an artistic avant-garde in English culture. Avant-garde groups, according to Bürger, aim to overcome the relegation of art to the margins in bourgeois societies, to transcend its status as an irrelevance or a mere pastime when art is "unassociated with the life praxis of men." See Bürger, *Theory of the Avant-Garde,* 49.

11. Thomas Carlyle, *Past and Present* (London, 1843; reprint, London, 1960), 6, 7. Emphasis in the original.

12. There are, however, no significant modern life subjects in the P.R.B. canon before 1852. That year represents a turn toward modern subjects after attempts to encapsulate modern experience in older forms. Rossetti's short stories, which I discuss below, are fictionalized attempts to assert this encapsulation as an accomplished fact. See, on this general subject, Jerome McGann, "Medieval *versus* Victorian *versus* Modern: Rossetti's Art of Images," *Modernism/Modernity* 2, no. 1 (1995): 97–112.

13. Carlyle, *Past and Present,* 8; John Ruskin, "Academy Notes, 1859," in *Works,* ed. Cook and Wedderburn, 24:244.

14. Carlyle, *Past and Present,* 121.

15. Jerome McGann, *Dante Gabriel Rossetti and the Game That Must Be Lost* (New Haven, Conn., 2000), 36, 7.

16. See *The Art Criticism of John Ruskin,* ed. Robert L. Herbert (Gloucester, Mass., 1969), 395, cited in McGann, *Dante Gabriel Rossetti,* 77.

17. F. G. Stephens, *Dante Gabriel Rossetti* (London, 1894), 10.

18. W. Holman Hunt, *Pre-Raphaelitism and the Pre-Raphaelite Brotherhood,* (London, 1905), 1:150. As I note later, there are many minor changes in the text of the second edition (1913).

I have used the first edition cited here except where I specify otherwise.

19. F. G. Stephens [John Seward], "The Purpose and Tendency of Early Italian Art," *The Germ* 2 (1850): 58.

20. Ibid., 59, 60. Stephens and Rossetti had a close intellectual relationship at this and later periods. It is likely that Rossetti originated the idea.

21. Ibid., 64.

22. Dante Gabriel Rossetti, "St Agnes of Intercession," in *The Works of Dante Gabriel Rossetti,* ed. William Michael Rossetti (London, 1911), 558.

23. Writing in support of the P.R.B. in 1851, Ruskin picked up Stephens's linkage of modernity and his call for "closer communion with nature" ("Purpose and Tendency," 58): "The Pre-Raphaelites . . . intend to return to early days in this one point only—that, as far as in them lies, they will draw either what they see, or what they suppose might have been the actual facts of the scene they desire to represent, irrespective of any conventional rules of picture-making" (Ruskin, letter to *The Times,* 13 May 1851, in *Works,* ed. Cook and Wedderburn, 12:321–22).

24. See Virginia Surtees, *The Paintings and Drawings of Dante Gabriel Rossetti (1828–1882): A Catalogue Raisonné* (Oxford, 1971), 1:7, cat. 31.

25. For Rossetti's reluctance, see Stephens, *Dante Gabriel Rossetti,* 11, and W. Holman Hunt, *Pre-Raphaelitism,* 1:107–8 and passim.

26. Alastair Grieve, *The Art of Dante Gabriel Rossetti: The Pre-Raphaelite Period, 1848–50* (Hingham, U.K., 1973), 2. Grieve sees connections to the drawings Rossetti produced from this period. In them, he similarly "seems to have questioned the basic purpose of composition and space in pictures" (4). According to Grieve, Rossetti's graphic technique was as radical as his oil painting. This is achieved in Rossetti's case partly by translation across media, so that "the pen strokes resemble the engraving style of contemporary illustrators like John Leech" (3).

27. William Bell Scott, *Autobiographical Notes,* ed. W. Minto (New York, 1892), 1:250. Hunt later remembered Millais declaring during their early meetings: "Last year it was the rage to talk about 'Collinson's finish.' . . . I'll show 'em that wasn't finish at all." See W. Holman Hunt, *Pre-Raphaelitism,* 1:84.

28. Prettejohn, *The Art of the Pre-Raphaelites,* 140, 145. See also John Gage, *George Field and His Circle: From Romanticism to the Pre-Raphaelite Brotherhood,* exh. cat., Fitzwilliam Museum (Cambridge, 1989).

29. John Gage, *Colour and Culture: Practice and Meaning from Antiquity to Abstraction* (London, 1993), 221 and 295 n. 51, where Gage relates the palette of *Ecce Ancilla Domini!* and the presence of pots of primary colors on the window ledge of *Dante Drawing an Angel* (1853, Ashmolean Museum, Oxford) to Rossetti's "interest in Field on the primaries," an observation that could also be made of *Bottles.* See also George Field, *Chromatography; or, a Treatise on Colours and Pigments, and of Their Powers in Painting* (London, 1835); Gage, *George Field;* Prettejohn, *The Art of the Pre-Raphaelites,* 148–50; and Allen Staley, *The Pre-Raphaelite Landscape,* rev. ed. (New Haven, Conn., 2001), 27–28.

30. Staley, *The Pre-Raphaelite Landscape,* 26; see W. Holman Hunt, *Pre-Raphaelitism,* 1:275–76.

31. All cited in Staley, *The Pre-Raphaelite Landscape,* 27.

32. George Field, *A Grammar of Colouring: Applied to Decorative Painting and the Arts, new edition revised, enlarged and adapted to the use of the Ornamental Painter and Designer,* ed. Ellis A. Davidson (London, 1875), 1–2. Something of the influence of Field's writings can be gauged from the publishing history of this book, which appeared in 1850 as *Rudiments of the Painter's Art, or, A Grammar of Colouring.* It was republished in 1858, and it appeared in a second edition with some revisions by R. Mallet in 1870 before being revised by Davidson, whose own version went through at least six editions up to 1903. The passage I have cited does not appear in either the 1850 or 1858 edition, and it thus represents the impact of Pre-Raphaelite thinking in its turn on color theory.

33. W. M. Rossetti, introduction to *The Germ,* 8.

34. Ibid.

35. As reported by Carr in *Some Eminent Victorians*, 66.

36. See Michael Baxandall, *Patterns of Intention: On the Historical Explanation of Pictures* (New Haven, Conn., 1985), chapter 1.

37. I cite these sonnets from *The Complete Writings and Pictures of Dante Gabriel Rossetti: A Hypermedia Research Archive*, ed. Jerome McGann, http://www.iath.virginia.edu/rossetti/index.html (accessed 19 August 2003). See the entry on *The Girlhood of Mary Virgin*.

38. Rossetti seems to have accorded the visual priority in his own ambition during this period and earlier. This is widely noticed in the biographical and early critical literature. Marillier, for instance, reports "a statement of his brother that he could not remember any date at which it was not an understood thing in the family that Gabriel was to be a painter." See H. C. Marillier, *Dante Gabriel Rossetti: An Illustrated Memorial of His Life and Art* (London, 1899), 6.

39. See W. M. Rossetti's comment in *The P.R.B. Journal: William Michael Rossetti's Diary of the Pre-Raphaelite Brotherhood, 1849–1853, Together with Other Pre-Raphaelite Documents*, ed. William E. Fredeman (Oxford, 1975), 33.

40. See Jan B. Gordon, "The Imaginary Portrait: Fin-de-Siècle Icon," *University of Windsor Review* 5 (Fall 1969): 81–104; D. M. R. Bentley, "Rossetti's 'Hand and Soul,'" *English Studies in Canada* 3 (Winter 1977): 445–57; John Pfordresher, "Dante Gabriel Rossetti's 'Hand and Soul': Sources and Significance," *Studies in Short Fiction* 19 (1982): 103–32; Richard Giles, "The House of Life: A Pre-Raphaelite Philosophy?" *Journal of Pre-Raphaelite and Aesthetic Studies* 2 (May 1982): 101–8; McGann, *Dante Gabriel Rossetti*, 88–93.

41. [Dante Gabriel Rossetti], "Hand and Soul," *The Germ: Thoughts Towards Nature in Poetry, Literature, and Art* 1 (1850): 23. Subsequent references to this work will appear parenthetically in the text.

42. See *P.R.B. Journal*, ed. Fredeman, 64, where in his entry for 21 March 1850 W. M. Rossetti records that "Gabriel [finished his design] of Chiaro's painting. He is now engaged, as regards writing, on a tale entitled 'An Autopsychology,' originally suggested to himself by an image he introduced into 'Bride-chamber Talk', that is, the poem eventually known as 'The Bride's Prelude.'" (Rossetti began "The Bride's Prelude" in 1848–50 and left it incomplete after later revisions.) Even at the very end of *The Germ*'s life, when the P.R.B. was tentatively costing a possible fifth number, the chance of printing "St Agnes of Intercession" proved attractive; see ibid., 229.

43. The "dual" work that partners this story is therefore proposed as the drawing "How They Met Themselves" (1851/1860). See Surtees, *Paintings and Drawings*, cat. 118, for Rossetti's references to the "bogie drawing." The story itself remains unfinished. See W. M. Rossetti's account in the notes to his 1911 edition of the *Works*, 680.

44. W. M. Rossetti, *The Complete Writings and Pictures*, 680.

45. I rely here on the analysis put forward by McGann in the pages devoted to this story on the *Complete Writings and Pictures* website. On Poe, see Alastair Grieve, "Rossetti's Illustrations for Poe," *Apollo* 97 (1973): 142–45.

46. Dante Gabriel Rossetti, "St Agnes of Intercession," in *Works*, ed. W. M. Rossetti, 566. Subsequent references to this work will appear parenthetically in the text. Evidence of Rossetti's interest in this subject can be gleaned from a contemporary poem, "Sudden Light," the first two stanzas of which begin "I have been here before" and "You have been mine before" (*Works*, ed. W. M. Rossetti, 200). See also Jan Marsh, *Dante Gabriel Rossetti: Painter and Poet* (London, 1999), 48, for Rossetti's contemporary identification with Dante.

47. Like the enthusiasm for Poe, the gothic reflects a staple of Rossetti's reading as a youth and young man. See Marsh, *Dante Gabriel Rossetti*, chapters 2–4.

48. Unlike his narrator, Rossetti did not submit *The Girlhood of Mary Virgin* to the test of the RA but showed at the Free Exhibition held at Hyde Park Corner. In the story, the RA represents an ambition unfulfilled, although one of which Rossetti is skeptical.

49. It seems likely that these reminiscences at the end of the story were added as part of the work Rossetti did on the original draft of 1850 when he returned to it around 1870. Both

the quotations at the start of the story appear in the 1850 draft manuscript now at Duke University (see the electronic version on McGann's *Complete Writings and Pictures* website). The draft breaks off about midway through the narrative, where the narrator reads the critic's poem in the gallery.

50. Compare the account, quoted above, that Rossetti's narrator gives of the moment of despair in "Hand and Soul": "Am I not as a cloth drawn before the light, that the looker may not be blinded; but which sheweth thereby the grain of its own coarseness; so that the light seems defiled, and men say, 'We will not walk by it'" (29).

51. This is not to imply that Millais shut himself away from public reception, as Rossetti did; of course, the opposite is true.

52. See Flint, *The Victorians and the Visual Imagination*, 68–71.

53. As noted by Malcolm Warner in *The Pre-Raphaelites,* ed. Parris, 134. Millais's wife preferred this interpretation, seeing it as "a subject full of pathos" (ibid.).

54. The landscape is in fact a composite, a mixture of Winchelsea in Hampshire and landscape near Perth in Scotland (ibid.).

55. M. Warner's *The Victorians* notes the evocation of the senses (72).

56. "Fine Arts," *The Athenaeum,* no. 1489 (10 May 1856): 590.

57. Correctly described with colors in reversed sequence—an effect corrected after an admonitory letter from a member of the public. See M. Warner in *The Pre-Raphaelites,* ed. Parris, 135–36.

58. Flint, *The Victorians and the Visual Imagination,* 90.

59. Ibid., 86.

60. See Prettejohn, *The Art of the Pre-Raphaelites,* 115; Paul Barlow, "Millais, Manet, Modernity," in *English Art, 1860–1914,* ed. Corbett and Perry; and Paul Barlow, *Time Past and Time Present: The Art of John Everett Millais* (London, forthcoming). In *Time Past,* Barlow discusses the competition between different styles of brushwork in Millais's painting.

61. Cited by M. Warner in *The Pre-Raphaelites,* ed. Parris, 141. This stands in contrast to the account Millais himself gave of the painting, which stresses the typological and a strong religious symbolism. Nevertheless, Millais describes his attempts to produce an effect of "the deepest religious reflection" in alternative terms—as "a matter of feeling and recollection" (ibid., 127, 139). See also Malcolm Warner, "John Everett Millais's *Autumn Leaves:* 'A Picture Full of Beauty and Without Subject,'" in *Pre-Raphaelite Papers,* ed. Leslie Parris (London, 1984), 126–42.

62. Stephens, *Dante Gabriel Rossetti,* 54.

63. Barbara Bryant in *The Age of Rossetti, Burne-Jones, and Watts: Symbolism in Britain, 1860–1910,* exh. cat., Tate Gallery (London, 1997), 96.

64. Elizabeth Prettejohn, *Rossetti and His Circle* (London, 1997), 30.

65. See Virginia M. Allen, "'One Strangling Golden Hair': Dante Gabriel Rossetti's *Lady Lilith,*" *The Art Bulletin* 66 (June 1984): 285–94.

66. On these paintings as "Venetian," see Alastair Grieve, "Rossetti and the Scandal of Art for Art's Sake in the Early 1860s," in *After the Pre-Raphaelites: Art and Aestheticism in Victorian England,* ed. Elizabeth Prettejohn (Manchester, 1999), 24–26.

67. Marillier, *Dante Gabriel Rossetti,* 133; Stephens, *Dante Gabriel Rossetti,* 68, 69.

68. Cited in Prettejohn, *Rossetti and His Circle,* 30.

69. W[illiam] M[ichael] Rossetti and A[lgernon] C[harles] Swinburne, *Notes on the Royal Academy Exhibition* (London, 1868; facsimile reprint, New York, 1976), 46.

70. See the entry for *Lady Lilith* on McGann's *Complete Writings and Pictures* website.

71. Parris, ed., *The Pre-Raphaelites,* 121.

72. It has been suggested that John William Waterhouse's *The Lady of Shalott* (1894, Leeds City Art Gallery) is also indebted to *The Awakening Conscience* in its use of the compositional device of a mirror behind the action that reflects a segment of nature not otherwise visible in the design. See Gail-Nina Anderson and Joanne Wright, *Heaven on Earth: The Religion of Beauty in Late Victorian Art,* exh. cat., University of Nottingham (Nottingham, U.K., 1994), 125. This use of a mirror within the composition occurs elsewhere in Waterhouse, and Anderson

and Wright suggest a connection to Hunt's *The Lady of Shalott* (fig. 22) and its companion illustration for the Moxon Tennyson. See *Heaven on Earth*, 120, and Waterhouse, *Destiny* (1900, Towneley Hall Art Gallery and Museums, Burnley).

73. This inaugurates a group of works, from Whistler's *Symphony in White, No 2—The Little White Girl* (fig. 66) and beyond, that takes up common themes of representation. See my discussion below.

74. Dante Gabriel Rossetti, "Body's Beauty," in *The Age of Rossetti*, 102.

75. My emphasis.

76. In this the subject of *Lady Lilith* resembles Sturge Moore's bacchante, who, "half-conscious," reflects back the world to herself and thus resembles Titian's painting. See Moore, "Lines on Titian's 'Bacchanal,'" and the discussion of the bacchante figure in the Introduction to this volume.

77. Cited in John Nicoll, *Dante Gabriel Rossetti* (New York, 1975), 125.

78. Bryant in *The Age of Rossetti*, 97.

79. Cited in Parris, ed., *The Pre-Raphaelites*, 215.

80. Psomiades, *Beauty's Body*, 3.

81. Freedman, *Professions of Taste*, 9. See Algernon Charles Swinburne, *William Blake: A Critical Essay* (London, 1868).

82. Cited in Penelope Fitzgerald, *Edward Burne-Jones: A Biography* (London, 1975), 50.

83. Wildman and Christian, *Burne-Jones*, 50.

84. Dante Gabriel Rossetti, *Letters of Dante Gabriel Rossetti*, ed. Oswald Doughty and John Robert Wahl (Oxford, 1965–67), 1:319.

85. In this context, it is significant that many of Burne-Jones's contemporaries attributed to him a powerful literary drive. "His outlook was that of a man of letters," wrote W. Graham Robertson in his memoir; "he saw nothing from the purely pictorial point of view" and "had not the painter's eye." See *Time Was: The Reminiscences of W. Graham Robertson* (London, 1945), 82. Burne-Jones himself said that he wished to "learn to read a picture as we do a poem." See G. Burne-Jones, *Memorials*, 1:124. Particularly in the early and middle stages of his career, he held to the Pre-Raphaelite desire to translate the realism of the word into visual form. But elsewhere Burne-Jones could be adamant in his repudiation of the word. According to Georgiana Burne-Jones, "after he became a painter he seemed to feel a kind of jealousy at the employment of any other means of expression than painting, and deliberately curbed the use of words in public, so that nothing would have induced him to make a speech or write an article" (*Memorials*, 1:124). Burne-Jones published two short stories, "The Cousins" and "A Northern Tale," as well as an essay on Thackeray's *The Newcomes* in the magazine of the Order of Sir Galahad that he published with William Morris and others while at Oxford.

86. Cited in Martin Harrison and Bill Waters, *Burne-Jones*, 2d ed. (London, 1989), 153.

87. William Waters, *Sir Edward Coley Burne-Jones, Bart, 1833–1898, Laus Veneris* (Newcastle upon Tyne, U.K., 1975), unpaginated.

88. Henry James, *The Painter's Eye: Notes and Essays on the Pictorial Arts*, ed. John L. Sweeney (London, 1956), 164. For a history of the painting, see Waters, *Sir Edward Coley Burne-Jones*.

89. "Dreading the darkening of oil and disliking its greasiness, he liked a stiff pigment of the texture of soft cheese": see T. M. Rooke, "Note on Burne-Jones's Medium," *Burne-Jones*, Mappin Art Gallery, 8.

90. Robertson, *Time Was*, 83.

91. Sometimes this effect results from an extended gestation or reworking at a later date. This is the case, for example, with *St George and the Dragon Series No 7—The Return* (c. 1866, reworked 1895, Bristol City Art Galleries), where the reworking has resulted in, or at least contributed to, a severely impacted material surface.

92. Sizeranne, *English Contemporary Art*, 287.

93. Didi-Huberman, "The Art of Not Describing," 154 and passim.

94. To some degree, this effect is the result of the Pre-Raphaelite devotion to derived fresco technique, the completion of the work in discrete sections, and the desire for clarity and forcefulness of colour. See Sizeranne, *English Contemporary Art*, 290–93. See also Craig Harrison, ed., *The Essence of Art: Victorian Advice on the Practice of Painting* (Aldershot, U.K., 1999).

95. G. Burne-Jones, *Memorials,* 1:261.

96. See Christine Poulson, *The Quest for the Grail: Arthurian Legend in British Art, 1840–1920* (Manchester, 1999), 146. See also the discussion in Stephen Kern, *Eyes of Love: The Gaze in English and French Culture, 1840–1900* (New York, 1996), 175–76. In other versions, Viviane is called Nimuë: hence "Study for the Head of Nimuë" in "The Beguiling of Merlin" in Wildman and Christian, *Burne-Jones,* 171, cat. 65.

97. See Wildman and Christian, *Burne-Jones,* 171, and Poulson, *The Quest for the Grail,* 149–50. For autobiographical readings of Burne-Jones's works as a principle of interpretation, see Fitzgerald, *Edward Burne-Jones.*

98. For an extended discussion of some of the issues I raise in this section, see David Peters Corbett, "Visuality and Unmediation in Burne-Jones's *Laus Veneris," Art History* 24, no. 1 (2001): 83–102.

99. Poulson, *The Quest for the Grail,* 148–49, and *Burne-Jones: The Paintings, Graphic, and Decorative Work of Sir Edward Burne-Jones, 1833–98,* exh. cat., Arts Council (London, 1975), 51.

100. See my discussion in the Introduction to this volume.

101. The painting is connected to a poem of the same title by Swinburne, who dedicated his *Poems and Ballads* (1866) "to my friend Edward Burne-Jones." Swinburne's poem obsessively investigates the spiritual agonies of the renegade knight of the Tannhäuser legend, who, falling under the spell of Venus, abandons morality and salvation for the fatal pleasures of sensuality. Burne-Jones's version is less frenetic, cooler than the overheated eroticism of Swinburne's verse while sharing its sense of menace and fatality: "To have known love, how bitter a thing it is,/And afterward be cast out of God's sight." See Algernon Charles Swinburne, "Laus Veneris," *Poems and Ballads (First Series)* (1866; London, 1927), 26. This is not to suggest that Swinburne's poem is the source for the picture. Burne-Jones painted a small watercolor called *Laus Veneris* in 1861, "shortly before Swinburne began his poem in June 1862" (*Burne-Jones,* Arts Council, 53, cat. 129). During the 1860s, Burne-Jones also illustrated the version of the Tannhäuser legend in William Morris's *The Hill of Venus,* part of *The Earthly Paradise.* The oil version of *Laus Veneris* was derived from the watercolor at the suggestion of the latter's owner, William Graham; see Waters, *Sir Edward Coley Burne-Jones.*

102. See J. B. Bullen, *The Pre-Raphaelite Body: Fear and Desire in Painting, Poetry, and Criticism* (Oxford, 1998).

103. Frederick Wedmore, "Some Tendencies in Recent Painting," *Temple Bar* 53 (July 1878): 339. For a critic in the *Illustrated London News* in 1879, "the ultra-sensual school . . . would destroy everything of value in the national character." For the quotation, see Susan Casteras, "Burne-Jones and the Pre-Raphaelite Circle at the Palace of the Aesthetes," in *The Grosvenor Gallery: A Palace of Art in Victorian England,* ed. Susan Casteras and Colleen Denny (New Haven, Conn., 1996), 89. Casteras has identified the "sensuality of Burne-Jones's work" as the focus of viewers' objections, a combination of sexual anxiety and dismay at the overt repudiation of the mid-Victorian and Ruskinian claim for moral meaning in the fine arts (88).

104. In Burne-Jones's painting, the presence of writing and of painted metaphors of depth that seek to transform writing into the visual manifest the anxiety that accumulates around this attempt to assert the authority of pure visuality as alternative space. It is for this reason that in *Laus Veneris,* as elsewhere, Burne-Jones uses music as an intermediary term between the word and the visual. Music, with its implication of the nonverbal communication of emotional states and circumstances, serves to undermine the authority of the word by transmitting the manuscript and the activity of the companions in a form that accommodates it to the nonverbal idiom of music. In this sense, as in *King Cophetua,* music is a halfway house. It preserves the word so that its authority can be used but also compromises that authority, dragging it toward the silent and nonverbal realm of painting. See, on this subject, Suzanne Fagence, "Representations of Music in the Art of Burne-Jones," *Apollo* (May 1998): 9–14; Asleson, *Albert Moore,* 94–95; Michael Musgrave, "Leighton and Music," in *Frederic Leighton: Antiquity, Renaissance, Modernity,* ed. Tim Barringer and Elizabeth Prettejohn (New Haven, Conn., 1999); and Elizabeth Prettejohn, "Walter Pater

and Aesthetic Painting," in *After the Pre-Raphaelites,* ed. Prettejohn, 42–43. On the general context and attempts to bring sound and vision together, see Beer, "Authentic Tidings," 91–92. I do not have space to bring out the connections between vision and the audible here, but they are widespread and linked to the themes of my discussion.

105. *Lord Leighton: Eminent Victorian Artist,* exh. cat., Royal Academy of Arts (London, 1996), 236. An earlier version of the *Briar Rose* series dating from 1870–73 is in the Museo de Arte de Ponce, Puerto Rico. The series has a complex history, but Burne-Jones had begun work on the theme at the end of the 1860s or in the early 1870s. *The Briar Rose: The Council Chamber* (1872–92, and in the Buscot Park version, 1885–90) features the distinction between the three-dimensional book and the decorative denial of realistic space that I have already identified; throughout the paintings, the idea of unmediation receives graphic treatment. The series also features the tangled growth of thorns—as in *The Briar Rose: The Briar Wood*—that stands as a principal metaphor/example of paint and paint surface as visual fact and that reappears in the *Romaunt of the Rose* series (1874–89) and, transformed, in *Phyllis and Demophoön* (1870) and *The Perseus Series: The Baleful Head* (1885), as well as *The Beguiling of Merlin* and, transformed again, in the tapestry of *Laus Veneris.*

106. An earlier version of this subject (1871–73), now in the Museo de Arte de Ponce, was extensively revised when the Buscot Park painting was made. In particular, the figure of the Prince was entirely recast, as were the shields and the surrounding briar. Burne-Jones introduced the elements I am discussing only in painting this new version.

107. They are discussed by Poulson, *The Quest for the Grail,* chapter 8, and include Arthur Hughes, *The Lady of Shalott* (1873, lost), and Sidney Harold Meteyard, *"'I Am Half-Sick of Shadows' Said the Lady of Shalott* (1913, private collection).

108. Waterhouse made another version of the subject as well: *The Lady of Shalott* (1894, Leeds City Art Gallery).

109. Alfred Tennyson, "The Lady of Shalott," in *Tennyson, Poems and Plays,* ed. T. Herbert Warren, rev. and enl. by Frederick Page (London, 1971), 27. For the image of the boat used to express the soul's journey through life, compare Thomas Cole's *Voyage of Life* series (1840).

110. On the quarrel with Rossetti and Hunt's temperament generally, see Jeremy Maas, *Holman Hunt and the Light of the World* (London, 1984), 92–95 and passim.

111. W. Holman Hunt, *Pre-Raphaelitism,* 2:332. Subsequent references to this work will appear parenthetically in the text.

112. W. Holman Hunt, *Pre-Raphaelitism and the Pre-Raphaelite Brotherhood,* 2d ed., rev. from the author's notes by M. E. H.-H. (London, 1913), footnote to 2:2.

113. Rossetti's design appeared as "The Lady of Shalott," illustration to *Poems* by Alfred Tennyson, published by Edward Moxon (London, 1857). On the Moxon edition, see Richard L. Stein, "The Pre-Raphaelite Tennyson," *Victorian Studies* 24, no. 3 (1981): 279–301.

114. W. Holman Hunt, *Pre-Raphaelitism and the Pre-Raphaelite Brotherhood,* 2d ed., 2:102.

115. The wood engraving from Hunt's illustration for the Moxon Tennyson is reproduced in Prettejohn, *The Art of the Pre-Raphaelites,* 226.

116. There is a sizable literature on the poem and its Pre-Raphaelite visualizations. See, in particular, Isobel Armstrong, "Tennyson's 'The Lady of Shalott': Victorian Mythography and the Politics of Narcissism," in *The Sun is God,* ed. Bullen, 49–107; Lynne Pearce, *Woman/Image/Text: Readings in Pre-Raphaelite Art and Literature* (Toronto, 1991); Julia Saville, "'The Lady of Shalott': A Lacanian Romance," *Word & Image* 8, no. 1 (1992): 71–87; Prettejohn, *The Art of the Pre-Raphaelites,* 223–31.

117. W. Holman Hunt, *Pre-Raphaelitism,* 2d ed., 2:401.

118. Ibid., 2:401–2.

119. Ibid., 2:401.

120. Hunt completed the painting with the assistance of Edward Robert Hughes, with the result that the technique differs from much of his later work. See Prettejohn, *The Art of the Pre-Raphaelites,* 261. On Hunt's facture generally (and with an interpretation congruent with my

thesis in this book), see Carol Jacobi's "William Holman Hunt: Revealing and Disguising the Object," forthcoming in *Visual Culture in Britain.* I also profited from seeing Dr. Jacobi's unpublished book manuscript, "William Holman Hunt: Painter, Painting, Paint," and I am grateful to her for the opportunity.

121. Samuel J. Wagstaff Jr. suggests that *The Awakening Conscience* is referred to in *The Lady of Shalott* and forms a middle link in a chain that connects the 1850 illustration to the eventual oil painting. He also ties these mirrors to Van Eyck's *Arnolfini Portrait,* which entered the National Gallery in 1842 and became a touchstone for several Pre-Raphaelites, including Hunt. See Wagstaff, "Some Notes on Holman Hunt and *The Lady of Shalott,*" *Wadsworth Atheneum Bulletin* (Summer 1962): 1–21.

122. On this painting, see George P. Landow, *William Holman Hunt and Typological Symbolism* (New Haven, Conn., 1979), 126–39.

123. "The Lady of Shalott," in *The Poems of Tennyson,* ed. Christopher Ricks, 2d ed. (Harlow, U.K., 1987), 1:390–391, 393 (lines 46–50, 109–117).

Chapter 2

References to material held in the Whistler archive in Glasgow University Library Special Collections are given in the form GUL. The volumes of press cuttings are identified as PC, followed by the number of the volume and the folio number.

1. Pater published the "Conclusion" for the first time as a section of his review "Poems by William Morris" in the *Westminster Review* (October 1868). It appeared in the first edition of *The Renaissance* in 1873. See Pater, *The Renaissance,* 443–44.

2. Pater, *The Renaissance,* 186–87.

3. Ibid., 187.

4. Ibid., 188.

5. Ibid.

6. See Levenson, *A Genealogy of Modernism,* 16–17.

7. Pater, *The Renaissance,* 190.

8. Sidney Colvin, "English Painters and Painting in 1867," *Fortnightly Review,* n.s., 2 (October 1867): 473–76. I owe this reference to Elizabeth Prettejohn's introduction to *After the Pre-Raphaelites,* ed. Prettejohn, 3, where it is cited and discussed.

9. See *The Grosvenor Gallery,* ed. Casteras and Denny; Christopher Newall, *The Grosvenor Gallery Exhibitions* (Cambridge, 1995); and Michele Archambault, "The Grosvenor Gallery, 1877–1890" (Ph.D. diss., Courtauld Institute of Art, 1978).

10. On Aestheticism, see Elizabeth Aslin, *The Aesthetic Movement: Theory and Practice* (London, 1972); Richard Dellamora, *Masculine Desire: The Sexual Politics of Victorian Aestheticism* (Chapel Hill, N.C., 1999); Freedman, *Professions of Taste;* Lionel Lambourne, *The Aesthetic Movement* (London, 1996); and Robin Spencer, *The Aesthetic Movement: Prelude to Art Nouveau* (London, 1969). Contemporary discussions include Walter Hamilton, *The Aesthetic Movement in England* (London, 1882). For a recent and very helpful discussion of the difficulties of the term "Aestheticism" and of its salient characteristics, see Prettejohn's introduction to *After the Pre-Raphaelites,* ed. Prettejohn.

11. Gillett, *Worlds of Art,* 7.

12. Pater, *The Renaissance,* 104. "The School of Giorgione," the essay from which this comes, was not included in the first edition of *The Renaissance* (1873); it appeared only in the third edition of 1888. It was first published in the *Fortnightly Review* in October 1877. There is good reason to believe that it was included when the text of the 1873 edition was sent to the publishers in 1872 and was later withdrawn. See Donald Hill's "Critical and Explanatory Notes" to *The Renaissance* in the edition I am citing (384).

13. Pater, *The Renaissance,* 102, 106.

14. Ibid., 103.

15. A. L. Baldry, "Albert Moore: An Appreciation," *The Art Journal* 65 (February 1903): 34.

16. As Asleson notes in *Albert Moore,* 81.

17. William Michael Rossetti, "The Royal Academy Exhibition," *Fraser's Magazine* 71 (June 1865): 744.

18. Sidney Colvin, "The Grosvenor Gallery," *Fortnightly Review,* n.s., 27 (June 1877), 831. See also Colvin's comments in "English Painters of

the Present Day," *Portfolio* 1 (1870): 4–6. There Colvin speaks of Moore's paintings as having "borne the marks not only of a special ocular predilection, a special susceptibility to a certain class of beauties in the visible world, but of a special theoretical conviction . . . making the decorative aspect of his canvas, regarded as an arrangement of beautiful lines and refreshing colours, the one important matter in his work" (5).

19. Baldry, "Albert Moore: An Appreciation," 34.

20. H. Heathcote Statham, "The Grosvenor Gallery," *Macmillan's Magazine* 36 (1877): 113.

21. Asleson, *Albert Moore,* 130.

22. *Apples* and *A Sofa* (both 1875, in private collections) repeat the design, with the minor addition of a few examples of the fruit in *Apples,* but with different color schemes.

23. Asleson, *Albert Moore,* 133.

24. Cited in ibid., 114. In 1868, Swinburne had used the opportunity afforded by Moore's exhibition of *Azaleas* (1867–68, Hugh Lane Municipal Gallery of Modern Art, Dublin)—a picture that the *Daily Telegraph* called "a strange, wild performance," "brimful of undeniable talent . . . but daringly eccentric in design and execution"— to make a programmatic statement of the Aestheticist position this refusal of narrative implied. Swinburne wrote, "his painting is to artists what the verse of Théophile Gautier is to poets: the faultless and secure expression of an exclusive worship of things formally beautiful. . . . The melody of colour, the symphony of form is complete: one more beautiful thing is achieved, one more delight is born into the world; and its meaning is beauty; and its reason for being is to be." See Algernon Charles Swinburne, "Notes on Some Pictures of 1868," *Essays and Studies* (London, 1875), 360–61. Quotation from *Daily Telegraph* cited in A. L. Baldry, *Albert Moore: His Life and Works* (London, 1894), 35.

25. GUL, PC 3/33. There is no note of the source in the press-cuttings book, although the spelling suggests the U.S.; the place in the sequence and the nature of the challenge suggest a date toward the end of the 1870s and probably after 1878.

26. Leighton originally resisted overtures from the Grosvenor and expressed annoyance that the Grosvenor might "draw off . . . good work from the Academy," but "after a time . . . calmed down" and "promised some of his works to our first exhibition." See Charles Hallé, *Notes from a Painter's Life, Including the Founding of Two Galleries* (London, 1909), 143–44.

27. Elizabeth Prettejohn, "Leighton: The Aesthete as Academic," in *Art and the Academy in the Nineteenth Century,* ed. Rafael Cardoso Denis and Colin Trodd (Manchester, 2000), 37.

28. See *Lord Leighton: Eminent Victorian Artist,* 117. See also Anna Gruetzner Robins, "Leighton: A Promoter of the New Painting," in *Frederic Leighton,* ed. Barringer and Prettejohn. The *Saturday Review* certainly discerned in the 1869 show not only the replacement by "classicism" of "the mediaevalism which threatened to take possession of the English school" but also a "tendency to exchange naturalism for idealism, to substitute individual forms for generic types, to surrender styles which were illusive to the eye in favour of treatments which appeal to the imagination" (*Saturday Review,* 5 June 1869, 743).

29. This can be seen in Leighton's relationship with Albert Moore. When Moore's work was prominently hung at the Royal Academy exhibition of 1869 (despite the fact that he was not an Academician), he found himself part of what seemed the first positive step forward in English art since the Pre-Raphaelites, potentially "transforming the face of British art overnight." This partly took the form of a revival of large-scale female nude painting during these years. See Alison Smith, *The Victorian Nude: Sexuality, Morality, and Art* (Manchester, 1996), 101–61, and see *Exposed: The Victorian Nude,* exh. cat., Tate Gallery (London, 2002), 94. By the late 1860s, Moore was a leading figure—along with Watts and Leighton, the newly elected RAs who had hung the show—in the reintroduction of antiquity as model and subject for English painting. In 1869 Moore's *Venus* (1869, York City Art Gallery) hung next to Leighton's *Electra at the Tomb of Agamemnon* (1868–69, Ferens Art Gallery, Hull), and Leighton's *Daedalus and Icarus* (1869, Buscot Park, Oxfordshire, The Faringdon Collection

Trust) hung next to Moore's *Quartet: A Painter's Tribute to the Art of Music, AD 1868* (1868, private collection) as examples of the new art. Leighton proved a strong supporter of Moore and, according to Asleson, he was reported to have "threatened to withdraw all of his own pictures if Moore's *A Venus* was not exhibited" (*Albert Moore*, 108). On this important exhibition, see Robyn Asleson, "Classic into Modern: The Inspiration of Antiquity in English Painting, 1864–1918" (Ph.D. diss., Yale University, 1993).

30. Leighton, *Addresses*, 9, 10. Subsequent references to this work will appear parenthetically in the text. On the *Addresses*, see Joseph A. Kestner, "Poynter and Leighton as Aestheticians: The *Ten Lectures* and *Addresses*," *Journal of Pre-Raphaelite and Aesthetic Studies* 2, no. 2 (1989): 108–20.

31. Leighton echoes Pater here: "art addresses not pure sense, still less the pure intellect, but the 'imaginative reason' through the senses." See "The School of Giorgione," in *The Renaissance*, 102.

32. *Pomegranates*, for instance (1865–66, Guildhall Art Gallery, London), has an extraordinary surface, densely worked around the contours of the figures and accordingly evoking for its first audiences the surfaces of Roman wall painting in Pompeii. See J. B. Atkinson, "Exhibitions of the Year," *Fine Arts Quarterly Review*, n.s., 1 (October 1866): 347, as well as Asleson's discussion in *Albert Moore*, 84, 86–87. Baldry believed that with *Pomegranates* and *Apricots* (1866, Fulham Public Library, London Borough of Hammersmith), Moore "put himself at once in the front rank of the artists of his time" (*Albert Moore*, 32). Restricting his use of the oil medium to the smallest quantities, Moore mixed a pigment that gave a "dry, chalky appearance" to his pictures (Asleson, *Albert Moore*, 87; see also Baldry, *Albert Moore*, 75–78).

33. George Moore, "Royal Academy Criticism," *The New Budget Extra* 1 (1895): 15. See Prettejohn, "Aestheticising History Painting," in *Frederic Leighton*, ed. Barringer and Prettejohn, 105.

34. Leighton's remarks are cited in Mrs. Russell Barrington, *The Life, Letters, and Work of Frederic Leighton* (London, 1906), 2:188. Barrington's book contains correspondence between Leighton and A. H. Church, who was Professor of Chemistry at the Royal Academy from 1879. The extracts she gives show Leighton as a careful and conscientious technician. His questions to Church seek reassurance that his latest method will not lead to cracking, short life, or a similar fate. Clearly deeply concerned about the technical aspects of what he does, Leighton's interest in the kitchen is conducted in a spirit of caution rather than fascination for its own sake. It is part of Leighton's "thoroughness"—his prime quality, according to Barrington (see 2:20–21). See also A. H. Church, *The Chemistry of Paints and Painting* (London, 1890), which was dedicated to Leighton and had the straightforward aim of "explaining to artists . . . the chief chemical and physical characters of the materials with which they deal and of the operations they practice" (vii).

35. See Charles Rosen and Henri Zerner, "The Ideology of the Licked Surface: Official Art," in *Romanticism and Realism: The Mythology of Nineteenth-Century Art* (London, 1984).

36. Barrington, *Frederic Leighton*, 2:20, 31. For an earlier discussion of Leighton's technique, see E. F. S. Pattison, "Sir Frederic Leighton, PRA," in *Illustrated Biographies of Modern Artists*, ed. F. G. Dumas (London, 1882), 18–24.

37. In this context, Prettejohn notes that, as part of a "'decadent' turn" in English criticism, Leighton's highly finished academic surfaces came to seem polished "at the expense of deeper emotional or spiritual meaning" (see "Leighton: The Aesthete as Academic," 37). This is the context of Barrington's defense in her critical biography of Leighton: "he spared no labour, time, or patience, in working over and over on a picture in order to attain the finest quality in the actual surface which his material—paint—could possibly produce" (*Frederic Leighton*, 2:24).

38. "The Royal Academy," *The Art Journal*, n.s., 8 (July 1869): 199.

39. Carr, *Some Eminent Victorians*, 100. See, though, Carolyn Dakers, *The Holland Park Circle: Artists and Victorian Society* (New Haven, Conn., 1999), 201–5.

40. Cited in Dakers, *The Holland Park Circle*, 201. James is contemplating a short story with a

protagonist based on the otherwise unlikely convergence of Leighton and Robert Browning. On this topic, see the discussion in Prettejohn, "Leighton: The Aesthete as Academic," 33–52.

41. Barrington, *Frederic Leighton,* 2:32.

42. Ibid., 2:62, cites this letter from Leighton to his father.

43. For a discussion of Leighton's complex relation to Academic history painting even at the height of his career, see Prettejohn, "Aestheticising History Painting."

44. See Stephen Jones in *Lord Leighton: Eminent Victorian Artist,* 169, 170. The catalogue names *Summer Moon* (c. 1872, Leighton House Museum and Art Gallery), *Idyll* (c. 1880–81, private collection), *Summer Slumber* (c. 1894, private collection), and *Flaming June* as highlights of this period of Leighton's work.

45. Quotation from *Fraser's Magazine* in Prettejohn, "Leighton: The Aesthete as Academic," 37.

46. Barrington, *Frederic Leighton,* 2:30.

47. For a discussion of the sleeping figure in Victorian painting in the context of *Flaming June,* see Christopher Newall in *Lord Leighton: Eminent Victorian Artist,* 236. Leighton produced a large number of paintings featuring sleeping models (e.g., *Summer Moon*).

48. There are many examples, including, among Leighton's last paintings, *Perseus Hastening to the Rescue of Andromeda* (c. 1895–96, Leicestershire Museums, Arts and Records Service). For a discussion of the care Leighton took over the drapery in *Daedalus and Icarus,* see Stephen Jones in *Lord Leighton: Eminent Victorian Artist,* 165.

49. As is the case in Burne-Jones, I have argued. See the discussion of *The Beguiling of Merlin* (fig. 19) in Chapter 1.

50. Paul Barlow, "Transparent Bodies, Opaque Identities: Personification, Narrative, and Portraiture," in *Frederic Leighton,* ed. Barringer and Prettejohn, 196.

51. See *Lord Leighton: Eminent Victorian Artist,* 236.

52. Barrington, *Frederic Leighton,* 2:33. Barrington makes Leighton sound perhaps too much like Watts, her other principal subject. Nonetheless, the general claim is justified.

53. Although contemporary with the opening, *Elijah in the Wilderness* was not shown at the Grosvenor. It was exhibited first at the Paris Exposition Universelle in 1878 and then at the Royal Academy the following year. Barrington reported that "Leighton told a friend he had put more of himself into that picture than into any other he had ever invented" (ibid., 2:188).

54. Christopher Newall suggests that "it is possible that the conscious classicism and grand scale of the . . . painting, combined with its biblical theme, were adopted deliberately with the Exposition [Universelle in Paris] of 1878 in mind" (*Lord Leighton: Eminent Victorian Artist,* 185). Leighton was the president of the jury that selected the British contributions.

55. Leonée Ormond in *Lord Leighton: Eminent Victorian Artist,* 234–35. Ormond notes that there is "a group of nude drawings for both *Fatidica* and *Flaming June* on one sheet at Leighton House," arguing for a close association and the possibility "that *Flaming June* began life as a study for *Fatidica*" (235).

56. This suggestion calls up Michael Fried's writings on absorption, to which I owe a debt in thinking about these issues. See Fried's *Absorption and Theatricality; Courbet's Realism* (Chicago, 1990); and *Manet's Modernism, or, the Face of Painting in the 1860s* (Chicago, 1996).

57. *After the Deluge* was first exhibited at the New Gallery in 1891. Leighton's *Clytie* (c. 1890–92, Fitzwilliam Museum, Cambridge), a subject earlier treated sculpturally by Watts (c. 1867–78, marble), appears to be in direct dialogue with Watts's painting, as does *Lachrymae. The Age of Rossetti* suggests a similar conversation between *Solitude* and Watts's *Hope* (258).

58. As I have already hinted, there is frequently the impression of a dialogue between the two in words and images. Each will cite the other, often in new contexts. See, on Watts, Colin Trodd and Stephanie Brown, eds., *G. F. Watts: Cultural Enchantment in Victorian Art* (Aldershot, U.K., forthcoming).

59. This is not to suggest that Leighton did not imagine such a role for his art (see Barrington, *Frederic Leighton,* 2:33). But his is a more diffuse and theoretical possibility than for his

friend. For Watts, art had to act in the world and create positive consequences.

60. David Loshak, "George Frederic Watts, OM, RA," in *George Frederic Watts, 1817–1904*, exh. cat., Arts Council (London, 1954–55), 9. For a less convinced commentator, Watts paints "to serve his generation . . . to teach cockneys morality, and to make clubmen consider their destinies" (Sizeranne, *English Contemporary Art*, 86).

61. Cited in Rowland Alston, *The Mind and Work of G. F. Watts, OM, RA: With Introduction and Special Reference to the Watts Gallery, Compton, Guildford* (London, 1929), ix. A fascinating example of Watts's moral influence is H. W. Shrewsbury, *The Visions of an Artist: G. F. Watts, RA, OM, with Verse Interpretations* (London, 1918), which interprets Watts within a heavily devotional, Christian context aimed at Sunday and other schools and which offers "to bring young students under the spell of G. F. Watts, and to put into their hands a key to the meaning of some of his greatest allegorical pictures" (7).

62. G. F. Watts, "Prefatory Note," in *The Works of G. F. Watts, RA*, exh. cat., New Gallery (London, 1896), 9. Ronald Chapman called Watts "a thinker in paint," although in keeping with the twentieth-century view of the painter, he added that his work led to an "over-emphasis of the intellectual qualities at the expense of the pictorial" (*The Laurel and the Thorn: A Study of G. F. Watts* [London, 1945], 148). Watts himself thought of the intellectual "faculties" in this sense as central to humanity and as the necessary foundation of any meaningful expression in art. See "The Aims of Art" in *George Frederick Watts: Annals*, by M. Watts, 3:231.

63. G. F. Watts, catalogue note in *The Works of G. F. Watts*, 29–30.

64. G. F. Watts, "The Aims of Art," 232.

65. M. Watts, *George Frederick Watts: Annals*, 3:166.

66. In 1882—unlike in 1850—Watts could count on a public eye educated by social realist painters like Fred Walker, Luke Fildes, and Hubert von Herkomer. Allen Staley notes that Herkomer made a special trip to see Watts's paintings in 1882, and he suggests that *Hard Times* (1885, Manchester City Art Galleries), one of the great moments of social realism in England, is "basically a reworking of Watts's social-realist paintings [*sic*] *The Irish Famine*." See Staley, "Art Is Upon the Town," in *The Grosvenor Gallery*, ed. Casteras and Denny, 72–73; on the general issue, also see David Alan Stewart, "G. F. Watts: The Social and Religious Themes" (Ph.D. diss., Boston University, 1988). Watts's *The Good Samaritan* (c. 1849–52, Manchester City Art Galleries), which is contemporary with the four social realist pictures but was completed after them, offers a less direct model of compassion than they do and may represent Watts's withdrawal from the assertiveness of the 1849 paintings, perhaps because they were of an unfamiliar type.

67. G. F. Watts, "The Aims of Art," 228.

68. "The Present Conditions of Art," in *George Frederick Watts: Annals*, by M. Watts, 3:148. Subsequent references to this work will appear parenthetically in the text.

69. In his understanding of the character of nineteenth-century culture, Watts draws directly on the famous formulations of the 1820s, through which Carlyle defines his time as "the Mechanical Age": "It is the Age of Machinery, in every outward and inward sense of that word; the age which, with its whole undivided might, forwards, teaches and practises the great art of adapting means to ends." See Carlyle, "Signs of the Times," 465.

70. Pater, *The Renaissance*, 103, 102.

71. G. K. Chesterton, *G. F. Watts* (1904; London, 1920), 125, 126.

72. Walter Bayes, *The Landscapes of G. F. Watts* (London, 1907), ix.

73. Cited in Alston, *The Mind and Work of G. F. Watts*, 5. In an apparently similar spirit, Watts wrote to Ruskin that "if I worked to please myself only . . . I should make outline compositions filled upon a monochromatic principle," although he goes on to associate with this "the highest & noblest beauty of form, truth of movement and general colour." Letter from Watts to Ruskin, reproduced in Chapman, *The Laurel and the Thorn*, 161–62.

74. Watts conceived of fresco as an instrument for the social effectiveness of his art. After the failure of his offer to decorate Euston

Station with a fresco without payment, he successfully designed and executed a 40 ft. × 45 ft. fresco known as *Justice: A Hemicycle of Lawgivers* in the New Hall of Lincoln's Inn (1853–59) as part of this ambition. It began to degrade early, swiftly surrendering to the attacks of climate, and this may have contributed to Watts's decision to turn to easel painting as the instrument of his social ambitions for his art. See Wilfred Blunt, *England's Michelangelo: A Biography of George Frederic Watts, OM, RA* (London, 1975), 97–98 and 67–68.

75. Cited in Chris Mullen, "G. F. Watts: The Home of Life," in *G. F. Watts, 1817–1904: A Nineteenth-Century Phenomenon*, exh. cat., Whitechapel Art Gallery (London, 1974), unpaginated.

76. Colin Trodd, "Turning Back the Grotesque: G. F. Watts and the Matter of Painting and the Oblivion of Art," in *Victorian Culture and the Idea of the Grotesque*, ed. Colin Trodd and Paul Barlow (Aldershot, U.K., 1999), 185.

77. He also showed three portraits, including one of Burne-Jones (c. 1870, now in Birmingham Museums and Art Gallery). The Grosvenor painting is one of more than a dozen versions of the picture. The first, smaller version (c. 1868–76, Bristol City Art Gallery) was shown at the Dudley Gallery in 1870 as a "design for a large picture," presumably that in Manchester. See *Victorian High Renaissance: George Frederic Watts, 1817–1904; Frederic Leighton, 1830–96; Albert Moore, 1841–93; Alfred Gilbert, 1854–1934*, exh. cat., Minneapolis Institute of Arts (Minneapolis, 1978), 78.

78. Bryant, "G. F. Watts at the Grosvenor Gallery," 116. Bryant argues that the overt visual qualities of such paintings as *Love and Death* were a means of seeking "universal appeal" and asserting oil paint as a medium capable of living up to the seriousness of Watts's ambitions for it.

79. M. Watts, *George Frederic Watts: Annals*, 3:180.

80. Mrs. Russell Barrington, *G. F. Watts: Reminiscences* (London, 1905), 134–35.

81. Cited in Blunt, *England's Michelangelo*, 194.

82. Barbara Bryant in *The Age of Rossetti*, 201; the quotation from Watts is also cited here (200).

83. Loshak, "George Frederic Watts," 10.

84. For an attack on Watts in these terms—one written in the 1940s, at the height of Watts's unpopularity—see Chapman, *The Laurel and the Thorn*.

85. J. E. Phythian, *Fifty Years of Modern Painting, Corot to Sargent* (London, 1908), 300.

86. Ibid.

87. Ibid., 301.

88. According to A. L. Baldry, "Whistler and Albert Moore," *Pall Mall Budget* 1323 (1 February 1894): 14. On the relationship between Moore and Whistler, see Asleson, *Albert Moore*, 89–99, 152–54.

89. Robertson, *Time Was*, 83. Whistler scholars tend to give less weight to the joint project and to allow Moore less importance in formulating its tenets and technical procedures than Asleson does (see Asleson, *Albert Moore*, 98). See also Joyce Hill Stoner, "Textured Surfaces: Technique, Facture, and Friendship in the Work of James McNeill Whistler" (Ph.D. diss., University of Delaware, 1995).

90. Andrew McLaren Young, Margaret MacDonald, Robin Spencer, and Hamish Miles, *The Paintings of James McNeill Whistler* (New Haven, Conn., 1980), 64.

91. Cited in ibid. See *The Times*, 14 November 1871.

92. Otto H. Bacher, *With Whistler in Venice* (New York, 1908), 75–76. See also, for an account of working methods, T. R. Way, *Memories of James McNeill Whistler, the Artist* (London, 1912).

93. Bacher, *Whistler in Venice*, 68, 57, 58.

94. Mortimer Menpes, *Whistler as I Knew Him* (London, 1904), 74.

95. Bacher, *Whistler in Venice*, 58–59.

96. Arthur Jerome Eddy, *Recollections and Impressions of James A. McNeill Whistler* (Philadelphia, 1903), 232, 235.

97. Cited in John Siewert, "Whistler's Decorative Darkness," in *The Grosvenor Gallery*, ed. Casteras and Denny, 95.

98. *The Times*, 5 May 1864, GUL, PC 1/13; *The Saturday Review*, 1 June 1867, GUL, PC 1/3. It is

worth noting that Whistler annotated the latter press cutting, which also claimed that "no picture ever exhibited at the Royal Academy contained so little manual labour as Mr Whistler's 'Sea and Rain,'" with the words "utterly and stupidly false."

99. *Examiner,* 22 June 1872, GUL, PC 1/9. As an example of this, consider the following comment on *Purple and Rose: The Lange Leizen of the Six Marks* (1864, Philadelphia Museum of Art): "the most glorious arrangement of colour in the Exhibition, exhausting to a highly sensitive eye. Beyond this let no one think of it. The woman is hideous, absurdly ill-drawn" ([illegible periodical], 4 June 1867, GUL, PC 1/13). *The Hour* summed it up in 1874: "the principle—if principle it can be called—on which this artist has lately worked, and which has caused him to ignore every element of art but one, is founded on a fallacy. Colour, however pure and perfect in tone, when divorced from the forms with which it is associated in nature has no significance and appeals only to the senses" (GUL, PC 1/71).

100. Andrew Stephenson has shown that color was "coded as . . . superficial, 'treacherous and unstable'" and that it "carr[ied] connotations of the subjective and the unreasoned." See "Refashioning Modern Masculinity: Whistler, Aestheticism, and National Identity," in *English Art, 1860–1914,* ed. Corbett and Perry, 142.

101. Flint, *The Victorians and the Visual Imagination,* 204.

102. Deanna Marohn Bendix, *Diabolical Designs: Paintings, Interiors, and Exhibitions of James McNeill Whistler* (Washington, D.C., 1995), 10.

103. James McNeill Whistler, *The Gentle Art of Making Enemies* (London, 1912), 135.

104. Cited in Bendix, *Diabolical Designs,* 9.

105. Stephenson, "Refashioning Modern Masculinity." See also Jonathan Shirland, "The Construction of Artistic Masculinity in James McNeill Whistler, Walter Sickert, and Wyndham Lewis, c. 1880–1914" (Ph.D. diss., University College, London, 2002).

106. Elizabeth and Joseph Pennell, *The Life of James McNeill Whistler* (London, 1908), 2:107.

107. *The Graphic,* 2 November 1872, GUL, PC 2/2; William Rothenstein, *Men and Memories: Recollections of William Rothenstein, 1872–1900* (London, 1931), 82–83, 85.

108. Cited in Ronald Anderson, *The Gentle Art of Making Enemies: "An Extraordinary Practical Lot . . . a Great Literary Curiosity,"* pamphlet, Michael Parkin Gallery (London, 1990), unpaginated. See Max Beerbohm, *Yet Again* (London, 1909), 105–19; *The Saturday Review,* 16 June 1890. Charges of eccentricity were very common against Whistler after the Ruskin trial in 1878. The press response to the 1885 "Ten O'Clock Lecture" almost entirely concentrated on Whistler as a comedy turn—and discussion of his opinions or aesthetics vanished almost completely.

109. Whistler spoke of "the usual *complete perfection of finish* which is the great characteristic of the Whistler shows." Cited by Margaret F. MacDonald in *Whistler,* ed. Margaret F. MacDonald, exh. cat., Tate Gallery (London, 1994), 221.

110. *Queen,* cited in ibid.

111. Cited in Bendix, *Diabolical Designs,* 214.

112. Ibid., 9.

113. See Stephenson, "Refashioning Modern Masculinity," and Shirland, "The Construction of Artistic Masculinity."

114. For 21 and 28 February 1885. In Chapter 3, I take up some of the implications of this form of public combat in the context of Wilde's equally fraught relationship with Charles Ricketts.

115. See Richard Ellmann, *Oscar Wilde* (London, 1988), 254–58.

116. Cited in ibid., 257.

117. On the trial, see Linda Merrill, *A Pot of Paint: Aesthetics on Trial in* Whistler v. Ruskin (Washington, D.C., 1992).

118. Whistler, *Gentle Art,* 5.

119. Cited in R. Anderson, *Gentle Art.* See Max Beerbohm, *The Metropolitan Magazine* 20, no. 6 (1904). Whatever the confidence, there is plenty of reason to question the success of Whistler's publicity campaigns. It was only late in his career, with the purchase of the *Arrangement in Grey and Black: Portrait of the Painter's Mother* (1871) by the Musée du Luxembourg in

1891, that Whistler came to be generally regarded as an established master, and the tone of reviews and references became uniformly respectful. Until then, the reputation for "eccentricity" tended to obscure engagement with the art.

120. Bendix, *Diabolical Designs,* 11.

121. Cited in Flint, *The Victorians and the Visual Imagination,* 171.

122. Cited by Richard Dorment in *Whistler,* ed. MacDonald, 122.

123. See Roy McMullen, *Victorian Outsider: A Biography of J. A. M. Whistler* (London, 1973), 162–63; Eddy, *Recollections and Impressions,* 231–32.

124. Cited by Dorment in *Whistler,* ed. MacDonald, 131.

125. Didi-Huberman, "The Art of Not Describing," 135.

126. Ibid., 153.

127. Didi-Huberman, *Fra Angelico,* 9.

128. John Ruskin, *Fors Clavigera,* in *Works,* ed. Cook and Wedderburn, 29:160.

129. Dorment, in *Whistler,* ed. MacDonald, 138.

130. Cited by MacDonald in ibid., 224.

131. Ibid., 223. See also Margaret F. MacDonald, *James McNeill Whistler's Drawings, Pastels, and Watercolors: A Catalogue Raisonné* (New Haven, Conn., 1995), 324–25. See Oscar Wilde, "The Decay of Lying," in *Intentions: The Decay of Lying; Pen, Pencil, and Poison; The Critic as Artist; The Truth of Masks* (London, 1891), for a well-known commentary on the London fog and its representation in art and literature.

132. Cited in *Whistler,* ed. MacDonald, 223. Commenting on the three *Nocturnes* exhibited at the Grosvenor in 1878, the *Magazine of Art* thought them "clever renderings of various effects of London fog." Cited in Young et al., *The Paintings of James McNeill Whistler,* 91.

133. Whistler, *Gentle Art,* 144.

134. Ibid.

135. Ibid. Sickert inherited this concern with the transformation of the world in painting, as I discuss in Chapter 4.

136. Elizabeth Prettejohn, "Art and 'Materialism': English Critical Responses to Alma-Tadema, 1865–1913," in *Sir Lawrence Alma-Tadema,* ed. Edwin Becker et al., exh. cat., Van Gogh Museum (Amsterdam, [1996]), 104.

137. See Flint, *The Victorians and the Visual Imagination,* chapters 7 and 8, as well as her "Moral Judgement," 59–66; see also Elizabeth Prettejohn, "Aesthetic Value and the Professionalization of Victorian Art Criticism, 1837–78," *Journal of Victorian Culture* 2, no. 1 (1997): 71–94.

138. Flint, *The Victorians and the Visual Imagination,* 203.

Chapter 3

1. On Ricketts generally, see Calloway's *Subtle and Fantastic Decorator;* Darracott, *The World of Charles Ricketts;* and Delaney, *Charles Ricketts.*

2. Charles Ricketts, Diary, 5 December 1900, British Library, Add. MS 58098. The text is reprinted without the excisions in Ricketts, *Self-Portrait,* 49–50.

3. The excision of the phrase beginning "and the end" was apparently made separately from the other cancellations.

4. Ricketts, Diary, 17 December 1900, British Library, Add. MS 58098; Ricketts, *Self-Portrait,* 50.

5. Ricketts, Diary, 31 December 1900, British Library, Add. MS 58098; Ricketts, *Self-Portrait,* 50.

6. Many contemporaries had powerful reactions to Wilde's arrest and trial (see Gordon Bottomley's account, reproduced in Ricketts, *Self-Portrait,* 299, for a typical response), but Ricketts is unusual in being reserved at the trial and overcome only when Wilde died.

7. Although Beardsley's role as Wilde's illustrator was tiny compared to that of Ricketts, commentators have preferred to consider *Salome* in this context. Beardsley's work is less interesting than Ricketts's in the context of this book, but it also resists. Almost all the writing on *Salome* stresses the negative and antagonistic view of Wilde's text taken up by the illustrations. The exception is a 1983 article by Elliot L. Gilbert that argues the opposite: see his "'Tumult of Images': Wilde, Beardsley, and *Salome,*" *Victorian Studies* 26, no. 2 (1983): 133–59. More recently, Jeffrey Walden has

reverted to the standard line in "Illustrating *Salome:* Perverting the Text?" *Word & Image* 8, no. 2 (1992): 124–32. See also Susan Owens, "Aubrey Beardsley, *Salome,* and Satire" (Ph.D. diss., University College, London, 2002).

8. Ricketts designed the binding and/or the decoration for the following books by Wilde: *The Picture of Dorian Gray* (1891), *Intentions* (1891), *Lord Arthur Saville's Crime* (1891), *Poems* (1892), and the Collected Edition of 1908. He was responsible for every aspect of the physical appearance of *The Sphinx* (1894); with Charles Shannon, he designed *A House of Pomegranates* (1891). Shannon alone designed the binding for Wilde's plays *Lady Windermere's Fan* (1893), *A Woman of No Importance* (1894), *The Importance of Being Earnest* (1899), and *An Ideal Husband* (1899).

9. Denys Sutton, "A Neglected Virtuoso: Charles Ricketts and His Achievements," *Apollo* 83 (1966): 141.

10. Pollock, *Avant-Garde Gambits,* 15.

11. Charles Shannon, *A Catalogue of Mr Shannon's Lithographs, with Prefatory Notes by Charles Ricketts, and a Portrait Engraved by Charles Ricketts After a Medal by Alphonse Legros* (London, [1902]), 6.

12. Ricketts, *Self-Portrait,* 51.

13. Ricketts, "Century of Art," 48.

14. Ibid., 50.

15. In fact, Ricketts frequently deprecated his abilities as a painter. This did not stop him from being preoccupied with them and what they implied.

16. Ricketts, *Self-Portrait,* 104.

17. Ricketts, *The Prado,* 136.

18. Ibid., 140, 144.

19. Ibid., 150.

20. Ricketts, *Self-Portrait,* 97–98.

21. Ricketts, Diary, 22 January 1900.

22. W. B. Yeats, *Autobiographies* (London, 1980), 518.

23. Ricketts, *The Prado,* 162.

24. Ibid., 163.

25. Ricketts, *Self-Portrait,* 105.

26. Ricketts's periodical *The Dial,* for instance, in the words of a contemporary commentator, "conferred upon all its works the important gift of free expression, in absolute disregard to [*sic*] the traditions of the publishing world." See "Theocritus," "The Vale Artists—IV," *The Sketch,* 25 April 1895, 683. This was the last of four articles, all with the same title; the others appeared in the *Sketch* numbers for 23 January, 13 March, and 17 April 1895.

27. Bürger, *Theory of the Avant-Garde,* 46.

28. Wilde, "The Decay of Lying," 53.

29. This is the basis of the critique of avant-garde practice mounted by Bürger in *Theory of the Avant-Garde.*

30. *Speaker,* 28 November 1891.

31. *The Letters of Oscar Wilde,* ed. Rupert Hart-Davis (London, 1962), 300.

32. Bürger, *Theory of the Avant-Garde,* 47 and passim.

33. J. Hillis Miller, *Illustration* (London, 1992).

34. Calloway, *Subtle and Fantastic Decorator,* 16. Toward the end of his life, Ricketts designed a completely new set of illustrations to *The Sphinx,* which Calloway reproduces, commenting that they serve as a homage to Wilde's memory (see *Subtle and Fantastic Decorator,* 84 and 86–91). This revisionist homage bears ample witness to Wilde's continuing emotional power as a figure in Ricketts's internal life.

35. See Delaney, *Charles Ricketts,* 44. Delaney has identified contributions by Ricketts to *Woman's World* from 1888.

36. Ibid., 45.

37. [Jean Paul Raymond {pseud.} and] Charles Ricketts, *Oscar Wilde: Recollections* (London, 1932), 36. Subsequent references to this work will appear parenthetically in the text.

38. Michael Field, Journal, 1900, fol. 165^{v}, cited in Delaney, *Charles Ricketts,* 45.

39. *Letters of Oscar Wilde,* ed. Hart-Davis, 249, and reported by Sturge Moore in Ricketts, *Self-Portrait,* 16; there is another version in Ricketts, *Recollections,* 36–37.

40. W. Rothenstein, *Men and Memories,* 172.

41. Laurence Housman, *The Unexpected Years* (London, 1939), 115.

42. Holmes, *Self and Partners,* 166.

43. Ricketts, *Self-Portrait,* 124.

44. See ibid., 178–79, and Ricketts, *Recollections.*

45. Holmes, *Self and Partners,* 168.

46. Cited in Delaney, *Charles Ricketts,* 57. Ricketts discusses Wilde's delivery at length throughout *Recollections.* Wilde's self-presentation owed much to Whistler, according to Ellmann in *Oscar Wilde,* 127–28, 201.

47. Ricketts said *Beyond the Threshold* "was written in one of those crises in a man's life" (Delaney, *Charles Ricketts,* 357).

48. Hesketh Pearson, *The Life of Oscar Wilde* (London, 1946), 322–24. According to Delaney, Ricketts actually did hope to print the play, but Wilde subsequently lost the manuscript; the Vale printed nothing by Wilde. See Delaney, *Charles Ricketts,* 109.

49. *Letters of Oscar Wilde,* ed. Hart-Davis, 541.

50. Ricketts, "Century of Art," 49.

51. Ricketts, *The Prado,* 126.

52. Ibid., 127–28. He later wrote a separate book on Titian: see Charles Ricketts, *Titian* (London, 1910).

53. Ricketts, *The Prado,* 163.

54. Within the argument I am making here, this refers back to the thinking I have identified in the early P.R.B. as well as to the adaptation identifiable in Watts and Whistler; see Chapters 1 and 2.

55. Ricketts, *The Prado,* 150.

56. See *Letters of Oscar Wilde,* ed. Hart-Davis, 250.

57. Michael Field, *Works and Days* (London, 1933), 136.

58. Wilde, "The Decay of Lying," 54.

59. Ibid., 4.

60. *Letters of Oscar Wilde,* ed. Hart-Davis, 301.

61. See Ricketts, *Self-Portrait,* 112–13, 425.

62. Portraiture and critical interest in it saw a dramatic rise during this period. Much of the debased popular success of the painter Norbert Franks in Gissing's *Will Warburton* is based on meretricious portraiture.

63. On relevant questions of identity, see T. C. Heller, M. Sosna, and D. Wellbery, eds., *Reconstructing Individualism: Autonomy, Individuality, and the Self in Western Thought* (Stanford, 1986); Scott Lash and Jonathan Friedman, *Modernity and Identity* (Oxford, 1992); and Charles Taylor, *Sources of the Self: The Making of Modern Identity* (Cambridge, 1989).

64. On portraiture, see *The Art Journal* 46, no. 3 (1987), a special issue on portraiture; Richard Brilliant, *Portraiture* (London, 1991); Marcia Pointon, *Hanging the Head: Portraiture and Social Formation in Eighteenth-Century England* (New Haven, Conn., 1993); and Joanna Woodall, ed., *Portraiture: Facing the Subject* (Manchester, 1997).

65. See Joanna Woodall's introduction to *Portraiture,* ed. Woodall, 1.

66. This was partly because Watts had begun his career as a portrait painter. Barrington thought that in his early career, "by most of his fellow-artists, as well as by the world in general, Watts . . . had been viewed as a portrait-painter only. . . . I remember more than one artist speaking of him as such, and rather contesting his wisdom in attempting any other line of art. One of the greatest in the Pre-Raphaelite school was of this opinion . . . saying to me, referring to Watts' portraits, 'He is no good at anything else.'" See Barrington, *G. F. Watts,* 9.

67. Blunt, *England's Michelangelo,* 59.

68. M. Watts, *George Frederic Watts: Annals,* 3:35.

69. Ibid. On the Hall of Fame, see *G. F. Watts, The Hall of Fame: Portraits of His Famous Contemporaries,* exh. cat., National Portrait Gallery (London, 1975).

70. M. Watts, *George Frederic Watts: Annals,* 3:35. For a discussion of this aspect of the portraits, see Paul Barlow, "Facing the Past and Present: The National Portrait Gallery and the Search for 'Authentic' Portraiture," in *Portraiture,* ed. Woodall, 219–38.

71. Chesterton, *G. F. Watts,* 153; reported in Blunt, *England's Michelangelo,* 59.

72. Mary Elizabeth Braddon, *Lady Audley's Secret* (London, 1862), 1:133, 143.

73. Ibid., 1:143. Compare this with Tennyson's account of Watts as portraitist (cited in Blunt, *England's Michelangelo,* 59):

> *As when a painter, poring on a face,*
> *Divinely thro' all hindrance finds the man*
> *Behind it, and so paints him that his face,*

The shape and colour of a mind and life,
Lives for his children, ever at its best.

74. Barlow, "Facing the Past and Present," 234–35. See also, for a discussion of Watts's portraiture, Lewis Johnson, "Pre-Raphaelitism, Personification, Portraiture," in *Pre-Raphaelites Re-Viewed,* ed. Marcia Pointon (Manchester, 1989), 140–58.

75. Barlow, "Facing the Past and Present," 236.

76. For instance, "Ricketts has just done for me a lovely cover for *Dorian Gray*—grey pastel paper with a white back and tiny gold marigolds" (*Letters of Oscar Wilde,* ed. Hart-Davis, 276). Wilde's language assigns Ricketts's work to an inferior ("tiny") and minor realm.

77. Wilde, "The Critic as Artist, Part 1," in *Intentions,* 134. The two parts of "The Critic as Artist" contain a sustained denigration of the visual arts and a celebration of literature.

78. *Pall Mall Gazette,* 21 February 1885. For accounts of the Whistler-Wilde argument, see Ellmann, *Oscar Wilde,* 254–58, and Ronald Anderson and Anne Koval, *James McNeill Whistler: Beyond the Myth* (London, 1994), 265–71.

79. M. Field, *Works and Days,* 135.

80. Oscar Wilde, "The Portrait of Mr W. H.," in *The Complete Works of Oscar Wilde* (London, 1971), 1151. This is the "Clouet" that Ricketts painted for Wilde.

81. Oscar Wilde, *The Picture of Dorian Gray,* in *Complete Works,* 112.

82. Ibid., 166.

83. Ibid., 119. "Soul" is Pater's word in the essay on "Style" for the force of personality in the artwork. See Walter Pater, *Appreciations with an Essay on Style* (London, 1889).

84. Wilde, *Dorian Gray,* 122–23.

85. Ibid., 167.

86. Ibid., 17.

87. Wilde, "Mr W. H.," 1150.

88. Wilde, *Dorian Gray,* 111, 112.

89. Ibid., 112. See, in this context, Flint's discussion of Victorian interest in physiognomy in *The Victorians and the Visual Imagination,* 13–19, especially 18. See also Mary Cowling, *The Artist as Anthropologist: The Representation of Type and Character in Victorian Art* (Cambridge, 1989).

90. Wilde, "Mr W. H.," 1163.

91. Ibid.

92. Cited in ibid., 1164.

93. Ricketts and Sturge Moore saw Titian's *Bacchanal* in 1900 during their trip to Spain to research *The Prado and Its Masterpieces*—and hence before Wilde's death in December of the same year. The writing, however, of both *The Prado* and Moore's poem "Lines on Titian's 'Bacchanal'" post-dated the death.

94. Ricketts, *The Prado,* 136.

95. Ricketts's journals of the trips he made to Italy in 1899 and, at other times, to Italy, Germany, and Spain are particularly good sources for his art criticism; they contain notes and observations that later found their way into his published writings. The journals of 1899 and 1903 are kept at the British Library, Ricketts and Shannon Papers, vol. 10, Add. MS 58094, and vol. 11, Add. MS 58095, respectively. Selections from these and from the diaries and letters were published posthumously in Ricketts, *Self-Portrait,* but Ricketts's editor deliberately chose to omit the greater part of his comments on works of art from what was published. See *Self-Portrait,* 23 n. 1 and 90 n. 2.

96. Ricketts, *The Prado,* 137.

97. See Delaney, *Charles Ricketts.* In the chapter on technique in *Titian,* Ricketts gives an account of the evolution of oil painting into the sixteenth century, and he argues for Titian's use of glazing and overpainting as essential to the achievement of "the tranquil glow and tender lustre of his best preserved pictures" (*Titian,* 162). Ricketts aimed for this effect in his own work, and he valued it in the work of others. Hence the preoccupation in his commentary with restoration, repainting, and cleaning and with the survival (or otherwise) of glazes he believed to have been present originally. This concentration on the condition of the canvas gives a distinctive flavor to much of Ricketts's writing.

98. British Library, Ricketts and Shannon Papers, vol. 11, Add. MS 58095.

99. British Library, Ricketts and Shannon Papers, vol. 10, Add. MS 58094.

100. Ibid.

101. Keith Moxey has some relevant observations on a parallel process in art history as an academic discipline. See Keith Moxey, "Motivating History," *Art Bulletin* 77, no. 3 (1995): 392–401.

102. Ricketts, translating *Las Hilanderas,* calls the painting *The Spinners.*

103. Ricketts, *The Prado,* 86.

104. Ibid., 86–87.

105. Ibid., 81, 83, 82.

106. *Titian,* 60.

107. Ibid., 88–89.

108. For recent work on ekphrasis, see W. J. T. Mitchell, "Ekphrasis and the Other," *South Atlantic Quarterly* 91 (Summer 1992): 695–719, and his *Picture Theory,* chapter 5, as well as James W. Heffernan, *Museum of Words: The Poetics of Ekphrasis from Homer to Ashbery* (Chicago, 1993). See also John Dixon Hunt, "Making Vergil Look English," in *Word & Image Interactions,* ed. Martin Heuser (Basel, 1993).

109. Ricketts, *Self-Portrait,* 108.

110. See *Letters of Oscar Wilde,* ed. Hart-Davis, 341.

111. Oscar Wilde, *The Sphinx* (London, 1894), unpaginated.

112. Wilde, "The Decay of Lying," 19.

113. Ellmann, *Oscar Wilde.*

114. Wilde, "The Critic as Artist," 127.

115. For an excellent account of Ricketts, *The Sphinx,* and their cultural context, see the discussion in Lorraine Janzen Kooistra, *The Artist as Critic: Bitexuality in Fin-de-Siècle Illustrated Books* (Aldershot, U.K., 1995), especially 94–107. Kooistra's book appeared after the first version of this argument was published in my "Collaborative Resistance: Charles Ricketts as Illustrator of Oscar Wilde," *Word & Image* 10, no. 1 (1994): 22–37. She stresses Ricketts's confirmation of the depth and complexity of Wilde's text: "Ricketts's designs are at least as esoteric, self-conscious, and intertextual as Wilde's poem" (99).

116. This arrangement is common in the Vale Press books that Ricketts designed, though. See, for instance, Michael Field, *The World at Auction* (1898), *A Race of Leaves* (1901), and *Julia Domna* (1903), all of which have a similar layout. The same is true of Charles Ricketts, *A Defence of the Revival of Printing* (1899). In these cases, however, the relationship between text and image in the book as a whole is not contested as forcefully as in *The Sphinx* (although they continue to express the tensions that I identify between the illustrator and the text).

117. Here, too, things are not as straightforward as they seem. In the spring of 1894, Wilde returned corrected proofs to Ricketts and commented: "Don't you think the pages are terribly few in number? Why not put fewer verses on each page? We could easily have four or five pages more." See *More Letters of Oscar Wilde,* ed. Rupert Hart-Davis (London, 1985), 123.

118. M. Field, *Works and Days,* 139.

119. Wilde, "The Decay of Lying," 31.

120. Ibid., 30–31.

121. Wilde used a similar explanation to account for what he perceived to be Ricketts's insensitivity to A. E. Housman's poems: "Ricketts . . . is dominated by the sense of definite design and intellectual architecture, nor can he see the wonderful strangeness of simple things in art and life" (*More Letters of Oscar Wilde,* ed. Hart-Davis, 153).

Chapter 4

References to material held in the Sickert archive in the Islington Libraries Local History Collection are given in the form IC. The volumes of press cuttings are identified as PCB, followed by the dates covered by the volume and, where one exists, by the folio number. Throughout the text and notes I give the catalogue number in Wendy Baron, *Walter Sickert* (London, 1973), for works that I do not illustrate in this book.

1. I do not mean to suggest by this that Sickert explores these themes only in the music-hall series. I have chosen to concentrate on them here not only for reasons of space but also because they formulate the issues with particular clarity over a number of different works.

2. The exhibitors were Francis Bate, Fred Brown, Francis James, Paul Maitland, Theodore Roussel, Bernhard Sickert, Walter Sickert, Sidney Starr, Philip Wilson Steer, and

George Thompson; see Anna Gruetzner Robins, "The London Impressionists at the Goupil Gallery: Modernist Strategies and Modern Life," in *Impressionism in Britain,* by Kenneth McConkey, exh. cat., Barbican Art Gallery (New Haven, Conn., 1995); and Robins, "The London Impressionists" (Ph.D. diss., Courtauld Institute of Art, 1988). See also Baron, *Walter Sickert,* chapter 3; Baron, *Perfect Moderns: A History of the Camden Town Group* (Aldershot, U.K., 2000), 16–17; and Denys Sutton, *Walter Sickert* (London, 1976), 62–70.

3. See T. J. Clark, *The Painting of Modern Life,* for the most influential version of this reading of the relations between art and modernity.

4. Walter Sickert, "Introduction to the Catalogue of the 'London Impressionists' Exhibition" (Goupil Gallery, December 1889), reprinted in *Sickert: The Complete Writings,* ed. Robins, 59–61, 60.

5. See Kenneth McConkey, *British Impressionism* (Oxford, 1989), 85, 88. But also see Baron, *Sickert,* for an identification of this as a Symbolist influence.

6. Sickert, "Introduction to the 'London Impressionists,'" 60.

7. See Baron, *Sickert,* 23–24, for her association of this passage with Whistler's "Ten O'Clock Lecture" and more general refusals of content in painting in favor of its visual qualities.

8. Symbolism brings with it a well-established narrative: it is said to have passed to its modernist successors a "suppression of meaning," the subordination of content that is essential to abstraction. In the Tate's 1997 exhibition *The Age of Rossetti,* this understanding of the relationship with modernism seems dominant. Modernism's inheritance is said to derive from the Symbolist aim "to create a language of pure 'mood' . . . achieved entirely by means of colour and form" and "independent of any narrative element" (see "The Suppression of Meaning" in *The Age of Rossetti,* 108). In the catalogue, Andrew Wilton writes: "In painting, the inner turbulence of much Symbolist thinking was increasingly to be seen on the surface of pictures which sought no longer to express the transcendental glimpsed through a dreamlike mist but to embody directly the emotional life of the artist" ("Symbolism in Britain," 33). MaryAnne Stevens adds, "French Symbolism . . . radically severed the link between art and representation and laid the foundations for a celebration of the individual artist's right to seek out the most effective mode of expressing the new subject-matter, the Idea. Released from the shackles of representation . . . it contained within it the programme for abstraction" ("Symbolism—A French Monopoly?" 63). (See also Stevens in *The Last Romantics.*) As part of the general argument of this chapter, I want to offer an alternative account of the relationship between Symbolism and modernism.

9. For a recent attempt to use Symbolism as a catch-all term, see *The Age of Rossetti.*

10. See McConkey, *Impressionism in Britain,* for a recent and comprehensive survey.

11. See Leighton's idealist/realist dichotomy in his *Addresses.*

12. See, for instance, Anderson and Koval, *James McNeill Whistler,* 187–88, 243.

13. *The Age of Rossetti,* 207.

14. James McNeill Whistler, "The Ten O'Clock Lecture," in *Strangeness and Beauty: An Anthology of Aesthetic Criticism, 1840–1910,* ed. Eric Warner and Graham Hough (Cambridge, 1983), 2:81. For instances of this modernity of subject matter, see, for example, *Whistler,* ed. MacDonald, cat. 46, cat. 123, and cat. 49.

15. Cited in *The Age of Rossetti,* 169.

16. See McConkey, *British Impressionism,* for a discussion of the aesthetics of Realism in this period.

17. Sickert made the argument for Realism in art in a chapter entitled "Modern Realism in Painting" that he contributed to A. Theuriet, *Jules Bastien-Lepage and His Art: A Memoir* (London, 1892), 133–43. Sickert wrote there that "the important fact about Millet is not that he struggled with poverty, or that he expressed on canvas the dignity of labour, but that he was a great artist," one able "to render" his motifs "in fitting terms in accordance with the tradition which governs the use of each material" (133, 134).

18. For contemporary comments on some of the music-hall works, see Anna Gruetzner Robins, "Sickert 'Painter-in-Ordinary' to the Music Hall," in *Sickert,* ed. Wendy Baron and

Richard Shone, exh. cat., Royal Academy of Arts (New Haven, Conn., 1992), 13.

19. *Pall Mall Gazette,* IC, PCB 1906–9 [unpaginated].

20. W. H. Meyers, *Onlooker,* 22 July 1911, IC, PCB 1906–9, 2.

21. *Saturday Review,* 1 December 1906, IC, PCB 1906–9 [unpaginated].

22. Claude Phillips, "Goupil Gallery: Contemporary Art Society," *Daily Telegraph,* 7 April 1913, IC, PCB 1908–14, 102.

23. Two of the most sophisticated and developed attempts to do so work by defining Sickert as a wholly realist artist, unresponsive to the mediating function of the painter. See Robert Ross, "The Stafford Gallery: Paintings by Mr Walter Sickert," *Morning Post,* 19 July 1911, and Roger Fry, "Mr Walter Sickert's Pictures at the Stafford Gallery," *Nation,* 8 July 1911, both of which were provoked by a successful one-man show. For Fry, Sickert's "vision is curiously detached. . . . Things for him have only their visual values, they are not symbols, they contain no key to unlock the secrets of the heart and spirit." For Ross, Sickert's subjects "must . . . satisfy a severe aesthetic formula which admits nothing so artificial as poetry, nothing so obvious as physical beauty, to disturb the functions of paint." The point, for both critics, is that Sickert is a creature only of the visual and that for him, his subject matter is accordingly inconsequential.

24. *Observer,* 28 November 1909, IC, PCB 1906–9 [unpaginated].

25. See Bruce Laughton, *Philip Wilson Steer, 1860–1942* (Oxford, 1971), 39 and chapters 2 and 3, and Ysanne Holt, *Philip Wilson Steer* (Bridgend, U.K., 1992). According to Holt, Steer's contributions were "generally perceived in the press to be inspired by Monet" (36), and Monet was a powerful influence on Steer at this time. Monet had shown twenty paintings at the Goupil Gallery earlier in 1889.

26. D. S. MacColl, "On Two Fallacies," *Spectator,* 1893 (cited in Holt, *Philip Wilson Steer,* 38).

27. For a very clear exposition of this and associated paradoxes, see Rosen and Zerner's "Ideology of the Licked Surface."

28. On Sickert's graphic works, see Aimée Troyen, *Walter Sickert as Printmaker,* exh. cat., Yale Center for British Art (New Haven, Conn., 1979).

29. On the significance and history of music halls, see Diana Howard, *London Theatres and Music-Halls, 1850–1950* (London, 1970); Peter Bailey, *Leisure and Class in Victorian England: Rational Recreation and the Contest for Control, 1830–1885* (London, 1978); Bailey, ed., *Music Hall: The Business of Pleasure* (Milton Keynes, U.K., 1986); and J. S. Bratton, *Music Hall: Performance and Style* (Milton Keynes, U.K., 1986). On Sickert, see John Stokes's "Prudes on the Prowl" in his *In the Nineties* (New York, 1989); Robins, "Sickert 'Painter-in-Ordinary'"; and Robert Emmons, *The Life and Opinions of Walter Richard Sickert* (London, 1941), chapter 5.

30. For a reproduction of Sickert's first music-hall painting, now destroyed—*Collins Music Hall, Islington Green,* c. 1887–88—see Frederick Wedmore, *Some of the Moderns* (London, 1909), figs. after p. 50. On this painting, see also Baron, cat. 50, 24, 29.

31. Later, between 1919 and 1926, he produced several paintings with related themes, including *That Old-Fashioned Mother of Mine* (c. 1920, private collection; Baron, cat. 400). After this, with the exception of one or two paintings such as the well-known *Plaza Tiller Girls* (1928, private collection; Baron, cat. 420), Sickert abandoned themes related to the halls.

32. See Baron, *Sickert,* 24–25, for a discussion of the halls' appeal to Sickert and possible influences; see also Robins, "Sickert 'Painter-in-Ordinary.'"

33. Andrew Stephenson, "Buttressing Bohemian Mystiques and Bandaging Masculine Anxieties," *Art History* 17, no. 2 (1994): 276.

34. See Lisa Tickner, *Modern Life and Modern Subjects: British Art in the Early Twentieth Century* (New Haven, Conn., 2000).

35. See Baron, *Sickert,* 22–30, and Robins, "The London Impressionists."

36. Sickert, 1889, cited in Baron, *Sickert,* 24. The influence of Degas has been a strong concern of the literature; on the question of the influence of Whistler and Degas, see Baron, *Sickert,* 24, and Ronald Pickvance, "The Magic of the Halls and Sickert," *Apollo* (April 1962): 107–15.

37. Sickert was adamant in print that Degas's realism had influenced neither his choice of music-hall subjects nor their composition. He wrote that "it is surely unnecessary to go so far afield as Paris to find an explanation of the fact that a Londoner should seek to render on canvas a familiar and striking scene in the midst of the town in which he lives," and he goes on to describe *Collins Music Hall, Islington Green*. Quoted in Pickvance, "The Magic of the Halls," 109, from *The Scotsman*, 24 April 1889. See *Sickert: The Complete Writings*, ed. Robins, 41.

38. Robins discusses the spatial ambiguity in these paintings in "Sickert 'Painter-in-Ordinary,'" 16–17.

39. Enid Bagnold, *Autobiography* (London, 1969), 73. Bagnold describes Sickert's fascination with "the abated light that got muffled in the glass" of mirrors. She goes on, "he had his own term for this effect, 'blonde', he would mutter. It was a love-word. The folds of a dirty sheet in shadow, the model's naked body on the bed, her flesh, green-shadowed, melting into the surrounding wood, rep, leather, reverberating, softly in a splendour of unspoiled light."

40. See the discussion in Robins, "Sickert 'Painter-in-Ordinary,'" 13–16. Robins discusses the version of the painting in the Art Gallery of New South Wales in Sydney, which is the one shown at the NEAC. *Gatti's* has a complicated history; see Baron, cat. 42, 302, and Baron and Shone, eds., *Sickert*, 70.

41. This version of *Gatti's* was also known as *Ta-Ra-Ra-Boom-De-Ay*, according to Baron, cat. 42, 302–3; see also ibid., cat. 43.

42. The existence of multiple versions of this painting suggests the continuing fascination of the challenge to Sickert. Baron lists the evidence in *Sickert*, cat. 42 and cat. 43.

43. This is evident from the fact that the cartouches in the "rear wall" with the figures of the dancing women both reappear reflected at an angle between the columns.

44. In a short essay on Sickert's late work in *Late Sickert: Paintings, 1927–1942*, exh. cat., Hayward Gallery (London, 1981), Helen Lessore described the ways in which "one of the most striking characteristics of Sickert's late pictures is the consistent treatment of the canvas as a surface, with an all-over equality of tension between the flat shapes into which it is divided, irrespective of what they represent" (22). She adduces *Temple Bar* (c. 1941, private collection [not in Baron]), which has some claim to be the last picture Sickert ever painted, as evidence that "he did also eventually notice that the grid of squares on the canvas itself in some mysterious way contributed something to the painting" so that "he actually re-painted the squaring-up lines after their original purpose has been served." She comments, "part of the magic lay in seeming to bring everything up to the surface" (ibid.). This technique clearly has a longer history in Sickert's oeuvre than Lessore remembered.

45. Because the description and technique here is a mixture of wet on wet and heavy black outline (that is, it mixes Degas and Whistler), this inscription of a broken grid pattern over wet-on-wet painting may also declare that Sickert is using Degas as well as Whistler. See Wendy Baron's comments on the impact of Degas on Sickert's technique in "Sickert's Links with French Painting," *Apollo* (March 1970): 186–97. Baron argues that Sickert derived the use of squaring-up procedures, utterly alien to the technique of Whistler, from Degas (188–89). On Sickert's technical practice and squaring up, see the memoir by Clifford Hall, who was Sickert's pupil in the 1920s, printed in Marjorie Lillie, *Sickert: The Painter and His Circle* (London, 1971), 71–74, especially 72–73.

46. Sickert made drawings during performances directly into notebooks that he carried with him on his nocturnal visits to the music halls; see Emmons, *Life and Opinions*, 48.

47. See Didi-Huberman, "The Art of Not Describing," 135–69.

48. Sickert wrote in a letter to *The Times* that "the great painters painted from drawings that remained stable, and not in the presence of the 'movie' that is nature. To the extent that the moderns have not forgotten this, have they succeeded in doing work that could hang beside that of their predecessors and masters?" See Walter Sickert, "Whistler: The Artist in Practice" [letter], *The Times* [no date or issue given], IC, PCB 1906–9, June 1934–38 [unpaginated]. This argument is part of his repudiation of Whistler. See also *Sickert: The Complete Writings*, ed. Robins, 629.

49. As well as its capacity to act as an unmediated presentation of knowledge about the circumstances and conditions of experience.

50. Mitchell, *Iconology,* 5. See also the related concept of the "metapicture" that Mitchell elaborates in *Picture Theory,* 35–82, and that he describes as "a kind of summary image . . . that encapsulates an entire episteme, a theory of knowledge" (49). The founding discussion of the hypericon and its relevance for understandings of modernity is Michel Foucault's discussion of Velasquez's *Las Meninas* in *The Order of Things: An Archaeology of the Human Sciences* (London, 1970); see Baron, *Sickert,* 29–31, for a discussion of Sickert's use of mirrors and a comparison with *Las Meninas.* See also, for a useful history of modern critical responses to the idea of the hypericon, James Elkins, *Why Are Our Pictures Puzzles?* (London, 1999).

51. I rely on Baron's definition of the "Camden Town period" as 1905–14. See her introduction to *Sickert: Paintings, Drawings, and Prints of Walter Richard Sickert, 1860–1942,* exh. cat., Arts Council (London, 1977), 21. Also see Baron on the dating of *The Studio* in Baron and Shone, eds., *Sickert,* 182. I am indebted to comments on the spatial setting by these authors.

52. The works based on photographs Sickert produced later in his career make sense in the context of this argument. See *Late Sickert;* Baron and Shone, eds., *Sickert;* and David Peters Corbett, *Walter Sickert* (London, 2001), for discussion of these paintings.

53. See Michel de Certeau, *The Practice of Everyday Life* (Berkeley and Los Angeles, 1984). On de Certeau and the issues he raises for this discussion, see Victor Burgin, "Chance Encounters: *Flâneur* and *Detraquée* in Breton's *Nadja,*" *New Formations* 11 (1990).

54. See Jonathan Raban, *Soft City* (London, 1974), for a discussion of the psychic mechanisms provoked by life in the modern city.

55. James Donald, "The City, the Cinema, Modern Spaces," in *Visual Culture,* ed. Chris Jenks (London, 1995), 77. I am generally indebted to this formulation of the issues.

56. On this, see Susan Buck-Morss, *The Dialectics of Seeing: Walter Benjamin and the Arcades Project* (Cambridge, Mass., 1991), and see also Elizabeth Wilson, *Hallucinations: Life in the Post-Modern City* (London, 1988).

57. See, for instance, James Donald, "Metropolis: The City as Text," in *Social and Cultural Forms of Modernity,* ed. Robert Bocock and Kenneth Thompson (Cambridge, 1992), as well as his "The City, the Cinema," cited above.

58. I am using the term "Camden Town period" here to describe a more restricted period running from 1905 to 1910. Although I deal in detail almost exclusively with Sickert's painting, his drawing and graphic work of the time was entirely of a piece with the concerns I discuss.

59. Anna Gruetzner Robins, *Walter Sickert, Drawings, Theory, and Practice: Word and Image* (Aldershot, U.K., 1996), 33.

60. Ibid.

61. *Sickert: The Complete Writings,* ed. Robins, 243.

62. Ibid., 233.

63. Ibid., 229.

64. Ibid., 247–48.

65. See the discussion of the representation of "the 'real'" in Sickert's drawings in Robins, *Walter Sickert, Drawings;* 10 and 15 are particularly relevant.

66. According to Richard Shone, the Whiteley's sign in *Queens Road Station* refers to a large department store in Queensway, just outside the station. Shone reports that the founder, William Whiteley, was "fatally shot" in 1907 by "a man claiming to be his bastard son" and comments on the connections this establishes between the painting and the Camden Town Murder series. See Baron and Shone, eds., *Sickert,* 258.

67. T. S. Eliot's Prufrock measures out his life with "coffee spoons." There is an interest in the marginal and dingy in English modernism that goes well beyond Sickert. See *The Complete Poems and Plays of T. S. Eliot* (London, 1969), 14.

68. For instance, in *Off to the Pub* (c. 1912, Tate Britain, London; Baron, cat. 296) and the various versions of *Ennui* (Baron, cat. 313).

69. Cited in Baron and Shone, eds., *Sickert,* 9.

70. Consider Sickert's cultivation of models like "Hubby," who appears in *Off to the Pub* and

other contemporary works as the type of the dissolute working man.

71. See Sickert's article, "The Naked and the Nude," *The New Age,* 21 July 1910 (reprinted in *Sickert: The Complete Writings,* ed. Robins, 260–64), for an explicit repudiation of the academic conventions of representing the nude in the service of an argument for a greater realism.

72. Cited in Baron and Shone, eds., *Sickert,* 158.

73. Other examples of music-hall paintings from this period that confirm Sickert's interest in the audience include *The Old Middlesex* (c. 1906–7, The Beaverbrook Art Gallery, Fredericton, New Brunswick; Baron, cat. 231); *The Eldorado* (c. 1906, Barber Institute of Fine Arts, University of Birmingham; Baron, cat. 235); and *The New Bedford* (1908–9, private collection; Baron, cat. 238).

74. See Prettejohn, *Rossetti and His Circle,* for an analysis to which I am indebted; see also my discussion in Chapter 1.

75. *Observer,* 12 May 1912. According to Baron, "Fred Brown wrote to Sickert that the sordid nature of his pictures since the Camden Town Murder series made it impossible for there to be any friendship between them" (*Sickert,* 109).

76. *The Star,* 10 December 1912.

77. For an account of Sickert's interest in crime, see Stella Tillyard, "The End of Victorian Art: W. R. Sickert and the Defence of Illustrative Painting," in *Towards a Modern Art World,* ed. B. Allen. On the newspaper reporting of the case and for an interpretation of the series, see Tickner, *Modern Life and Modern Subjects.* See also the account in Baron and Shone, eds., *Sickert,* 206.

78. For an identification of *Summer Afternoon,* or, *What Shall We Do for the Rent?* (fig. 70) as one of these paintings, see Baron, *Sickert,* 349, cat. 275.

79. *The Observer,* 18 June 1911.

80. Robins has shown conclusively what has been known in general terms for a long time (i.e., Baron, *Sickert,* 110)—that is, that Sickert had not originated these works as representations of the murder. See *Walter Sickert, Drawings,* 39–41. She concludes, "viewed as part of a complicated process of interchangeable titles orchestrated by Sickert, they destabilise any one single meaning in these drawings and paintings of a clothed man and a nude woman" (41). This supports my own conclusion that beneath the apparent control of these works there is a pervasive instability and a deference before the threatening world.

81. See Robins's very interesting discussion of Sickert's choice of models whose bodies were "large" or "misshapen" and his deliberate enhancement of these characteristics in his representations of them (*Walter Sickert, Drawings,* 33–34).

82. For the complex Victorian history of the nude, see A. Smith, *The Victorian Nude.*

83. See Richard Shone, "Walter Sickert, the Dispassionate Observer," in *Sickert,* ed. Baron and Shone, 1–11.

84. On this topic, see the extended analysis and discussion of Sickert's paint surface in Baron, *Sickert.* Baron argues that "the entire development of Sickert's handling between 1907 and 1909 was, in a sense, a paradoxical interlude in the context of his technical representation" (116). Whereas the dominant interest over his career was in economy of application, during this period, he experimented with a method derived from NEAC practice involving "a clear and solid mosaic of thick paint" (ibid.). Baron sees the Mornington Crescent nudes as early examples of this experimentation, when Sickert held the advantages and disadvantages of the technique in successful balance (see 103). By the time of *L'Affaire de Camden Town* (fig. 71) and *Dawn, Camden Town* (fig. 65), the handling had evolved into a "brutal" and "exaggerated" crudity of application, a violence that Baron connects to the subject matter (111).

85. Cited in Baron and Shone, eds., *Sickert,* 198.

86. *Sunday Times,* 18 June 1911.

87. *Sickert: The Complete Writings,* ed. Robins, 264.

88. Ibid., 355.

89. Walter Sickert, *A Free House! Or, the Artist as Craftsman, Being the Writings of Walter Richard Sickert,* ed. Osbert Sitwell (London, 1947), xxxviii.

90. Given that Sickert had already become fascinated by the case as a schoolboy in the 1880s. See Emmons, *Life and Opinions,* 21.

91. See *Sickert: Paintings,* 306.

92. Sickert, *A Free House!,* xxxix.

93. Ibid.

94. Ibid., xxxix–xl.

95. Ibid., xl.

96. See Robins, *Walter Sickert, Drawings,* 39–40, for a recent review and discussion of this issue.

97. A characteristic noted and sustained by his biographers and historians. Emmons promotes the idea of Sickert as all performance and no essence: "It was impossible to tell what he would say next, wear next, or paint next. Sickert himself has always been critical of the habit of labelling artists by groups or theories. 'Let us leave the labels,' he says, 'to those who have little else wherewith to cover their nakedness.' Least of any can he himself be docketed and pigeon-holed under this heading or that. Label him to Calcutta and he will turn up at Pekin. Like a well-traveled suit-case he has had many pretty stamps affixed to him: pupil of Whistler, Impressionist, Neo-Realist, Academician, etc. Not one of them has stuck. Either the glue is not good enough or he is too slippery to be held. Like a boy after a butterfly, just when you have thrown your cap and think you have him pinned, he is away again, coquetting with a flower in your neighbour's garden" (*Life and Opinions,* 4). Emmons's answer to Sickert's possession of "no fixed point, no common denominator, that we can take hold of and say 'this is the real man'" is "his work" (ibid.). Sickert's impenetrability matches that of his nude subjects in the Camden Town Murder series.

98. Baron, *Sickert,* 170.

99. Robins has interpreted Sickert as a *flâneur* in "The London Impressionists at the Goupil Gallery," but she is content to remain at the level of interpretation allowed, to date, by the figure of the *flâneur.* She does not question it.

100. See Sally Munt, "The Lesbian Flâneur," in *Mapping Desire,* ed. David Bell and Gill Valentine (London, 1995); 117, Nancy Duncan, ed., *Body Space: Destabilizing Geographies of Gender and Sexuality* (London, 1996); and the first two sections of Jon Bird, Barry Curtis, Tim Putnam, George Robertson, and Lisa Tickner, eds., *Mapping the Futures: Local Cultures, Global Change* (London, 1993).

101. On the general question of the meanings of the female nude for early-twentieth-century painting, see Carol Duncan, "Virility and Male Domination in Early Twentieth-Century Vanguard Art," in *Feminism and Art History,* ed. Norma Broude and Mary D. Garrard (New York, 1982), 293–313. On the nude more generally, see Lynda Nead, *The Female Nude: Art, Obscenity, and Sexuality* (London, 1992); on the period immediately before Sickert was working, see A. Smith, *The Victorian Nude.*

102. Judith R. Walkowitz, *City of Dreadful Night: Narratives of Sexual Danger in Late Victorian London* (Chicago, 1992), 11.

103. Ibid. On this topic, see also Jenny Ryan, "Women, Modernity, and the City," *Theory, Culture, and Society* 11 (1994): 35–63.

104. Walkowitz, *City of Dreadful Night,* 80.

105. See the full discussion of the positioning of the figure and the use of the framing window in Baron, *Sickert,* 104. The model was the daughter of Sickert's frame maker (103).

106. Cited in Baron and Shone, eds., *Sickert,* 198, where the location is also identified.

107. For a compelling reading of this trope in modernist painting, see Meyer Shapiro, "The Social Bases of Art," reprinted in *Art in Theory,* ed. Harrison and Wood, 506–10.

Chapter 5

1. Walter Sickert, "A Perfect Modern," *The New Age* (9 April 1914), in *Sickert: The Complete Writings,* ed. Robins, 353. Subsequent references to this work will appear parenthetically in the text. Gore, who was president of the Camden Town Group, a founding member of the London Group, and a member of the committee of the Allied Artists' Association, died of pneumonia at the age of 36 on 27 March 1914.

2. According to Baron, "at least a dozen such paintings are known, besides about another ten of the gardens painted from an outdoor vantage spot" (*Perfect Moderns,* 118).

3. "Manifesto—I," *Blast* 1 (1914): 18–19.

4. Sickert's exploration of the modernity of this past was a lifelong occupation. The series of paintings known as "English Echoes" made in the 1930s rework Victorian periodical illustrations in a modernist visual language. The tone of the images remains difficult to read with any confidence. See *Late Sickert* and Corbett, *Walter Sickert,* chapter 4.

5. See W. C. Wees, *Vorticism and the English Avant-Garde* (Manchester, 1972); Richard Cork, *Vorticism and Abstract Art in the First Machine Age,* 2 vols. (London, 1976); and Anna Gruetzner Robins, *Modern Art in Britain, 1910–1914,* exh. cat., Barbican Art Gallery (London, 1997). A study that usefully discusses Camden Town and Bloomsbury together is Simon Watney, *English Post-Impressionism* (London, 1980).

6. Peter Stansky, *On or About December 1910: Early Bloomsbury and Its Intimate World* (Cambridge, Mass., 1996), 176. Stansky is referring to the first exhibition in 1910.

7. See Rosalind Krauss, *The Originality of the Avant-Garde and Other Modernist Myths* (Cambridge, Mass., 1984).

8. See Charles Harrison, *English Art and Modernism, 1900–1939* (London, 1981), especially chapter 3, and Robins, *Modern Art in Britain.*

9. Wyndham Lewis, "The Vorticists" (1956), reprinted in *Wyndham Lewis on Art: Collected Writings, 1913–1956,* ed. Walter Michel and C. J. Fox (London, 1969), 456; Lewis, "Creatures of Habit and Creatures of Change," *The Calendar of Modern Letters* 3 (1926): 28.

10. Wyndham Lewis, "Our Vortex," *Blast* 1 (1914): 147.

11. See Baron, *Perfect Moderns,* and Malcolm Easton, "'Camden Town' into 'London': Some Intimate Glimpses of the Transition and Its Artists, 1911–1914," in *Art in Britain, 1890–1914,* exh. cat., University of Hull (Hull, U.K., 1967).

12. Charles Ginner, "The Camden Town Group," *The Studio* 130 (1945): 132.

13. Ibid. As evidence of internal dissent, Baron cites the draft of a letter from Pissarro to Gore (as president of the Group) in which Pissarro protests the "rubbish" of Lewis's exhibits at the first Group show in 1911. See *Perfect Moderns,* 48.

14. Cited in Paul Edwards, *Wyndham Lewis: Painter and Writer* (New Haven, Conn., 2000), 53. Lewis made the comment in 1950.

15. This drawing is conventionally taken to be one of those Lewis exhibited, but the evidence, although persuasive, is only circumstantial. See Cork, *Vorticism and Abstract Art,* 1:14.

16. Lewis to T. Sturge Moore [September 1911], "The Sturge Moore Letters," ed. Victor M. Cassidy, *Lewisletter* 7 (1977): 15–16.

17. Cork, *Vorticism and Abstract Art,* 1:15.

18. Charles Harrison, *English Art and Modernism,* 18.

19. *The Times,* 11 December 1911; Frank Rutter, *Sunday Times,* 3 December 1911.

20. Cork, *Vorticism and Abstract Art,* 1:83. See also Andrew Wilson, "Our Little Gang," in *Blast: Vorticism, 1914–1918,* ed. Paul Edwards (London, 2000).

21. Cited in Easton, "'Camden Town' into 'London,'" 67. I rely on Easton for my discussion of the internal politics of the group.

22. "The Cubist Room," foreword to "Exhibition of the Work of English Post-Impressionists, Cubists, and Others" (Public Art Galleries, Brighton, December 1913–January 1914), reprinted in Walter Michel, *Wyndham Lewis: Paintings and Drawings* (London, 1971), 431.

23. See Emmons, *Life and Opinions,* 147, and Cork, *Vorticism and Abstract Art,* 1:135–36.

24. In a letter to Nan Hudson dated before March 1914. Cited in Richard Cork, *Vorticism and Its Allies,* exh. cat., Hayward Gallery (London, 1974), 13.

25. On the London Group, see Denys J. Wilcox, *The London Group, 1913–1939: The Artists and Their Works* (Aldershot, U.K., 1995).

26. See Walter Sickert, "Epstein and His Critics or Nietzsche and His Friends" and "On Swiftness," *The New Age* 14 (1914), reprinted in *Sickert: The Complete Writings,* ed. Robins, 346–49. Lewis's reply is "Modern Art," *The New Age* 14 (1914): 703.

27. Wyndham Lewis, "History of the Largest Independent Society in England," *Blast* 2 (1915): 80. Subsequent references to this work will appear parenthetically in the text.

28. There are closer intellectual links than this suggests. In "On Swiftness," Sickert offers a definition of art: *"Art may be said to be the individual quality of failure, or the individual co-efficient of error of each highly skilled and cultivated craftsman in his effort to attain to the expression of form."* He goes on to state that "art is a sport" (*Sickert: The Complete Writings*, ed. Robins, 346). In his "Essay on the Objective of Plastic Art in Our Time," which was published in his periodical *The Tyro* 2 (1922), Lewis makes the same comparison. Art for Lewis is "cut out of a similar substance" to sport (25). Moreover, art (like sport) is said to arise from "a feeling of gain and significance residing in [our] human fallibility" (26). Lewis's use of these ideas is much more developed than Sickert's brief throwaway remarks, but I suggest that Sickert's conversation may be behind Lewis's later elaboration. It is not surprising, in view of this, that in a review of *The Tyro* 2, Sickert praised the "Objective of Plastic Art" essay and quoted a passage from it that makes the points I have noted, with the comment, "has anything more genial and profound been said on art than the following?" See Sickert's untitled review in *The Burlington Magazine* 41 (1922): 200.

29. Jeffrey Meyers, *The Enemy: A Biography of Wyndham Lewis* (London, 1980), 39.

30. Setting an attendance record for the gallery, according to Wees, *Vorticism*, 27.

31. Charles Ginner, "Harold Gilman" (1919), cited in Charles Harrison, *English Art and Modernism*, 35.

32. Charles Harrison, *English Art and Modernism*, 50–51.

33. For a discussion of the complicated history of this painting, see Cork, *Vorticism and Abstract Art*, 1:37–42, and Michel, *Wyndham Lewis*, 57–58, 429, as well as Tickner, *Modern Life and Modern Subjects*, chapter 3. See also the related ink, wash, and gouache *Kermesse* (1912, Yale Center for British Art, New Haven, Conn.).

34. Ramiro de Maetzu, "Expressionism," *The New Age* 14 (1914): 122.

35. Clive Bell, *Art* (London, 1914), 8. "Significant Form" is Bell's formulation rather than Fry's, but it seems clear that Bell is popularizing—and to some extent vulgarizing—Fry's thought here. Fry was already thinking of form as separable from content as early as 1909. See Fry's "Essay in Aesthetics" (1909), reprinted in *Art in Theory*, ed. Harrison and Wood. On this topic, see also Frances Spalding, *Roger Fry: Art and Life* (London, 1980), 163–65, and Charles Harrison, *English Art and Modernism*, 59–60.

36. Roger Fry, "The Allied Artists at the Albert Hall," *The Nation* 11 (1912): 583.

37. Clive Bell [C. B., pseud.], "The London Salon at the Albert Hall," *The Athenaeum* 4422 (1912): 98.

38. Clive Bell, "The English Group," introduction to *The Second Post-Impressionist Exhibition, British, French, and Russian Artists*, exh. cat., Grafton Galleries (London, 1912), 9.

39. Ibid.

40. Fry praised Lewis's painting *Group* (lost) when it was shown at the AAA in 1913 as "Michaelangelesque in [the] sombre and tragic intensity" of its mood; see Roger Fry, "The Allied Artists," *The Nation* 13 (1913): 677. At about this time, Bell bought "a big canvas" from Lewis for £50, and Lewis noted in 1917 that Fry owned "drawings and paintings" of his. See Wees, *Vorticism*, 64, and Cork, *Vorticism and Abstract Art*, 1:42.

41. Roger Fry to Charles Vildrac, 1 April 1912, in *The Letters of Roger Fry*, ed. Denys Sutton (London, 1972), 1:356; Gertrude Stein, *The Autobiography of Alice B. Toklas* (New York, 1933), 122–23. Fry and Lewis visited Stein together in 1913.

42. The so-called rumpus has been extensively discussed. See Quentin Bell and Stephen Chaplin, "The Ideal Home Rumpus," *Apollo* 80 (1964): 284–91; Virginia Woolf, *Roger Fry: A Biography* (London, 1940), 191–94; John Rothenstein, *Modern English Painters* (London, 1984), 1:216–18; Michel, *Wyndham Lewis*, 64–70; Wees, *Vorticism*, 63–67; Cork, *Vorticism and Abstract Art*, 1:85–101; Jeffrey Meyers, *The Enemy*, 46–53; Paul O'Keeffe, *Some Sort of Genius: A Life of Wyndham Lewis* (London, 2000), 130–37; Judith Collins, *The Omega Workshops* (London, 1983), 54–61. See also S. P. Rosenblum, ed., *The Bloomsbury Group: A Collection of Memoirs, Commentary, and Criticism* (London, 1975), which usefully reprints an exchange of views that followed

Bell and Chaplin's original article. The Rebel Art Centre opened in March 1914.

43. Winifred Gill to Duncan Grant, cited in Cork, *Vorticism and Abstract Art,* 1:98.

44. Wyndham Lewis, "Round Robin," in *The Letters of Wyndham Lewis,* ed. W. K. Rose (London, 1963), 49. The "Round Robin" was circulated publicly by Lewis after the Omega incident. For the masculinism of the Vorticists and their contemporaries, see Lisa Tickner, "Men's Work? Masculinity and Modernism," in *Visual Culture: Images and Interpretations,* ed. Norman Bryson, Michael Ann Holly, and Keith Moxey (Hanover, N.H., 1994), 63–64.

45. *Letters of Wyndham Lewis,* ed. Rose, 49.

46. Levenson, *A Genealogy of Modernism,* 138.

47. The catalogue of *The Art of Bloomsbury* exhibition held at the Tate Gallery in 1999 points out that Bloomsbury's connections back into the Victorian past operated at the aesthetic and intellectual levels as well as the merely familial. Richard Shone describes Grant's enthusiasm for Burne-Jones, and Richard Morphet notes the interest Fry and others took in the art of Watts, at least before 1914. See Richard Shone, ed., *The Art of Bloomsbury: Roger Fry, Vanessa Bell, and Duncan Grant,* exh. cat., Tate Gallery (London, 1999). See also Prettejohn, "Out of the Nineteenth Century."

48. Fry, "An Essay in Aesthetics," 79. Subsequent references to this work will appear parenthetically in the text.

49. Prettejohn, "Out of the Nineteenth Century," 38. Also in *Art Made Modern,* ed. Green, see Caroline Elam's "Roger Fry and Early Italian Painting."

50. Roger Fry, review of George Gronau's *Titian, The Athenaeum* 4011, no. 7 (1904): 355, cited in Prettejohn, "Out of the Nineteenth Century," 41.

51. Vanessa Bell commented on this picture, "I mean one isn't supposed nowadays to paint what one thinks beautiful"—a statement that has been taken as evidence of "a mocking reference to Clive Bell's *Art,*" one arguing that "although she agreed with much of its aesthetic argument, she was by no means a slave to its theoretical tenets." See Shone, ed., *The Art of Bloomsbury,* 119.

52. Ibid., 90. The painting is *Studland Beach* (fig. 78).

53. See Tickner, *Modern Life and Modern Subjects,* chapter 4.

54. For a vigorous (if not entirely convincing) defense of Bloomsbury as radical social practice, see Christopher Reed, ed., *A Roger Fry Reader* (Chicago, 1996).

55. Richard Shone, "The Artists of Bloomsbury: Roger Fry, Vanessa Bell, and Duncan Grant," in *The Art of Bloomsbury,* ed. Shone, 17.

56. See Bürger, *Theory of the Avant-Garde.*

57. Lewis's politics have been the subject of extensive commentary, not all of it well informed. See, for recent and scholarly assessments, Edwards, *Wyndham Lewis,* and O'Keeffe, *Some Sort of Genius.*

58. See Jane Farrington, ed., *Wyndham Lewis,* exh. cat., Manchester City Art Galleries (London, 1980), cat. 38, 68.

59. "Manifesto—II," *Blast* 1 (1914): 34, 39–40.

60. "Manifesto—I," 23.

61. Gaudier-Brzeska reviewed the painting in *The Egoist* for 15 June 1914 and described it as "a composition of cool tones." Cited in Cork, *Vorticism and Its Allies,* 83.

62. Cork provides a good discussion of this aspect of Wadsworth's Vorticist work, and I am indebted to it. See *Vorticism and Abstract Art,* 2:369–71.

63. "Manifesto—II," 40.

64. See David Wragg, "Wyndham Lewis's Vorticism and the Aesthetics of Closure," in *Theorizing Modernism: Essays in Critical Theory,* ed. Steve Giles (London, 1993).

65. "Decorative" here recalls Sickert's use of the word in his introduction to the London Impressionists catalogue discussed in Chapter 4. See Sickert, "Introduction to the 'London Impressionists,'" 59.

66. Wyndham Lewis, "The London Group 1915 (March)," *Blast* 2 (1915): 79.

67. Wyndham Lewis, "A Review of Contemporary Art," *Blast* 2 (1915): 46.

68. In a slightly later work, *The Caliph's Design,* the "Fitzroy tinkerers and tasters" of the Omega are criticized for indulging in a "colour-matching, match-box-making, dressmaking,

chair-painting game," which is the polar opposite of "the credence or intensity of creative art." See Wyndham Lewis, *The Caliph's Design: Architects! Where Is Your Vortex?* (London, 1919), 64, 63–64.

69. Lewis, "Round Robin," 49.

70. On gender and Vorticism, see Jane Beckett, "(Is)land Narratives: Englishness, Visuality, and Vanguard Culture, 1914–18," in *English Art, 1860–1914,* ed. Corbett and Perry, 195–212; Jane Beckett and Deborah Cherry, "Modern Women, Modern Spaces: Women, Metropolitan Culture, and Vorticism," in *Women Artists and Modernism,* ed. Katy Deepwell (Manchester, 1998), 36–54; and Beckett and Cherry, "Reconceptualizing Vorticism: Women, Modernity, Modernism," in *Blast: Vorticism, 1914–1918,* ed. Edwards, 59–72.

71. Tickner, "Men's Work?" 63–64.

72. A. S. Byatt, "The Chinese Lobster," in *The Matisse Stories* (London, 1993), 66.

73. Wyndham Lewis, "Frederick Spencer Gore," *Blast* 1 (1914): 150.

74. Ysanne Holt, "An Ideal Modernity: Spencer Gore at Letchworth," in *The Geographies of Englishness: Landscape and the National Past in English Art, 1880–1940,* ed. David Peters Corbett, Ysanne Holt, and Fiona Russell (New Haven, Conn., 2002).

75. Frank Rutter, "F. Spencer Gore," *Sunday Times,* 5 April 1914. This is Rutter's obituary of Gore.

76. Lewis, "Frederick Spencer Gore," 150.

77. Sickert, "Introduction to the 'London Impressionists,'" 60.

78. Baron notes this interpretation in *Perfect Moderns,* 151.

79. *Pall Mall Gazette,* 12 December 1912.

80. Cork draws attention to the fact that *Blackpool* "was quite possibly inspired by the view to be seen from the top of Blackpool tower"—that is, it forms a view associated with the perpendicular sight lines of *A Short Flight* and other works. See *Vorticism and Abstract Art,* 2:372.

81. Lewis, "The London Group 1915 (March)," 77.

82. Lewis, "Frederick Spencer Gore," 150.

83. See Holt, "An Ideal Modernity," and, on Richmond, *Spencer Gore in Richmond,* exh. cat., Museum of Richmond (Richmond, U.K., 1996).

84. *Letters of Wyndham Lewis,* ed. Rose, 293.

85. I am thinking here of paintings like *Cambrian Road, Richmond* (1913–14, Yale Center for British Art, New Haven, Conn.) or *Nearing Euston Station* (fig. 90).

86. Robins speaks of Gore in this sense as able to cross the artistic "party lines with ease" (*Modern Art in Britain,* 149).

87. Although the title may have been conferred by Wadsworth (see Farrington, ed., *Wyndham Lewis,* cat. 41, 70), the stacked bays of skyscraper architecture and the bird's-eye viewing of urban mapping are unmistakable.

88. Periodization has received more attention from literary scholars and from historians. See, for instance, David Perkins, *Is Literary History Possible?* (Baltimore, 1992), and Ludmilla Jordanova, *History in Practice* (London, 2000), chapter 5.

89. See entries in Robert S. Nelson and Richard Shiff, eds., *Critical Terms for Art History* (Chicago, 1996).

90. F. R. Ankersmit, "Historiography and Postmodernism," in *The Postmodern History Reader,* ed. Keith Jenkins (London, 1997), 278.

91. For a pithy discussion of this issue, see Solkin, "The British and the Modern."

92. Virginia Woolf, cited in Stansky, *On or About December 1910,* 2.

93. Ibid., 1.

94. Ibid., 2, 251.

95. Ibid., 213.

96. Cited in ibid., 219.

97. Delaney, "Ricketts, Shannon, and Their Circle," 45.

98. Stansky, *On or About December 1910,* 219.

99. Ricketts, *Pages on Art,* 149–50, cited in Stansky, *On or About December 1910,* 219.

100. Ricketts, *Pages on Art,* 47.

101. See Bürger, *Theory of the Avant-Garde,* 47–54. Significantly, Bürger's historical context for this—the opening of the gap between art and life as the bourgeois world order takes hold and supersedes older, "sacral" arrangements—

echoes Ricketts's diagnosis in the passage I quote.

102. Stansky, *On or About December 1910,* 218.

103. Laurence Binyon, *The Art of Botticelli: An Essay in Pictorial Criticism* (London, 1913), 17.

104. Hence, at least in part, Binyon's fascination with the art of the Far East. See Laurence Binyon, *The Flight of the Dragon: An Essay on the Theory and Practice of Art in China and Japan* (London, 1911).

105. Binyon, *Botticelli,* 15–16.

106. Ibid., 14.

107. Ibid., 16, 17. Part I of Binyon's book, from which these quotations come, is called "Botticelli's Significance for Modern Art."

108. Stansky, *On or About December 1910,* 218, 219

109. Wilde, "The Decay of Lying," 53.

110. Wyndham Lewis, *Blasting and Bombardiering* (London, 1937), 278–79.

111. For the British Museum Group, see note 27 to the introduction to this volume.

112. See Corbett, *The Modernity of English Art.*

113. Wyndham Lewis, "Dean Swift with a Brush: The Tyroist Explains His Art," *Daily Express,* 11 April 1921.

114. For examples of readings that bring some of these figures into convergence with modernism, see Prettejohn, *The Art of the Pre-Raphaelites,* and Robins, *Walter Sickert, Drawings.*

115. Schwartz, *The Matrix of Modernism,* 8.

116. Recently, Barringer and Prettejohn have made a very clear case for new histories of academic artists like Leighton at the latter end of the nineteenth century that complicate the established modernist readings in ways similar to those I have suggested. See their introduction to *Frederic Leighton,* ed. Barringer and Prettejohn.

117. See Corbett, *The Modernity of English Art.*

Bibliography

The Age of Rossetti, Burne-Jones, and Watts: Symbolism in Britain, 1860–1910. Exh. cat., Tate Gallery. London, 1997.

Allen, Brian, ed. *Towards a Modern Art World*. New Haven, Conn., 1995.

Allen, Virginia M. "'One Strangling Golden Hair': Dante Gabriel Rossetti's *Lady Lilith*." *The Art Bulletin* 66 (June 1984).

Alston, Rowland. *The Mind and Work of G. F. Watts, OM, RA: With Introduction and Special Reference to the Watts Gallery, Compton, Guildford*. London, 1929.

Anderson, Gail-Nina, and Joanne Wright. *Heaven on Earth: The Religion of Beauty in Late Victorian Art*. Exh. cat., University of Nottingham. Nottingham, U.K., 1994.

Anderson, Ronald. *The Gentle Art of Making Enemies: "An Extraordinary Practical Lot . . . a Great Literary Curiosity."* Pamphlet, Michael Parkin Gallery. London, 1990.

Anderson, Ronald, and Anne Koval. *James McNeill Whistler: Beyond the Myth*. London, 1994.

Ankersmit, F. R. "Historiography and Postmodernism." In *The Postmodern History Reader*, ed. Keith Jenkins. London, 1997.

Archambault, Michele. "The Grosvenor Gallery, 1877–1890." Ph.D. diss., Courtauld Institute of Art, 1978.

Armstrong, Isobel. "Transparency: Towards a Poetics of Glass in the Nineteenth Century." In *Cultural Babbage: Technology, Time, and Invention*, ed. Francis Spufford and Jenny Uglow. London, 1996.

Art in Britain, 1890–1914. Exh. cat., University of Hull. Hull, U.K., 1967.

The Art Journal 46, no. 3 (1987).

Asleson, Robyn. "Classic into Modern: The Inspiration of Antiquity in English Painting, 1864–1918." Ph.D. diss., Yale University, 1993.

———. *Albert Moore*. London, 2000.

Aslin, Elizabeth. *The Aesthetic Movement: Theory and Practice*. London, 1972.

Atkinson, J. B. "Exhibitions of the Year." *Fine Arts Quarterly Review*, n.s., 1 (October 1866).

Bacher, Otto H. *With Whistler in Venice*. New York, 1908.

Bagnold, Enid. *Autobiography*. London, 1969.

Bailey, Peter. *Leisure and Class in Victorian England: Rational Recreation and the Contest for Control, 1830–1885*. London, 1978.

———, ed. *Music Hall: The Business of Pleasure*. Milton Keynes, U.K., 1986.

Bal, Mieke. *Reading "Rembrandt": Beyond the Word-Image Opposition*. Cambridge, 1991.

———. "What Do We Want Pictures to Be?" *Critical Inquiry* 22 (1996).

Bal, Mieke, and Norman Bryson. "Semiotics and Art History." *Art Bulletin* 73, no. 2 (1991).

Balakian, Anna, ed. *The Symbolist Movement in the Literature of European Languages*. Budapest, 1984.

Baldry, A. L. *Albert Moore: His Life and Works*. London, 1894.

———. "Whistler and Albert Moore." *Pall Mall Budget* 1323 (1 February 1894).

———. "Albert Moore: An Appreciation." *The Art Journal* 65 (February 1903).

Baron, Wendy. "Sickert's Links with French Painting." *Apollo* (March 1970).

———. *Walter Sickert*. London, 1973.

———. *Perfect Moderns: A History of the Camden Town Group*. Aldershot, U.K., 2000.

Baron, Wendy, and Richard Shone, eds. *Sickert*. Exh. cat., Royal Academy of Arts. New Haven, Conn., 1992.

Barringer, Tim. *The Pre-Raphaelites: Reading the Image.* London, 1988.
Barringer, Tim, and Elizabeth Prettejohn, eds. *Frederic Leighton: Antiquity, Renaissance, Modernity.* New Haven, Conn., 1999.
Barrington, Mrs. Russell. *G. F. Watts, Reminiscences.* London, 1905.
———. *The Life, Letters, and Work of Frederic Leighton.* 2 vols. London, 1906.
Baudelaire, Charles. *The Painter of Modern Life and Other Essays.* Translated by Jonathan Mayne. Oxford, 1964.
Baxandall, Michael. *Painting and Experience in Fifteenth-Century Italy: A Primer in the Social History of Pictorial Style.* Oxford, 1972.
———. *Patterns of Intention: On the Historical Explanation of Pictures.* New Haven, Conn., 1985.
Bayes, Walter. *The Landscapes of G. F. Watts.* London, 1907.
Becker, Edwin, et al., eds. *Sir Lawrence Alma-Tadema.* Exh. cat., Van Gogh Museum. Amsterdam, [1996].
Beckett, Jane, and Deborah Cherry. "Modern Women, Modern Spaces: Women, Metropolitan Culture, and Vorticism." In *Women Artists and Modernism,* ed. Katy Deepwell. Manchester, 1998.
———. "Reconceptualizing Vorticism: Women, Modernity, Modernism." In *Blast: Vorticism, 1914–1918,* ed. Paul Edwards. London, 2000.
Beer, Gillian. *Darwin's Plots: Evolutionary Narrative in Darwin, George Eliot, and Nineteenth-Century Fiction.* London, 1983.
———. "Darwin and the Growth of Language Theory." In *Nature Transfigured: Science and Literature, 1700–1900,* ed. John Christie and Sally Shuttleworth. Manchester, 1989.
———. "Authentic Tidings of Invisible Things." In *Vision in Context: Historical and Contemporary Perspectives on Sight,* ed. Teresa Brennan and Martin Jay. New York, 1996.
———. *Open Fields: Science in Cultural Encounter.* Oxford, 1996.
Bell, Clive. "The English Group." Introduction to *The Second Post-Impressionist Exhibition, British, French, and Russian Artists.* Exh. cat., Grafton Galleries, October 1912–January 1913. London, 1912.
——— [C. B., pseud.]. "The London Salon at the Albert Hall." *The Athenaeum* 4422 (1912).
———. *Art.* London, 1914.
Bell, Ian F. A. *Critic as Scientist: The Modernist Poetics of Ezra Pound.* London, 1981.
Bell, Quentin, and Stephen Chaplin. "The Ideal Home Rumpus." *Apollo* 80 (1964).
Bendix, Deanna Marohn. *Diabolical Designs: Paintings, Interiors, and Exhibitions of James McNeill Whistler.* Washington, D.C., 1995.
Bentley, D. M. R. "Rossetti's 'Hand and Soul.'" *English Studies in Canada* 3 (Winter 1977).
Berman, Russell A. *Modern Culture and Critical Theory: Art, Politics, and the Legacy of the Frankfurt School.* Madison, Wisc., 1989.
Bernstein, J. M. *The Fate of Art: Aesthetic Alienation from Kant to Derrida and Adorno.* Cambridge, 1992.
Binyon, Laurence. *The Flight of the Dragon: An Essay on the Theory and Practice of Art in China and Japan.* London, 1911.
———. *The Art of Botticelli: An Essay in Pictorial Criticism.* London, 1913.
Birch, Dinah, ed. *Ruskin and the Dawn of the Modern.* Oxford, 1999.
Bird, Jon, Barry Curtis, Tim Putnam, George Robertson, and Lisa Tickner, eds. *Mapping the Futures: Local Cultures, Global Change.* London, 1993.
Blast 1–2 (1914–15).
Bloom, Harold. *The Anxiety of Influence.* New York, 1973.
Blunt, Wilfred. *England's Michelangelo: A Biography of George Frederic Watts, OM, RA.* London, 1975.
Bois, Yves-Alain. *Painting as Model.* Cambridge, Mass., 1993.
Bradbury, Malcolm, and James McFarlane, eds. *Modernism.* Harmondsworth, U.K., 1976.
Braddon, Mary Elizabeth. *Lady Audley's Secret.* 3 vols. London, 1862.

Brake, Laurel. *Subjugated Knowledges: Journalism, Gender, and Literature in the Nineteenth Century.* London, 1994.
Brake, Laurel, Bill Bell, and David Finkelstein. *Nineteenth-Century Media and the Construction of Identities.* Basingstoke, U.K., 2000.
Bratton, J. S. *Music Hall: Performance and Style.* Milton Keynes, U.K., 1986.
Brilliant, Richard. *Portraiture.* London, 1991.
Bryson, Norman. *Word and Image: French Painting of the Ancien Régime.* Cambridge, 1981.
———. *Vision and Painting: The Logic of the Gaze.* Basingstoke, U.K., 1983.
Bryson, Norman, Michael Ann Holly, and Keith Moxey, eds. *Visual Theory: Painting and Interpretation.* Cambridge, 1988.
Buck-Morss, Susan. *The Dialectics of Seeing: Walter Benjamin and the Arcades Project.* Cambridge, Mass., 1991.
Bullen, J. B. *The Pre-Raphaelite Body: Fear and Desire in Painting, Poetry, and Criticism.* Oxford, 1998.
———, ed. *The Sun Is God: Painting, Literature, and Mythology in the Nineteenth Century.* Oxford, 1989.
Bürger, Peter. *Theory of the Avant-Garde.* Translated by Michael Shaw. Manchester, 1984.
Burgin, Victor. "Chance Encounters: *Flâneur* and *Detraquée* in Breton's *Nadja.*" *New Formations* 11 (1990).
Burne-Jones. Exh. cat., Mappin Art Gallery. Sheffield, U.K., 1971.
Burne-Jones, Georgiana [G. B.-J., pseud.]. *Memorials of Edward Burne-Jones.* 2 vols. London, 1904.
Burne-Jones: The Paintings, Graphic, and Decorative Work of Sir Edward Burne-Jones, 1833–98. Exh. cat., Arts Council. London, 1975.
Burns, Sarah. *Inventing the Modern Artist: Art and Culture in Gilded Age America.* New Haven, Conn., 1996.

Cahan, David, ed. *Hermann von Helmholtz and the Foundations of Nineteenth-Century Science.* Berkeley and Los Angeles, 1993.
Calloway, Stephen. *Charles Ricketts: Subtle and Fantastic Decorator.* London, 1979.
Calloway, Stephen, and Paul Delaney. *Charles Ricketts and Charles Shannon: An Aesthetic Partnership.* Exh. cat., Orleans House Gallery, Twickenham. London, 1979.
Cantor, G. N. *Optics After Newton: Theories of Light in Britain and Ireland, 1704–1840.* Manchester, 1983.
Carlyle, Thomas. *Past and Present.* London, 1843. Reprint, London, 1960.
———. *Complete Works of Thomas Carlyle.* 24 vols. New York, 1901.
Carr, J. Comyns. *Some Eminent Victorians: Personal Recollections in the World of Art and Letters.* London, 1908.
Carter, Robert Brudenell. *Eyesight, Good and Bad: A Treatise on the Exercise and Preservation of Vision.* London, 1880.
Cartwright, Julia. "Sir Edward Burne-Jones, Bart: His Life and Work." *The Art Annual,* "Christmas Number" (1894).
Casteras, Susan. *Images of Victorian Womanhood in English Art.* London, 1987.
Casteras, Susan, and Colleen Denny, eds. *The Grosvenor Gallery: A Palace of Art in Victorian England.* New Haven, Conn., 1996.
Certeau, Michel de. *The Practice of Everyday Life.* Berkeley and Los Angeles, 1984.
Chapman, Ronald. *The Laurel and the Thorn: A Study of G. F. Watts.* London, 1945.
Chesterton, G. K. *G. F. Watts.* 1904. London, 1920.
Church, A. H. *The Chemistry of Paints and Painting.* London, 1890.
Cianci, Giovanni, and Peter Nicholls, eds. *Ruskin and Modernism.* Basingstoke, U.K., 2001.
Clark, Howard. "The British Museum Group, 1885–1920." Master's thesis, University of York, 1998.
Clark, T. J. *The Painting of Modern Life: Paris in the Art of Manet and His Followers.* London, 1984.

———. *Farewell to an Idea: Episodes from a History of Modernism.* New Haven, Conn., 1999.
Collins, Judith. *The Omega Workshops.* London, 1983.
Colvin, Sidney. "English Painters and Painting in 1867." *Fortnightly Review,* n.s., 2 (October 1867).
———. "English Painters of the Present Day." *Portfolio* 1 (1870).
———. "The Grosvenor Gallery." *Fortnightly Review,* n.s., 27 (June 1877).
Corbett, David Peters. *The Modernity of English Art, 1914–30.* Manchester, 1997.
———. "Visuality and Unmediation in Burne-Jones's *Laus Veneris.*" *Art History* 24, no. 1 (2001).
———. *Walter Sickert.* London, 2001.
Corbett, David Peters, and Andrew Thacker. "Raymond Williams and Cultural Formations: Movements and Magazines." *Prose Studies* 16, no. 2 (1993).
Corbett, David Peters, and Lara Perry, eds. *English Art, 1860–1914: Modern Artists and Identity.* Manchester, 2000.
Corbett, David Peters, Ysanne Holt, and Fiona Russell, eds. *The Geographies of Englishness: Landscape and the National Past in English Art, 1880–1940.* New Haven, Conn., 2002.
Cork, Richard. *Vorticism and Its Allies.* Exh. cat., Hayward Gallery. London, 1974.
———. *Vorticism and Abstract Art in the First Machine Age.* 2 vols. London, 1976.
Cowling, Mary. *The Artist as Anthropologist: The Representation of Type and Character in Victorian Art.* Cambridge, 1989.
Crary, Jonathan. *Techniques of the Observer: On Vision and Modernity in the Nineteenth Century.* Cambridge, Mass., 1990.
———. *Suspensions of Perception: Attention, Spectacle, and Modern Culture.* Cambridge, Mass., 1999.
Curtis, Gerard. *Visual Words: Art and the Material Book in Victorian England.* Aldershot, U.K., 2002.

Dakers, Carolyn. *The Holland Park Circle: Artists and Victorian Society.* New Haven, Conn., 1999.
Darracott, Joseph. *The World of Charles Ricketts.* New York, 1980.
Delaney, J. G. P. *Charles Ricketts: A Biography.* Oxford, 1990.
Dellamora, Richard. *Masculine Desire: The Sexual Politics of Victorian Aestheticism.* Chapel Hill, N.C., 1999.
Denis, Rafael Cardoso, and Colin Trodd, eds. *Art and the Academy in the Nineteenth Century.* Manchester, 2000.
Didi-Huberman, Georges. "The Art of Not Describing: Vermeer—The Detail and the Patch." *History of the Human Sciences* 2, no. 2 (1989).
———. *Fra Angelico: Dissemblance and Figuration.* Translated by Jane Marie Todd. Chicago, 1995.
Donald, James. "Metropolis: The City as Text." In *Social and Cultural Forms of Modernity,* ed. Robert Bocock and Kenneth Thompson. Cambridge, 1992.
———. "The City, the Cinema, Modern Spaces." In *Visual Culture,* ed. Chris Jenks. London, 1995.
Dowling, Linda. *Language and Decadence in the Victorian Fin de Siècle.* Princeton, N.J., 1986.
Dumas, F. G., ed. *Illustrated Biographies of Modern Artists.* London, 1882.
Duncan, Carol. "Virility and Male Domination in Early Twentieth-Century Vanguard Art." In *Feminism and Art History,* ed. Norma Broude and Mary D. Garrard. New York, 1982.
Duncan, Nancy, ed. *Body Space: Destabilizing Geographies of Gender and Sexuality.* London, 1996.

Eagleton, Terry. *Criticism and Ideology: A Study of Marxist Literary Theory.* London, 1977.
Eddy, Arthur Jerome. *Recollections and Impressions of James A. McNeill Whistler.* Philadelphia, 1903.
Edwards, Paul. *Wyndham Lewis: Painter and Writer.* New Haven, Conn., 2000.
———, ed. *Blast: Vorticism, 1914–1918.* London, 2000.
Elkins, James. *On Pictures and the Words That Fail Them.* Cambridge, 1998.
———. *Why Are Our Pictures Puzzles?* London, 1999.
———. *What Painting Is: How to Think About Oil Painting, Using the Language of Alchemy.* New York, 2000.
Ellmann, Richard. *Oscar Wilde.* London, 1988.

Emmons, Robert. *The Life and Opinions of Walter Richard Sickert*. London, 1941.
Exposed: The Victorian Nude. Exh. cat., Tate Gallery. London, 2002.

Fagence, Suzanne. "Representations of Music in the Art of Burne-Jones." *Apollo* (May 1998).
Farrington, Jane, ed. *Wyndham Lewis*. Exh. cat., Manchester City Art Galleries. London, 1980.
Fellows, Jay. *The Failing Distance: The Autobiographical Impulse in John Ruskin*. Baltimore, 1975.
Feltes, N. N. *Literary Capital and the Late Victorian Novel*. Madison, Wisc., 1993.
Field, George. *Chromatography; or, a Treatise on Colours and Pigments, and of Their Powers in Painting*. London, 1835.
———. *A Grammar of Colouring: Applied to Decorative Painting and the Arts, new edition revised, enlarged and adapted to the use of the Ornamental Painter and Designer*. Edited by Ellis A. Davidson. London, 1875.
Field, Michael. *Works and Days*. London, 1933.
Fitzgerald, Penelope. *Edward Burne-Jones: A Biography*. London, 1975.
Flint, Kate. "Moral Judgement and the Language of English Art Criticism, 1870–1910." *Oxford Art Journal* 6, no. 2 (1983).
———. *The Victorians and the Visual Imagination*. Cambridge, 2000.
Foster, Hal, ed. *Vision and Visuality*. Seattle, Wash., 1988.
Foucault, Michel. *The Order of Things: An Archaeology of the Human Sciences*. London, 1970.
Fredeman, William E., ed. *The P.R.B. Journal: William Michael Rossetti's Diary of the Pre-Raphaelite Brotherhood, 1849–1853, Together with Other Pre-Raphaelite Documents*. Oxford, 1975.
Freedman, Jonathan. *Professions of Taste: Henry James, British Aestheticism, and Commodity Culture*. Stanford, 1990.
Fried, Michael. *Absorption and Theatricality: Painting and Beholder in the Age of Diderot*. Chicago, 1980.
———. *Courbet's Realism*. Chicago, 1990.
———. *Manet's Modernism, or, the Face of Painting in the 1860s*. Chicago, 1996.
Fry, Roger. "The Allied Artists at the Albert Hall." *The Nation* 11 (1912).
———. "The Allied Artists." *The Nation* 13 (1913).
———. *The Letters of Roger Fry*. Edited by Denys Sutton. 2 vols. London, 1972.

Gage, John. *George Field and His Circle: From Romanticism to the Pre-Raphaelite Brotherhood*. Exh. cat., Fitzwilliam Museum. Cambridge, 1989.
———. *Colour and Culture: Practice and Meaning from Antiquity to Abstraction*. London, 1993.
Gagnier, Regenia. *Idylls of the Marketplace: Oscar Wilde and the Victorian Public*. Aldershot, U.K., 1987.
———. *The Insatiability of Human Wants: Economics and Aesthetics in Market Society*. Chicago, 2000.
George Frederic Watts, 1817–1904. Exh. cat., Arts Council. London, 1954–55.
The Germ: Thoughts Towards Nature in Poetry, Literature, and Art (1850). Facsimile reprint, ed. William Michael Rossetti, London, 1901.
G. F. Watts, 1817–1904: A Nineteenth-Century Phenomenon. Exh. cat., Whitechapel Art Gallery. London, 1974.
G. F. Watts, The Hall of Fame: Portraits of His Famous Contemporaries. Exh. cat., National Portrait Gallery. London, 1975.
Gilbert, Elliot L. "'Tumult of Images': Wilde, Beardsley, and *Salome*." *Victorian Studies* 26, no. 2 (1983).
Giles, Richard. "The House of Life: A Pre-Raphaelite Philosophy?" *Journal of Pre-Raphaelite and Aesthetic Studies* 2 (May 1982).
Gillett, Paula. *Worlds of Art: Painters in Victorian Society*. New Brunswick, N.J., 1990.
Ginner, Charles. "The Camden Town Group." *The Studio* 130 (1945).
Gissing, George. *New Grub Street: A Novel*. London, 1891. Reprint, Oxford, 1993.

———. *Will Warburton: A Romance of Real Life.* London, 1905.

Gordon, Jan B. "The Imaginary Portrait: Fin-de-Siècle Icon." *University of Windsor Review* 5 (Fall 1969).

Green, Christopher, ed. *Art Made Modern: Roger Fry's Vision of Art.* London, 1999.

Grieve, Alastair. *The Art of Dante Gabriel Rossetti: The Pre-Raphaelite Period, 1848–50.* Hingham, U.K., 1973.

———. "Rossetti's Illustrations for Poe." *Apollo* 97 (1973).

Gwynn, Frederick L. *Sturge Moore and the Life of Art.* Lawrence, Kans., 1951.

Hallé, Charles. *Notes from a Painter's Life, Including the Founding of Two Galleries.* London, 1909.

Hamilton, Walter. *The Aesthetic Movement in England.* London, 1882.

Harrison, Charles. *English Art and Modernism, 1900–1939.* London, 1981.

———. "On the Surface of Painting." *Critical Inquiry* 15, no. 2 (1989).

Harrison, Charles, and Paul Wood, eds. *Art in Theory, 1900–1939: An Anthology of Changing Ideas.* Oxford, 1992.

Harrison, Craig, ed. *The Essence of Art: Victorian Advice on the Practice of Painting.* Aldershot, U.K., 1999.

Harrison, Martin, and Bill Waters. *Burne-Jones.* 2d ed. London, 1989.

Hatcher, John. *Laurence Binyon: Poet, Scholar of East and West.* Oxford, 1995.

Heffernan, James W. *Museum of Words: The Poetics of Ekphrasis from Homer to Ashbery.* Chicago, 1993.

Heller, T. C., M. Sosna, and D. Wellbery, eds. *Reconstructing Individualism: Autonomy, Individuality, and the Self in Western Thought.* Stanford, 1986.

Heyck, T. W. *The Transformation of Intellectual Life in Victorian England.* London, 1982.

Holloway, John. *The Victorian Sage: Studies in Argument.* London, 1953.

Holly, Michael Ann. *Past Looking.* Ithaca, N.Y., 1996.

Holman Hunt, W. *Pre-Raphaelitism and the Pre-Raphaelite Brotherhood.* 2 vols. London, 1905.

———. *Pre-Raphaelitism and the Pre-Raphaelite Brotherhood.* 2d ed. Revised from the author's notes by M. E. H.-H. [Mrs. Marion Edith Holman Hunt]. 2 vols. London, 1913.

Holmes, Charles. *Self and Partners (Mostly Self): Being the Reminiscences of Sir Charles Holmes.* London, 1936.

Holt, Ysanne. *Philip Wilson Steer.* Bridgend, U.K., 1992.

Housman, Laurence. *The Unexpected Years.* London, 1939.

Howard, Diana. *London Theatres and Music-Halls, 1850–1950.* London, 1970.

Hunt, John Dixon. "Making Vergil Look English." In *Word & Image Interactions,* ed. Martin Heuser. Basel, 1993.

Jacobi, Carol, "Mimesis, Materiality, and *The Shadow of Death.*" *Art History* 25, no. 2 (2002).

James, Henry. *The Painter's Eye: Notes and Essays on the Pictorial Arts.* Edited by John L. Sweeney. London, 1956.

Jenkins, Keith, ed. *The Postmodern History Reader.* London, 1997.

Jordanova, Ludmilla. *History in Practice.* London, 2000.

Joselit, David. "Notes on Surface: Toward a Genealogy of Flatness." *Art History* 23, no. 1 (2000).

Kayman, Martin A. *The Modernism of Ezra Pound: The Science of Poetry.* Basingstoke, U.K., 1986.

Kermode, Frank. *Romantic Image.* London, 1976.

Kern, Stephen. *Eyes of Love: The Gaze in English and French Culture, 1840–1900.* New York, 1996.

Kestner, Joseph A. "Poynter and Leighton as Aestheticians: The *Ten Lectures* and *Addresses.*" *Journal of Pre-Raphaelite and Aesthetic Studies* 2, no. 2 (1989).

Kirsh, Andrea, and Rustin S. Levenson. *Seeing Through Paintings: Physical Examination in Art Historical Studies.* New Haven, Conn., 2000.

Knight, David M. *Atoms and Elements: A Study of Theories of Matter in England in the Nineteenth Century.* London, 1967.
Knights, Ben. *The Idea of the Clerisy in the Nineteenth Century.* Cambridge, 1978.
Kooistra, Lorraine Janzen. *The Artist as Critic: Bitextuality in Fin-de-Siècle Illustrated Books.* Aldershot, U.K., 1995.
Krasner, James. *The Entangled Eye: Visual Representation and the Representation of Nature in Post-Darwinian Narrative.* Oxford, 1992.
Krauss, Rosalind. *The Originality of the Avant-Garde and Other Modernist Myths.* Cambridge, Mass., 1984.

Lago, Mary, ed. *Burne-Jones Talking: His Conversations, 1895–1898, Preserved by His Studio Assistant Thomas Rooke.* London, 1982.
Lambourne, Lionel. *The Aesthetic Movement.* London, 1996.
Landow, George P. *William Holman Hunt and Typological Symbolism.* New Haven, Conn., 1979.
Lash, Scott, and Jonathan Friedman. *Modernity and Identity.* Oxford, 1992.
The Last Romantics: The Romantic Tradition in British Art, Burne-Jones to Stanley Spencer. Exh. cat., Barbican Art Gallery. London, 1989.
Late Sickert: Paintings, 1927–1942. Exh. cat., Hayward Gallery. London, 1981.
Laughton, Bruce. *Philip Wilson Steer, 1860–1942.* Oxford, 1971.
Leighton, Frederic. *Addresses, Delivered to Students at the Royal Academy.* London, 1896.
Lessing, G. E. *Laocoön: An Essay on the Limits of Painting and Poetry.* Translated with an introduction and notes by Edward Allen McCormick. Baltimore, 1984.
Levenson, Michael H. *A Genealogy of Modernism: A Study of English Literary Doctrine, 1908–1922.* Cambridge, 1984.
Lewis, Wyndham. *The Caliph's Design: Architects! Where Is Your Vortex?* London, 1919.
———. "Dean Swift with a Brush: The Tyroist Explains His Art." *Daily Express,* 11 April 1921.
———. "Creatures of Habit and Creatures of Change." *The Calendar of Modern Letters* 3 (1926).
———. *Blasting and Bombardiering.* London, 1937.
———. *The Letters of Wyndham Lewis.* Edited by W. K. Rose. London, 1963.
———. *Wyndham Lewis on Art: Collected Writings, 1913–1956.* Edited by Walter Michel and C. J. Fox. London, 1969.
———. "The Sturge Moore Letters." Edited by Victor M. Cassidy. *Lewisletter* 7 (1977).
Lillie, Marjorie. *Sickert: The Painter and His Circle.* London, 1971.
de Lisle, Fortunée. *Burne-Jones.* 2d ed. London, 1906.
Lord Leighton: Eminent Victorian Artist. Exh. cat., Royal Academy of Arts. London, 1996.

Maas, Jeremy. *Holman Hunt and the Light of the World.* London, 1984.
MacColl, D. S. *Life, Work, and Setting of Philip Wilson Steer.* London, 1945.
MacDonald, Margaret F. *James McNeill Whistler's Drawings, Pastels, and Watercolors: A Catalogue Raisonné.* New Haven, Conn., 1995.
———, ed. *Whistler.* Exh. cat., Tate Gallery. London, 1994.
MacLeod, Dianne Sachko. "The Dialectics of Modernism and English Art." *British Journal of Aesthetics* 35 (1995).
———. *Art and the Victorian Middle Class: Money and the Making of Cultural Identity.* Cambridge, 1996.
Marillier, H. C. *Dante Gabriel Rossetti: An Illustrated Memorial of His Life and Art.* London, 1899.
Marsh, Jan. *Dante Gabriel Rossetti: Painter and Poet.* London, 1999.
McConkey, Kenneth. *British Impressionism.* Oxford, 1989.
———. *Impressionism in Britain.* Exh. cat., Barbican Art Gallery. New Haven, Conn., 1995.
McGann, Jerome. "Medieval *versus* Victorian *versus* Modern: Rossetti's Art of Images." *Modernism/Modernity* 2, no. 1 (1995).

———. *Dante Gabriel Rossetti and the Game That Must Be Lost.* New Haven, Conn., 2000.
McMullen, Roy. *Victorian Outsider: A Biography of J. A. M. Whistler.* London, 1973.
Menpes, Mortimer. *Whistler as I Knew Him.* London, 1904.
Merrill, Linda. *A Pot of Paint: Aesthetics on Trial in* Whistler v. Ruskin. Washington, D.C., 1992.
Meyers, Jeffrey. *The Enemy: A Biography of Wyndham Lewis.* London, 1980.
Michel, Walter. *Wyndham Lewis: Paintings and Drawings.* London, 1971.
Miller, Andrew H. *Novels Behind Glass: Commodity Culture and Victorian Narrative.* Cambridge, 1995.
Miller, J. Hillis. *Illustration.* London, 1992.
Mirzoeff, Nicholas. *An Introduction to Visual Culture.* London, 1998.
Mitchell, W. J. T. *Iconology: Image, Text, Ideology.* Chicago, 1986.
———. "Ekphrasis and the Other." *South Atlantic Quarterly* 91 (Summer 1992).
———. *Picture Theory.* Chicago, 1994.
Moore, Thomas Sturge. *The Gazelles and Other Poems.* London, 1904.
Moxey, Keith. "Motivating History." *Art Bulletin* 77, no. 3 (1995).
Müller, Max. *Lectures on the Science of Language, Delivered at the Royal Institution of Great Britain in February, March, and April 1863.* 2d ser. London, 1864.
Munt, Sally. "The Lesbian Flâneur." In *Mapping Desire,* ed. David Bell and Gill Valentine. London, 1995.

Nead, Lynda. *The Female Nude: Art, Obscenity, and Sexuality.* London, 1992.
———. *Victorian Babylon: People, Streets, and Images in Nineteenth-Century London.* New Haven, Conn., 2000.
Nelson, Robert S., and Richard Shiff, eds. *Critical Terms for Art History.* Chicago, 1996.
Newall, Christopher. *The Grosvenor Gallery Exhibitions.* Cambridge, 1995.
Nicholls, Peter. *Modernisms: A Literary Guide.* Basingstoke, U.K., 1995.
Nicoll, John. *Dante Gabriel Rossetti.* New York, 1975.

O'Keeffe, Paul. *Some Sort of Genius: A Life of Wyndham Lewis.* London, 2000.
Owens, Susan. "Aubrey Beardsley, *Salome,* and Satire." Ph.D. diss., University College, London, 2002.

Parris, Leslie, ed. *Pre-Raphaelite Papers.* London, 1984.
———. *The Pre-Raphaelites.* Exh. cat., Tate Gallery. London, 1984.
Pater, Walter. *Appreciations with an Essay on Style.* London, 1889.
———. *The Renaissance: Studies in Art and Poetry: The 1893 Text.* Edited by Donald L. Hill. Berkeley and Los Angeles, 1980.
Pearce, Lynne. *Woman/Image/Text: Readings in Pre-Raphaelite Art and Literature.* Toronto, 1991.
Pearson, Hesketh. *The Life of Oscar Wilde.* London, 1946.
Pennell, Elizabeth and Joseph. *The Life of James McNeill Whistler.* 2 vols. London, 1908.
Perkins, David. *Is Literary History Possible?* Baltimore, 1992.
Pfordresher, John. "Dante Gabriel Rossetti's 'Hand and Soul': Sources and Significance." *Studies in Short Fiction* 19 (1982).
Phythian, J. E. *Burne-Jones.* London, 1908.
———. *Fifty Years of Modern Painting, Corot to Sargent.* London, 1908.
Pickvance, Ronald. "The Magic of the Halls and Sickert." *Apollo* (April 1962).
Pointon, Marcia. *Hanging the Head: Portraiture and Social Formation in Eighteenth-Century England.* New Haven, Conn., 1993.
———, ed. *Pre-Raphaelites Re-Viewed.* Manchester, 1989.
Pollock, Griselda. *Avant-Garde Gambits, 1888–1893: Gender and the Colour of Art History.* London, 1992.

Poulson, Christine. *The Quest for the Grail: Arthurian Legend in British Art, 1840–1920*. Manchester, 1999.
Prettejohn, Elizabeth. "Aesthetic Value and the Professionalization of Victorian Art Criticism, 1837–78." *Journal of Victorian Culture* 2, no. 1 (1997).
———. *Rossetti and His Circle*. London, 1997.
———. "Out of the Nineteenth Century: Roger Fry's Early Art Criticism, 1900–1906." In *Art Made Modern: Roger Fry's Vision of Art*, ed. Christopher Green. London, 1999.
———. *The Art of the Pre-Raphaelites*. London, 2000.
———, ed. *After the Pre-Raphaelites: Art and Aestheticism in Victorian England*. Manchester, 1999.
Psomiades, Kathy Alexis. *Beauty's Body: Femininity and Representation in British Aestheticism*. Stanford, 1997.

Raban, Jonathan. *Soft City*. London, 1974.
Reed, Christopher. "Making History: The Bloomsbury Group's Construction of Aesthetic and Sexual Identity." In *Gay and Lesbian Studies in Art History*, ed. Whitney Davis. Binghamton, N.Y., 1994.
———, ed. *A Roger Fry Reader*. Chicago, 1996.
Ricketts, Charles. *The Prado and Its Masterpieces*. London, 1903.
———. *Titian*. London, 1910.
———. *Pages on Art*. London, 1913.
——— [Jean Paul Raymond, pseud.]. *Beyond the Threshold*. Plaistow, U.K., 1929.
———. *Self-Portrait Taken from the Letters and Journals of Charles Ricketts, R.A.* Collected and compiled by T. Sturge Moore. Edited by Cecil Lewis. London, 1939.
——— [Jean Paul Raymond {pseud.} and]. *Oscar Wilde: Recollections*. London, 1932.
Robertson, W. Graham. *Time Was: The Reminiscences of W. Graham Robertson*. London, 1945.
Robins, Anna Gruetzner. "The London Impressionists." Ph.D. diss., Courtauld Institute of Art, 1988.
———. *Walter Sickert, Drawings, Theory, and Practice: Word and Image*. Aldershot, U.K., 1996.
———. *Modern Art in Britain, 1910–1914*. Exh. cat., Barbican Art Gallery. London, 1997.
Rosen, Charles, and Henri Zerner. *Romanticism and Realism: The Mythology of Nineteenth-Century Art*. London, 1984.
Rosenblum, S. P., ed. *The Bloomsbury Group: A Collection of Memoirs, Commentary, and Criticism*. London, 1975.
Ross, Dorothy, ed. *Modernist Impulses in the Human Sciences, 1870–1930*. Baltimore, 1994.
Rossetti, Dante Gabriel. *The Works of Dante Gabriel Rossetti*. Edited by William Michael Rossetti. London, 1911.
———. *Letters of Dante Gabriel Rossetti*. Edited by Oswald Doughty and John Robert Wahl. 4 vols. Oxford, 1965–67.
———. *The Complete Writings and Pictures of Dante Gabriel Rossetti: A Hypermedia Research Archive*. Edited by Jerome McGann. http://www.iath.virginia.edu/rossetti/index.html (accessed 19 August 2003).
Rossetti, William Michael. "The Royal Academy Exhibition." *Fraser's Magazine* 71 (June 1865).
Rossetti, W[illiam] M[ichael], and A[lgernon] C[harles] Swinburne. *Notes on the Royal Academy Exhibition*. London, 1868. Facsimile reprint, New York, 1976.
Rothenstein, John. *Modern English Painters*. 3 vols. London, 1984.
Rothenstein, William. *Men and Memories: Recollections of William Rothenstein, 1872–1900*. London, 1931.
Ruskin, John. *The Works of John Ruskin*. Edited by E. T. Cook and Alexander Wedderburn. 39 vols. London, 1903–12.
———. *The Art Criticism of John Ruskin*. Edited by Robert L. Herbert. Gloucester, Mass., 1969.
Rutter, Frank. "Spencer F. Gore." *Sunday Times*, 5 April 1914.
Ryan, Jenny. "Women, Modernity, and the City." *Theory, Culture, and Society* 11 (1994).

Saville, Julia. "'The Lady of Shalott': A Lacanian Romance." *Word & Image* 8, no. 1 (1992).
Schaffer, Talia, and Kathy Alexis Psomiades, eds. *Women and British Aestheticism.* Charlottesville, Va., 1999.
Schwartz, Sanford. *The Matrix of Modernism: Pound, Eliot, and Early Twentieth-Century Thought.* Princeton, N.J., 1985.
Scott, William Bell. *Autobiographical Notes.* Edited by W. Minto. 2 vols. New York, 1892.
Shannon, Charles. *A Catalogue of Mr Shannon's Lithographs, with Prefatory Notes by Charles Ricketts, and a Portrait Engraved by Charles Ricketts After a Medal by Alphonse Legros.* London, [1902].
Shaw, W. David. *The Lucid Veil: Poetic Truth in the Victorian Age.* London, 1987.
Shirland, Jonathan. "The Construction of Artistic Masculinity in James McNeill Whistler, Walter Sickert, and Wyndham Lewis, c. 1880–1914." Ph.D. diss., University College, London, 2002.
Shone, Richard, ed. *The Art of Bloomsbury: Roger Fry, Vanessa Bell, and Duncan Grant.* Exh. cat., Tate Gallery. London, 1999.
Shrewsbury, H. W. *The Visions of an Artist: G. F. Watts, RA, OM, with Verse Interpretations.* London, 1918.
Shuttleworth, Sally. *George Eliot and Nineteenth-Century Science: The Make-Believe of a Beginning.* Cambridge, 1984.
Sickert, Walter. "Idealism." *Art News* (12 May 1910).
———. *A Free House! Or, the Artist as Craftsman, Being the Writings of Walter Richard Sickert.* Edited by Osbert Sitwell. London, 1947.
———. *Walter Sickert: The Complete Writings on Art.* Edited by Anna Gruetzner Robins. Oxford, 2000.
Sickert: Paintings, Drawings, and Prints of Walter Richard Sickert, 1860–1942. Exh. cat., Arts Council. London, 1977.
Sizeranne, Robert de la. *English Contemporary Art.* Translated by H. M. Poynter. Westminster, U.K., 1898.
Smiles, Sam. "'Splashers,' 'Scrawlers,' and 'Plasterers': British Landscape Painting and the Language of Criticism, 1800–1840." *Turner Studies* 10, no. 1 (1990).
Smith, Alison. *The Victorian Nude: Sexuality, Morality, and Art.* Manchester, 1996.
Smith, Lindsay. *Victorian Photography, Painting, and Poetry: The Enigma of Visibility in Ruskin, Morris, and the Pre-Raphaelites.* Cambridge, 1995.
Solkin, David. "The British and the Modern." In *Towards a Modern Art World,* ed. Brian Allen. New Haven, Conn., 1995.
Spalding, Frances. *Roger Fry: Art and Life.* London, 1980.
Spencer, Robin. *The Aesthetic Movement: Prelude to Art Nouveau.* London, 1969.
Spencer Gore in Richmond. Exh. cat., Museum of Richmond. Richmond, U.K., 1996.
Staley, Allen. *The Pre-Raphaelite Landscape.* Rev. ed. New Haven, Conn., 2001.
Stansky, Peter. *On or About December 1910: Early Bloomsbury and Its Intimate World.* Cambridge, Mass., 1996.
Statham, H. Heathcote. "The Grosvenor Gallery." *Macmillan's Magazine* 36 (1877).
Stein, Richard L. "The Pre-Raphaelite Tennyson." *Victorian Studies* 24, no. 3 (1981).
Steiner, George. *In Bluebeard's Castle: Some Notes Towards the Re-definition of Culture.* London, 1971.
Stephens, F. G. [John Seward, pseud.]. "The Purpose and Tendency of Early Italian Art." *The Germ* 2 (1850).
———. *Dante Gabriel Rossetti.* London, 1894.
Stephenson, Andrew. "Buttressing Bohemian Mystiques and Bandaging Masculine Anxieties." *Art History* 17, no. 2 (1994).
Stewart, David Alan. "G. F. Watts: The Social and Religious Themes." Ph.D. diss., Boston University, 1988.
Stokes, John. *In the Nineties.* New York, 1989.
Stoner, Joyce Hill. "Textured Surfaces: Technique, Facture, and Friendship in the Work of James McNeill Whistler." Ph.D. diss., University of Delaware, 1995.

Surtees, Virginia. *The Paintings and Drawings of Dante Gabriel Rossetti (1828–1882): A Catalogue Raisonné*. 2 vols. Oxford, 1971.
Sutton, Denys. "A Neglected Virtuoso: Charles Ricketts and His Achievements." *Apollo* 83 (1966).
———. *Walter Sickert*. London, 1976.
Swinburne, Algernon Charles. *William Blake: A Critical Essay*. London, 1868.
———. *Essays and Studies*. London, 1875.

Taylor, Charles. *Sources of the Self: The Making of Modern Identity*. Cambridge, 1989.
"Theocritus." "The Vale Artists—I–IV." *The Sketch*, 23 January, 13 March, 17 April, and 25 April 1895.
Theuriet, A. *Jules Bastien-Lepage and His Art: A Memoir*. London, 1892.
Tickner, Lisa. "Men's Work? Masculinity and Modernism." In *Visual Culture: Images and Interpretations*, ed. Norman Bryson, Michael Ann Holly, and Keith Moxey. Hanover, N.H., 1994.
———. *Modern Life and Modern Subjects: British Art in the Early Twentieth Century*. New Haven, Conn., 2000.
———. "Messing About in Boats: E. J. Gregory's *Boulter's Lock: Sunday Afternoon* (R.A., 1897)." *Oxford Art Journal* 25, no. 2 (2002).
Tillyard, Stella. *The Impact of Modernism, 1900–1920: Early Modernism and the Arts and Crafts Movement in Edwardian England*. London, 1988.
Trodd, Colin, and Paul Barlow, eds. *Victorian Culture and the Idea of the Grotesque*. Aldershot, U.K., 1999.
Trodd, Colin, and Stephanie Brown, eds. *G. F. Watts: Cultural Enchantment in Victorian Art*. Aldershot, U.K., forthcoming.
Troyen, Aimée. *Walter Sickert as Printmaker*. Exh. cat., Yale Center for British Art. New Haven, Conn., 1979.
Tyndall, John. *Fragments of Science for Unscientific People: A Series of Detached Essays, Lectures, and Reviews*. London, 1871.
———. *Advancement of Science: The Inaugural Address of Prof. John Tyndall, DCL, LLD, FRS, Delivered Before the British Association for the Advancement of Science at Belfast, August 19, 1874*. New York, 1874.

Victorian High Renaissance: George Frederic Watts, 1817–1904; Frederic Leighton, 1830–96; Albert Moore, 1841–93; Alfred Gilbert, 1854–1934. Exh. cat., Minneapolis Institute of Arts. Minneapolis, 1978.

Wagstaff, Samuel J., Jr. "Some Notes on Holman Hunt and *The Lady of Shalott*." *Wadsworth Atheneum Bulletin* (Summer 1962).
Walden, Jeffrey. "Illustrating *Salome*: Perverting the Text?" *Word & Image* 8, no. 2 (1992).
Walkowitz, Judith R. *City of Dreadful Night: Narratives of Sexual Danger in Late Victorian London*. Chicago, 1992.
Warner, Eric, and Graham Hough, eds. *Strangeness and Beauty: An Anthology of Aesthetic Criticism, 1840–1910*. 2 vols. Cambridge, 1983.
Warner, Malcolm. *The Victorians: British Painting, 1837–1901*. Exh. cat., National Gallery of Art. Washington, D.C., 1997.
Waters, William. *Sir Edward Coley Burne-Jones, Bart, 1833–1898, Laus Veneris*. Newcastle upon Tyne, U.K., 1975.
———. *Burne-Jones: An Illustrated Life of Sir Edward Burne-Jones, 1833–1898*. Princes Risborough, U.K., 1989.
Watney, Simon. *English Post-Impressionism*. London, 1980.
Watts, Mary S. *George Frederic Watts: The Annals of an Artist's Life*. 3 vols. New York, n.d.
Way, T. R. *Memories of James McNeill Whistler, the Artist*. London, 1912.
Wedmore, Frederick. "Some Tendencies in Recent Painting." *Temple Bar* 53 (July 1878).

———. *Some of the Moderns.* London, 1909.
Wees, W. C. *Vorticism and the English Avant-Garde.* Manchester, 1972.
Whistler, James McNeill. *The Gentle Art of Making Enemies.* London, 1912.
Whiteley, Nigel. "Readers of the Lost Art: Visuality and Particularity in Art Criticism." In *Interpreting Visual Culture: Explorations in the Hermeneutics of the Visual,* ed. Ian Heywood and Barry Sandywell. London, 1999.
Wilcox, Denys J. *The London Group, 1913–1939: The Artists and Their Works.* Aldershot, U.K., 1995.
Wilde, Oscar. *Intentions: The Decay of Lying; Pen, Pencil, and Poison; The Critic as Artist; The Truth of Masks.* London, 1891.
———. *The Sphinx.* London, 1894.
———. *The Letters of Oscar Wilde.* Edited by Rupert Hart-Davis. London, 1962.
———. *The Complete Works of Oscar Wilde.* London, 1971.
———. *More Letters of Oscar Wilde.* Edited by Rupert Hart-Davis. London, 1985.
Wildman, Stephen, and John Christian. *Burne-Jones: Victorian Artist-Dreamer.* Exh. cat., Metropolitan Museum of Art. New York, 1998.
Wilson, Elizabeth. *Hallucinations: Life in the Post-Modern City.* London, 1988.
Winters, Yvor. *Uncollected Essays and Reviews.* London, 1974.
Woodall, Joanna, ed. *Portraiture: Facing the Subject.* Manchester, 1997.
Woolf, Virginia. *Roger Fry: A Biography.* London, 1940.
The Works of G. F. Watts, RA. Exh. cat., New Gallery. London, 1896.
Wragg, David. "Wyndham Lewis's Vorticism and the Aesthetics of Closure." In *Theorizing Modernism: Essays in Critical Theory,* ed. Steve Giles. London, 1993.

Yeats, W. B. *Autobiographies.* London, 1980.
Young, Andrew McLaren, Margaret MacDonald, Robin Spencer, and Hamish Miles. *The Paintings of James McNeill Whistler.* New Haven, Conn., 1980.

Index

Page numbers in *italics* refer to illustrations in the text.

Works of visual art are physical objects. Art history as a discipline neglects that materiality at its peril. Perhaps we really are now coming to the end of a phase when that foundational fact has seemed less compelling than a variety of other things—social, historical, cultural—one can say about art. But, if the work of painting has historical or social meaning, then those meanings can only arise from the signifying potentialities of its material substance. Any analysis that refuses to engage with that signification and its processes, which neglects, that is, to develop an account of the historical resonance of the physical manipulation of material in painting, must be inadequate as an account. Such a project does not necessarily or desirably take place outside history, but if we are to make of the "return to the object" anything worthwhile we will need to develop ways of speaking about materiality and objectness that can track the making of meaning in non-verbal, visual forms. I find it hard to imagine a credible art history that does not have that aspiration at its core.

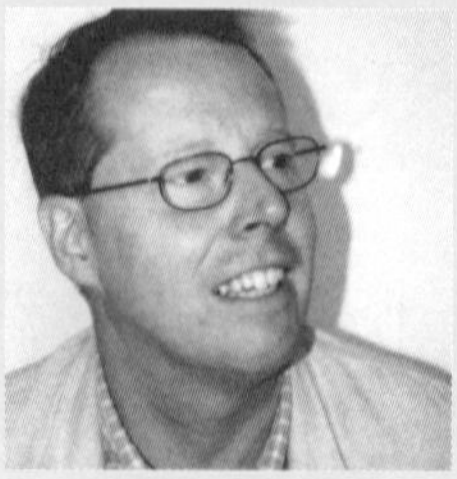

DAVID PETERS CORBETT IS PROFESSOR OF ART HISTORY AND DIRECTOR OF THE RESEARCH SCHOOL IN BRITISH ART AT THE UNIVERSITY OF YORK.